Albert Bandura
Stanford University

AGGRESSION

a

social learning

analysis

PRENTICE-HALL, INC., ENGLEWOOD CLIFFS, NEW JERSEY

Library of Congress Cataloging in Publication Data

BANDURA, ALBERT
   Aggression: a social learning analysis.

   (The Prentice-Hall series in social learning theory)
   Bibliography: p.
   1. Aggressiveness (Psychology)   2. Violence.
I. Title.
HM281.B25   301.1   72-12990
ISBN 0-13-020743-8

The Prentice-Hall Series in Social Learning Theory
Albert Bandura, editor

Printed in the United States of America

10 9 8 7 6

PRENTICE-HALL INTERNATIONAL, INC., *London*
PRENTICE-HALL OF AUSTRALIA, PTY. LTD., *Sydney*
PRENTICE-HALL OF CANADA, LTD., *Toronto*
PRENTICE-HALL OF INDIA PRIVATE LIMITED, *New Delhi*
PRENTICE-HALL OF JAPAN, INC., *Tokyo*

to Ginny, Mary, and Carol

contents

v

preface

This book is concerned with why man aggresses. There are several reasons for addressing this issue, despite the great deal of attention that has already been devoted to it. Although aggression pervades our lives, few concerted efforts have been made to substantiate its causes or to devise constructive ways of reducing the level of societal violence. Man's technological capacity for massive destruction has now developed to the point where he can no longer continue to settle conflicts by destructive means. In addition to the threats posed to survival, violence increasingly encroaches on daily human affairs to impair the quality of life. These developments make it all the more necessary to understand the determinants of injurious conduct.

Theories of human behavior have been undergoing drastic change in the last decade. Interest in traditional approaches that depict behavior as either instinctively determined or impelled by drive forces declined as their deficiencies became apparent. New perspectives based on social learning principles have emerged that substantially advance understanding of human behavior. In this book I have attempted to formulate a social learning theory of aggression sufficiently broad in scope to integrate evidence on all facets of aggression, whether individual or collective, personal or institutionally sanctioned. The aim of this undertaking is not only to offer a better basis for explaining, predicting, and modifying aggression, but also to provide impetus for new lines of research likely to augment the explanatory power of social learning theory.

The worth of a psychological theory should be partly measured in terms of the effectiveness of the modification procedures that it produces. A sizable portion of this book is therefore devoted to demonstrating how social learning principles can be applied individually and at the social systems level to reduce deleterious forms of aggression. There will always be social conflicts, but they need not require violent solutions. Some forceful measures have functional value in promoting constructive social changes which lessen the likelihood that people will resort to violent action. The exercise of social power as an instrument of change receives detailed consideration.

No account of aggression can be complete without discussing the social labeling and ethics of aggressive action. Findings bearing on these issues, along with evidence that aggressive conduct can be rapidly and drastically altered by moral sanctions, strongly indicate that the determinants of human aggression are best sought in man's social practices.

Many people have contributed to this book in various stages of its growth, and I am pleased to take this opportunity to acknowledge my indebtedness to them. Fellowship grants from the National Institute of Mental Health and the John Simon Guggenheim Foundation greatly aided my work. This project was begun during my residence as a Fellow at the Center for Advanced Study in the Behavioral Sciences. The opportunity to pursue one's studies in the company of distinguished scholars free from intrusive routines is an experience that will be long treasured and for which I am deeply grateful to the staff of the Center. Violence was more than a topic for intellectual discussion at the Center that year. It personally touched the lives of the Fellows and the staff. In the predawn hours on April 24, 1970 ten studies were gutted by fire-bombs in a calculated attempt to burn the Center to the ground. It was tragic to see a facility devoted to the enlightenment and betterment of man selected as a target for destruction.

I am thankful to Ted Rosenthal and Leonard Berkowitz who took time from their crowded schedules to comment on preliminary versions of the manuscript. To Jane Crane, whose diligent efforts in preparing the manuscript eased my task considerably, I owe a large debt of gratitude. My daughter, Mary, helped me along the way with typing and proofreading. I was most fortunate to have the able services of Julia Baskett in preparing the final version of the manuscript for publication.

Writing a book at times takes possession of the household as well as the author. I am thankful to my family for their forebearance. It is to them that I dedicate this work.

Albert Bandura

chapter one

THEORIES OF AGGRESSION

Among the various human activities that are the subject of attention, none has aroused deeper concern than man's aggressiveness. Though aggression has always been an important social problem, developments during the past few decades have fully justified increased concern. With the progressive growth of instruments of destruction, simple aggressive acts can produce widespread disastrous consequences. The hazards of ill-judged actions have thus become enormously magnified. Man's aggressive potential has also been increased, independently of expanding destructive accouterments, by changes in the social conditions of life. When populations were widely dispersed, the consequences of any given aggressive act were principally confined to persons toward whom the behavior was directed. Under conditions of urbanized life, in which the welfare of hordes of residents depends upon smooth functioning of intricate interdependent systems, destructive behavior that can be easily performed without requiring elaborate apparatus instantaneously harms vast numbers of people.

Concern over the adverse consequences of aggression obscures the fact that such behavior often has functional value for the user. Indeed, there is a property unique to aggression that generally creates conditions fostering its occurrence. Unlike other social behaviors that cannot be effective without some reciprocity acceptable to the participants, aggression does not require willing responsiveness from others for its success. One can injure and destroy to self-advantage regardless of whether the victim likes it or not. By aggressive behavior, or dominance through physical and verbal force, individuals can obtain valued resources, change rules to fit their own wishes, gain control over and extract subservience from others, eliminate conditions that adversely affect their well-being, and remove barriers that block or delay attainment of desired goals. Thus, behavior that is punishing for the victim can, at least on a short-term basis, be rewarding for the aggressor. Although, as we shall see later, aggression has many different causes, its utilitarian value undoubtedly contributes heavily to the prevalence of such behavior in the interactions of everyday life.

Over the years a number of theories have been proposed to explain why people behave aggressively. This chapter is focused on a comparison of the tenets of instinct and drive theories, which historically attributed aggression to internal aggressive forces, with the explanatory system based upon social learning theory. The basic principles of social learning are then applied in succeeding chapters to the explanation of both individual and collective aggression. This formulation differs in several important respects from the alternative lines of theorizing not only in the factors considered to be the causes of aggression, but also in its implications for the management and control of human aggression.

LABELING OF AGGRESSION

Attempts to define a concept essentially represent an invitation for a stroll through a semantic jungle. The journey, however, is instructive because it reveals important issues about the phenomena selected for analysis. Aggression, like most other concepts, has been characterized in many different ways. Variations in defining features arise mainly because some authors describe aggression solely in terms of attributes of the behavior, while others include assumptions about the instigators, the emotional concomitants, or the intent of potentially injurious actions.

In the theory originally advanced by Dollard, Doob, Miller, Mowrer, and Sears (1939), which occupies a prominent historical position, aggression is defined as "any sequence of behavior, the goal response to which is the injury of the person toward whom it is directed." Most subsequent theorizing and research have adopted injurious intent as an essential aspect of aggression (Berkowitz, 1962; Feshbach, 1970; Sears, Maccoby and Levin, 1957). A major limitation of such a definition is that it assumes that aggression serves only a single purpose, namely, to inflict injury.

If aggression is restricted to behavior that is performed solely for the purpose of injuring others, then a wide range of activities that are commonly judged as aggressive, including some of the most violent forms of interpersonal assault, would be excluded from consideration. Some writers (Berkowitz, 1965a; Feshbach, 1970) have attempted to deal with this problem by proposing different types of aggression. Instrumental aggression, which is aimed at securing extraneous rewards other than the victims' suffering, is distinguished from hostile aggression, the sole aim of which is presumably to inflict injury on others. Since hurtful and destructive actions were largely attributed to aggressive drive forces, so-called instrumental aggression received only passing notice. The differentiation generally conveys the impression that aggressive behavior performed for rewarding outcomes represents a form of pseudoaggression relegated to the subsidiary status of a means to other ends. According to this valuation, the holocaust in Hiroshima, which was ordered to force a quick end to war, would represent a mere instrumental act. So would any act of war, for that matter.

In point of fact, so-called hostile aggression is equally instrumental except that the actions are used to produce injurious outcomes rather than to gain status, power, resources, or some other types of results. Whatever its merits, the distinction reflects differences in desired outcomes, not in instrumentality. It would therefore be more accurate to differentiate aggressive actions in terms of their functional value rather than in terms of whether or not they are instrumental. Most aggressive acts serve ends other than solely to produce injury. Hence, when researchers report that instrumental aggression is excluded from their theoretical analysis, it is unclear whether they are mislabeling what is being studied or whether, in fact, they are concerned with only a small aspect of aggression.

As a rule, aggressive acts not only hurt the victim, but create a variety of results for the aggressor. It is therefore difficult to determine, in any given instance, whether the aggressive behavior is primarily reinforced by signs of injury, by associated noninjurious outcomes, or by both sets of consequences. A given action is most apt to be misjudged as rewarded by the suffering of others when the purposes served by aggression are not fully understood and when it produces no evident material gains. In many social groups, for example, aggression has powerful status-conferring value. Under these types of contingencies homicidal assaults are sometimes performed mainly to gain the approval and admiration of peers and to maintain one's status in the social hierarchy of a deviant reference group (Yablonsky, 1962). The way in which threat of loss of "rep" may compel a person to engage in a homicidal assault is graphically illustrated in the following excerpt from an interview with one of the boys studied by Yablonsky:

> Momentarily I started to thinking about it inside; I have my mind made up I'm not going to be in no gang. Then I go on inside. Something comes up, then here comes all my friends coming to me. Like I said before, I'm intelligent and so forth. They be coming to me—then they talk to me about what they gonna do. Like, "Man, we'll go out there and kill this cat." I say, "Yeah." They kept on talkin'. I said, "Man, I just gotta go with you." Myself, I don't want to go, but when they start talkin' about what they gonna do, I say, "So, he isn't gonna take over my rep. I ain't gonna let him be known more than me." And I go ahead. (p. vii)

The pull of status rewards rather than the push of an aggressive drive also appears to account for the behavior of another youth involved in a gang killing:

> If I would of got the knife, I would have stabbed him. That would have gave me more of a build-up. People would have respected me for what I've done and things like that. They would say, "There goes a cold killer." (p. 8)

The operation of similar reinforcement contingencies is illustrated by a gang that used attacks upon strangers without provocation as its main admissions requirement (*San Francisco Chronicle*, 1964). Each physical assault, which had to be observed by a club member to be valid, was valued at 10 points, a total of 100 points was required for full-fledged membership.

A large body of research will be cited later to demonstrate that aggressive behavior declines when social reactions to it are withheld. Such evidence further supports the view that much interpersonal aggression that appears to have no utilitarian value may be extensively regulated by the social consequences it produces. Physical aggression is also often employed to gain control over other people, to secure material resources, and to force changes in social practices that adversely affect one's everyday life. In other words, people frequently resort to aggressive acts because they produce desired results that cannot as readily be achieved through nonaggressive means, rather than simply to generate expressions of suffering. A comprehensive theory of aggression must therefore account not only for aggressive actions that are primarily reinforced by satisfactions derived from hurting others, but also for much broader classes of aggressive behavior in which the infliction of suffering is essentially irrelevant or serves, at best, a secondary purpose.

For purposes of the present discussion, *aggression* is defined as behavior that results in personal injury and in destruction of property. The injury may be psychological (in the form of devaluation or degradation) as well as physical. Although this formulation delimits the phenomenon in a meaningful way, it should be made clear that aversive effects cannot serve as the sole defining characteristic of aggression. Individuals who hurt others while performing a socially sanctioned function (for example, dentists repairing teeth or surgeons making painful incisions) would not be considered as acting in an aggressive manner. Nor would bulldozer operators destroying condemned buildings to make way for new construction be charged with committing aggressive acts. Conversely, some forms of conduct would be judged aggressive even though no personal injury or property damage occurred. A person who attempted to hurt another individual by firing a gun at him or by striking him with a lethal object, but who happened to miss the unsuspecting victim, would be judged as behaving violently. As the preceding examples show, additional criteria for distinguishing between accidental and intended injury must be used both to exclude numerous pain-producing responses from the category of aggression and to include others that do not injure anyone because they are poorly executed.

In social learning theory, aggression is treated as a complex event including behavior that produces injurious and destructive effects as well as social labeling processes. According to this view, a full explanation of aggression must consider both *injurious behavior* and *social judgments* that determine which injurious acts are labeled as aggressive. The behavioral component has been studied in considerable detail. Subsequent chapters describe fully the mechanisms by which potentially injurious and destructive behaviors are acquired and the conditions regulating their expression. The judgmental component, on the other hand, has received relatively little attention, so that the factors that lead people to attach aggressive labels to social behavior are less well understood.

Social Labeling Processes

People come to judge certain actions as aggressive on the basis of a variety of criteria, some of which are grounded in the behavior, while others are extraneous to it and quite subjective. The *characteristics of the behavior itself* undoubtedly exert a strong influence on how it will be judged by others. As is evident in virtually all formal definitions of aggression, behavior that is likely to produce aversive consequences, such as physical assaults, humiliation, social rebuffs, and property destruction, is generally designated as aggressive, quite apart from the actual effects it may have on recipients.

The *intensity of responses* also often influences the labeling of behavior as aggressive. Behaviors of high magnitude, even relatively acceptable ones, such as addressing a person loudly, performing activities that exceed the tolerance levels of others, and almost any actions that are executed impetuously, tend to be interpreted as aggressive. Since the intensity of the response is an important factor in determining whether or not it will be painful or damaging, intensity is often a major distinguishing feature of aggressive responses that otherwise differ widely in character.

It follows from the conceptualization of aggression in terms of high-magnitude responses (Bandura and Walters, 1963) that teaching people to behave forcefully on a variety of nonaggressive tasks would, other factors being constant, increase the likelihood of behavior judged to be aggressive. In a test of this hypothesis, Walters and Brown (1963) found that children who were rewarded for responding vigorously either in hitting an automated Bobo doll or in depressing a lever later displayed more physically aggressive behavior in an interpersonal situation than children trained to respond in a less intense manner.

Expressions of pain and injury by recipients is another important determinant of how the associated behavior will be evaluated. Scuffles between children are likely to be labeled aggressive if a member cries or otherwise conveys the impression that he has been injured, whereas the same behavior is apt to be viewed as youthful exuberance if the participants display no pain reactions. This feature of an aggressive event reflects the ruggedness and endurance of the target person rather than properties of the actions. At the broader social level, coercive behavior of enforcement agents that is denounced by the victims is more apt to be viewed as unwarranted brutality than treatment to which they acquiesce.

The discussion thus far has been concerned with observable aspects of behavior and its evident consequences. Whether or not a given action is construed as aggressive is also strongly affected by factors extraneous to the behavior being evaluated. The *intentions* attributed to the performer will alter the way his actions are categorized. If they are judged to be unintended, then his behavior is not thought to be aggressive. The same actions would be interpreted as aggressive, even though no injury was in fact inflicted, by observers who assumed that the person wanted to hurt others.

The task of assessing a person's intentions is no simple matter. Intent is typically inferred from, among other factors, the social context of the act, the role status of the perpetrator of the act, and recent or more remote antecedent conditions. Injuries produced through physical assaults on a football field, for example, are less likely to be ascribed to pernicious intent than identical wounds caused by similar actions on city streets. The painful behavior performed by agents in socially sanctioned roles, as in the case of physicians, veterinarians, trial lawyers, and policemen, and the destructive activities of lumberjacks and house-wreckers, are rarely attributed to evil purposes. In these instances, general standards of acceptable conduct are delineated and grievance procedures are created to discourage legitimate agents from exhibiting unwarranted punitiveness. Disputes, however, often arise over whether hurtful practices reflect vigorous enactment of agents' roles or thinly veiled aggression.

Injurious intentions are also inferred from knowledge of earlier provocations. A baseball pitcher who strikes, with a supposedly wild throw, an opposing pitcher who had "beaned" a star performer in a preceding inning will be judged by most fans as exhibiting retaliatory aggression rather than momentary loss of control. Although high consensus may be achieved in inferring hostile intent from an obvious immediate provocation, agreement in labeling behavior as aggressive is relatively low if the instigation for vengeful actions is more subtle, far removed in time, or generalized from other sources of provocation. Under these types of conditions, which predominate in interpersonal interactions, the alleged causes of injurious actions are difficult to verify. The validity of causal attribution is especially debatable when hurtful consequences are presumed to be intended unconsciously, since confirmable criteria are even more elusive. In many instances the attribution of injurious intentions is, in fact, determined more by liking for the performer than by information about the instigators of his actions. People tend to ascribe evil designs to those whom they dislike and well-meaning intentions to those they like.

As alluded to in the preceding comments, *characteristics of the labelers* may significantly affect the way in which particular patterns of behavior are interpreted. It has been repeatedly shown that individuals tend to ascribe to others attributes that they themselves are known to possess (Holmes, 1968). Whether the assumed similarity represents a form of imputation or predictions about others made on the basis of one's own response tendencies remains unclear. The empirical findings nevertheless suggest that the individuals who are strongly disposed to behave aggressively would be most inclined to attribute hostile intent to others and to perceive their actions as aggressive. One might also expect persons who have a low threshold for aversive stimulation to classify a wider variety of activities as aggressive than those whose pain tolerance is appreciably higher. The manner in which social training for attending to violent activities may enhance responsiveness to aggressive cues is illustrated in a study by Toch and Schulte (1961), who presented subjects with violent pictures to one eye and matched neutral pictures to the other in a binocular rivalry procedure. Advanced police administration students, who had completed a three-year course in law enforcement, reported seeing more violent activities than novices in the same police training program.

It is evident from informal observation that people who differ in socioeconomic level, sex, ethnic background, and in educational and occupational status often vary in the way they view the same behavior with respect to its aggressive qualities. When social learning experiences associated with these diverse backgrounds give rise to different normative standards for judging behavior, it is not uncommon for activities promoted as suitable forms of conduct by members of some groups to be considered antisocially aggressive by people who adhere to different codes.

An additional source of influence on labeling behavior is the *characteristics of the aggressor*. On the basis of direct experiences and knowledge of cultural norms, people develop stereotypes of behaviors that are considered appropriate for given ages and sexes, and for members of different religious, ethnic, occupational, and socioeconomic groups. Evaluation of particular forms of behavior will vary depending on the normative standard against which they are compared. Thus, physical assertiveness is more likely to be defined as aggression if performed by a female than by a male because such behavior departs more widely from common expectations of appropriate female conduct. Conversely, similar assertiveness by boys in a delinquent gang would in all probability be underrated with respect to aggressiveness.

Definitions of aggression generally convey the impression that they are concerned solely with factors that reside in the performer, namely, his behavior and his intentions. It is apparent from the preceding discussion that social labeling processes are also a fundamental feature of the phenomenon. For this reason, aggression is characterized as *injurious and destructive behavior that is socially defined as aggressive on the basis of a variety of factors, some of which reside in the evaluator rather than in the performer*. The characteristics of the performer's behavior, carry a great deal of weight in the interpretation, and the basis for excluding certain injurious behaviors is commonly accepted so that, in practice, people generally agree on what forms of behavior should be designated as aggressive.

Judgmental controversies are most likely to arise when injurious actions take subtle or indirect forms. People ordinarily refrain from direct personal assaults because such obvious actions carry high risk of retaliation. Rather, they favor disguised modes of aggression that, being difficult to interpret or to consider blameworthy, afford protection against counterattack. For similar reasons, people often hurt others indirectly by setting in motion a series of detrimental events or by fostering certain environmental conditions that eventually produce injurious consequences for others. Here the causal link between a person's behavior and the harm experienced by others is remote, circuitous, and impersonal. When aversive conditions are collectively promoted, as is typically the case, no one individual bears responsibility for causing the injurious effects. Indeed, decision-making systems are specifically designed so as to diffuse or obscure responsibility for detrimental actions. To the victims, however, people who endorse prejudicial social practices, who oppose reforms that would alleviate suffering in disadvantaged members, and who press for military attacks on foreign populations are acting in a destructive manner. Thus, an individual who votes for social practices that have injurious physical and psychological effects on others is, in his view, engaging in democratic action, but to the victims who must endure the harmful consequences, he is behaving aggressively. Social scientists have examined direct assaultive behavior in minute detail, whereas remote circuitous acts, which produce widespread devastating consequences, are rarely given consideration.

Disputes over the labeling of aggressive acts assume special significance in the case of collective behavior. What one calls it entails more than semantic issues. Because the way in which civil disturbances are labeled partly determines the countermeasures employed, such labeling can have far-reaching consequences. As Grimshaw (1970) has noted, civil strife characterized as lawlessness or insurrection arouses widespread fears and demands for suppressive controls. On the other hand, if the same activities are designated as legitimate protest against deleterious conditions, people are more disposed to seek remedies rather than coercive countercontrols. The established leadership and their constituencies who come under attack are understandably quick to apply criminal labels to collective protest.

Social labeling of forcible tactics is not entirely an arbitrary matter. Turner (1969) identifies several factors that are likely to influence public interpretations of collective disruptions. When justifiable grievances are combined with restrained, selective pressure and principled rejection of violent tactics, protest activities gain legitimacy that makes them less amenable to labeling as antisocial outbursts. The balance between appeal and coercive threats in the protests affects whether or not the actions of participants are viewed as transgressive. Challengers appear more villainous when their professed aims are radical change in the social system or its leadership than when they seek to ameliorate inequitable conditions. Dissident leaders are prone to exaggerate the magnitude and gravity of their impending actions, either through miscalculation or in efforts to gain compliance by threatening rhetoric with revolutionary overtones. To the extent that such alarming self-labeling leads others to view subsequent coercive behavior as violence rather than protest, it is more apt to usher in the police than social reforms.

Social scientists, like other people, are not immune to the influence of their own ideological biases in their interpretations of collective aggression. When social scientists theorized about the aggression of the disadvantaged, they characterized group aggression as an impulsive, emotional, pathological manifestation. More recently, as social scientists and their close associates themselves began to participate in coercive protest and to take aggressive action against deleterious social practices, a different perspective of aggression and its determinants emerged. What appears irrational and pathological to onlookers or to those attacked often serves the aggressor as a method of getting what he wants when other options fail or remain unavailable. Group aggression, which had long been regarded in sociological theory as an irrational "mob" phenomenon, came to be viewed by some theorists as a highly principled form of collective bargaining intended to sway an irrational social system (Currie and Skolnick, 1970). Less partisan approaches treat collective aggression as multiply determined like other forms of social conduct, without attributing to participants either psychic aberrations or selfless morality (Marx, 1970a). As in designations of disturbances in terms of crime or protest, people respond differently depending upon whether pathological or problem-solving labels are attached to collective acts of aggression.

A closely related issue concerns the use of a double standard in judging dissident and institutionally sanctioned aggression. Agencies of government are entrusted with considerable coercive power designed to protect the citizenry. When countries wage wars in the name of national security, their supporters view military combat as an admired act of patriotism, whereas opponents consider it an unauthorized use of government authority to kill human beings. They insist that violence per se should be deplored, regardless of whether it is under governmental or private sanction.

Similar controversies arise about how people evaluate domestic use of governmental force. Those whose social and economic interests are well served by the system applaud coercive law enforcement practices as acceptable means of keeping lawlessness under control. By contrast, dissident factions tend to regard military and police forces as control agents of political authority more intent on preserving the status quo than impartially protecting the welfare of all segments of society. Few would deny that governmental agencies are dispensers of aggression. Authoritarian states rule by force. Nor is institutionally sanctioned violence foreign to democratic systems in checking oppositional behavior that challenges the existing order (Iglitzin, 1970; Marx, 1970b). When the dispenser of aggression is a sanctioned authority, his injurious behavior is minimized as vigorous pursuit of duty, but if a free-lancing individual does it, he is judged to be acting violently. The rhetoric of recent years demonstrates how one man's violence is another man's self-defined altruism.

Adoption of a definition of aggression primarily serves to delimit the range of phenomena that a given theory is designed to explain. But it does not necessarily aid in identifying causal relationships, because one selects for study only specific classes of behavior and not an abstract "aggression." That is, research workers investigate the factors that cause people to commit murder, to destroy certain property, to engage in prejudicial practices that have harmful effects, or other specific forms of injurious behavior. A high degree of specificity is required at the investigatory level because there is little reason to believe that the diverse activities subsumed under the omnibus label "aggression," though sharing some ingredients in common, have the same determinants. In fact, apparent inconsistencies in findings relating to aggression arise in part from the fact that writers frequently use the generic term rather than specifying the particular injurious behaviors they have in mind. The preceding comments apply equally to other areas of functioning. Creativity, for example, is a heterogeneous phenomenon that subsumes a vast array of diverse activities. To advance understanding of the determinants of inventiveness, one would select specific endeavors such as painting, sculpting, composing, or writing, rather than omnibus artistry. It matters little what the activity is called as long as it is clearly designated.

THEORETICAL ANALYSES OF AGGRESSION

Early psychological theories sought to explain human behavior principally in terms of instinctual forces. During the period when such interpretations were in vogue, many writers advanced the view that man is by nature aggressive. Although eventually the instinct doctrine fell into disrepute, the belief that man is innately endowed with an aggressive drive still enjoys a sizable following. Proponents of this view usually draw heavily on the doctrine of biological determinism in accounting for aggressive actions. The reasoning typically proceeds along the following lines: Under primitive conditions of life aggression had high survival value. Consequently, survivors of the process of natural selection were those who possessed strong aggressive tendencies. Over the years, environmental conditions have been radically altered, but unfortunately man's instinctual aggressive drive and his innate responses, though no longer serviceable in contemporary society, remain unchanged. As man's destructive powers are markedly augmented by technological advances, his evolutionary heritage continuously threatens his very survival. Other versions of this thesis convey the impression that the neuroendocrine system with which man is endowed by heredity generates energy under stress in quantities more fitting for fight or flight under primitive than under contemporary conditions. These characterizations rarely acknowledge that without the energy-mobilizing system, man would lack the capacity for emotional experience or for coping with the common challenges of everyday life.

Instinctual explanations of aggression assumed many different forms, depending on whether they posited inborn motivational mechanisms, innately organized responses, or innate stimulus functions wherein external cues evoke aggressive actions supposedly without any prior learning. These theories ranged from McDougall's (1931) view that virtually all social behavior is under instinctual control, to Freud, for whom aggression represented overt expressions of the death instinct, to some present-day ethologists who regard aggression as innately organized response patterns that are released in each species by specific external stimuli.

Psychoanalytic Instinctual Theory

Freud (1920) initially believed that aggression was a "primary response" to the thwarting of pleasure-seeking or pain-avoiding behavior. His explanation of aggression changed markedly, however, as he modified his instinct theory of motivation. Freud originally assumed that human behavior was regulated by two opposing sets of instincts—the sexual instincts and the self-preservative ego instincts that altered, deferred, or inhibited pleasure-striving in the service of the reality principle. There were certain behavioral phenomena, however, such as compulsive repetitions of unpleasant experiences, sadism, and especially self-destructive actions, that could not be adequately understood in terms of the dual instinctual impulses. Freud (1922, 1933) therefore adopted a new instinctual system of motivation, with the opposition being between life instincts (Eros) aimed at enhancing and prolonging life and death instincts (Thanatos) that continuously strove for destruction of life within the organism. Specific actions are presumably generated by various admixtures of the two instinctual impulses. In this conceptual revision, aggression became an inborn drive rather than a by-product of thwarting libidinal strivings. Sadism and other forms of interpersonal aggression represented the death instinct discharged outward; self-injurious actions were considered manifestations of the self-destructive instinct directed inward.

The social implications of this theory for the modification of human aggression provide little basis for optimism. In an exchange of letters with Einstein on how mankind might be spared future wars, Freud (1950) reiterated his belief that destruction satisfies an instinctual inclination and that it is therefore fruitless to attempt to eliminate aggressiveness. Neither satisfaction of material needs, establishment of equality, nor other improvements in the conditions of life can alter the level of aggression. Though in Freud's view aggression is unavoidable, the intensity and the form of its expression are modifiable. Aggression could presumably be attenuated by the antagonistic influence of the life instincts. Development of emotional ties between people was suggested by Freud as one indirect means of curtailing extreme destructiveness. The provision of opportunities for outward discharge of the innate aggressive impulse was also proposed as a regulatory device. For Freud (1933) maintained that when expression of aggression is impeded, people are forced to behave destructively in order to protect themselves from self-destruction.

Freud won few adherents to his position even among enthusiastic advocates of psychoanalytic theory. Apparently the notion that people harbored an inborn impulse constantly striving to kill them exceeded the bounds of credibility. In recent years much more parsimonious—and empirically verifiable—explanations of why people repeatedly behave in self-injurious ways have been advanced by learning theorists. It is amply documented in psychological research that immediate reinforcement outweighs the effects of delayed punishment in controlling behavior. Through appropriate temporal arrangement of positive and negative outcomes, one can cause any organism, be it man, chimpanzee, or flatworm, to engage in self-hurtful behavior. Most detrimental actions such as self-defeating defensive behavior, excessive drinking, overeating, and other addictive behaviors are powerfully maintained by their immediate and automatic reinforcing effects, whereas the aversive consequences are often slowly cumulative and not experienced for some time. Evidence that self-injurious behavior in humans can be turned off and on by environmental cues and reduced in frequency by varying its immediate consequences provides further support for the view that such behavior is primarily under social rather than instinctual control.

As Gillespie (1971) has noted at a recent Vienna Congress devoted to aggression, most psychoanalysts have compromised with Freud's theory, treating aggression as an instinctual drive but rejecting the self-directed death instinct. Aggression presumably originates internally like other endogenous drives. The lack of evidence for a physiological drive mechanism in aggression is either dismissed as unimportant because the instinctual drive is only a "construct," or it is believed that an internal drive will be discovered by future research.

It is doubtful that the instinctual drive theories of aggression are capable of empirical verification. Most of them are formulated in such broad terms that they do not generate specific predictions that could be put to experimental tests. When a nonmeasurable instinctual force is combined with many qualifying factors that are also somewhat elusive, the theory can explain any variety of events that have already happened, though it cannot predict them. The postdictions, of course, are compatible with alternative theories that do not invoke the operation of an innate aggressive drive. The conceptual status of an instinctual drive is especially dubious if it is presented as an autonomous energy-generating system, as in the case of the aggressive instincts posited by Freud and by Lorenz. Innate drives usually have an identifiable biological source such as food deprivation in hunger, water deprivation in thirst, and gonadal hormones and evocative external stimuli in sexual urges. Their strength is therefore externally modifiable and at least indirectly measurable.

Ethological Theories

The writings of some ethologists and their popularizers renewed interest in explanations of aggressive behavior in terms of instinctual mechanisms. The view that man possesses a fighting instinct was engagingly presented in an anecdotal blend of ethology, anthropology, and moral philosophy by the distinguished ethologist Lorenz (1966) in his publicly acclaimed book *On Aggression*. Certain aspects of this position were further popularized by a former playwright, Ardrey (1966), who contended that humans are driven to fight each other by a property instinct designated as a territorial imperative. Other books, published under catchy titles, similarly proclaim that man is instinctively aggressive.

For Lorenz, aggression involves an instinctual system that generates its own source of aggressive energy independently of external stimulation; this fighting urge gradually builds up until relieved by an appropriate releasing stimulus. The property of being self-generating rather than reactive to external conditions accounts for its danger and its unmodifiability. Intraspecies aggression in subhumans, however, serves a number of positive functions. Fighting disperses populations over a habitable area and thus ensures optimal utilization of food resources. It produces selective breeding of strong members of the species. And the aggressive urge can provide the driving force for activities that outwardly do not appear aggressive. The potential benefits of aggression are realized by animals because, through the evolutionary process, they have developed aggression inhibitions that prevent them from destroying members of their own species. For example, animals typically ward off dangerous combat by threatening displays that presumably convey information innately to the protagonists. When animals aggress toward each other, they do so in harmless ritualized ways that establish the victor more through endurance than serious physical injury. And as an additional protection, overpowered combatants can promptly terminate further attacks on themselves by submission signals that instinctively inhibit the victors' aggressive behavior.

Lorenz contends that man is endowed with the same fighting instinct as lower animals, but that it is poorly controlled because he lacks inborn inhibitions against severely injuring and killing his fellow human beings. The following evolutionary explanation is offered for this tragic state of affairs: Natural selection ensured that animals with powerful destructive potential evolved strong aggression-inhibiting mechanisms to prevent self-extermination of the species. Since man is "a basically harmless, omnivorous creature, lacking in natural weapons with which to kill big prey," he never developed built-in inhibitors against aggression as did the dangerously armed carnivores. Although man's natural fighting equipment may be puny, his intelligence gave him lethal weaponry for which he has no innate inhibitors. Paradoxically, man's highest qualities —his capacity for thought and verbal communication—drive him out of the "paradise in which he could follow his instincts with impunity." The proverbial Martian, viewing the skeletons of dinosaurs in natural history museums and the masses of lively people inhabiting the earth, would undoubtedly leave unconvinced that intelligence and the capacity to learn through experience are necessarily life-shortening attributes. Interestingly, Montagu (1968) argues the opposite position, that man has been favored in the process of natural selection because most of his behavior is not under instinctual control and thus can be adjusted to changing environmental circumstances.

In point of fact, animals do not possess innate signals for stopping attacks, and the stereotyped signals they do use have variable effects on the responses of their foes (Barnett, 1967). Lorenz's widely cited account of defeated wolves turning off their assailants by exposing the jugular vein turned out to represent faulty observation. What Lorenz interpreted as vulnerable exposure by the defeated that automatically blocks aggression was actually a challenging posture by the victor preparatory to dangerous attack (Schenkel, 1967). Defeated rivals can best forestall further assaults by surrender, by relinquishing claims, or by escape. Those that are unskilled in defense or escape may meet with serious injury or even death. Under conditions of confinement animals are known to kill members of their own species, a phenomenon that is not readily explainable in terms of innate signal control of lethal responses. It is true that man does not rely heavily on auditory, postural, and olfactory signals for conveying aggressive intent or appeasement. He has a much more intricate system of communication—namely, language—for controlling aggression. National leaders can therefore better safeguard against catastrophic violence by verbal communiqués than by snapping their teeth or erecting their hair, especially in view of the prevalence of baldness among the higher echelons.

In the closing chapter of his book, Lorenz offers some suggestions for how a society might cope with a poorly controlled aggressive drive. He cautions against either social prohibitions or genetic engineering on the grounds that negative sanctions dam up aggressive impulses to dangerous levels and that breeding out the fighting instinct could remove a generalized source of motivation. Believing firmly in cathartic drainage, Lorenz recommends that aggression should be encouraged toward substitute targets and in sublimated forms. International competitive sports are considered especially well suited for this purpose, though in fact such contests often breed discord. Occupying privileged positions in society, theorists of different persuasions readily prescribe gladiatorial combat for mass viewing and other recreational activities supposedly conducive to the release of pent-up aggressive impulses. But to the less advantaged who rely on aggression to improve their life circumstances, the recreational prescriptions would be ineffectual remedies for misdiagnosed conditions.

As additional preventive measures, Lorenz advises people to laugh more and to embrace all humanity with love and friendship. Finally, militant enthusiasm widely used by demagogues to breed discord can be enlisted to promote international friendships by channeling the devotion to transnational values of art, science, and medicine. The latter humanitarian practices, which stand in sharp contrast to the fatalistic view of human aggression, seem grafted on rather than derivable from Lorenz's theory of behavior. According to the hydraulic motivational system, no amount of laughter or friendship can stop the self-generating aggressive drive from welling up and discharging periodically. Prescriptions of benevolent remedies increase the appeal of instinctual doctrines.

In professional circles, the works of Lorenz and Ardrey were admired for their literary quality, but severely criticized for their weak scholarship. A volume edited by Montagu (1968) contains critiques by a number of scientists who evaluated the validity of the views advanced in these books. Ardrey's case for an innate territorial drive, which is disputed by a sizable body of evidence, was dismissed as grossly misleading. Lorenz was similarly taken to task, though with less enmity, on a variety of grounds; many of his generalizations about animal behavior and cultural patterns contain errors of fact; questionable causal interpretations are assuredly proffered without substantiating data; and evidence that fails to support the instinctual theory is either slighted or disregarded. Nowhere does Lorenz provide adequate criteria for differentiating inborn patterns of behavior from those developed and maintained by experiential influences. Since he attributes most social behaviors to instinctual sources, usually by analogy to subhuman patterns, the disregard of learning influences comes as no particular surprise. Thus, for instance, defense of one's own beliefs and customs is depicted as a "phylogenetically programmed behavior mechanism" and likened to the instinctual "triumph ceremony" of geese. Instinctual attribution constitutes explanation in this scheme.

In a scholarly critique of the principles later used to explain aggression, Lehrman (1953) marshaled considerable evidence to dispute many of Lorenz's nativistic interpretations. Complex behavior does not emerge as a unitary pattern, but is formed through integration of many component activities of differing origins. Thorough causal analyses of behavior reveal that instinctual explanations are often not only misleading, but discourage examination of developmental processes. Animals are sometimes raised in isolation from members of their species to show that responses can appear without learning. However, practice of component activities, which is never completely controlled in isolation experiments, may make a considerable contribution to the development of supposedly innate patterns.

Although some researchers have sought the nature of animals by observing how they behave under impoverished or limited natural circumstances, others have explored how their nature may vary depending upon their social experiences. The classic experiments by Kuo (1930) illustrate the latter approach. Kittens were raised by themselves, with rat-killing mothers, or with rat companions. Within each of these conditions half were brought up as vegetarians and the other half as carnivores. The different rearing conditions produced cats with pacifistic and vicious natures. Those raised with rat-killing mothers became avid rat killers (85 percent); less than half of those reared in isolation (45 percent) ever killed any rats; whereas those that grew up with rats developed a strong attachment to them and rarely killed any members of their species (17 percent). Vegetarianism reduced rat-eating but not rat-killing. Kittens that failed to attack any rats after several months of testing under hungry or satiated conditions were then exposed to modeling influences in which they observed adult cats kill rats. Aggressive modeling converted 82 percent of the pacifistic kittens with the isolation background into vigorous rat killers, but even the power of example and severe hunger could not induce rat-raised kittens to attack rats (only 7 percent did so).

Neutral contact with customary prey also drastically reduces attack behavior and susceptibility to aggressive modeling, although early positive contact serves as a greater aggression-neutralizing influence (Kuo, 1938). Given appropriate reinforcement conditions, animals can adapt to a noncompetitive social system within which they function amicably, or they can organize themselves into dominance hierarchies based on fighting that maintain orderly relations by threat and submission (Kuo, 1960). Examining the habits of humans raised alone or in a particular environment would likewise yield a different view of man's nature than if one studies how man behaves under diverse cultural practices. The higher the evolutionary development of a species, the greater is its plasticity.

Lorenz's motivational model, which assumes special importance in the explanation of aggression, is open to even more serious criticism than his speculations about the origins of behavior. As a number of researchers (Hinde, 1960; Lehrman, 1953; Scott, 1972) have pointed out, there exists no neurophysiological evidence that functional activities generate their own motivating energy which accumulates with time in the absence of appropriate releasing stimuli. Nor is there any means by which energy can become "dammed up" in the nervous system, forcefully discharging without external elicitation or spilling over to brain centers controlling other activities. In other words, the neurophysiological mechanisms that mediate aggression do not themselves create stimulation for fighting.

Researchers working in this field not only questioned the partial and casual treatment of empirical evidence, but they also objected to uncritical extrapolations from a dubious hereditarian model and to analogical reasoning based on superficial similarities in cross-species behavior. Considering that the factors regulating behavior often tend to be specific to a given species, most theorists understandably rejected the notion that mechanisms governing aggressive behavior in greylag geese and sticklebacks apply equally to human suburbanites. Even if this assumption were valid, how could alleged instinctual mechanisms of aggression that do not apply even to all lower animals explain the behavior of man? Territorial fighting, which figures prominently in the writings of both Ardrey and Lorenz, is a good case in point. Many herd animals, including some of man's closest forebears, do not stake out territories, nor do they jealously defend areas they inhabit at any given time. Even in animals that exhibit territorial aggression, such behavior tends to be quite variable depending upon environmental characteristics, population densities, sex hormonal states, scarcity of food, and other external factors (Crook, 1968; Hinde, 1956). The specificity and variable nature of territorial fighting in lower animals casts grave doubt on the notion that man is impelled by a territorial instinct to wage warfare against trespassers. Indeed, as Carrighar (1968) has noted, nations' need for resort to military conscription suggests that their citizens are far from moved by an overpowering urge to fight for territory.

Unlike coral fish that are quick to repulse approaches by members of their own species, trespassers on a person's property do not as a rule evoke territorial fighting. Under most conditions interlopers are more likely to elicit curiosity than combat. On the occasions when people do fight over territorial intrusions, the phenomena can be much better explained in terms of learning processes than instinctual mechanisms. Some types of intruders have no particular effect on the proprietor's well-being; the appearance of others may produce positive outcomes; and still others appropriate or destroy valued resources, creating adverse effects. People may thus incline to be initially wary of a stranger, but they base their reactions toward him on judgments of probable consequences. They will welcome a visitor of good will and threaten a menacing one. Differential experiences, either direct or vicarious, with different types of intruders produce discriminative responses that cannot be readily explained by an indiscriminate property instinct that automatically compels an organism to chase whatever approaches its territorial boundaries.

Carefully conducted ethological studies (Carthy and Ebling, 1964; van Lawick-Goodall, 1971) have produced a large body of descriptive data on the way animals of different species behave in their natural habitats. Some of this information is specifically concerned with environmental situations that stimulate fighting. In certain species aggressive responses are regularly elicited by specific environmental stimuli. Stickleback fish, for example, vigorously attack male members of their species during periods when their bellies have a red coloration. Their assault on red-bellied facsimiles that otherwise differ markedly in shape from actual sticklebacks shows that their aggressiveness is controlled by color cues (Tinbergen, 1951).

Territorial encroachment, as previously noted, is another event that evokes fighting in some animal species and in many fish and birds. After proprietors establish rights over a given locality, they generally attack rivals who intrude on their domain. A number of other factors have been identified as determinants of aggressive behavior, though as in territorial fighting, the degree of behavioral control exerted by the evocative stimuli is significantly affected by a variety of conditions. Males of some species fight over possession of females, especially during mating periods. Animals also fight over food, over rank in a dominance hierarchy, in defense of their young offspring, in warding off attacks from predators on members of their own species, and they often behave aggressively when subjected to painful stimulation (Hamburg, 1970).

Field studies have been principally concerned with environmental elicitors of aggression, perhaps because the cues that evoke combat can be easily observed and documented. On the other hand, identification of social learning determinants of aggression under natural conditions of life requires painstaking analyses of interaction processes and therefore tends to be neglected. Few researchers are willing to follow selected animals continuously as they wander through their natural habitats in order to record incidents in which aggressive responses are modeled and are affected by the consequences of fighting various adversaries. Detailed observations would also be needed to trace the manner in which social stimuli become endowed with fight-eliciting properties through associations with combat experiences. When elicitors are favored over causal processes in field observations, the selective data tend to convey the impression that aggressiveness is a preestablished phenomenon triggered by more or less fixed stimulus events.

Lower species usually come equipped with rudimentary preformed habits and high initial susceptibility to modeling influences that enable them to respond adaptively from the outset to their environmental circumstances. By contrast, man is furnished with few inborn habits, but with vast potentialities for learning. Not only are people more malleable than biologically simpler organisms, but advanced information-processing capacities render human behavior more subject to social and cognitive control. Rather than responding instinctively to releasing sign stimuli, humans regulate their behavior in accordance with judgments of anticipated consequences for prospective actions. In other words, innate releasing and inhibiting mechanisms have been largely replaced by cortical control. For these reasons, causal relationships established in lower species may be misleading when applied to man without empirical confirmation of the equivalence. Interspecies studies of the mechanisms governing sexual behavior provide an excellent illustration of this point.

Hormonal control of sexual behavior decreases with advancing evolutionary status (Beach, 1969; Ford and Beach, 1951). In lower mammalian species, for instance, sexual activities are closely regulated by gonadal hormones; among primates, sexual responsiveness is partially independent of hormone secretions; human sexual arousal is exceedingly variable and relatively independent of hormonal conditions. Thus, to produce a rodent Don Juan would require repeated administration of testosterone, whereas showing him lascivious pictures of well-endowed female mice would have no stimulating effects. One would, on the other hand, rely on sexually valenced displays rather than on hormonal injections to produce erotic arousal in human males.

Cross-cultural studies of sexual behavior (Ford and Beach, 1951) disclose further that the regions of the body, the physical characteristics, the social acts, and the extrinsic sensory events that function as sexual arousers all vary considerably from society to society. What is erotically stimulating in one culture—corpulence or skinniness; upright hemispherical breasts or long pendulous ones; shiny white teeth or black pointed ones; deformed ears, nose, and lips or naturally shaped ones; broad or slim hips; light or dark skin color—may be neutral or repulsive to members of another social group. A similar diversity exists in the age at which sexual interest first emerges, in the forms that sexual behavior takes, and in the choice of sexual objects. Considering that human sexual responsiveness is, in large part, socially rather than hormonally determined, findings based on studies of subhuman species concerning regulatory mechanisms have limited generalizability to humans. There is every reason to believe that the evolutionary decrease in innate determinants of behavior holds true for aggression as well.

Studies of hormonal influences have shown that androgen fosters aggressiveness in animals (Conner and Levine, 1969; Rothballer, 1967). In addition to their effects on brain organization, sex hormones can influence combative behavior indirectly by stimulating physical growth and muscular development. Moreover, during mating periods when sex hormone levels are high, male species are especially combative. Animals must rely upon their biological equipment for whatever success they can achieve in combat. Hence, those with large canine teeth, powerful jaw muscles, and imposing size become belligerent fighters through victories; the physically less well-endowed become submissive through defeats. By contrast, man's capacity to use destructive weapons greatly reduces his dependence upon structural equipment to aggress successfully. A puny man with a gun can easily triumph over powerfully built opponents who are unarmed. In violent human encounters other than fisticuffs, weapons will almost always beat physical build. Man's capacity for social organization likewise reduces the importance of structural characteristics in aggressive attainments. At the social level, aggressive power derives from organized collective action rather than from biological advantage. Victory is thus assured by the force of numbers acting in concert, and the physical stature of individual challengers does not matter much, if at all. Organized fighting between groups, as in internation warfare, domestic rebellion, and intergang combat, is a human creation that does not exist except in the most rudimentary form among animals.

Animal studies have shown that testosterone treatment of fetal or newborn females masculinizes them and increases their aggressiveness. In humans, excess fetal androgens, produced by either enzyme defect or administration of progestin to pregnant mothers, causes masculinization of external genitalia in female offspring and fosters male orientations. These females are, however, no more physically aggressive than nonandrogenized girls (Ehrhardt, Epstein, and Money, 1968). Interpretation of the differences in interest patterns is complicated by the fact that approximately half of the androgenized girls were raised as males during the early months of life before their condition was correctly diagnosed. If excessive prenatal testosterone is highly associated with later tomboyishness, further research would be needed to determine whether hormones exert their effect through neurosexual organization, physical structure, or by some other means (Hamburg, 1969). Androgenized girls who selectively associate with boys because of their physical characteristics might be expected to develop male orientations through peer modeling and participation in masculine play activities.

Structural characteristics related to aggressiveness also have somewhat different evolutionary and survival consequences for animals and man. In some animal species, physical strength determines which males do the mating. Combat victors gain possession of females so that the most dominant males have the highest reproduction rates. With humans, most of whom practice monogamy, mate selection is based more on such qualities as good looks, winsome style, intelligence, and financial standing than on fighting prowess. Within such social arrangements, differential reproduction rates are primarily determined by religious and ecological beliefs, as well as by access to birth control devices. For these reasons, variations in fertility do not necessarily favor aggressiveness.

Questions of generality likewise arise in evaluating the influence of genetic factors on aggressiveness. The propensity of laboratory animals to behave aggressively can be significantly altered by selective breeding. Descendants of aggressive strains tend to be increasingly more combative across succeeding generations than offspring of docile stocks. The matter is more complicated, however, than it might appear from limited assessments. Contrasting strains can vary widely in their relative combativeness depending upon the circumstances under which they are tested and the nature of their targets. Thus, members of docile strains may behave submissively in one setting but aggressively in a different situation; similarly, fighting breeds may be vicious toward certain targets and pacific in relation to others (Fredericson and Birnbaum, 1954; Ginsburg and Allee, 1942).

Corning and Corning (1972) put it well when they noted that genes do not produce behavior; rather, they generate enzymes that affect biochemical processes and structural development which, in turn, can influence response potentialities. Therefore, to understand the means by which genetic variations affect aggressive responsiveness requires knowledge about the links between genes, neurophysiological mechanisms, and behavioral capabilities to act aggressively. When animals are bred with respect to an outstanding characteristic, they may display other features that largely account for observed differences between strains. This is especially true of activities that require a variety of functions (for example, perceptual, cognitive, locomotor, emotional, and motivational), as is usually the case. By selective breeding, for example, researchers produced populations of animals bright and dull in maze learning. Further analysis revealed that not only did the relative superiority of the groups change on different learning tasks, but that differences in motivation and emotionality were largely responsible for the variation in learning performances (Searle, 1949). With regard to fighting, combative strains have been found to be more active motorically and less emotionally upset by stress (Lagerspetz, 1969). Such factors might be expected to determine success in physical combat.

To complicate the picture further, some of the variability attributed to genetic factors may stem from other sources. When animals are reared by their own mothers, postnatal maternal influences can contribute to interstrain differences in behavior (Denenberg, 1970). Offspring from aggressive strains nursed by their own mothers are likely to turn out to be more combative than those reared by docile foster mothers. Behavioral differences can result from maternal handling during the nursing period and from maternal modeling of aggression in later developmental phases, as convincingly demonstrated by Kuo (1930).

Some characteristics are highly heritable and difficult to modify, whereas others, which are only indirectly affected by genetic factors, may be highly susceptible to environmental influences. The importance attached to genetically mediated effects on aggressiveness therefore depends upon their modifiability through experience. Several investigators have shown that aggression in combative strains can be markedly reduced by repeated defeats, whereas submissive animals can be made somewhat more aggressive through combat victories (Ginsburg and Allee, 1942; Lagerspetz, 1964, 1969). Since even victors are likely to receive painful bruises while fighting, the experienced punishment may detract from the value of eventual success. To take a human example, a person who triumphed over an opponent but in the process lost his teeth would be somewhat hesitant about violent encounters even if assured victory. The relative influence of reinforcement and genetic determinants is best tested under conditions in which conquests gain victors access to food, mates, territories, and social rank. These are the types of purposes that aggression serves for animals in their natural habitat. In the case of man, although some may derive self-esteem rewards from disposing of opponents, few go around picking hurtful fights merely to win them. They too risk the costs of aggression to obtain a variety of outcomes extrinsic to the act itself.

On the assumption that the male-determining chromosome is related to aggressiveness, researchers explored whether a genetic abnormality involving an extra male chromosome increases propensity to violent conduct. (Normal males possess an XY pair of sex chromosomes, whereas females have an XX pair; the Y is considered to be the chromosome determining maleness.) Surveys of newborn children reveal that approximately 1 in 500 males possesses an extra Y chromosome (XYY).

Little interest was shown in the XYY anomaly until Jacobs and her colleagues (Jacobs, Brunton, and Melville, 1965) reported that mentally defective men institutionalized for various forms of criminal behavior show a higher prevalence of the extra Y chromosome (2.9 percent of all those tested) than might be expected in the general public (0.2 percent). Since the XYY condition is comparatively rare but goes with tallness, many of the subsequent studies used biased sampling procedures by selecting only tall imprisoned men for chromosomal analysis. On the basis of further reports of higher prevalence rates, some investigators concluded that XYY males are genetically predisposed to violent and antisocial conduct. The stereotype of the XYY males as dangerously assaultive was quickly established by publicized murder trials in which legal responsibility for homicidal acts was disclaimed on the grounds of chromosomal defect. Richard Speck, a ruthless mass murderer, was reported in the press and in professional journals as an XYY aberration, although in fact he had no genetic defect. Some medical practitioners even advocated genetic counseling for parents about the antisocial propensities of XYY children. Such a stigmatizing practice could very well lead apprehensive adults to overreact to misconduct in ways likely to confirm the prophecy. Lost in the publicity was the notable feature that XYY inmates in the original survey rarely aggressed against people and, of their total convictions, 88 percent were for offenses against property. The XYY prisoners in fact have a lower incidence of physical and sexual assaults than suitably matched XYs (Price and Whatmore, 1967). Perhaps the most striking aspect of the chromosome story is the ready proclivity to blame crime on "bad genes."

The alleged relationship between the double Y chromosome and aggressiveness was strongly disputed by some researchers on a number of grounds (Kessler and Moos, 1970; Owen, 1972; Shah, 1970). To begin with, the prevalence studies confounded, among other things, chromosomal anomaly with height and social influences. Given evidence that the XYY karyotype is found more often among tall men, its prevalence among tall inmates should be compared not against the general population, but against a subsample of tall noninstitutionalized individuals matched with the prisoners on social factors conducive to antisocial aggression. The misleading results of biased sampling are shown by Clark *et al.* (1972), who report that when only tall prisoners are selected for chromosomal screening, the prevalence of XYY is higher (2.7 percent) than when prisoners under 6 feet are also included (1.8 percent). Although XYYs who run afoul of the law are not especially assaultive, they are nevertheless arrested at an earlier age and more often. This differential arrest pattern, which can have a decisive impact on the course of future behavior, may conceivably be related to physical stature. Apart from the psychological strains and older companionship fostered by conspicuous tallness, large offenders are likely to be treated by arresting officers as older and more dangerous than are smaller ones. Early commitment to a reformatory populated with delinquents is apt to launch one on an antisocial career, regardless of genetic makeup.

An extra male chromosome was believed to enhance aggressiveness by producing hypermasculinity. Results of a comparative study by Clark *et al.* (1972) cast serious doubt on this line of reasoning. They conducted a chromosomal survey of men in several penal institutions for the rate of XYY anomaly and the Klinefelter syndrome (XXY), which is presumed by many to be associated with nonaggressive tendencies. The XYYs are no more prevalent (1.8 percent) than XXYs (2.6 percent), nor is there any discernible difference in their criminal records. It might be noted in passing that results of a large number of chromosomal surveys yield a lower prevalence of XYY prisoners (2.3 percent) than originally reported, and even this figure overestimates the rate for prison populations because, with few exceptions, only tall males are selected for analysis (Owen, 1972).

What effects, if any, an extra Y chromosome has on behavioral development can be satisfactorily answered only by a double-blind prospective study in which psychological functioning is periodically assessed in children with the XYY karyotype and in suitably matched controls who have no chromosomal anomaly. A longitudinal investigation of this type would most likely demonstrate that the vast majority of XYY males, like others, are engaged in prosocial pursuits. The data already reviewed suggest that the small numbers who may get into legal difficulty are, if anything, apt to be less interpersonally assaultive than transgressors of normal genetic makeup.

It is interesting that people vigorously disclaim that instincts or genes cause them to behave the way they do, but are quick to believe that man is instinctively aggressive. The wide popular appeal of such interpretations cannot be attributed to the attraction of simple explanations, nor to the prevalence of aggressive behavior, because other social practices found to be widespread or universal, such as bartering behaviors, are rarely ascribed to an economic instinct. One possible explanation is that most people find it exceedingly difficult to understand how socialized human beings can repeatedly commit atrocities, often at the risk of self-extermination, unless driven by an inherent viciousness. Also, by attributing aggression to inherited tendencies, people are absolved from the responsibility of changing social conditions that benefit their self-interests at the risk of provoking aggression in disadvantaged members of society.

The dichotomous view that behavior is either learned or innate has dwindling support as knowledge about human functioning increases. Though radical hereditarians and environmentalists still exist, most theorists acknowledge that social and physiological influences are not that easily separable, since both sets of factors interact in subtle ways in determining behavior. Where certain biological equipment is needed to perform manual aggressive acts, structural factors, which have a genetic basis, may partly determine whether initial aggressiveness proves successful and is further developed, or whether it fails and is discarded. Possession of a brawny physique, for example, increases the probability that physically aggressive modes of behavior will prove effective.

Physical characteristics can also indirectly affect the development of aggressive behavior through their influence on associational preferences. The social acquaintances and activities of robust boys, for instance, are likely to differ substantially from those of frail boys or of petite girls. Association preferences, in turn, determine to a large degree the types of models repeatedly observed and, consequently, the patterns of behavior that will be most thoroughly learned. The groups with which children choose to affiliate also define the forms of behavior that are normatively sanctioned, rewarded, and selectively perfected.

Even in instances in which new patterned responses are formed entirely on the basis of learning experiences, physiological factors still serve as contributing influences. Learning capacity is affected by genetic characteristics. And while the organization of behavioral components into novel intricate patterns is a product of experience, the rudimentary elements are present as part of the natural endowment. Thus, for example, children begin with a set of elementary sounds that they subsequently learn to combine into an infinite variety of larger verbal units to form grammatical speech. The basic phonetic elements may appear trivial compared to the learned intricate compounds, but they are nevertheless essential. But it would be misleading to designate social behavior as instinctual simply because it employed a few innate elements. The fact that a child is born with the capacity to strike objects with his hand does not mean that the elaborate fighting skills of a boxer reflect an inherited tendency. One of the basic issues in dispute with regard to instinctual interpretations of aggression is whether complex patterned responses themselves come preformed or are fashioned through experiential influences.

Many so-called instinctual behaviors may contain a large learning component even in the common patterns displayed by members of a species. Observational learning is a principal means of acquiring new response patterns in animals and humans alike (Bandura, 1971d). Developmental studies of modeling processes disclose that animals readily learn adaptive responses soon after their eyes become functional by observing the behavior of skilled models (Adler and Adler, 1968). In the natural enviroment young offspring are provided with countless opportunities to observe and to learn the behavior exhibited by members of the same species.

Observational learning may play an especially important role in species that are highly susceptible to imprinting. This is a process wherein young offspring develop a strong attachment to, and rapidly learn general characteristics of the model to which they were first exposed during a developmentally sensitive period (Hess, 1959). Although some response patterns are transmitted during the impressionable period itself, the formation of a close social attachment to a model greatly enhances observational exposure and thereby assures further learning of the modeled behavior.

Not all species are susceptible to imprinting. Apparently those whose locomotor abilities mature rapidly are most prone to display the phenomenon, whereas higher mammalian species that are born biologically incompetent and hence require extended dependence on caretakers do not (Klopfer, 1962). These notable evolutionary differences further underscore the need for caution in generalizing across species. Moreover, modeling and reinforcement influences, which are universally present, have powerful effects on the behavior of species that are influenceable throughout life rather than mainly at an early optimal period of development. For this reason, informal ethological observations cannot provide full understanding of the origins of behavior. When the effects of social experiences are not systematically measured, behaviors that result from observational and reinforcement learning are readily ascribed to biological inheritance. Denenberg (1970) has shown that neonatal rearing practices not only have a profound effect on aggressiveness, but produce lasting changes in the animals' physiology as reflected in adrenocortical activity. Evidence that behavioral potentialities can be significantly affected by fetal environment further complicates identification of instinctually determined behavior. Finally, given some indications of fetal conditioning (Spelt, 1948), the possibility of prenatal learning must be considered in evaluating simple response patterns present at birth.

The coordination of aggressive behavior, like other forms of visceral and motor responsiveness, depends on neurophysiological mechanisms. Substantial research has been conducted on animals to determine whether the mechanisms mediating aggression are localized in specific brain regions. The results show that subcortical structures, principally the hypothalamus and the limbic system, are involved in facilitating and inhibiting aggressive behavior. Lesioning these areas or stimulating them chemically or electrically can modify the expression of threat displays and stereotyped attack responses. The effects induced by such methods are not entirely specific, however. Not only are behaviors other than aggression similarly affected, but activation of any one of several regions can produce similar behavioral effects (Clemente and Lindsley, 1967; Garattini and Sigg, 1969). While the hypothalamus is a prominent mediator of attack responses, animals can be prompted to aggress by external events even after the hypothalamus has been surgically isolated from the rest of the brain (Ellison and Flynn, 1968). The same neural structure can thus serve a variety of behavioral functions, and different structures can mediate the same social behavior.

Although aggressive actions are partly coordinated at subcortical levels, these neural systems are selectively activated and controlled by higher cortical functions. Consequently, responding is regulated to a large extent by sensory inputs that are centrally processed. An ingenious study by Delgado (1967) shows how experiential influences can govern response selection during electrical activation of the same neural center. It has been shown that electrical stimulation of the hypothalamus in the vicinity of the ventromedial nucleus generally evokes attack-like behavior in animals. Delgado added a social dimension to the research that threw new light on thalamic control of aggression. He recorded the social behavior of a small colony of monkeys at normal times and at periodic intervals when selected members with brain-implanted electrodes were electrically stimulated through radio transmission.

Hypothalamic stimulation of a monkey who assumed a dominant role in the colony instigated him to attack subordinate male members, but the stimulated boss monkey did not assault the females. Nor did he attack his immediate subordinate, with whom he was on friendly terms. By contrast, hypothalamic stimulation elicited cowering and submissive behavior in a monkey of low social rank. Even more impressive is evidence that electrical stimulation of the same cerebral mechanism can evoke markedly different behavior in the same animal as his social rank is modified by changing the membership of the colony. Thus, hypothalamic stimulation elicited submissiveness in the animal when he occupied a low hierarchical position, but marked aggressiveness when he was the dominant member in the group.

Other investigators (Panksepp, 1971; Panksepp and Trowill, 1969; Roberts, Steinberg, and Means, 1967) also report that electrical stimulation of the same brain region produces no attacks in some animals, that attacks are more readily elicited in normally aggressive animals than in more docile members of the same species, that hypothalamically stimulated aggressive responses are inhibited under threat of counterattack, and that assaultive responses decline and even disappear with repeated electrical stimulation. Aggressive responses are not, in fact, directly and automatically elicited, but vary depending upon the types of targets available. Such evidence indicates considerable environmental control of centrally stimulated effects.

For the most part, researchers studying neural regulation of attack responses directly stimulate subcortical areas with an artificial electrical input in a relatively barren social environment without varying prior learning experiences. Experimental arrangements of this sort are advantageous for localizing lower brain functions. However, Delgado's finding that social influences can determine the nature of the cerebrally evoked behavior indicates that such procedures may exaggerate the degree of neural control under natural conditions, in which environmental activators transmitted by informative sensory messages are modulated through higher memory and learning mechanisms. The functional organization of these higher control systems is largely determined by learning experiences. It is therefore only by varying neural and experiential influences that a full understanding can be obtained of how the various brain structures interact in regulating aggressive behavior.

It is valuable to know how biological equipment works internally, but from the standpoint of explaining aggression it is even more important to understand how it is socially activated for different courses of action. In everyday life, biological systems are roused in humans by provocative sensory inputs from the environment and by anticipated response outcomes and other types of ideational activation. Hence, a remark interpreted as an insult will doubtless generate activity in the hypothalamus, whereas the same comment viewed innocuously will leave the hypothalamus undisturbed. Given a negative interpretation, social factors are likely to determine how the recipient will respond.

The social learning theory of human aggression adopts the position that man is endowed with neurophysiological mechanisms that enable him to behave aggressively, but the activation of these mechanisms depends upon appropriate stimulation and is subject to cortical control. Therefore, the specific forms that aggressive behavior takes, the frequency with which it is expressed, the situations in which it is displayed, and the specific targets selected for attack are largely determined by social experience.

A problem of clinical interest that has implications for neural regulatory functions is concerned with whether brain injuries affect expression of aggressive behavior. Literature on the neural correlates of human aggression is sparse. In exploratory studies of assaultive patients with brain pathologies, Delgado and his associates (1968) have occasionally been able to elicit aggressive responses by telemetered stimulation of the amygdala, but as a rule, the stimulation mainly evokes strange sensations and feelings.

Mark and Ervin (1970) report a high incidence of neurological dysfunctions in both self-referred violent patients and repetitively assaultive prisoners. According to these authors, the aggressiveness may reflect impairment of cortical control that leaves the person vulnerable to excitation by stimuli that would ordinarily be ineffective. Alternatively, external stimulation of a malfunctioning area of the brain may trigger neural discharges that prompt actions, sometimes at reduced levels of consciousness.

In judging how much importance to attach to neural dysfunctions, one also needs to know in how many cases brain damage is present but physical aggression does not occur. Incidence rates are less subject to misinterpretation when individuals are selected because they possess the condition supposedly conducive to aggression rather than because they display a history of aggressive conduct. Let us assume, for the sake of illustration, a 30 percent incidence of brain damage in the criminally assaultive, whereas in the total population of brain-damaged people 3 percent are physically aggressive. Knowing only the proportion of incarcerated offenders who suffer neurological impairment, it would be easy to overrate the influence of neural factors.

Cerebral disorder can accompany aggression either as cause, as effect, or as a joint product of other conditions. Abnormal electroencephalograms (EEGs) have been reported by some investigators to be more common among assaultive persons than in the general population (Mark and Ervin, 1970). The meaning of differential incidence rates can change, however, depending upon what groups are compared. In a study reported by Ostrow and Ostrow (1946), for example, abnormal EEGs were just as prevalent among conscientious objectors who eschew violence and other inmates jailed for nonaggressive offenses as among assaultive prisoners. It is conceivable that deviant EEG patterns may, in many cases, be merely accompaniments of aggression and not its cause. Considering the impoverished backgrounds from which most prisoners come, they probably show a higher incidence of physiological deficiencies of almost any kind. Moreover, assaultive people are repeatedly involved in fights, in auto accidents, and in forcible arrests that might easily result in head injuries (Bach-y-Rita et al., 1971; Bandura and Walters, 1959). Thus, some cerebral damage would not be a surprising product of an aggressive style of life. A longitudinal study of boxers would attest to progressive cerebral damage with continued fighting. Finally, a person who suffers brain injury that impairs his level of functioning may be treated by others in a rejecting, disparaging manner productive of aggression. If a neurologically intact person were dealt with in a similar fashion, he too might be prompted on occasion to respond assaultively. If the effects operate principally through social consequences, brain damage with maltreatment may increase the likelihood of aggression, but brain damage with considerate treatment may not.

Theories appear comprehensive when they contain an all-embracing analysis to the effect that aggressive behavior is determined by biological, psychological, and sociological factors. Such general propositions, which apply equally to almost anything people may do, hardly advance our understanding of aggression. It is also easy to misjudge learning approaches on the grounds that, as their name seems to imply, they must ignore biological determinants. The critical issue is not whether aggressive behavior is multiply determined, but to what extent do biological, psychological, and social influences contribute to variations in aggression between different people and in the same individual at different times and under different circumstances. It is evident from the preceding discussion and material presented later that the proportion of variance accounted for by these determinants differs across species, types of aggressive behavior, and social conditions.

Aggressive Drive Theories

Until recent years most theorists subscribed to an energy model of aggression, but they rejected instincts as the driving forces. In an effort to resolve the motivational problem, drives eventually replaced instincts as internal impellers of action. According to these theories, man is motivated to behave aggressively by a frustration-produced drive rather than by an innate aggressive force. This view, which gained widespread popular acceptance, was originally expounded in a set of testable propositions by Dollard and his co-authors (1939) and elaborated further in later publications (Feshbach, 1964, 1970; Sears, Whiting, Nowlis, and Sears, 1953; Whiting and Child, 1953).

The frustration-aggression hypothesis contended that interference with goal-directed activity induces an aggressive drive which, in turn, motivates behavior designed to injure the person toward whom it is directed. Infliction of injury was assumed to reduce the aggressive drive. In the form in which it was originally presented, the hypothesis presupposed that frustration always produces aggression. In later modifications of the hypothesis, aggression was still considered the naturally dominant response to frustration, but nonaggressive reactions could occur if aggressive behavior had previously been eliminated through punishment or nonreward. Although some members of the Yale group (Miller, 1941; Sears, 1941) discarded the notion that aggression is the only unlearned response to frustration, frustration nevertheless continued to be regarded as an inevitable cause of aggression; in other words, whenever an aggressive act occurred, frustration was assumed to be always present as the instigating condition. For years the standard explanation of aggression was in terms of frustration.

A number of factors were identified by Dollard and his associates as major determinants of aggressive behavior and the specific forms it takes. Since this formulation drew heavily on psychoanalytic theory, the variables singled out for attention are similar to those with which psychoanalysts concerned themselves at the time, rather than to those that have subsequently been found to be powerful controllers of aggressive behavior. One set of conditions that was proposed concerned antecedent factors governing degree of frustration, from which strength of the aggressive drive is inferred. The strength of instigation to aggression was assumed to vary directly with how strongly the thwarted response was motivated, the extent to which the thwarted response was interfered with, and the number of actions that were frustrated.

Criticism of the frustration-aggression hypothesis focused at first on the nature of responses to frustration. Anthropologists (Bateson, 1941) pointed out that in some cultures aggression was by no means a typical response to frustration. Barker, Dembo, and Lewin (1941) and Wright (1942, 1943) demonstrated that young children were inclined to regress rather than to aggress when frustrated. Other critics argued that only some kinds of frustration evoke aggressive behavior and that other forms do not. Maslow (1941), Rosenzweig (1944), and more recently Buss (1961) noted that personal insult and threat are more likely to evoke aggression than blocking of ongoing behavior, an issue that will be examined more fully later. And finally, Pastore (1952) emphasized the role of justifiability of the frustration in determining whether or not an aggressive response will occur. For example, a person who is passed by a municipal bus returning to a garage for repairs will display much less aggression than if the bus he has been waiting for drives by without justification, even though the goal-directed behavior of the ignored passenger has been equally thwarted in both instances. The effects of justifiability of frustration have not been tested behaviorally, but people typically report more aggression to hypothetical thwartings that appear unwarranted than to those for which excusable reasons exist (Cohen, 1955; Pastore, 1952).

Frustration subsumes such a diverse set of conditions that it no longer has a specific meaning. As new instigators of aggression were identified, the definition of frustration was stretched to accommodate them. In experimental studies, for example, people are frustrated by being personally insulted, subjected to physically painful treatment, deprived of valued rewards, blocked from reaching desired goals, and by experiencing failure. A large body of evidence exists showing that punishment, extinction, delay of reward, and response obstruction do not have uniform behavioral effects (Bandura, 1969a). Even the same treatment can elicit markedly different responses at different intensities and with different learning histories.

Not only is there great heterogeneity on the antecedent side of the relationship, but the consequent part of the formula—the aggressive behavior—also subsumes a vast array of activities colored by value judgments. As we already have seen, whether or not a given action is considered aggressive depends on a variety of factors, many of which reside in the definer rather than in the performer. The same injurious behavior can be labeled aggressive or not depending on subjective judgments of whether it was intentional or accidental; whether or not it is socially sanctioned; and among other factors, on the age, sex, role, and socioeconomic level of the performer. Considering the mixed items that are included under both frustration and aggression, it is questionable whether any general statements about the relationship between the two events have much meaning or validity.

The widespread acceptance of the frustration-aggression notion is perhaps attributable more to its simplicity than to its demonstrated predictive power. In point of fact, the formula that frustration breeds aggression does not hold up well under empirical scrutiny in laboratory studies in which conditions regarded as frustrative are systematically varied. They may sometimes increase aggression (Berkowitz, 1965a; Hartmann, 1969; Ulrich, Hutchinson, and Azrin, 1965); they may have no effect on aggressive behavior (Buss, 1966a; Jegard and Walters, 1960; Walters and Brown, 1963); or they may reduce aggressive responding (Kuhn, Madsen, and Becker, 1967). In experiments reporting positive results, frustration usually exerts an influence only in conjunction with prior training in aggression or exposure to aggressive modeling influences. The fact that negative findings occurred in studies in which social learning variables were highly influential lends support to the view that frustration, as commonly defined, is only one—and not necessarily the most important—factor affecting the expression of aggression.

There are two possible approaches to the problem of frustration. One may define it in terms broad enough to encompass heterogeneous conditions that could conceivably be judged to be frustrating. This strategy provides the convenience of a single shorthand label, but for reasons given earlier, the diverse operations subsumed under the omnibus term will yield inconsistent and contradictory empirical relationships to aggressive behavior. Alternatively, one may distinguish between dissimilar antecedent conditions and study how each type affects different classes of aggressive behavior. The latter approach is selected in social learning analyses of aggression.

Since frustration does not always produce aggression, inhibitory factors were introduced by drive proponents as additional controlling influences. A frustrated person will tend to suppress overt aggressive actions that are likely to be punished. The strength of inhibition was postulated, in this theory, to vary positively with the severity of punishment anticipated for behaving in an aggressive manner. There is substantial evidence, to be reviewed later, that punishment does indeed exert a regulatory function over aggressive behavior. However, the relationship between punishment and aggressive behavior proved to be more complex than was originally believed. The degree of behavioral control exerted by punishment is, in addition to its intensity, determined by the type and distribution of aversive consequences; their temporal relation to the behavior to be modified; the strength with which punished responses are concurrently reinforced; the availability of alternative modes of behavior for securing rewards; and the characteristics of punishing agents (Bandura, 1969a). Depending on its nature and interaction with other determinants, punishment can thus increase, reduce, or have no appreciable effect on aggressive behavior.

The relative strengths of the competing instigative and inhibitory tendencies served as the basis for explaining two other features of aggressive behavior, namely, displacement of aggression to substitute targets and change in the form of the aggressive behavior. According to Miller's (1959) conflict model, the objects and strength of displaced responses can be predicted from knowledge of three variables—the strength of aggressive instigation, the severity of punishment of aggressive behavior, and the similarity of alternative targets to the original frustrator. In empirical tests of this paradigm it was additionally assumed that both aggressive and inhibitory tendencies developed toward the original instigator were generalized to other people as well, the extent of the generalization being a function of the degree of similarity; and that inhibitory responses were generalized less than aggressive ones. It follows from this model that the stronger the inhibitions, the further out on the dissimilarity continuum the aggressive response is likely to be displaced. Thus, aggression will be diverted to other persons who are similar to the original instigator when fear of punishment is relatively weak, but to dissimilar people when it is strong.

The process of response displacement is depicted in the same way as victim displacement, except that the generalization dimension represents a continuum of directness of response (for example, physical aggression, verbal aggression, covert fantasy aggression) rather than differing characteristics of people. The effect of increasing the inhibitory tendency is to shift the mode of aggression to more indirect forms.

Deductions from this model were evaluated on the basis of findings derived from field studies of aggression and from controlled laboratory situations. It is difficult to assess the theoretical implications of the field studies (Bandura and Walters, 1959; Sears, Whiting, Nowlis, and Sears, 1953; Whiting and Child, 1953; Wright, 1954) because the ordering and locating of targets of aggression on the similarity dimension are somewhat arbitrary (and usually post hoc), and additional assumptions are often introduced to explain discrepancies between findings and predictions based on Miller's conflict model. Moreover, selective aggressiveness cannot be fully understood without knowledge of the patterns of reinforcement associated with expression of aggression toward different target persons. Antisocially aggressive boys, for example, have been found to have parents who strongly disapprove of and punish aggression in the home (Bandura, 1960; Bandura and Walters, 1959; Glueck and Glueck, 1950), a finding that has frequently been interpreted as an instance of displacement. However, since parents of such boys encourage and reward aggression outside the home, the apparently displaced aggression may be primarily an outcome of discrimination training (Bandura, 1960; Bandura and Walters, 1959).

The conflict model was tested most systematically in experimental studies of the scapegoat theory of prejudice. Applied in this context, the theory predicted that when a frustrating agent is feared, aggression will be displaced to people who differ from the social group to which the frustrator belongs. Evidence for this formulation is, at best, equivocal (Bandura and Walters, 1963; Berkowitz, 1958, 1962). Nor do informal observations of prejudicial behavior appear to provide much support for derivations from the conflict paradigm—namely, people will be most prejudiced toward highly dissimilar minorities when inhibitions are strong, but they will divert their hostility to minorities that are similar to the original frustrator if their inhibitions are weak. Holding inhibitory tendencies constant, the theory would also predict that the more strongly a person is angered, the more likely he is to displace his aggression to someone who is similar to the instigator.

The displacement model has limited predictive power when applied to the problem of human aggression because it adopts a basically non-social approach to a phenomenon that involves intricate social learning. Prejudices, like other aggressive acts, are developed through modeling and social reinforcement, and they make their appearance relatively early in a child's life (Stevenson, 1967; Radke-Yarrow, Trager, and Miller, 1952). Parents and other influential people, through precept, example, and their approving reactions, teach children whom they should hate and for what reasons, and how they should express their aggression toward the stigmatized targets. Reports of Ku Klux Klan rallies (*San Francisco Chronicle*, 1963) provide illustrations of how fear and hatred can be transmitted through modeling and social sanction to the Klansmen's observant offspring. People similarly come to abuse Irishmen, Italians, Poles, Jews, and other minority groups as a result of the prevailing sanctions in different communities, rather than on the basis of their resemblance to frustrators. Indeed, frustrators come in too many diverse forms to aid much in victim selection.

Displaced aggression is further modified by the reactions it elicits from the people who are aggressed against. Acquiescent targets will be victimized more often than retaliative ones. Moreover, the theory makes no provision for self-imposed restraints arising from self-devaluative reactions for hurting others, which may be more influential in controlling aggressive behavior than inhibitions motivated by fear of external punishment. One might expect the conflict paradigm to prove most successful under circumstances in which individuals have had no prior experiences, either direct or vicarious, with potential scapegoats who receive attacks but otherwise do not counterreact, since this factor would significantly alter the generalization gradients. Such conditions rarely, if ever, obtain in everyday life.

The preceding comments in no way question the existence of aggression displacement. One can readily cite examples in which an individual who inhibits aggressing toward a feared antagonist later mistreats another person without adequate justification. A social learning interpretation of the phenomenon, however, takes into account a number of factors that are ignored in Miller's paradigm. The degree of provocation and punitiveness of the frustrator is, of course, relevant. In addition, however, accurate prediction requires knowledge about the individual's learned responses to thwarting; about the types of reactions modeled by influential figures to potential victims; about the social sanctions for aggressing toward different classes of people; about the likelihood of counteraggression by different victims; and about the self-evaluative reactions the aggressor experiences whenever he hurts people possessing certain characteristics.

Catharsis of aggression is another hypothesized process that is assigned a prominent role in drive theories. After the aggressive drive has been aroused, it presumably remains active as a motivating force until discharged by some form of aggressive behavior. In accord with the original formulation, theorists working within this tradition assume that expression of aggression reduces the urge or drive to behave aggressively. This energy discharge is designated *catharsis*. The theory further postulates that all forms of aggression are functionally equivalent; that is, one type of aggressive response can serve as a substitute for another in reducing the aggressive drive. Thus, for example, a person who was blocked from striking someone who annoyed him could drain the aroused drive by fantasizing physical assaults or by observing others acting violently.

Of the various propositions advanced by drive theorists, those pertaining to catharsis have been studied most extensively, perhaps because of their important social implications for the management and control of human aggression. The catharsis issue was debated by the illustrious Greek savants long before the advent of the frustration-aggression hypothesis. Aristotle contended that emotional displays purged emotions, whereas Plato maintained that they aroused them. As in most of their disputes over the nature of man, Plato turned out to be the better psychologist. The catharsis hypothesis has fared even less well than other aspects of the drive theory. A large body of research evidence shows that direct or vicarious participation in aggressive activities tends to maintain the behavior at its original level or to increase the likelihood of subsequent aggression. The relevant findings and their theoretical and practical implications are fully discussed in a later chapter.

The problem of catharsis has been further reformulated (Feshbach, 1970) so that neither increases, decreases, nor absence of changes in aggressive behavior necessarily refute the occurrence of cathartic discharges of an aggressive drive. According to this revised position, direct or vicarious participation in aggression can have three separable effects that work in different directions: It can reduce the aggressive drive; it can reinforce aggressive responses; and it can alter the strength of inhibitions. Under conditions in which the aggression-augmenting effects of reinforcement and disinhibition outweigh the reductive effects of drive discharge, it could be argued that catharsis occurred even though aggression increased. Similarly, if these hypothesized counteracting influences are of equal strength, catharsis could be claimed on the basis of no evident changes in the level of aggressive behavior. Since there exist no adequate measures of these subprocesses that are independent of changes in aggressive behavior, the catharsis hypothesis cannot be subjected to a decisive empirical test.

In the most recent version of the drive theory, Feshbach (1970) retains the notion that frustrating events elicit an aggressive drive that causes people to aggress. However, the properties ascribed to the underlying aggressive drive differ in several respects from traditional conceptions of how an energetic drive system operates. After defining hostile aggression as behavior for which the goal is hurting a disliked person, Feshbach states that infliction of injury is not really the principal goal of most hostile aggression; rather, producing pain in others serves to restore the aggressor's self-esteem and sense of power. It follows from this redefined purpose that esteem-enhancing experiences could discharge the aggressive drive without any aggressive behavior ever being performed. Indeed, bolstering self-esteem through positive accomplishments may serve as a more direct and effective means of reducing aggression than having people try to derive esteem rewards from the suffering of others. What remains to be explained by drive theorists is how a non-aggressive activity discharges an aggressive source of energy. In theories employing drive concepts, drives are characteristically altered by drive-related activities. Conceptual ambiguities arise when aggressive acts are attributed to a drive that is claimed to be satisfied only by infliction of injury—and then the actual purpose of aggression is redefined as restoration of self-esteem.

A similar interpretive problem arises in Feshbach's observation that aggression is frequently eliminated when people reinterpret situations they had erroneously perceived as insulting. Redefinition of a social situation can eliminate further aggressive instigation, but what happens to the aggressive drive that has already been induced? Dollard and his collaborators assumed that after the original instigation is removed, the residual drive still remains and must be reduced through some form of aggressive behavior. The questions posed here do not dispute the notion that esteem-enhancing experiences and favorable redefinition of social events can diminish aggressive behavior, the issue is whether it is necessary to invoke an aggressive drive to explain human aggression. Doing so creates more conceptual problems than it explains.

A given theory prescribes the factors that will be regarded as determinants of behavior and those that will be excluded from consideration. Since drive theories viewed aggression as impelled by the action of an aggressive drive, a number of important processes, including the conditions governing acquisition of injurious modes of behavior, the powerful influence of response consequences in regulating behavior, and symbolic activities that enable people to hurt others without experiencing self-contempt, were essentially ignored. Obviously, people are not innately equipped with military combat repertoires or with proficient means of insulting others. A complete theory of aggression must therefore explain how intricate behaviors that are potentially injurious and destructive are learned in the first place. Inasmuch as the frustration-produced drive accounted for the occurrence of aggressive behavior, the main function of response consequences was a negative, inhibitory one. Punishment was singled out as a factor that inhibits, attenuates, and displaces aggression, but the positive value of aggressive behavior in attaining desired outcomes was overlooked. Feshbach gives somewhat greater recognition to learning variables than did his theoretical forerunners. In his view, the frustration–aggressive-drive relationship is innately furnished, but the frustration–aggressive-behavior linkage can be increased through reinforcement and modeling. Evidence will be presented later to show that aggression is generally better explained in terms of its rewarding consequences than on the basis of frustrative conditions and the punishments it incurs. In effect, despite their avowed relationship to learning principles, drive theories failed to provide an adequate starting point for a social learning approach to aggression.

Although the motivation forces for aggression differ in instinctual and drive theories in terms of whether they are innately supplied or externally stimulated, they are much alike in their implications for the regulation of aggressive behavior. Since frustration is ever present in one form or another, in both approaches man is burdened with a continuous source of aggressive energy that requires periodic release. And both assume that aggression is reduced by behaving aggressively.

Social Learning Theory

Until recently, most personality theories depicted behavior as impelled by inner forces in the form of needs, drives, and impulses, often operating below the level of consciousness. Since the principal causes of behavior resided in forces within the individual, that is where one looked for explanations of man's actions. Although this view enjoyed widespread professional and popular acceptance, it did not go unchallenged.

Theories of this sort were criticized on both conceptual and empirical grounds. Because the inner determinants were typically inferred from the behavior they supposedly caused, the result was pseudoexplanations. Thus, for example, a hostile impulse was deduced from a person's irascible behavior, which was then attributed to the action of the inferred impulse. In a similar manner, various traits and dynamics, which represent the descriptive constructs of the assessor, frequently become entities within the individual that supposedly cause his behavior. Different personality theories proposed diverse lists of motivators, some containing a few all-purpose drives, others embracing a varied assortment of specific drives.

The conceptual structure of psychodynamic theories was further criticized for disregarding the tremendous complexity of human responsiveness. An internal motivator cannot possibly account for the marked variation in the incidence of a given behavior in different situations, toward different persons, at different times, and in different social roles. One can predict with much greater accuracy the expression of aggressive behavior from knowledge of the social contexts (for example, church, school, ghetto sidewalk, athletic gymnasium), the targets (for example, parent, priest, teacher, or peer), the role occupied by the performer (for example, policeman, soldier, teacher, sales clerk), and other cues that reliably signify potential consequences for aggressive actions, than from assessment of the performer (Bandura, 1960; Bandura and Walters, 1959). When diverse social influences produce correspondingly diverse behaviors, the inner cause implicated in the relationship cannot be less complex than its effects.

It should be emphasized here that it is not the existence of motivated behavior that is being questioned, but rather whether such behavior is at all explained by ascribing it to the action of drives or other inner forces. The deficiencies of this type of simplistic analysis can be illustrated by considering a common activity, such as reading printed matter, which has the qualities of a highly motivated behavior. People spend large sums of money purchasing reading material; they expend effort obtaining it from libraries; they engage in reading for prolonged periods; and they become emotionally upset over being deprived of reading material (as when their daily newspaper is not delivered through an oversight or when a library is unable to locate a desired book in its collection). Following the common practice of inferring drives from prepotent behaviors, one could ascribe the activated reading to the force of a reading drive. However, in predicting what a person reads, when he chooses to read it, and the order in which different contents are read, one would appeal not to drives, but rather to the stimulus inducements and consequences of reading, and to a variety of specific factors that influence reading behavior. On the stimulus side, one would want to know the person's reading assignments, their deadlines, the type of information he requires to deal effectively with projects he has undertaken, and the presence of other reading instigators; on the consequences side, knowledge about the contents the person finds rewarding and those he dislikes and the effects of reading or ignoring certain materials would constitute important controlling influences. There is a marked difference between ascribing motivating properties to social inducements and acquired incentives, a quality that is easily demonstrable, and invoking acquired drives, a concept that has been found lacking in explanatory power (Bolles, 1967).

Although the conceptual adequacy of psychodynamic formulations was debatable, their empirical limitations could not be ignored indefinitely. They provided intriguing interpretations of events that had already happened, but they lacked power to predict how people would behave in given situations (Mischel, 1968). Moreover, it was difficult to demonstrate that persons who had undergone psychodynamically oriented treatment benefited more than untreated cases (Bandura, 1969a; Rachman, 1971). Acquisition of insight into the underlying impulses, through which behavioral changes were supposedly achieved, turned out to represent more of a social conversion than a self-discovery process. As Marmor (1962), among others, pointed out, each psychodynamic approach had its own favored set of inner causes and its own preferred brand of insight. The presence of these determinants could easily be confirmed through suggestive proving and selective reinforcement of clients' verbal reports in self-validating interviews. For these reasons, advocates of differing theoretical orientations repeatedly discovered their favorite motivating agents, but rarely found evidence for the hypothesized causes emphasized by proponents of competing views. The content of a particular client's insights and emergent "unconscious" could therefore be better predicted from knowledge of the therapist's belief system than from the client's actual social learning history.

It eventually became apparent that if progress in the understanding of human behavior was to be accelerated, more stringent requirements would have to be applied in evaluating the adequacy of explanatory systems. Theories must demonstrate predictive power, and they must accurately identify causal factors, as shown by the fact that varying the postulated determinants produces corresponding changes in behavior.

The attribution of behavior to inner forces can perhaps be likened to early explanatory schemes in other branches of science. At one time diverse chemical reactions were supposedly caused by movements of a material substance called phlogiston, physical objects were internally propelled by intangible essences, and physiological functioning was ascribed to the action of humors.

Developments in learning theory shifted the focus of causal analysis from hypothesized inner determinants to detailed examination of external influences on responsiveness. Human behavior was extensively analyzed in terms of the stimulus events that evoke it and the reinforcing consequences that alter it. Researchers repeatedly demonstrated that response patterns generally attributed to underlying forces could be induced, eliminated, and reinstated simply by varying external sources of influence. These impressive findings led many psychologists to the view that the causes of behavior are found not in the organism, but in environmental forces.

The idea that man's actions are under external control, though amply documented, was not enthusiastically received for a variety of reasons. To most people it unfortunately implied a one-way influence process that reduced man to a helpless reactor to the vagaries of external rewards and punishments. Popular descriptions of the potential for social influence conjured up macabre associations of *1984* and *Brave New World,* in which people are manipulated at will by occult technocrats. By associating the term *behaviorism* with odious images of salivating dogs and animals driven by carrots and sticks, critics of behavioral approaches skillfully employ Pavlovian conditioning procedures on their receptive audiences to endow this point of view with degrading properties. The fact that valuation of places, persons, or things is affected by one's emotional experiences, whether they be fearful, humiliating, disgusting, mournful, or pleasurable, does not mean that such learning outcomes reflect a base animal process. To expect people to remain unaffected by paired experiences is to require that they be less than human. Moreover, to be sensitive to the consequences of one's actions indicates intelligence rather than subhuman functioning. Nevertheless, promoters of various causes often lobby against social practices they do not like by designating them as Pavlovian or as harrowing precursors of *1984.*

The view that behavior is environmentally determined also appeared to contradict firm but ill-founded beliefs that people possess generalized personality traits leading them to behave in a consistent manner, however variable the social influences might be. Fortunately for survival purposes, cultural practices are much too diverse to produce undiscerning generalized traits (Mischel, 1968). A person who behaved in a church the same way he acted in a nightclub would be a forced recipient of an extended rest in a psychiatric facility. A high degree of behavioral flexibility is required if a person is to deal effectively with the complexities of ever-changing environmental demands.

A more valid criticism of extreme situational determinism is that, in a vigorous effort to avoid spurious inner causes, it neglected determinants of man's behavior arising from his cognitive functioning. Man is a thinking organism possessing capabilities that provide him with some power of self-direction. People can represent external influences symbolically and later use such representations to guide their actions; they can solve problems mentally without having to enact the various alternatives; and they can foresee the probable consequences of different actions and alter their behavior accordingly. These higher mental processes permit both insightful and foresighted behavior. By managing the stimulus determinants of given activities and producing consequences for their own actions, people are able to control their own behavior to some degree. As will be illustrated later, cognitive and self-regulative influences often serve important functions in causal sequences. To the extent that traditional behavioral theories could be faulted, it was for providing an incomplete rather than an inaccurate account of human behavior.

In the social learning view, man is neither driven by inner forces nor buffeted helplessly by environmental influences. Rather, psychological functioning is best understood in terms of continuous reciprocal interaction between behavior and its controlling conditions. Early attempts to incorporate both individual and environmental determinants in personality theory simply depicted behavior as caused by these two sets of influences. The problem with this type of formulation is that it treated response dispositions and the environment as independent entities. Contrary to this assumption, the environment is only a potentiality, not a fixed property that inevitably impinges upon individuals and to which their behavior eventually adapts. Behavior partly creates the environment and the resultant environment, in turn, influences the behavior. In this two-way causal process the environment is influenceable, just as the behavior it controls is.

In examining social interactions, Rausch (1965) found that the immediately preceding act of one person was the major determinant of the other person's response. In approximately 75 percent of the instances, hostile behavior elicited unfriendly responses, whereas cordial acts seldom did. Aggressive children thus created through their actions a hostile environment, whereas children who displayed friendly interpersonal modes of response generated an amicable social milieu. With little effort one could readily identify individuals who predictably create negative social climates wherever they go. People thus play an active role in constructing their own reinforcement contingencies through their characteristic modes of response.

A complete theory of aggression, whatever its orientation, must explain how aggressive patterns of behavior are developed, what provokes people to behave aggressively, and what maintains their aggressive actions. These major issues are treated at length in subsequent chapters. The remainder of this chapter is devoted to a general discussion of social learning principles of how patterns of behavior are acquired and how their expression is continuously regulated by the interplay of self-generated and external sources of influence.

Development of new modes of behavior.   Patterns of behavior can be acquired through direct experience or by observing the behavior of others. The more rudimentary form of learning, rooted in direct experience, is largely governed by the rewarding and punishing consequences that follow any given action. People are repeatedly confronted with situations with which they must deal in one way or another. Some of the responses they try prove unsuccessful, while others produce more favorable effects. Through this process of differential reinforcement, successful modes of behavior are eventually selected from exploratory activities, while ineffectual ones are discarded.

Although behavior can be shaped into new patterns to some extent by rewarding and punishing consequences, learning would be exceedingly laborious and hazardous if it proceeded solely on this basis. Most of the intricate responses people display are learned, either deliberately or inadvertently, through the influence of example. Indeed, virtually all learning phenomena resulting from direct experiences can occur on a vicarious basis through observation of other people's behavior and its consequences for them. Man's capacity to learn by observation enables him to acquire complex patterns of behavior by watching the performances of exemplary models. Emotional responses toward certain places, persons, or things can also be developed by witnessing the affective reactions of others punished for their actions. And, finally, the expression of previously learned responses can be socially regulated through the actions of influential models.

The preceding remarks are not meant to imply that new modes of behavior are fashioned solely through experience, either of a direct or observational sort. Biological structure obviously sets limits on the types of aggressive responses that can be successfully perfected, and genetic endowment influences the rate at which learning progresses.

Regulatory functions.   A comprehensive theory of behavior must explain not only how response patterns are acquired, but how their expression is regulated and maintained. In social learning theory, human functioning relies on three regulatory systems. They include antecedent inducements, response feedback influences, and cognitive processes that guide and regulate action. Human aggression is a learned conduct that, like other forms of social behavior, is under stimulus, reinforcement, and cognitive control. These control functions will be discussed separately for explanatory purposes, although in reality they are closely interrelated.

Stimulus control.   To function effectively a person must be able to anticipate the probable consequences of different events and courses of action and regulate his behavior accordingly. Without a capacity for anticipatory or foresighted behavior, man could not profit much from experience. Information about probable consequences is conveyed by environmental stimuli, such as verbal communications; pictorial cues; distinctive places, persons, or things; or the actions of others.

In the earliest years of development, environmental events, except those that are inherently painful, exert little or no influence on infants and young children. As a result of paired experiences, direct, symbolic, or vicarious, formerly neutral stimuli begin to acquire motivating and response-directive properties. Environmental stimuli gain the capacity to activate physiological reactions and emotional behavior through association with evocative events. Such learning often occurs on the basis of direct experience. People come to fear and to avoid individuals who are commonly associated in their experience with pain or distress. Through a similar learning process they become easily angered by the sight or thought of individuals with whom they have had hostile encounters.

Social characteristics generally acquire evocative power through processes that are more subtle and complex than is commonly believed. Emotional responses are frequently acquired on the basis of vicarious rather than direct experiences. The emotional responses exhibited by others toward certain people tend to arouse in observers strong emotional reactions that can become conditioned to the same targets. It is not uncommon for unpopular minority groups or nationalities to become endowed with anger-evoking potency in the absence of personal contact through exposure to modeled animosity. Emotion-arousing words and pictures that conjure up hostile reactions likewise often function as the vehicle for symbolic conditioning of hatreds.

The emotional responses that become established to paired events can be evoked by not only direct experience, observation of another's affective expression, and symbolic stimuli, but also by provocative thoughts. People can easily make themselves nauseous by imagining revolting experiences. They can become sexually aroused by generating erotic fantasies. They can frighten themselves by fear-provoking thoughts. And they can work themselves up into a state of anger by ruminating about mistreatment from offensive provocateurs. The cognitive capacities of humans thus enable them to invest things with positive or negative valence by pairing them repeatedly with thought-produced emotions. This self-arousal process is illustrated in a husband's slaying of a friend who kissed his wife at a New Year's Eve party (*Portland Press Herald,* 1963). The husband had brooded almost incessantly about the kiss over a period of two years. As Thanksgiving approached he further intensified his anger by imagining his foe enjoying a family Thanksgiving dinner while his own family life was irreparably ruined. Shortly after observing how easy it was to kill a man from seeing Oswald shot on television, the brooding husband sought and shot his former friend.

The preceding discussion has shown how things can become invested with response-activating properties on the basis of paired experiences. Environmental cues also acquire response-directing functions when they are associated with differential response consequences. The same actions can produce markedly different results depending upon the time, the place, and the persons toward whom they are expressed. Insulting an irascible aggressor, for example, will have painfully different effects from treating a submissive individual in the same manner. People therefore pay close attention to cues that signify probable consequences, and they partly regulate their behavior on the basis of such information. Stimuli indicating that given actions will be punished or unrewarded tend to inhibit their performance, whereas those signifying that the actions are permissible or rewardable facilitate their occurrence. The following quotation provides a telling example of an autistic boy who freely expressed destructive behavior with his lenient mother but rarely did so in the presence of his father, who tolerated no aggression.

> Whenever her husband was home, Billy was a model youngster. He knew that his father would punish him quickly and dispassionately for misbehaving. But when his father left the house, Billy would go to the window and watch until the car pulled out. As soon as it did, he was suddenly transformed. . . . "He'd go into my closet and tear up my evening dresses and urinate on my clothes. He'd smash furniture and run around biting the walls until the house was destruction from one end to the other. He knew that I liked to dress him in nice clothes, so he used to rip the buttons off his shirts, and used to go in his pants." (Moser, 1965, p. 96)

Social behavior is extensively regulated by verbal cues. We influence people's actions in innumerable situations by suggestions, requests, commands, and written directives. Often these operate in subtle ways. To take a common example, parents are quick to issue commands to their children, but they do not always see to it that their requests are heeded. Children are therefore inclined to ignore demands voiced in mild or moderate tones. The parents' mounting anger usually serves as the cue that they will enforce compliance, so that only shouts produce results. Because of the differential signal value of parental directives, many households are run at a fairly high decibel level.

Of the numerous cues that influence how people will behave at any given moment, none is more ubiquitous or effective than the actions of others. People applaud when others clap, they exit from social functions when they see others leaving, they wear their hair like others, they dress alike, and on countless other occasions their behavior is prompted and channeled by the power of example. Modeling influences play an especially important role in the rapid contagion of aggression. The actions of others acquire response-directing properties through selective reinforcement in much the same way as do physical and symbolic cues in nonsocial forms. When behaving like others produces rewarding outcomes, modeling cues become powerful determinants of analogous behavior; conversely, when imitative actions are treated negatively but dissimilar behavior proves rewarding, models' responses prompt divergent performances in observers.

In everyday life the likely consequences of a given course of action depend upon the presence of several factors, including combinations of temporal, social, and situational features. It may be permissible to aggress toward a peer during a physical contact sport, for example, but punishable to do so at other times or in other settings. When subtle variations in stimulus events carry diverse outcomes for similar conduct, it is easy to misjudge what effects aggressive actions will have. Moreover, the force of activating circumstances may at times prompt a person to behave aggressively without paying much heed to subsequent consequences.

Reinforcement control.   A second control system involves behavior feedback influences, mainly in the form of reinforcing consequences. An organism that responded foresightedly on the basis of informative environmental cues but remained unaffected by the results of its actions would be too obtuse to survive for long. In fact, behavior is extensively controlled by its consequences. Responses that cause unrewarding or punishing effects tend to be discarded, whereas those that produce rewarding outcomes are retained and strengthened. Human behavior therefore cannot be fully understood without examining the regulatory influence of reinforcement.

Reinforcement control of behavior is most convincingly demonstrated by intrasubject replication. In these types of studies interpersonal modes of response, many of long standing, are successively eliminated and reinstated by altering the effects they produce. The susceptibility of behavior to reinforcement control is further shown by the fact that even subtle variations in the frequency and patterning of outcomes result in different types of performances. Those who have been rewarded each time they respond are likely to become easily discouraged and to give up quickly when their efforts fail. On the other hand, individuals whose behavior has been reinforced intermittently tend to persist for a considerable time despite setbacks and only occasional success.

In the minds of most people, reinforcement is usually equated with tangible rewards and punishments. Actually, human behavior is largely sustained and modified by symbolic reinforcers. As a result of repeated association with primary experiences, social reactions in the form of verbal approval, reprimands, attention, affection, and rejection acquire powerful reinforcing functions. Such interpersonal reinforcers assume a prominent role in regulating the interactions of everyday life, including aggressive responsiveness. Similarly, after accomplishments become a source of personal satisfaction, knowledge that one has done well can function as a reward that sustains activities independently of social or material incentives. Many forms of behavior (such as communicative and motor skills) that enable an individual to deal effectively with his environment likewise persist with little external support because they produce desired results. Finally, the sensory experiences that are naturally produced by the behavior itself can be effective in modifying and maintaining it over a long period. One rarely has to resort to extrinsic rewards to get people to read interesting books, to watch entertaining television programs, or to play pleasing musical selections.

Vicarious reinforcement.   Human functioning would be exceedingly inefficient, not to say dangerous, if behavior were influenced only by directly experienced consequences. Fortunately, one can profit greatly from the experiences of others. People repeatedly observe the actions of others and the occasions on which they are rewarded, ignored, or punished. Observed reinforcement influences behavior in much the same way as outcomes that are directly experienced (Bandura, 1971b; Kanfer, 1965). Observed rewards generally enhance, and observed punishments reduce, similar behavior in observers.

Observed consequences also provide reference standards that determine whether particular outcomes will assume positive or negative value. The same compliment, for instance, is likely to be punishing for persons who have seen similar performances by others more highly acclaimed, but rewarding when others have been less generously praised. Thus, through social comparison processes, observation of other people's response outcomes can drastically alter the effectiveness of direct reinforcements. Since both direct and vicarious reinforcement inevitably occur together in everyday life, the interactive effects of these two sources of influence on human behavior are of much greater significance than their independent controlling power.

Self-reinforcement.   At the highest level of psychological functioning, individuals regulate their own behavior by self-evaluative and other self-produced consequences (Bandura, 1971b). In this process people set themselves certain standards of conduct and respond to their own behavior in self-satisfied or self-critical ways in accordance with their self-imposed demands. Comparative studies show that people can manage their own behavior by self-reinforcement as well as or better than through consequences arising from external sources.

After a self-monitored reinforcement system has been established, a given action produces two sets of consequences—a self-evaluative reaction as well as some external outcome. These two sources of reinforcement can occur in several different patterns. Sometimes people are rewarded socially or materially for behavior that they devalue. Anticipation of self-reproach for personally repudiated actions provides an important motivating influence to keep behavior in line with adopted standards in the face of opposing influences. There is no more devastating punishment than self-contempt. Under conditions in which self-devaluative consequences outweigh the force of rewards for accommodating behavior, external influences prove relatively ineffective. On the other hand, when external inducements, whether rewarding or coercive, prevail over self-reinforcing influences, individuals exhibit cheerless compliance. Humans, of course, possess facile cognitive capacities for reconciling distressing conflicts. Devalued actions can be, and often are, justified so that losses in self-respect are minimized as long as the self-deception remains convincing.

An opposite type of conflict between external and self-produced consequences arises when people are punished for engaging in activities they value highly. The rebels, the dissenters, and the nonconformists often experience this type of counterinfluence. Here, the relative strengths of self-approval and external censure determine whether the behavior will be discarded or maintained. If the negative sanctions are relatively weak, socially disapproved but personally valued actions will be readily expressed. If the threatened consequences are severe, however, transgressive behavior is apt to be inhibited under high risk of penalty and freely performed in the absence of prohibitive agents. There are individuals whose sense of self-worth is so strongly linked to certain convictions that they will submit to prolonged maltreatment rather than accede to social practices they regard as unjust.

External reinforcement exerts its greatest influence when it is consonant with self-produced consequences—as when rewarded actions are a source of self-pride, and punished ones are self-censured. Indeed, people strive actively to achieve and to maintain such conditions. They do this by selectively associating with persons who share similar standards of conduct, thus ensuring social support for their own system of self-evaluation. Some of the most drastic changes in behavior are achieved in large part by modifying a person's basis for self-evaluation. By legitimizing aggression and dehumanizing potential victims, individuals who have been strictly socialized against brutalizing and slaying people can be led to do so in military situations without experiencing tormenting self-devaluative consequences. A later chapter presents the various antidotes for self-contempt. Among those who fully adopt the new standards of conduct, skillfully executed carnage may even serve as a basis for self-commendation.

Cognitive control.   If human behavior could be fully explained in terms of external inducements and response consequences, there would be no need to postulate any additional regulatory mechanisms. However, actions are not always predictable from these external sources of influence. Man's cognitive capacities tremendously increase the information he can derive from his experiences, and thus partly determine how he will be affected by them. There are several ways in which cognitive functioning enters into the regulation of human behavior. These are discussed next.

Cognitive representation of reinforcement contingencies.   Popular portrayals of behavioral approaches would lead one to believe that people can be easily conditioned and manipulated without their awareness. This melodramatic sketch receives little support in numerous studies of how awareness of reinforcement contingencies affects the process of behavior change. In fact, repeated paired stimulation generally fails to produce conditioned emotional responses as long as the connection between stimulus events goes unnoticed. The responses that get conditioned are to a large extent cognitively induced rather than directly elicited by external stimuli. Response consequences similarly have weak effects on behavior when the relationship between one's actions and outcomes is not recognized. On the other hand, awareness of conditions of reinforcement typically results in rapid changes in behavior, which is indicative of insightful functioning. People who are aware of what is wanted and who value the contingent rewards change their behavior in the reinforced direction; those who are equally aware of the reinforcement contingencies but who devalue the required behavior or the reinforcers show little change; those who remain unaware achieve, at best, small increments in performance even though the appropriate responses are reinforced whenever they occur.

Human behavior is regulated to a large extent by anticipated consequences of prospective actions. Individuals may accurately assess the customary effects of given activities but fail to act in accordance with existing conditions or reinforcement because of hope that their actions may eventually bring favorable results. Many a social reformer has sustained his efforts in the face of repeated failures by the belief that the rightness of his cause will ultimately produce desired changes. Sometimes people lead themselves astray by inaccurate expectations when they wrongly assume that certain changes in their behavior will alter future consequences. The deterrent value of threatened punishment, for example, is weakened when lawbreakers misjudge their chances of escaping apprehension for antisocial acts. Judgment of consequences can also be seriously impaired by intoxicants. Felonies are typically committed (72 percent) under the influence of alcohol (Shupe, 1954). Under laboratory conditions drunk subjects are more willing to risk punitive attack than sober ones (Shuntich and Taylor, 1972).

The notion that behavior is controlled by its immediate consequences holds up better under close scrutiny for anticipated consequences than for those that actually impinge upon the organism. In most instances customary outcomes are reasonably good predictors of behavior because the consequences that people anticipate for their actions are accurately derived from, and therefore correspond closely to, prevailing conditions of reinforcement. However, belief and actuality do not always coincide because anticipated consequences are also partly inferred from observed response consequences of others, from what one reads or is told, and from a variety of other cues that, on the basis of past experiences, are considered reliable forecasters of likely outcomes. When actions are guided by anticipated consequences derived from predictors that do not accurately reflect existing contingencies of reinforcement, behavior is weakly controlled by its actual consequences until cumulative experiences produce more realistic expectations.

In some of the more severe behavior disorders, psychotic actions are so powerfully controlled by bizarre subjective contingencies that the behavior remains essentially unaffected by its external consequences. This process is vividly illustrated in a patient's account of his psychotic experiences in an insane asylum during the early nineteenth century (Bateson, 1961). The narrator had received a scrupulously moralistic upbringing, according to which actions ordinarily viewed as fully acceptable were judged by him to be sinful and likely to provoke the wrath of God. Consequently, many innocuous acts elicited dreadful apprehensions of hellish torment; these in turn motivated and maintained self-torturing rituals for hours on end, designed to forestall the imagined disastrous consequences. Reduction in acute distress accompanying the nonoccurrence of subjectively feared, but objectively nonexistent, threats powerfully reinforced the self-punitive defensive behavior. Given fictional contingencies with a powerful internal reinforcing system, the patient persisted in his atonement rituals even in the face of severe external punishment and blatant disconfirming experiences. The attendants' punitive measures were pale compared to the feared Hadean torture imaginally represented in visions of clanking iron and massive flames fanned by huge forge bellows. When the prophecies of divine inner voices failed to materialize, the disconfirming experiences were discounted as tests by the Almighty of the strength of his religious convictions.

Instances of bizarre thought control of grotesque murders occur from time to time. In one such case reported by Reich and Hepps (1972), a student became convinced that his commune companions were, in fact, conspirators from another planet plotting to destroy his mind with LSD. Seeking refuge in Europe, he fled in terror from city to city in the belief that he was escaping a Nazi scheme to exterminate him. Upon arriving in Tel Aviv, he concluded that the Nazis had already taken over and were gassing the population. While sitting in a sidewalk cafe resignedly drinking what he thought was poisoned wine, he interpreted an over-heard conversation between Israeli soldiers as Nazis boasting about their kill rates. Enraged by imagined massacres, the student drew a knife, killing the soldier and wounding two other persons.

Cognitive guidance of behavior.   Cognitive processes play a prominent role in the acquisition and retention of response patterns as well as in their expression. The memory trace of momentary influences is short-lived, but such experiences often have lasting behavioral effects. This is made possible by the fact that transitory external events are coded and stored in symbolic form for memory representation. Patterns of behavior that have been observed and other experiences long past can thus be reinstated by visualizing them or by representing them verbally. These internal models of the outside world can serve as guides to overt action on later occasions. It will be recalled from the earlier discussion of learning processes that internal representations of patterned behavior are constructed from observed examples and from informative feedback to one's trial-and-error performances.

Cognitive functioning is especially important in observational learning in which a person reads about or observes a pattern of behavior, but does not perform it overtly until appropriate circumstances arise. Evidence will be cited later to illustrate how modeled activities are acquired in symbolic form without behavioral enactment, how they can be strengthened by mental rehearsal, and how they provide the basis for action on later occasions given suitable inducements.

Thought control of action through mental problem-solving.   Man's efforts to understand and to manage his environment would be exceedingly wearisome if optimal solutions to problems could be arrived at only by performing alternative actions and suffering the consequences. Actually, most problem-solving occurs in thought rather than in action. Man's higher mental capacities, for example, enable him to design sturdy dwellings and bridges without having to build them until he hits upon a structure that does not collapse. Alternative courses of action are generally tested in symbolic exploration and either discarded or retained on the basis of calculated consequences. The best symbolic solution is then executed in action.

The three major systems by which behavior is regulated do not operate independently; most actions are simultaneously controlled by two or more of the component influences. Moreover, the various systems are closely interdependent in acquiring and retaining their power to determine behavior. In order to establish and to maintain effective stimulus control, for example, the same actions must produce different consequences depending on the cues that are present. Stimulus and cognitive influences, in turn, can alter the impact of prevailing conditions of reinforcement. Certain stimuli can acquire such powerful control over defensive behavior that people avoid renewed encounters with feared or hated persons, places, or things. In instances in which the original threats no longer exist, their self-protective behavior is insulated from realistic reinforcement influences.

Even when the things one dislikes or fears are not completely avoided, cues having strong emotion-arousing potential provoke defensive behaviors that predictably create adverse reinforcement contingencies where they may not ordinarily exist. To the extent that an individual's distrust of certain people leads him to behave in ways that provoke hostile counterreactions from them, their negative valence is further strengthened and it, in turn, prompts actions that produce reciprocal negative reinforcement. Both processes thus support each other.

The way in which beliefs and conscious recognition of environmental contingencies can enhance, distort, or even negate the influence of reinforcing consequences has already been amply documented and needs no further illustration. Cognitive events, however, do not function as autonomous causes of behavior. Their nature, their emotion-arousing properties, and their occurrence are under stimulus and reinforcement control. Analysis of cognitive control of behavior is therefore incomplete without specifying what influences a person's thoughts. Detailed exposition of social learning theory falls beyond the scope of this book, but the principles are presented in other sources (Bandura, 1969a, 1971c).

DIFFERENTIAL IMPLICATIONS
OF DRIVE AND SOCIAL LEARNING THEORIES

A number of predictions that follow from the social learning formulation differ from the traditional frustration-aggression hypothesis. It will be recalled that drive theories of aggression assume that frustration arouses an aggressive drive that can be reduced only through some form of aggressive behavior. Frustration, in this view, is a necessary and sufficient condition for aggression. The diverse events subsumed under the omnibus term frustration have one feature in common—they are all aversive in varying degrees. In social learning theory, rather than frustration generating an aggressive drive, aversive treatment produces a general state of emotional arousal that can facilitate a variety of behaviors, depending on the types of responses the person has learned for coping with stress and their relative effectiveness. When distressed, some people seek help and support; others increase achievement strivings; others show withdrawal and resignation; some aggress; others experience heightened somatic activity; still others anesthetize themselves against a miserable existence with drugs or alcohol; and most intensify constructive efforts to overcome their adversities. The major differences among the instinctual, reactive drive, and social learning theories in the ways they conceptualize the motivational component of aggression are depicted schematically in Figure 1.1.

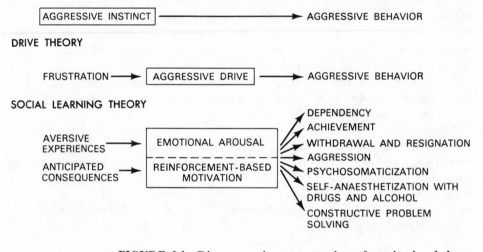

FIGURE 1.1 Diagrammatic representation of motivational determinants of aggression in instinct, reactive drive, and social learning theories.

There are several lines of evidence that lend support to the social learning formulation. Psychophysiological studies have been conducted in which people undergo fear- and anger-provoking experiences while changes in their physiological reactions are simultaneously recorded. Interpretation of findings is complicated because no efforts have been made to ensure that the two emotional experiences are equally intense. Should differences be obtained, they may arise from dissimilarities in the nature of the affective experiences or in their relative intensities. Moreover, as Duffy (1962) has noted, unless it has been shown that dissimilar stimuli within the same emotional class produce identical patterns of physiological arousal, the generality of findings yielded by a single fear stimulus and a single anger stimulus is open to question.

In a study in which adults were either frightened or treated in a rude manner, Ax (1953) found a few subtle differences in somatic reactions, but the physiological manifestations of these two emotions were much alike. Schachter (1957), using analogous methods, obtained essentially similar cardiovascular responsiveness to fear and anger stimulation, although on the basis of subjective categorization of the data, he extracts greater physiological specificity than the actual findings warrant. If the emotions of fear and anger had different physiological determinants, injections of drugs that selectively induce the distinguishing visceral reactions should produce qualitatively different emotions and social behavior. Although such an experiment has not been performed, it would most likely reveal that people do not rely on visceral cues for judging what emotion they are experiencing.

It would appear from the available evidence that fear and anger have similar physiological correlates. Looking at the physiological records alone, one could not distinguish whether the individuals had been frightened or angered. The varied array of emotions experienced phenomenologically apparently stem from a common diffuse state of emotional arousal rather than from distinct drive states. It seems unlikely that small differences in an otherwise identical pattern of physiological arousal are sufficiently distinguishable, if at all, to serve as the cues for differentiating among diverse emotional states. Whether people experience their emotional arousal as fear, anger, euphoria, or some other state depends not on particular somatic cues, but on a number of external defining influences.

People judge their emotions partly from the nature of the instigating conditions. Visceral arousal generated by threat is experienced as fear, arousal produced by thwarting is experienced as anger, and that resulting from irretrievable loss of valued objects as sorrow (Hunt, Cole, and Reis, 1958). Even the same source of physiological arousal may be experienced as different emotions depending on the emotional reactions of others. Affective modeling cues can give definition to emotional states of uncertain origin, or in ambiguous situations where people know the source of their arousal but are unsure how they are supposed to react to it. Schachter and Singer (1962) provide suggestive evidence that people under drug-induced arousal, who do not know what to attribute it to, experience the arousal as aggression when others respond hostilely, but they experience the same state as euphoria when they see others behaving in a jocular manner. Emotional states produced by environmental stress are likewise susceptible to relabeling to some extent (Ross, Rodin, and Zimbardo, 1969; Nisbett and Schachter, 1966).

Evidence that the same physiological arousal can be experienced subjectively as different kinds of emotion has several implications for a theory of aggression. First, it calls into question the validity of invoking an inborn aggressive drive from observations that infants display diffuse emotional upset to physical restraints and painful stimulation (Munroe, 1955; Feshbach, 1970). Second, the general arousal model predicts that under conditions in which individuals are prone to behave aggressively, any source of emotional arousal may enhance aggressive behavior. Results of several experiments have a bearing on this prediction. Zillmann (1971) exposed adults to physiologically arousing aggressive scenes, to erotic displays, or to nonarousing contents, and then provided them with an opportunity to behave punitively by shocking their antagonist. Both aggressive and sex arousal enhanced punitiveness, compared to nonaroused subjects. Indeed, aggressiveness was determined more by level of arousal than by its source. A series of ingenious experiments by Tannenbaum (1972) designed to test the general instigational effects of arousal further demonstrate that nonaggressive sources of arousal enhance aggressive behavior under conditions in which this is the only mode of response available. Geen and O'Neal (1969) similarly found that arousing though nonirritating noise increased subjects' punitiveness, especially if they had prior exposure to aggressive models.

It might be argued that high sex arousal and noise have some frustrating properties. An experiment performed by Christy, Gelfand, and Hartmann (1971) therefore provides a more definitive test of predictions from the *frustration-aggression* and the *arousal-prepotent response* formulations. After observing aggressive or nonaggressive models, groups of children engaged in competitive activities in which one member consistently won and the other was a consistent loser. Other pairs played noncompetitively. Following these experiences, the children's imitative aggressiveness was measured. Competitors showed more imitative aggression than noncompetitors; however, victors increased their aggression just as much as those who experienced failure-induced frustration. These findings are especially interesting, since Lorenz (1966), among others, prescribes rivalrous activities as a means of reducing aggressive behavior.

There are, of course, certain limiting conditions to the emotional facilitation of aggressive behavior. Some sources of arousal, such as joyful or rewarding experiences, tend to be incompatible with hostile actions and may thus serve as inhibitors rather than as instigators of aggressive responses. Even more important, in everyday life informative cues and response consequences serve as influential regulators of aggressive actions. By arranging social learning determinants such that arousal-linked aggression is negatively sanctioned but aggression without arousal is well received, one could undoubtedly reverse the relationship between physiological state and action. In other words, arousal not only has the capacity to facilitate whatever responses are dominant in a given setting; through selective reinforcement, it also acquires informative value in determining the type of behavior that will be activated. Hence, if arousal-linked aggression repeatedly produces negative results, experienced arousal is likely to reduce rather than to increase the likelihood of aggression. Evidence will be presented later to show that activation of aggressive behavior is, in fact, better explained in terms of anticipated consequences than in terms of drive.

The role of emotional arousal in aggression is magnified when aggression is studied as a function of arousal-producing conditions within a permissive context only. It was previously noted that theories generally give disproportionate attention to aversively motivated aggression. In the social learning analysis of motivation, incentives also constitute important impellers of action. A great deal of aggression is prompted by its anticipated benefits. Here, the instigator is the pull of expected success, rather than the push of aversive treatment. As depicted in Figure 1–1, anticipatory functions provide a mechanism of response selection from among a variety of alternatives.

Under circumstances in which arousal facilitates aggression, the social learning formulation predicts that arousal decreased through noninjurious means will reduce aggression as well as, or even better than, acting aggressively. In drive theories the actuated aggressive drive presumably endures until discharged by some form of aggressive activity. From the social learning perspective, anger arousal dissipates, but it can be repeatedly regenerated on later occasions by ruminating on anger-provoking incidents. By thinking about past insulting treatment, a person can work himself into a rage long after the initial emotional reactions have subsided. Given this cognitive capacity, it is not necessary to invoke a drive to explain arousal that outlasts its original instigators. Persistence of elevated anger arousal, in this view, reflects self-generated arousal rather than the existence of an undischarged reservoir of aggressive energy. To illustrate the different views, let us consider the example of a person who becomes angered by an apparent social slight only to discover that the invitation to the social function has arrived in the next mail. He is likely to show an immediate drop in anger arousal and aggressiveness without having to assault or denounce someone so as to reduce a lingering aggressive drive.

A number of investigators have compared the relative effectiveness of different ways of reducing aggressive behavior. Mallick and McCandless (1966) found that explaining why a provocateur behaved obnoxiously reduced children's aggression toward him, whereas free expression of physical aggression did not lessen their punitive behavior. This finding is in agreement with Kaufmann and Feshbach (1963), who reduced students' inclination to behave aggressively by cognitively restructuring the provocative situation.

Research to be cited later reveals that ventilative therapies aimed at draining aggressive drives by having people behave aggressively may be inadvertently reinforcing their aggressive tendencies. By contrast, social learning treatments, which have proved successful (Bandura, 1969a), help people from the outset to acquire better ways of dealing with social problems so that they have less to get angry about. Aggressive behavior of long standing is reliably reduced by a variety of approaches, including modeling of alternative coping responses; selective reinforcement in which aggressive actions are nonrewarded while better solutions are actively supported; eliminating fantasied instigators of violent outbursts; developing competencies that provide new sources of reward; and reducing aversive social conditions.

There is a third implication of social learning theory that differs from traditional views. Frustration or anger arousal is a facilitative but not a necessary condition for aggression. Frustration is most likely to provoke aggression in people who have learned to respond to aversive treatment with aggressive attitudes and actions. In an early study bearing on this issue, Davitz (1952) demonstrated that following arbitrarily insulting treatment, aggressively trained children behaved more aggressively, whereas cooperatively trained children behaved more cooperatively. Responses to aversive treatment are also frequently patterned on the characteristic actions of salient models (Bandura and Walters, 1963).

In writings on the causes of aggression, factors such as broken homes, parental rejection, adverse socioeconomic conditions, thwarted strivings, and intrapsychic conflicts are usually identified as important determinants. If one examines the antecedents that have been invoked for other types of behavior disorders, such as drug addiction, alcoholism, and schizophrenia, essentially the same adverse conditions appear in roughly comparable rates. Nor are adversity and familial discord necessarily rare in the backgrounds of people who develop patterns of behavior that are valued in the larger society. Findings of these etiological studies suggest that aversive conditions increase the probability that deviant patterns will arise, but they do not determine what form the behavior will take. Ghetto conditions, for example, probably produce more alcoholism, drug addiction, and resignation and withdrawal than aggression. One cannot account for the presence of elaborate modes of behavior on the basis of deficits or frustrative conditions alone. Response patterns that are socially labeled as deviant, like emulative conduct, require the presence of appropriate social learning influences for their acquisition and maintenance.

One can distinguish among aggressive acts, emotional arousal experienced as anger, and aggressive attitudes exemplified in negative evaluations. No evidence is available that behavioral, affective, and cognitive responses are inherently linked in one way or another. They can be coupled through common consequences and dissociated by differential consequences. When people are free to voice aggressive attitudes but injurious acts are strictly prohibited, correspondence between word and deed will be low. It was previously shown how emotional arousal can either facilitate or inhibit aggressive acts depending upon its contingent outcomes. Thus, people often experience anger without taking any aggressive action; conversely, they can be induced to perform injurious acts without accompanying anger. Even the physiological manifestations that are subjectively experienced as anger arousal can be dissociated through selective reinforcement. If individuals are rewarded only when they increase both their heart rate and blood pressure, these two autonomic functions become linked, but if rewards are given only when one response goes up and the other goes down, these physiological reactions become differentiated (Schwartz, 1972). Miller (1969) provides further impressive demonstrations of how specific autonomic responses can be selectively increased or reduced by differential reinforcement. Consonance between affect and attitudes will likewise be reduced should emotionally charged attitudes produce negative results while calmly expressed ones are well received.

In short, people do not have to be angered or emotionally aroused to behave aggressively. A culture can produce highly aggressive people, while keeping frustration at a low level, by valuing aggressive accomplishments, furnishing successful aggressive models, and ensuring that aggressive actions secure rewarding effects. Since aggression does not originate internally and its social determinants are alterable, social learning theory holds a more optimistic view of man's capacity to reduce the level of human destructiveness.

chapter two

ORIGINS
OF
AGGRESSION

People are not born with preformed repertoires of aggressive behavior; they must learn them in one way or another. Some of the elementary forms of physical aggression can be perfected with minimal guidance, but most aggressive activities—dueling with switchblade knives, sparring with opponents, engaging in military combat, or indulging in vengeful ridicule—entail intricate skills that require extensive social learning. Various types of aggression can, of course, be attempted without skill learning at a high risk of serious or fatal injury, just as people sometimes hazard treacherous mountain slopes without knowing how to ski or venture into perilous traffic before they have developed proficient driving skills.

Examination of the origins of aggression must consider not only the behavior of free-lancing aggressors, but also that of professionals who are authorized to use aggression as a means of social control or who are officially trained for mass destruction in the service of national policies. Societies rely on military training establishments rather than on innate response repertoires to produce good fighters. It requires a great deal of complex learning to develop efficient weapons of destruction as well as the technical skills to use them. Nor were the infamous extermination procedures in Nazi concentration camps instinctively bestowed; they were perfected in laboratories using human victims as test subjects (Wechsberg, 1967). In this chapter we will examine the processes whereby aggressive patterns of behavior are learned. Before turning to substantive issues, however, the methods used to discover laws of human behavior require some discussion to clarify certain misunderstandings about experimental inquiry.

Strategies of Research

A major purpose of psychological research, whatever the approach may be, is to identify the determinants of human behavior. The search for the causes of behavior is complicated by a number of factors. In everyday life a wide variety of conditions impinges on individuals, and it is therefore exceedingly difficult to unravel which of them exert some influence and which are inconsequential. There is always the danger that a person who relies solely on observation of naturally occurring events will wrongly conclude that one or another of the supposedly causative factors is the critical determinant when, in fact, unidentified influences are responsible for the observed effects. In addition, it is often difficult to ascertain the direction of causal relationships derived from covariations of events in the natural environment. It has been found, for example, that hyperaggressive boys regularly view more televised violence than those who are disinclined to behave aggressively. What is cause and what is effect? One cannot determine on the basis of correlational evidence alone whether aggressive boys are attracted to displays of violence, or whether repeated observation of televised violence fosters aggressive behavior in viewers. To verify that a causal relationship does exist and, if so, whether it involves a unidirectional or a reciprocal influence process requires controlled studies in which potential determinants are systematically varied and their effects are measured. Interpretation of evident covariations is further complicated because correlated events may not be causally related at all; rather, both can be co-effects of a third factor. Crime and physical health, for instance, may be positively related because both are affected by socioeconomic status.

For the reasons given above, causal relationships can be established most reliably through experimental inquiry. Under laboratory conditions it is possible to hold constant a variety of influences while others are varied and their effects assessed. If this method is skillfully applied, it is possible to verify with a high degree of confidence whether or not an alleged determinant causes people to behave in a certain manner. Causal relationships are most impressively demonstrated through replicative control, in which a selected behavior is successively produced and eliminated by introducing and removing its controlling conditions. The potential benefits of experimental inquiry do not derive from whether the phenomenon under investigation occurs inside or outside a laboratory, but from the degree of control exercised over concurrent determinants. Poorly designed experiments involving uncontrolled or confounded variables can therefore yield erroneous generalizations, whereas carefully regulated variation of conditions in natural settings can provide valuable information. Unfortunately, the advantages of controlled field studies often go unrealized because faulty procedures are more readily excused than in laboratory investigations.

Findings from experimental studies are often discounted on the grounds that the artificiality of laboratory conditions precludes extrapolation to everyday situations. This attitude reflects a misunderstanding of the manner in which knowledge is advanced. Experiments are not intended to duplicate events as they occur in real life, and they would lose their value if they did. Laws are formulated on the basis of simulated conditions and then evaluated in terms of how well they enable one to predict and to control phenomena as they occur under natural circumstances. In other words, it is predictive power, not likeness, that should be the guiding criterion of research. For this reason, investigators study basic processes rather than exact reproductions of natural events. This view of experimentation is taken for granted in all other branches of science. Airliners are built on aerodynamic principles developed largely in artificial wind tunnels; bridges and skyscrapers are erected on structural principles derived from experiments that bear little resemblance to the actual constructions; and knowledge about physiological functioning is principally gained from artificially induced changes, often in animals. Indeed, preoccupation with matching actual conditions can retard advancement of knowledge—witness the demise of venturesome fliers who tried to remain airborne by flapping wings strapped to their arms in the likeness of soaring birds.

Experiments that precisely duplicated events as they occur naturally would have limited informative value. This point might be illustrated by considering how a scientist could best determine the effects of brain damage on behavior. In everyday life, brain lesions can occur as a result of a large variety of adverse circumstances, such as automobile accidents, falling objects, or as a by-product of disease. The brain lesions that nature provides vary considerably in extent and location, thereby precluding unequivocal generalizations concerning their effects on behavior.

Knowledge would be more effectively advanced if, instead of waiting for injuries to occur, an experimenter were to "artificially" produce lesions through surgical operations in which the locus and amount of damage were systematically varied. One would not expect him to re-create the misfortunes that occur in nature—for example, by striking or dropping his subjects on their heads, or infecting them with syphilis and waiting for paresis to develop. Of course, ethical considerations preclude experimental induction of brain injury in humans; researchers study subhuman organisms, on which they perform controlled operations.

Experiments should be judged not on the basis of artificiality criteria, but in terms of the explanatory and predictive value of the principles they yield. Air travelers rarely discount research utilizing artificial models in wind tunnels provided it produces reliable airliners; rather, they would question the wisdom of researchers who insisted on using actual airliners for discovering basic aeronautical principles. Nor do they require that airplanes flap their wings because that is the manner in which flying occurs in nature. If the processes governing behavior under natural conditions are not created in the laboratory situations, then, of course, the experimental analyses will furnish little useful data.

The benefits of experimental inquiry often cannot be fully realized in social science because, for ethical and humane reasons, some types of causal conditions may not be applied or, even if the determinants were unobjectionable, certain outcomes may be prohibited. A psychologist who wishes to study the effects of anxiety on intellectual functioning is debarred from using the whole gamut of threats people experience in their everyday lives. Experimental conditions therefore can cover only a limited range of those found in society, and usually the weaker forms. Nor are researchers at liberty to test, through controlled experimentation, the necessary and sufficient conditions for producing homosexuality, schizophrenia, alcoholism, and other conditions that may be socially or personally detrimental. The relatively slow progress in understanding human behavior may perhaps be as much attributed to justified limitations on the use of powerful experimental methods as to the complexity of human functioning.

As in medical science, behavioral phenomena that cannot be created in humans are investigated to some extent through animal experimentation. Such studies can provide helpful information in instances in which the behaviors are analogous and their determinants are similar in animals and in man. On the other hand, when conditions governing a behavioral phenomenon differ across species, as previously noted in the case of sexual behavior, then prediction from animal experimentation to humans may be misleading.

As long as conditions that obtain in everyday situations cannot be produced in laboratory settings, controlled investigations alone cannot provide a full understanding of aggression. Theoretically based natural-istic and longitudinal studies are thus indispensable adjuncts to labora-tory methods. Consequently, it is important to seek conditions in nature in which certain social practices are present and others in which they are absent and to note corresponding variations in aggressive behavior. Ideally, a concerted attack on the problem of aggression should include both field and laboratory studies, and the latter should be designed in such a way as to reproduce the essential processes operative in real-life phenomena. Results obtained from laboratory and field studies will not always be directly comparable, for controlled experiments often reveal relationships that are obscured by unnoticed contravening influences in everyday circumstances. Positive results yielded by laboratory studies not only increase confidence in conclusions drawn from field studies, but frequently elucidate causal processes and bring to light important interaction effects, the precise nature of which cannot be assessed from field data. However, it should be noted that negative results obtained in laboratory studies may sometimes simply reflect the weakness and the limited character of the experimental influences or deficiencies in the way in which the effects are measured.

Learning-Performance Distinction

The social learning theory of aggression distinguishes between acquisi-tion of behaviors that have destructive and injurious potential and fac-tors that determine whether a person will perform what he has learned. This distinction, which is generally overlooked in discussions of aggres-sion, is emphasized because not all that people learn is exhibited in their actions. Discrepancies between learning and performance are most likely to arise under conditions in which the acquired behaviors have limited functional value or carry high risk of punishment. The im-portance of this distinction is illustrated in a study of how imitative aggression is affected by seeing response consequences experienced by the aggressor (Bandura, 1965a).

Children observed a filmed model who behaved in a novel physically and verbally aggressive manner. In one condition, the model was pun-ished for displaying the aggressive behavior; in the second, the model was praised and rewarded for his actions; in the third condition, the model experienced no evident consequences. Compared to children who observed the modeled aggression punished, those who saw aggression either rewarded or without consequences spontaneously performed a

greater variety of imitative aggressive responses. Moreover, boys reproduced substantially more of the model's behavior than girls, the differences being particularly marked when the model's aggressiveness was
punished (Figure 2.1).

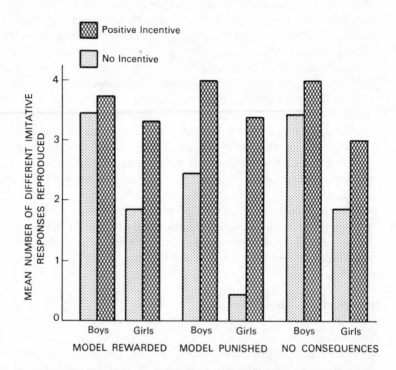

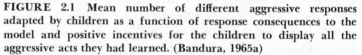

**FIGURE 2.1 Mean number of different aggressive responses
adapted by children as a function of response consequences to the
model and positive incentives for the children to display all the
aggressive acts they had learned. (Bandura, 1965a)**

Following the performance test, children in all three groups were
offered rewards for each modeled response they could accurately reproduce, in order to activate into performance all the behavior they had
acquired through observation. As shown graphically in Figure 2.1, the
rewards completely eliminated the previous performance differences,
revealing an equivalent amount of learning among children regardless
of how the model's aggression had been treated. The initially large
sex differential in performed aggression was likewise virtually eliminated
when the girls were provided with positive incentives to behave aggressively.

The results, considered together, thus show that boys, who are generally encouraged to emulate feats of physical prowess, spontaneously performed all they had learned when they saw aggression well received. When models were punished for their aggressive actions, boys performed less than they had learned, but they later readily exhibited additional imitative responses when they produced rewarding results. By contrast, girls, for whom physical aggression is traditionally regarded as sex-inappropriate and hence negatively sanctioned, kept much of what they had learned to themselves, regardless of how the male model's behavior was treated. Their learning was not manifested in action until they received direct assurance that it was acceptable. In predicting the occurrence of aggression, one should be more concerned with predisposing conditions than with predisposed individuals. Given that aggressive modes of conduct have been learned, social circumstances largely determine whether and when they will be performed.

It might be mentioned in passing that sex differences in modeling of aggression are commonly attributed to deficits in masculine role identification in girls. Results of the above study indicate, however, that in many instances the apparent lack of response capabilities primarily reflects performance rather than learning deficits. This conclusion is supported by findings of other studies showing that low aggressive modeling by females reflects differential inhibition rather than differential learning of aggression (Dubanoski and Parton, 1971; Madsen, 1968). With few exceptions, boys spontaneously perform substantially more imitative aggression than girls, but learning tests yield small or no sex differences. With simultaneous exposure to multiple models, sex differences in observational learning of aggression may arise because observers selectively attend to same-sex models who display different styles of behavior. When female models behave aggressively, sex differences disappear (Maccoby and Wilson, 1957).

The discussion thus far has centered on how discrepancies between learning and doing result from the inhibiting effects of adverse consequences accompanying the actions. Many of the things that people have learned are not revealed behaviorally either because the appropriate situations do not occur or because the equipment needed to execute the acquired pattern is lacking. Television viewers, for example, may learn from Western and crime series gun-fighting skills that are never exhibited because the viewers do not possess firearms—or, if they do, the occasion to use them does not arise.

Because of concern over the social consequences of aggression, most researchers have explored influences that lead people to aggress toward each other, but the mechanisms through which aggressive behavior is acquired in the first place have received comparatively little attention.

Since the conditions determining the acquisition of aggressive patterns differ substantially from those governing their subsequent performance, failure to distinguish between these two processes has created some confusion (to be discussed later) about the implications of research findings and the optimal methodologies for the study of human aggression.

Aggressive behavior is learned through essentially the same processes as those regulating the acquisition of any other form of behavior. People learn by observation and by direct experience. These two modes of learning are analyzed next in some detail as they apply specifically to the development of aggressive patterns of behavior.

LEARNING THROUGH MODELING

One of the fundamental means by which new behaviors are acquired and existing patterns are modified entails modeling and vicarious processes. It is evident from informal observation that human behavior is to a large extent socially transmitted, either deliberately or inadvertently, through the behavioral examples provided by influential models. Indeed, as Reichard (1938) noted some years ago, in many languages, "the word for 'teach' is the same as the word for 'show.' "

There are several reasons why modeling influences play a paramount role in learning in everyday life. When mistakes are costly or dangerous, skillful performances can be established without needless errors by providing competent models who demonstrate how the required activities should be performed. If learning proceeded solely through direct experience, most people would never survive their formative years because mistakes often result in fatal consequences. Some complex behaviors, of course, can be produced only through the influence of models. If children had no opportunity to hear speech, for example, it would be virtually impossible to teach them the linguistic skills that constitute a language. Where certain forms of behavior can be conveyed only by social cues, modeling is an indispensable aspect of learning. Even in instances in which it is possible to establish new skills through other means, the process of acquisition can be considerably shortened by providing appropriate models (Bandura and McDonald, 1963; Luchins and Luchins, 1961).

Three Major Effects of Modeling Influences

Modeling influences can produce three kinds of effects in observers, each of which explains different aspects of aggression. First, as noted above, observers can acquire new patterns of behavior through observation. A second major function of modeling influences is to strengthen or to weaken inhibitions of behavior that observers have previously learned. Inhibitory and disinhibitory effects are largely determined by observation of rewarding and punishing consequences accompanying models' responses. The actions of others also serve as social prompts that facilitate similar behavior in observers. Response facilitation effects can be distinguished from observational learning and disinhibition by the fact that no new responses are acquired, and the appearance of analogous actions is not attributable to weakening of inhibitions because the behavior is socially acceptable and hence unencumbered by restraints. Observational learning of aggression is analyzed in the present chapter; disinhibition and social facilitation are discussed in a later chapter concerned with instigators of aggressive actions.

Conceptualization of
Observational Learning

Learning by example depends upon four interrelated subprocesses. Before discussing the specific role played by modeling influences in the development of aggression, the four subsystems governing observational learning will be reviewed briefly because they specify the conditions that must obtain if the examples set by others are to have enduring behavioral effects.

Attentional processes. A person cannot learn much by observation if he does not attend to, or recognize, the important features of the model's behavior. One of the main component functions in observational learning therefore involves attentional processes. Exposure to models does not in itself ensure that people will attend closely to them, that they will necessarily select from models' numerous characteristics the most relevant ones, or that they will even perceive accurately the aspects they happen to notice.

Among the numerous factors that determine observational experiences, a person's associational preferences are undoubtedly of major importance. The people with whom a person regularly associates delimit the types of behavior that he will repeatedly observe and hence learn most thoroughly. Opportunities for learning aggressive modes of behavior obviously differ markedly for affiliates of delinquent gangs and of Quaker groups.

Within any social group, certain members are more likely to be selected as sources of behavior than others. The functional value of the behaviors displayed by different models is highly influential in determining which models will be closely observed and which will be ignored. A model's efficacy is inferred partly from tangible evidence of the results his actions typically produce and partly from status-conferring symbols that signify competence and past successes. The behavior of models who possess high status in prestige, power, and competence hierarchies is more likely to be successful and therefore to command greater attention from others than the behavior of models who are socially, occupationally, and intellectually inept.

Attention to models is channeled not only by the utilitarian value of their behavior, but also by their interpersonal attraction. Models who possess interesting and winsome qualities are actively sought, whereas those who lack rewarding characteristics tend to be ignored or actively rejected, even though they may excel in other ways. Control of attention through rewarding qualities is perhaps nowhere better illustrated than in televised modeling. Most televised stimulation commands the attention of people of all ages for extended periods. Indeed, models presented in televised form are so effective in holding attention that viewers learn the depicted behavior regardless of whether or not they are given extra incentives to do so (Bandura, Grusec, and Menlove, 1966). Psychological characteristics of viewers also exert selective influence on what they are most likely to attend to.

Observational learning is not a passive receptive process in which people simply absorb the vast array of models they encounter in their daily interactions. When people are exposed to a variety of models, as is invariably the case, they rarely confine their learning to a single source, nor do they reproduce all the characteristics even of preferred models. In experiments in which multiple models diplay different behaviors, the imitative patterns of observers generally represent amalgams of elements from the different models (Bandura, Ross, and Ross, 1963b). Moreover, the particular admixture of behavioral attributes varies from person to person. Conflicting modeling influences arising from adult and peer sources are likewise more apt to produce composite patterns than exclusively adult or peer identifiers (Bandura, Grusec, and Menlove, 1966).

Traditional theories of personality generally depict identification as a pervasive outcome that is firmly established early in the child's life in relation to parental figures and that then predetermines the direction of later development. Research findings reveal that modeling influences are considerably more complicated. Modeling is a continuous process in which new behaviors are acquired and existing patterns to some extent modified by exposure to influences from diverse actual and symbolic models at all periods of life (Bandura, 1969b).

Retention processes. A person cannot be much influenced by the behavior of a model if he has no memory of it. Another requisite function involved in observational learning, therefore, concerns long-term retention of activities that have been modeled at one time or another. In order to reproduce social behavior when the model is no longer present to serve as a guide, the response patterns must be represented in memory in symbolic form. Past events can achieve some permanence by being represented in images or in descriptive verbal symbols for future use. After modeled behaviors have been so transformed, these memory codes function as internal guides for imitative actions. Observers who preserve modeled activities in words and vivid imagery learn and retain the behavior better than those who passively observe or are mentally preoccupied with other matters while watching the performances of others (Bandura, Grusec, and Menlove, 1966; Bandura and Jeffery, 1972; Gerst, 1971).

In addition to symbolic coding, rehearsal also serves as an important memory aid. People who mentally rehearse or enact modeled patterns of behavior are much less likely to forget them than those who neither think about nor practice what they have seen. Most violent forms of behavior cannot be overtly practiced because of social prohibitions. It is therefore of considerable import that mental rehearsal, which can be readily engaged in when behavioral enactment is either impeded or impracticable, may increase retention of modeled behavior.

Motor reproduction processes.   The third component of modeling is concerned with behavioral enactment of what one has learned. To achieve behavioral reproduction, a learner must put together a given set of responses according to the modeled patterns. The amount of observational learning that a person can exhibit behaviorally depends on whether or not he has the required component skills. If he has the subskills, modeled behavior can be more faithfully enacted than if they are lacking. In the latter instance, the symbolic learning remains in abeyance until prerequisite skills are developed through further observation or practice.

Even though symbolic representations of modeled activities are developed and retained, behavioral enactment may be impeded because individuals do not have the physical capabilities with which to carry out the necessary activities. A young child can learn observationally the behavior for driving an automobile and be adept at executing the component responses, but if he is too short to operate the controls, he will be unable to coordinate the action sequences needed to maneuver a vehicle successfully.

Reinforcement and motivational processes.   A person can acquire, retain, and possess the capabilities for skillful execution of modeled behavior, but the learning may rarely be activated into overt performance if it is negatively sanctioned or otherwise unfavorably received. When positive incentives are introduced, observational learning that previously remained unexpressed is likely to emerge in action. Reinforcement influences not only regulate the overt expression of matching behavior, but also affect observational learning by determining the amount of attention people will pay to various models they encounter in their everyday life. Moreover, incentives aid selective retention of what has been learned by motivating observers to code and to rehearse modeled responses that have high functional value for them.

For reasons given above, exposure to models, even prestigious ones, does not automatically produce matching performances. In any given instance absence of imitative behavior may result from faulty observation, retention losses due to inadequate symbolic representation and rehearsal, motor deficiencies, or simply unwillingness to perform the exemplified behavior because of its unfavorable consequences.

Experimental Analysis of Aggressive Modeling

Social transmission of aggression through the power of example has been most clearly demonstrated in controlled experimental situations. Typically these studies make use of a modeling paradigm originally employed by Bandura, Ross, and Ross (1961) in which children observe models behaving in a physically and verbally aggressive manner toward a large inflated plastic figure. Since the studies are mainly concerned with issues of learning, the aggressive acts modeled are those that are rarely, if ever, displayed by children who have had no exposure to the modeled performances. In the general procedure, after addressing the figure belligerently, the model pummels it on the head with a mallet, hurls it down, sits on it and punches it in the nose repeatedly, kicks it across the room, flings it into the air, and bombards it with balls. These physically assaultive behaviors are accompanied by distinctive hostile remarks. Following exposure to the modeling influence, children are provided with opportunities to display what they have learned in a situation containing a variety of materials that can be used either for aggressive or nonaggressive purposes. Learning effects are measured either by recording the children's spontaneous behavior or by asking them to reproduce all the modeled aggressive actions and remarks they can recall (Bandura, 1965a). The latter measure provides the better index of observational learning because people generally learn more than they spontaneously perform.

In technologically developed societies, behavior is usually modeled in a variety of forms. Much social learning is fostered through the examples set by individuals one encounters in everyday life. People also pattern their behavior after symbolic models they read about or see in audiovisual displays. As linguistic competencies are acquired, written accounts describing the actions and successes of others can serve as guides for new modes of conduct. Another influential source of social learning, at all age levels, is the abundant and diverse modeling provided in television. Both children and adults can acquire attitudes, emotional responses, and complex patterns of behavior through exposure to pictorially presented models. Indeed, comparative studies (Bandura and Mischel, 1965; Bandura, Ross, and Ross, 1963a; Prentice, 1972) have shown that people can learn equal amounts from behavioral demonstration, pictorial representation, and verbal description, provided that they convey the same amount of response information, that they are equally effective in commanding attention, and that the learners are sufficiently adept at processing information transmitted by these alternative modes of representation. When some of these conditions do not obtain, aggression is learned more thoroughly from observed actions than from verbal descriptions (Grusec, 1972). Since large audiences in widely dispersed areas can be reached simultaneously through symbolic modeling, the aggression contagion potential of media presentations is greater than that of direct behavioral modeling.

One of the early analyses of observational learning of aggression (Bandura, 1962; Bandura, Ross, and Ross, 1963a) examined the relative potency of aggressive models presented in different forms. Nursery school children were matched individually in terms of their interpersonal aggressiveness and assigned to one of five conditions. One group observed adult models behaving aggressively toward the plastic figure. A second group saw a film of the same models performing the same aggressive acts. Half the children in each condition saw aggressive models of the same sex, the remainder were exposed to opposite sex models. A third group observed the model costumed as a cartoon cat enacting the same aggressive responses on the screen of a television console. This condition was included to test the notion that the more remote the models are from reality, the weaker is the tendency for children to imitate their behavior. In addition to the three modeling treatments, two control groups were included. The behavior of one group of children was measured without any prior exposure to the models to provide a baseline for the amount and form of aggression that children display in the same test situation when they have not experienced the modeling influence. It is conceivable that merely seeing the aggressive materials in the modeling situation could later increase children's use of them, quite apart from the model's actions. Therefore, in the fifth condition, the filmed models behaved in a calm, nonaggressive manner and did not handle the aggressive materials that were visibly displayed.

After the exposure, children in all groups were mildly frustrated and were then individually brought to a different situation containing a variety of play materials, where their behavior was recorded. The major findings are summarized graphically in Figure 2.2.

Results of this study show that exposure to aggressive models had two important effects on viewers. First, it taught them new ways of aggressing. Most of the children who had observed the aggressive models later emulated their novel assaultive behavior and hostile remarks, whereas these unusual aggressive acts were rarely exhibited by children in the control groups. Illustrations of how children patterned their aggressive actions after the model's example are presented in Figure 2.3. The top frames show the female model performing four uncommon aggressive responses; the lower frames depict a boy and a girl reproducing the behavior of the female model whom they had observed in the film presentation. Further analyses showed that a person displaying aggression on film was as influential in teaching distinctive forms of aggression as one exhibiting it in real life. The children were less inclined, however, to imitate the cartoon character than the real-life model.

Aggressive models not only furnished examples for learning, they also reduced the children's inhibitions against performing aggressive acts that they had previously learned but that were never modeled in the experiment itself. These nonimitative aggressive actions included such things as spanking and shooting dolls, killing animals, smashing automobiles, and other assaultive behaviors, sometimes accompanied by the children's own vituperative remarks. As shown in Figure 2.2, children who were exposed to the aggressive models subsequently exhibited substantially more total aggression than children in the nonaggressive model condition or the control group. Interestingly, the cartoon model served as a somewhat weaker teacher but an equally effective disinhibitor of aggression compared with the live and filmed counterparts. In addition, children who observed the nonaggressive adult displayed the restrained behavior characteristic of their model and expressed significantly less aggression than the no-model controls.

It was previously noted that cognitive representation of modeled responses aids in their acquisition and retention. A study by Bandura, Grusec, and Menlove (1966) specifically demonstrates that translating modeled actions into words facilitates observational learning of aggression. Children saw a filmed model perform a series of novel actions, some of which were physically aggressive. During the presentation, different groups of children simply observed the model's behavior attentively, verbalized every aggressive action as the model performed it, or were mentally preoccupied with other matters while watching the film to prevent them from coding the modeled responses into symbolic equi-

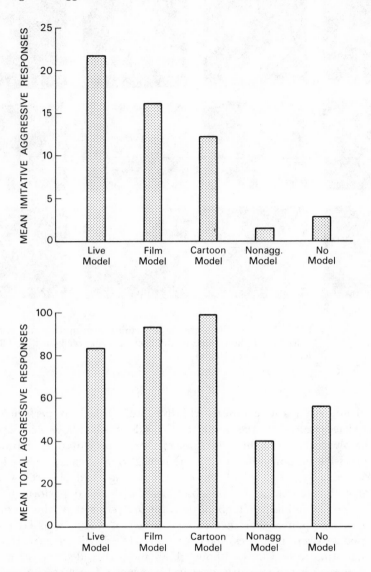

FIGURE 2.2   Mean imitative and total aggression performed by children who were either exposed to aggressive models, nonaggressive models, or who observed no models. (Plotted from data by Bandura, Ross, and Ross, 1963a)

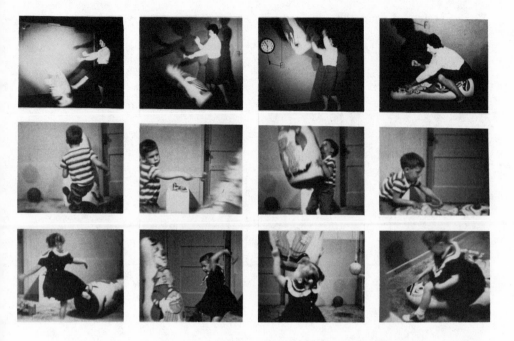

FIGURE 2.3 Photographs of children imitating the aggressive behavior of the female model they had observed on film. (Bandura, Ross, and Ross, 1963a)

valents. After the exposure, children were asked to perform all the' modeled aggressive responses they could recall. Those who converted the physical actions into words for memory representation retained more aggressive responses than the nonverbalizing viewers, who, in turn, showed a higher level of aggression learning than children who were mentally preoccupied while observing the modeled performances. Verbalizers reproduced a high proportion (62 percent) of the modeled aggressive responses that they had preserved in words, whereas noncoded responses were much less likely to be retrieved (26 percent). It was also interesting to find that, although boys and girls coded the same number of aggressive actions, girls retrieved somewhat fewer responses. Further research is needed to determine whether girls have poorer memory than boys for aggressive contents, whether they are more inclined to inhibit symbolic codes of aggressive actions because they are sex-role incongruent, or whether they are simply less disposed to display such behavior.

Whether aggressive responses acquired through modeling are retained or lost with the passage of time also depends on the extent to which rehearsal memory aids are employed. If a person casually observed a particular form of aggression but never practiced it or thought about it again, it is doubtful that he would retain it in memory for long. On the other hand, the contents of observational learning can become firmly established through either mental rehearsal or overt enactment of modeled responses. It might be noted here that assassins in some of the sensational mass slayings originally got the idea from reports of a mass killing. The incident remained salient in their thinking long after it had been forgotten by others, and it was repeatedly revivified and elaborated until, under appropriate instigating conditions, it served as the basis for an analogous murderous action. Robert Smith, an adolescent who shot four women and a young child in a beauty salon, reported being affected in this way by accounts of Speck's murder of eight nurses and Whitman's mass killing of students from atop a university tower (*The New York Times*, 1966d).

Relatively little research has been conducted on retention of observationally learned aggression over long periods, and even less on the factors that aid memory for past experiences. Hicks (1965) provides some evidence of enduring retention of modeled aggression in a study comparing models varying in age and sex as transmitters of aggressive modes of behavior. Children observed adult or peer aggressors presented on film and their imitative behavior was measured immediately after exposure and again six months later. In the postexposure test, groups that received the modeling influence performed more imitative aggression than the controls, who did not display a single imitative response. The different models had a comparable effect except for the male peer model, who produced the highest level of imitative aggression. When the children were retested six months later without any reference to the previous modeling experience, they spontaneously performed fewer imitative responses and it was the male adult model who had the most enduring effect. However, when the children were explicitly asked to demonstrate all they remembered, they revealed more of the modeled aggression than they displayed in action. In a second study, Hicks (1968a) reports that children were able to reproduce more than 70 percent of modeled aggressive responses shortly after exposure, and still retained about 40 percent of them eight months later.

The surprising finding of these experiments is not that some decrease occurred in observationally learned responses over time, but that children had any memory at all of a brief modeling experience that one would not expect to be especially salient or meaningful to them. There is some evidence, however, that filmed violence, particularly in realistic forms, is emotionally arousing to young children and that they retain substantially more aggressive than nonaggressive content (Osborn and Endsley, 1971). Since one is more apt to think about arousing than uninvolving events, emotionality probably enhances retention through its effects on symbolic rehearsal. In everyday life, of course, because people repeatedly observe the same models demonstrating their preferred modes of coping with diverse environmental demands, they have ample opportunities to relearn whatever they may have forgotten. If the model's behavior appears to have functional value, as it often does, observers have strong incentives to practice the modeled patterns and to overlearn them. Conditions of observational learning combining repeated exposure with opportunities for overt practice and symbolic rehearsal ensure more or less permanent retention of modeled activities.

Modeling of aggressive behavior has been studied as a function of a number of other variables. In some of the earlier experiments, when it was commonly believed that frustration was necessary for the occurrence of aggression, children were mildly frustrated after exposure to aggressive models. Kuhn, Madsen, and Becker (1967) found that modeling alone produced significant increases in aggression, whereas frustration, which took the form of arbitrary criticism and delay of reward, had no effect. If anything, frustration appeared to disrupt rather than to augment the effects of the prior modeling influence. This pattern of results is consistent with the view that frustration can have diverse effects and that it may inhibit responsiveness in young children, especially if it contains aversive features.

Experiments reported by Nelson, Gelfand, and Hartmann (1969) illustrate how prior emotional arousal may affect responsiveness to aggressive modeling. Children either succeeded or failed in competitive activities, or they engaged in noncompetitive play. After these experiences they observed a male model behaving either aggressively or nonaggressively. Children who were losers in competitive play were most prone to adopt aggressive behavior modeled by others; winners exhibited an intermediate level of imitative aggressiveness; children who observed the nonaggressive model showed virtually none of the novel assaultive responses regardless of whether they were winners, losers, or noncompetitors (Figure 2.4).

Modeling and competitiveness had similar effects on nonimitative aggression, though the differences are less striking and more dependent on sex characteristics than in the case of imitative responsiveness. The nonimitative aggression of boys seemed to be most affected by competitiveness and that of girls by aggressive modeling.

In a subsequent experiment designed to test predictions from the frustration-aggression theory and the arousal-prepotent response theory, Christy, Gelfand, and Hartmann (1971) had children participate in competitive or noncompetitive games, after which they were exposed to models who were aggressive, active but nonaggressive, or restrained in their behavior. Competitive experiences enhanced imitation of the

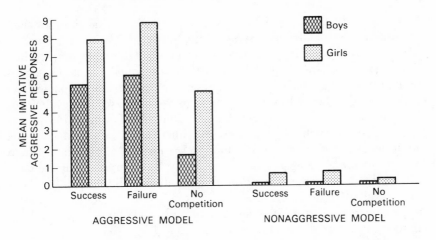

FIGURE 2.4 Mean imitative aggressive responses performed by children exposed to aggressive and nonaggressive models after they either succeeded or failed in competitive activities, or engaged in noncompetitive play. (Plotted from data by Nelson, Gelfand, and Hartmann, 1969)

types of behavior the children saw modeled. Compared to noncompetitors, the competitors behaved more aggressively when exposed to aggressive models and more energetically when exposed to active models, but they showed low aggressive and animated responsiveness when they were provided with restrained models. The effects of failure-induced frustration were thus largely determined by the behavioral examples set by models. Moreover, repeated success in rivalrous situations, in conjunction with modeling influences, enhanced both aggressive and nonaggressive behavior analogously to repeated failure. These findings are in closer agreement with derivations from social learning than from frustration-aggression formulations.

Another set of studies employing the standard modeling paradigm has explored the effects of social sanctions and response consequences to the model on children's imitative aggression. Observed punishment of assaultive actions generally reduces imitative aggression, whereas observed reward or the absence of adverse consequences tends to facilitate imitative responding (Bandura, 1965a; Bandura, Ross and Ross, 1963b; Rosekrans and Hartup, 1967). The influences of vicarious reinforcement on modeling are discussed at length in Chapter 4, which is primarily concerned with factors regulating the expression of aggression.

The role of sanctions in the performance of modeled aggression is elucidated by Hicks (1968b). While children observed a televised male model soundly pummeling his adversary, an adult, who also watched the program, responded approvingly, disapprovingly, or made no evaluative comments regarding the model's conduct. The behavioral evaluations had a substantial effect on children's subsequent imitative aggression provided the sanctioner was present in the test situation: Those who previously heard him praise the aggressor displayed a high level of imitative aggression (mean = 35); those who heard him condemn the aggressor seldom behaved in a similar manner (mean = 7); and when the adult had shown no reaction, children performed a moderately high amount of imitative aggression (mean = 25). By contrast, when the sanctioning adult was absent from the test situation, children paid no heed to his evaluative judgments and exhibited a similar amount of imitative aggression regardless of whether he had approved, condemned, or been indifferent toward the model's actions.

Most of the studies reviewed in this section probably underestimate the amount of aggression that was actually learned from the examples provided by models. With few exceptions, observational learning was measured in terms of the number of matching aggressive responses children were willing to perform spontaneously. As previously noted, people learn more than they usually perform, unless given positive incentives to do so. Therefore, the most precise measure of observational learning is obtained by explicitly instructing individuals, under optimal incentive conditions, to demonstrate all the responses they acquired from observing the modeled performances.

Some of the variables that have been shown to influence the incidence of imitative aggression are most likely operating on performance of observationally acquired behavior rather than on the learning process itself. This is shown in the experiment referred to earlier (Bandura, 1965a), in which learning and performance of modeled aggression were examined as a function of sex characteristics of observers and response consequences to the models. Results of a study by Madsen (1968) also have a bearing on this issue. Children were much more inclined to imitate a familiar aggressive model than an unfamiliar one. This was especially true of boys, who performed approximately three times as many matching responses as the girls. On the other hand, a prior nurturant relationship with the model, extending over a period of six weeks, had no appreciable effect on degree of aggressive modeling. A test for learning in which children were encouraged and rewarded for enacting the modeled patterns they had previously observed disclosed an equivalent amount of observational learning irrespective of model familiarity and nurturance; nor did boys and girls differ in this regard.

Kniveton and Stephenson (1970) tested the hypothesis that children would be more inclined to display imitative aggression in an unfamiliar environment than in a familiar one on the grounds that previous experiences create competing interests that "inoculate the observers against the model's example." Children who watched aggressive modeling, regardless of whether or not they had previously played in the situation portrayed in the film, performed more imitative aggression than control children who had received the familiarizing preexperience without exposure to filmed aggression. However, aggressive modeling without preexperience produced the highest imitative aggression. The authors report that the effect of the filmed influence was short-lived, but their findings actually support the opposite conclusion.

Control children in the foregoing experiment displayed a surprisingly high initial level of imitative aggression. This was probably because punching responses, which are considered common and therefore excluded from the imitative category in other studies, were here scored as imitative acts. Children assigned to the control group, in fact, performed approximately twice as much "imitative" aggression as the preexperience modeling group to begin with, but this sizable initial difference in aggressiveness was ignored in the analysis. A different picture emerges when children's subsequent aggressive responsiveness is compared against their initial baseline aggression. Whereas controls showed a marked drop in imitative aggression when retested (-24) and virtually no change a week later (2), children who received the familiarizing experience with aggressive modeling exhibited an increase in imitative aggression both immediately after exposure to the filmed aggression (23) and in the follow-up test (31). Similarly, when all forms of imitative behavior are considered, controls manifested a progressive loss in succeeding tests (-18, -28), while children who were exposed to the filmed modeling progressively increased in imitative responding (33, 46).

The generality of the hypothesis that familiarity attenuates modeling may also be questioned. Whether familiarity enhances or impedes imitation will largely depend on the functional value of the modeled behavior. It seems highly improbable that people who have previously patronized boxing gymnasiums would be less inclined to imitate a boxing instructor than those who had never been in such places, or that flight trainees who have had prior exposure to the numerous instruments in cockpits would be handicapped by that experience in learning how to fly through modeling. On the contrary, preexperience may enhance and focus attentiveness to critical features of the models' performances and thereby augment modeling effects. On the other hand, people who have developed successful ways of behaving in given situations might be less willing to adopt new modeled patterns of unknown value than would observers who are uncertain about what actions would be most appropriate or effective. Reluctance to give up familiar responses for modeled ones does not mean that exemplified patterns have not been learned or that they will not be adopted on future occasions if the originally preferred modes should prove ineffective. Modeling influences add to a person's repertoire a new response that may vary in preferability in different circumstances and at different times, depending on its value relative to alternative courses of action.

The generalizability of findings based on the modeling paradigm is sometimes mistakenly questioned on the assumption that tests of modeling effects must include human targets whom subjects actually hurt with injurious intent (Hartley, 1964). These requirements fail to recognize that aggression is rarely learned under such conditions even in everyday life. Behavior that has dangerous or costly consequences is typically acquired and perfected in simulated learning situations. Airline pilots, for example, develop basic flying skills in simulators that reproduce rolls, yaws, pitches, and vertical and lateral motions of actual airplanes. Similarly, aggressive behavior is largely learned under non-frustrating conditions in the absence of injurious intent and often with inanimate objects. Army recruits develop and perfect combat skills through many hours of target practice and simulated battle skirmishes. Military instructors who angered enlistees and then gave them live grenades to toss at humans would be judged grossly deranged. Aggression simulators are by no means confined to military training. Boxers develop pugilistic skills by using punching bags and sparring partners whom they do not necessarily intend to injure; hunters acquire the basic rudiments of hunting by shooting at inanimate targets before they venture into the woods in search of game; and parents rarely follow their children around to teach them how to fight in the context of actual battles. Indeed, if aggressive skills were taught only while individuals were angered and entertained injurious designs, many of the tutors and learners would probably be maimed during the acquisition phase.

In studying aggression, researchers must decide whether they are investigating learning or performance effects and choose their experimental procedures accordingly. Learning effects of aggressive modeling are best assessed under test conditions in which subjects are able and willing to reveal all they have learned. To use human targets for this purpose would be as nonsensical as to require bombardiers to bomb San Francisco, New York, or some other inhabited area in testing whether they have acquired bombing skills.

On the other hand, studies designed to identify conditions that lead people to use behavior they have learned for injurious purposes do require human targets. In such investigations, which receive detailed consideration in Chapters 3 and 4, people are provided with opportunities to hurt others. These experiments help explain what causes people to behave punitively, but they throw no light on learning determinants because the aggressive actions are already part of the subjects' repertoires. A complete understanding of aggression therefore requires both types of experimentation.

Although research using nonhuman targets is principally designed to advance understanding of learning processes, the question is sometimes raised whether such influences do affect interpersonal aggression. Considering that in everyday life the actions used to hurt others are usually developed under simulated conditions, one might expect some transfer to occur. There is evidence to indicate that this is indeed so. Walters and Brown (1963) found that boys who had been intermittently rewarded for punching an automated Bobo doll—a training situation devoid of pernicious intent and social injury—later exhibited more physically aggressive behavior toward other children in a competitive situation than boys who received no prior training in punching responses. Conversely, elimination of aggressive styles of behavior toward nonhuman targets can produce corresponding decreases in interpersonal assaultiveness. Hyperaggressive children who were taught through reinforced modeling to favor cooperative over aggressive solutions to problems in doll-play situations were much less prone to respond aggressively to interpersonal thwarting, both in structured situations and in their regular social interactions (Chittenden, 1942).

For those who attach special significance to observational learning exhibited toward human targets, the modeling paradigm has been applied in this manner too. After children have seen filmed models assault a person in novel ways, the imitative and nonimitative aggression they direct at a similar human target is recorded. Viewing interpersonal assaults fosters imitative aggressive acts toward people, whereas the unusual conduct rarely occurs when the example is not provided (Hanratty, O'Neal, and Sulzer, 1972; Savitsky, Rogers, Izard, and Liebert, 1972). For reasons given earlier, children reveal more observational learning of aggression in relation to inanimate than to human targets (Hanratty, Liebert, Morris, and Fernandez, 1969). Learning is a necessary though not a sufficient condition for performance. In later chapters we shall specify the conditions under which learned behavior is expressed in action.

Another issue that requires some comment concerns the criteria used for determining whether observers have learned anything new from modeled examples. Some writers (Aronfreed, 1969; Patterson, Littman, and Bricker, 1967) have questioned whether behavior formed through unique combinations of available actions represents response learning, inasmuch as the components already exist in subjects' repertoires. According to this line of reasoning, a pianist who has mastered a piano concerto has learned nothing new because all the finger movements already existed in his repertoire. Most intricate responses are composed of common behavioral elements.

An observer can learn a variety of things, even from relatively simple modeled performances. First, he can learn through example how to combine different actions, which themselves are not novel, into new forms of patterned behavior. Response novelty must be defined in terms of empirical criteria rather than a priori estimations. Any behavior that has an extremely low or zero probability of occurrence given appropriate stimulus conditions qualifies as a novel response. Second, a person can learn to make common responses to situations to which he previously did not respond at all, or to which he reacted in a substantially different manner. In the latter case, learning involves bringing existing behavior under new stimulus control rather than forming new response configurations. And third, he can learn the consequences that are likely to follow certain actions.

Findings of modeling studies are sometimes incorrectly interpreted on the grounds that inflated objects invite physical aggression (Aronfreed, 1969). This type of analysis not only disregards the experimental controls instituted for the target influence, but reflects a view of aggression that is refuted empirically. Aggressive acts are not internally impelled in the absence of any external instigators. On the contrary, aggressive responsiveness is generally under appropriate stimulus control. For this reason, people rarely go around assaulting innocuous targets. In real life the targets, whether they be boxing opponents, enemy troops, oppressors, or more common provocateurs, all have aggression-activating potential. Aggression does not occur in a vacuum. Research in this field is principally designed to explain variations in the form, direction, intensity, and frequency of aggression under certain eliciting conditions. Demonstrating that observationally learned aggression is seldom displayed when there are no suitable targets for it would have no more practical or theoretical significance than showing that hunters are disinclined to fire their guns as long as they see no game.

The effects of aggressive modeling are evaluated by measuring how people behave in the same situation as compared to their previous conduct or to that of others who have never been exposed to assaultive examples. Obviously, one cannot attribute differences in aggression under modeling and control conditions to the nature of the target, because it is identical in both situations. Moreover, the models purposely display uncommon ways of aggressing toward the figure, rather than the usual punching responses. Some of the responses involve unusual patterns of actions accompanied by distinctive hostile remarks. These particular configurations are almost never spontaneously performed by children who have not seen them modeled. Other modeled activities include common responses, but ones that children rarely if ever direct toward inflated dolls without the influence of example. Indeed, the behavior displayed by control children in a variety of modeling experiments consistently shows that inflated dolls, by themselves, do not invoke pummeling with mallets, bombardment with balls, or irate punting.

Modeling General Tactics

The research reported thus far has been concerned with the transmission through example of specific aggressive actions. However, models can teach more general lessons as well. From observing the behavior of others one can learn general strategies that provide guides for actions which go well beyond the specific modeled examples.

In studies of this higher form of modeling (Bandura, 1971d), people observe models respond successfully in a consistent manner to diverse incidents. When observers are later confronted with dissimilar situations, they are inclined to respond in a style resembling the models' dispositions, although their specific reactions cannot be mimicked because of the altered circumstances. In this modeling process, observers abstract the common features exemplified in specific modeled responses and formulate a general principle for fashioning similar models of behavior. Responses performed by subjects that embody the observationally derived principle resemble the behavior that models would be apt to exhibit under similar circumstances, even though subjects have never observed the models responding to these particular events. Naturalistic data will be cited later to illustrate how people adopt from models both specific aggressive actions and general tactics for dealing with diverse interpersonal situations.

Modeling of Attitudes and Values

Exposure to modeled aggression can affect not only observers' actions, but also their attitudes and values. If certain people are portrayed as behaving in aggressive and violent ways, one would expect such observational experiences to produce, through modeled associations, certain attitudes toward them. Siegel (1958), for example, had children listen to radio presentations in which taxi drivers resolved conflicts either by physical violence or through nonaggressive means. Children who had been exposed to the aggressive modeling were more inclined to ascribe aggressive characteristics to different taxi drivers encountered in new situations than those observing amiable examples. Many of the attitudes that people hold toward members of different occupations, races, and ethnic groups are undoubtedly cultivated through the modeling of stereotypes.

Results of a study by Bandura, Ross, and Ross (1963c) indicate that the evaluative reactions observers develop toward aggressors is partly dependent upon the success of their behavior. Children who had observed the aggressor's actions produce punishing consequences did not imitate his behavior, and they rejected him as a model for emulation when asked to select the person they would prefer to be like. On the other hand, when the aggressor's behavior was effective in amassing rewarding resources, he was readily chosen by most of the children as a desirable model for imitation. The surprising finding, however, is that without exception these children were critical of the tactics he used, which they characterized as *harsh, rough, mean,* and *wicked.* Evidently, the utility of aggression rather than its moral value served as the primary basis for emulation. These findings lend support to Toch's (1969) view that behavior is often discarded not because it is bad or wrong, but because it is ineffective. Moral justifications can always be found for practices that are beneficial to the user.

Children resolved the conflict arising from emulation of a person employing reprehensible tactics by derogating the unfortunate victim, thereby justifying the aggressor's exploitive assaultive actions. They criticized the victim for his inability to control the aggressor, for his unwillingness to cede some of his resources, and they ascribed to him demeaning characteristics that would excuse the aggressor's behavior. This study illustrates how rewarding consequences to the model may outweigh the value systems instilled in observers—children adopted the behavior of a successful aggressor and held him in high regard even though they considered his specific actions objectionable and morally reprehensible.

Anxiety-reduction Theory of
Aggressive Identification

Modeling of aggression has been widely interpreted in psychoanalytically oriented theories in terms of a process of defensive identification originating in the Oedipus complex (Freud, 1923; A Freud, 1946). According to this formulation, boys experience high anxiety over anticipated punishment by castration for their incestuous wishes toward their mothers and rivalrous feelings toward their fathers. Oedipal boys both reduce their anxiety and derive vicarious gratification of their sexual feelings by emulating the characteristics of the threatening father. Behaving like a feared aggressor presumably alleviates anxiety by assimilating the external threat. Alternatively, one might hypothesize that, except for adoption of parental prohibitions, acting like a threatening antagonist would accent the rivalry and thus exacerbate rather than diminish anticipatory fear of punishment.

Evidence for an anxiety-reduction mechanism in aggressive modeling is based almost entirely on anecdotal reports furnished by Anna Freud (1946) and Bettelheim (1943). Most of the examples of aggressive behavior that these authors attribute to defensive identification can be adequately accounted for without invoking an identificatory process at all. And in instances in which actions have been patterned on an aggressor, more parsimonious explanations can be offered for the occurrence of modeled behavior.

In a number of Freud's cases, for example, the person who supposedly serves as the model in fact displays no aggression, and it is simply assumed that the aggressive child expects him to be assaultive. Anticipatory aggression can be interpreted as a defensive maneuver, but it could hardly represent identification with the aggressor, any more than swatting a menacing mosquito represents insect identification by a threatened adult. In others of Freud's illustrations a child who was accidentally hurt by a teacher in an outdoor game wears military apparel the following day, and a boy who had undergone dental treatment later displays aggressively demanding and destructive behavior during a therapeutic session. It is, of course, entirely possible that the boys' behavior and the previous hurtful experiences are totally unrelated. Even if the events were causally linked, the theory of defensive identification does not explain why the forms of the boys' aggression were unlike that of the menacing models. Numerous studies, to be reviewed later, disclose that painful stimulation can elicit aggressive behavior, especially in animals. Explanations of this relationship never assume, however, that the animals' aggressive behavior represents defensive identification with the punisher.

The clearest example Freud gives of actual imitative behavior involves the case of a boy who mimicked his teacher's angry grimaces while the latter was reprimanding him. Freud's interpretation that the boy "through his grimaces was assimilating himself to or identifying himself with the dreaded external object" (p. 118) is complicated because the boy's imitative grimaces provoked bursts of laughter from his classmates, thus providing him with social rewards. It is therefore doubtful, even in the latter case, that the imitative behavior was maintained by anxiety reduction.

It is likewise apparent in Bettelheim's (1943) account of prisoners' behavior in a Nazi concentration camp, which is also frequently cited as evidence of defensive identification, that most of the behavioral outcomes may not, in fact, have involved identificatory processes. Bettelheim reports that many of the older prisoners were verbally and physically aggressive toward newcomers and potential troublemakers, sometimes behaving more aggressively than their guards when placed in charge of others. They enforced nonsensical rules that the Gestapo had at one time or another imposed on the group; some of the older captives even modified their uniforms to resemble those of the guards and resented sympathetic foreign correspondents who criticized the Germans.

It is true that the older prisoners often imposed on their fellow captives aversive controls similar to those they themselves had endured, but it is by no means clear that their behavior represented identification with the aggressor in the sense that the concept is employed in psychoanalytic theory. The Gestapo consistently imposed group-oriented punishments in which the transgressions of any individual resulted in brutal torture of the entire group. When two prisoners attempted to escape, for example, all the prisoners were punished by being forced to stand at attention for hours in a snowstorm without overcoats, during which time some died from exposure, and several hundred later had to undergo amputations of their badly frozen extremities. Since the group consequences were often severely painful and the demands of the guards highly capricious, it is not surprising that, in order to avoid brutal and degrading treatment, experienced prisoners often enforced their captors' demands. The prisoners' punitive rule enforcement may thus represent straightforward avoidance behavior designed to minimize transgressions that would endanger the whole group, rather than emulative behavior. Indeed, the explicit purpose of the hostage and group-punishment system was to make every prisoner feel responsible for the acts committed by others. Similarly, antagonism toward foreign correspondents and former fellow prisoners who had publicly reported cruelties perpetrated in the concentration camps, also interpreted by Bettelheim as an example of identification with the aggressor's ideology, may reflect a protective measure in that unfavorable newspaper accounts written by these persons brought severe punishment on the prisoners.

Bettelheim does provide evidence that, in some cases, prisoners went to great lengths to emulate the guards. Some of the older captives, for example, collected pieces of Gestapo uniforms and sewed their own uniforms so as to resemble those of the guards. However, such imitative behavior was punished by the guards and hence could hardly have served anxiety-reducing functions. Indeed, since this particular modeled behavior persisted in the face of aversive consequences, it requires an alternative explanation. The Gestapo elite possessed potent rewarding and coercive power. It has been shown in controlled experiments (Bandura, Ross, and Ross, 1963b; Mischel and Liebert, 1967) that people tend to model their behavior after sources of power. Given the additional evidence that authoritarian personalities are prone to imitative behavior of aggressive models (Epstein, 1966), one might expect that prisoners who had developed authoritarian attitudes prior to their imprisonment (some were formerly prominent politicians) would be disposed to admire and to imitate these attributes in domineering guards. Striving to emulate the elite who control desired privileges and resources is also noted in upwardly mobile persons who, like the prisoners in question, persist in imitative behavior despite the rebuffs they incur from their peers and high-status models.

The case material discussed above and empirical investigation of defensive identification (Sarnoff, 1951) illustrate the loose criteria often used in designating aggressive patterns as outcomes of a defensive identificatory process. There is considerable evidence, of course, that both children and adults imitate aggressive models presented on film, who obviously constitute no personal threat. Moreover, studies in which modeled aggressive acts incur either rewarding or punishing consequences demonstrate that the success of the model's behavior is an influential factor in determining the degree to which an aggressive pattern of behavior will be spontaneously reproduced by others. On the basis of the response-consequences interpretation of modeling effects, it would be predicted that if aggressors are highly successful in securing desired outcomes, observers will identify with them even if they ordinarily regard such attributes with disfavor (Bandura, Ross, and Ross, 1963c; Baron and Kepner, 1970). If, on the other hand, the aggressor's behavior fails to gain power and control over persons and their resources, or in fact produces punishing outcomes, identification with the aggressor will not occur. There is a sense in which aggressive identification may reduce anxiety. A person who adopts effective aggressive patterns is less apt to be victimized by others and is therefore less vulnerable to external threats. In this interpretation aggressive identification reduces anxiety not by assimilating the external threat, but by appropriating forceful tactics that ensure better control over the social environment.

In naturalistic studies the possible influence of the threat value of an aggressive model and the success of his behavioral style are confounded. That is, an aggressor may represent a threat to the observer, but he also repeatedly demonstrates that he can get what he wants by coercive means. It has been shown that fear of an aggressive model is not a necessary condition for aggressive identification. Whether fear is a facilitative, impeding, or irrelevant factor in the identification process can be best answered through controlled studies in which models' threat and the functional value of their aggressive behavior are independently varied.

LEARNING THROUGH PRACTICE

People rarely teach social behaviors that are never exemplified by anyone in their environment. Although modeling influences are universally present, it is possible to establish new response patterns solely on the basis of trial-and-error experiences. Moreover, observational learning usually produces rough approximations of desired activities that are then further refined through reinforced practice. In learning by experience, behavior is shaped into new patterns by its consequences. During the course of trial-and-error experimentation, unsuccessful responses tend to be discarded, whereas rewarded alternatives are progressively strengthened. New response patterns are similarly created by making reinforcement contingent upon novel combinations of actions. Since in this mode of learning the appropriate behavior must be discerned from differential consequences that accompany various actions, it is much less efficient than having a good example to follow.

The literature contains ample evidence that aggressive behavior is powerfully controlled by its consequences, but no experimental attempts have been made to fashion novel forms of aggression through differential reinforcement alone. The principal reason for this lack is that demonstration rather than unguided experience is the best teacher. It would be foolhardy to try to instruct novices in how to handle firearms or hand grenades by selectively reinforcing their trial-and-error efforts. In the case of less hazardous aggressive activities, however, they may be formed to some extent by response feedback.

Learning through combat experience has been explored to a limited extent in experiments with subhuman species designed to train nonaggressive animals to become ferocious fighters. This outcome is achieved by arranging a series of bouts with progressively more experienced fighters under conditions in which the trainee can win fights without being hurt. Initially, the animals used to provoke defensive fighting are either physically restrained or such weak combatants that the trainees can easily emerge as victors. As fighting skills are developed and reinforced through repeated victories, tougher opponents that can be beaten only by vigorous, hard fighting are introduced. Results show that as training progresses, formerly noncombative animals become more and more vicious in their aggressive behavior (Ginsburg and Allee, 1942; Kahn, 1951; Scott and Marston, 1953).

Some indications of the importance of social learning in animal aggressiveness are provided in studies of the long-term effects of infantile fighting experiences and in comparisons of physiological and training determinants of combativeness. Fredericson (1951) found that a brief experience in competitive aggression over food during infancy produced mice that fought over food in adulthood even when not motivated by hunger. By contrast, animals that did not receive the infantile fighting experience never battled over food when they were not hungry. Results of an experiment that varied castration and androgen injections before and after aggression training showed victorious fighting experiences to be the most influential determinant of subsequent aggressiveness, regardless of the point at which the physiological modifications occurred (Bevan, Daves, and Levy, 1960).

Although successful fighting produces brutal aggressors, severe defeats create enduring submissiveness. The power of injury to inhibit aggression is determined by a number of factors. Kahn (1951) found that the younger the animals are when they first suffer defeat, the more passively they behave later in the face of attack. Animals that have been subjected to many painful defeats likewise do not fight even when confronted with harmless opponents, whereas less frequent defeats result in only partial inhibition of aggressive behavior (Scott and Marston, 1953). Indeed, fighting success largely determines animals' social organization. In the course of a series of tournament bouts a stable social order eventually emerges that corresponds closely to the rate of triumphs and defeats of individual members (Ginsburg and Allee, 1942; Scott, 1944). Consistent victors assume a dominant social position; repeated losers become subordinates that submit passively; animals with a history of both wins and losses occupy intermediate ranks. Naturally evoked dominance relationships can be modified by systematically altering the reinforcing consequences of fighting. It is somewhat easier, however, to lower the aggressiveness and social status of superior fighters by a series of defeats than to transform meek appeasers into swaggering aggressors. Their extreme reluctance to perform any aggressive responses limits opportunities to influence them through positive reinforcement.

People are often confronted with provocative situations calling for some type of aggressive action. To the extent that forcible responsiveness produces good results, the rewarding consequences can shape aggressive styles of behavior. Patterson, Littman, and Bricker (1967) report a field study of the development of aggression in passive children through a process of victimization and successful counteraggression. Nursery school children were observed over a nine-month period for the frequency with which they aggressed toward each other and the immediate consequences that such behavior produced for them. Passive children who seldom resorted to defensive aggression because they were rarely picked on and those who were often victimized but whose counterattacks generally failed to terminate assaults by aggressors remained submissive in their behavior. By contrast, equally passive children who were frequently victimized by their peers but who counteraggressed successfully showed a marked increase in aggressive tendencies. Considering that the children had innumerable opportunities to learn observationally how to aggress from examples provided by their peers and assailants, it is debatable whether the particular forms of aggression they displayed were created solely by reinforcement influences. The findings nevertheless clearly show that if aggression, however learned, is positively reinforced, it will become a preferred mode of response. The development of aggressors through a process of tyrannization and reinforcement for counteraggression bears some similarity to how the more active members of oppressed segments of society are shaped into aggressors by people who themselves model, but decry, such behavior.

LEARNING OF AGGRESSION
UNDER NATURALLY OCCURRING CONDITIONS

There are many naturalistic studies demonstrating that people behave in aggressive ways that resemble patterns exemplified by salient models. Naturally occurring resemblances are difficult to interpret, however, for a number of reasons. Unlike laboratory studies in which the nature of the modeling influences is carefully delineated, in everyday life people are concurrently exposed to a number of models, including adults, peers, and all sorts of television personalities. There is no reliable way either of identifying which of these examples are selected as sources of behavior or of gauging their relative influence.

It was previously shown that when the examples set by others differ in significant ways, observers often pattern their behavior after a composite model embodying features taken from the different sources. The net result may be a novel pattern of aggression that does not bear exact likeness to any of the individual models, even though the composite pattern is created entirely from the examples provided. Resemblances arising from modeling influences are also less discernible when observers adopt the general tactics but not the specific actions modeled by others. It is not uncommon for people whose efforts to produce desired changes have been repeatedly thwarted to emulate coercive strategies, but in their own way, after seeing other groups successfully attain what they want through aggressive means.

Behavioral similarity does not invariably indicate a modeling outcome. Some performances, especially relatively simple ones, can be acquired on the basis of common direct experiences. To complicate matters further, the effects of modeling are often counteracted, attenuated, or augmented by the effects that imitative aggression produces when it is tried. The changes created by modeling, in turn, obscure the effects of reinforcement. In instances in which aggressive behavior is learned observationally but inhibited due to unfavorable consequences, positive reinforcement later may increase aggressive actions simply by conveying permissiveness for the previously learned behaviors rather than acting through its reinforcing and shaping functions, as is commonly assumed.

Within a modern society, three major sources of aggressive behavior are drawn upon to varying degrees. One is the aggression modeled and reinforced by family members. Though familial influences play a major role in setting the direction of social development, the family is embedded in a network of other social systems. The subculture in which a person resides and with which he has repeated contact provides a second source of aggression. The types of behaviors that are exemplified and valued in community subsystems may support or counteract familial influences. The third source of aggressive behavior is the symbolic modeling provided by the mass media, especially television. In heterogeneous and rapidly changing societies the specific patterns of behavior exemplified by parental models may have limited value for their offspring. Television can teach viewers how to behave in a variety of situations that extend well beyond the learning experiences available within the family or the immediate community.

Familial Transmission of Aggression

There are several published studies specifically comparing the quality of parental models of children who develop hyperaggressive personalities with those of nonaggressive models. In an analysis of information on familial conditions collected over an extended period, McCord, McCord, and Zola (1959) found that sons of criminals tended to become criminals themselves, especially if their fathers were cruel and neglecting (85 percent), whereas similar adverse treatment was associated with a lower rate of criminality (40 percent) in families where the father did not provide a grossly deviant model of behavior. Other investigators (Glueck and Glueck, 1950) have reported a much higher incidence of aggressive paternal modeling for delinquent than for nondelinquent boys. That violence breeds violence is further suggested by Silver, Dublin, and Lourie (1969). Their longitudinal study of child abuse cases over three generations shows that children who suffer brutal treatment at the hands of assaultive parents are themselves inclined to use abusive behavior in the future.

Most assaultive youngsters do not have criminally violent parents. In slum districts, where children generally spend more time in the streets than in their homes, peers and various extrafamilial adults serve as the primary transmitters of aggressive life styles. And in middle-class families that produce violence-prone offspring, parental aggressive modeling usually takes less blatant forms. This is shown in two studies (Bandura, 1960; Bandura and Walters, 1959) that examined the social learning determinants of aggressive disorders in boys who lived in privileged neighborhoods that are not conducive to antisocial behavior. Rather than examine why people who grow up under adverse familial and community conditions develop delinquent tendencies, we asked instead why intelligent boys who came from intact middle-class homes where the neighborhood standards of conduct support law-abiding behavior become antisocially aggressive (Bandura and Walters, 1959). Families of adolescents who exhibited repetitive antisocial aggression were compared with those of boys who were neither markedly aggressive nor passive.

The families differed most strikingly in the extent to which they trained their sons, through precept and example, to be aggressors. Parents of nonaggressive boys encouraged their sons to be firm in defending their principles, but they did not condone physical aggression as a means of settling disputes. In familial interactions the parents modeled considerate behavior and relied mainly on reasoning in handling social problems. By contrast, parents of the aggressive boys displayed little antisocial aggression, but they repeatedly modeled and reinforced combative attitudes and behavior. While intolerant of aggression toward themselves, one or the other of the parents almost invariably encouraged their sons to aggress toward peers, teachers, and other adults outside the family. During the early childhood years, the instigation often took the form of demands that the boy use his fists in dealing with antagonists, as illustrated in the following interview excerpts.

> **Interviewer (I):** Have you ever encouraged Glen to use his fists to defend himself?
>
> **Father (F):** . . . Well, Glen has always been a kid where kids have pushed him over at school. We've had to encourage him, "Now, son, you just stand right up there." That comes right back to the point that he's never played with children until five years ago. In fact, he was the type of kid that, when he was small, he'd rather sit down and play paper dolls than get in the yard and play with the boys, kicking a football around. . . . But lots of times he'd come home and kids would throw a left or right at him and he didn't know what to do about it. I used to want to teach him to protect himself but my wife didn't go for it. She said, "You're putting things in his head," that I was training him to fight. So we dropped it. (Bandura and Walters, 1959, pp. 106–7)

This father's method of training was depicted in greater detail by his wife, and it is easy to see why she felt that she had to intervene.

> **Mother (M):** When he was about six or seven years old, all the kids were fussing and fighting and he would never fight. His sister would always have to take up his battle for him. Always fighting. So one day my husband took off his belt and said, "Listen, you're

coming home and crying all the time, saying 'Somebody hit me.'"
So my husband was watching through the bedroom window one
day and he saw two little boys. They were really fighting him. So
he went up, took off his belt, and he said, "Glen, I'm going to tell
you something. You're going to whip these boys or else I'm going
to whip you." So he made him stand up and fight both of them.
(p. 107)

Although because of his wife's objections the father apparently
toned down the fighting instructions, he continued to demand that his
son accept and enjoy aggressive activities.

> **F:** One day we went to see Bobo Olson fight. We tried to get him
> to go. "No, I don't want to go." Well, he hated it. I said, "No,
> you're going." Of course, if he didn't want to go, that's fine. But
> he'd rather be home calling his friends over the telephone. That's
> what just burns me up; it makes me so mad. I never turned down
> anything like that when I was a kid. You get a chance maybe one
> out of five years to see Olson fight, the champion of the world, and
> he turns it down flat. (pp. 106–8)

Some of the most aggressive boys came from families in which both
parents demanded, instigated, and condoned assaultive behavior.

> **I:** Have you ever encouraged Earl to stand up for himself?
> **M:** Yes. I've taught young Earl, and his Dad has. I feel he should
> stand up for his rights, so you can get along in this world.
> **I:** How have you encouraged him?
> **M:** I've told him to look after himself and don't let anybody shove
> him around or anything like that, but not to look for trouble. I
> don't want him to be a sissy.
> **I:** Have you ever encouraged Earl to use his fists to defend him-
> self?
> **M:** Oh yes. Oh yes. He knows how to fight.
> **I:** What have you done to encourage him?
> **M:** When he was a little boy, he had a little pair of boxing gloves.
> His dad has been an athlete all his life, so his dad taught him.
> **I:** Has he ever come to you and complained that another fellow
> was giving him a rough time?
> **M:** Oh yes, when he was younger. I told him, "Go on out and
> fight it out yourself."
> **I:** If Earl got into a fight with one of the neighbor's boys, how
> would you handle it?
> **M:** Oh, he should fight it out himself. When he was a little fellow
> he used to fight his own battle . . .
> **I:** What would you do if you found Earl teasing another fellow
> or calling him bad names?
> **M:** That would be up to Earl. If the other boy wants to lick him,
> that would be up to Earl. He deserves it. (pp. 115–16)

In disputes with adults, the parents would insist that their sons not allow themselves to be "pushed around"; they would side with the boys against their teachers; and they would criticize protagonists in ways that excused their sons' assaultive actions.

The generality of these findings is confirmed by a second study (Bandura, 1960) that compared the social learning antecedents of hyper-aggression and withdrawal in preadolescent boys. Parents of the aggressive boys consistently punished aggression directed toward themselves, but they encouraged and intermittently reinforced aggression outside the home. The withdrawn boys, on the other hand, had undergone pervasive inhibitory training in relation to aggression, dependency, and sex behavior. In addition, parents of the aggressive boys, with their relatively frequent use of physical and verbal punishment, provided more aggressive models for their sons than parents of the withdrawn group, who were emotionally restrained in their behavior.

During early childhood years, perhaps the most salient parental modeling of interpersonal behavior occurs in the context of disciplinary activities. Here children are furnished with vivid examples of how one might attempt to influence and control the behavior of others. And, indeed, children often do draw on parental practices in coping with the interpersonal problems they encounter in their daily interactions. Hoffman (1960) found that mothers who forced compliance with their demands through domineering methods, which included verbal and physical aggression, had children who employed similar aggressive tactics in controlling the behavior of their peers.

In many instances the modeling provided in disciplinary actions is inconsistent with, and therefore contravenes, the effects of direct training. If, for example, a parent beats his child for having struck a playmate, the intended objective of the punishment is that the child should refrain from hitting others. Concomitantly with the intended training, however, the parent is unwittingly exemplifying the very behavior he is trying to eliminate. From fear of retaliation, children are unlikely to counter-aggress toward their parents, but the influence of parental example may outweigh parental dictates in guiding behavior in extrafamilial situations. Findings of laboratory studies in which modeling and direct tuition are systematically varied (McMains and Liebert, 1968; Mischel and Liebert, 1966; Rosenhan, Frederick, and Burrowes, 1968) reveal that people are most influential when they are consistent in what they practice and what they preach, whereas the impact of their behavioral prescriptions is considerably weakened by discrepant modeling.

Johnson and Szurek (1952) have identified another set of subtle familial influences that may create and maintain antisocial aggression in children even though extrafamilial conditions provide weak support for such behavior. It is not uncommon for parents to foster in their children patterns of behavior that they approve but cannot themselves engage in for various reasons, and to derive vicarious gratification from their children's successes. Such processes are clearly operative in the case of achievement behavior. However, socialized parents cannot openly instigate and delight in the aggressive exploits of their children without incurring censure. For this reason, the process, according to the observations of Johnson and Szurek, operates in a covert manner.

Antisocial behavior is often initiated by repeated warning of possible transgressions presented more in the form of suggestive prescriptions than prohibitions. Provocative negative modeling thus informs the child of courses of action that otherwise might never have occurred to him. Transgressive behavior is less likely to recur when desired behavior is clearly defined and actions that exceed acceptable limits are dealt with firmly without apology, guilt, or vacillation. The unwitting condoner, however, tends to respond to antisocial behavior in ways that serve to maintain it. Transgressions are overlooked, dismissed as unimportant, or excused; detailed accounts of the exploits are relished with feigned distress; and antisocial actions are met with covert permissiveness and approval. These detrimental parental practices are presumably reinforced by gratifications derived from the child's actions.

Unwitting condoning of socially disallowed forms of aggression is, of course, not confined to familial situations. Disputes often arise over whether societal agents entrusted with coercive power, such as the police, employ unwarranted forms of aggression in apprehending suspected lawbreakers and in controlling protesters. Proposed solutions to this problem generally center around offering police recruits better training, especially along psychiatric lines, elevating the status of police work, and establishing grievance review boards to monitor police departments. Although such programs can improve law enforcement practices, it should be recognized that excessive use of aggression is primarily determined by sanctions rather than by education. Police administrators who condone brutal tactics will find a great deal of such behavior exhibited by their officers, whereas those who censure such behavior will encounter little of it. The cruel third degree, for example, was eliminated by firmly imposed prohibitions, not by psychiatric training of interrogators.

Subcultural Transmission of Aggression

The highest rates of aggressive behavior are found in environments where aggressive models abound and where aggressiveness is regarded as a highly valued attribute. In these delinquent subcultures (Short, 1968;

Wolfang and Ferracuti, 1967) one gains status primarily through fighting prowess. Consequently, good aggressors are the prestigious models upon whom members pattern their behavior. The combination of prestigious aggressive modeling with positive reinforcement of fighting and other manifestations of toughness creates the most effective condition for cultivating aggressiveness.

The challenging question requiring explanation is not why people who inhabit an aggression-breeding milieu should develop aggressive modes of response, but why anyone residing in such an environment should adopt a markedly different style of life. How does a child develop in a divergent direction when models of alternative modes of behavior are lacking in his immediate environment and prosocial patterns are not only weakly rewarded but may even be devalued, whereas adherence to norms of the corner gang provides comradeship and the valued recognition of peers? Sociological studies of lower-class neighborhoods (Whyte, 1955) show that although most of the young residents conform to street-corner codes of behavior, some do come to value scholastic performance and strive hard for self-advancement through educational pursuits.

The processes whereby differential development is achieved within the same milieu are clarified in studies investigating the sources of high educational aspirations among lower-class children (Ellis and Lane, 1963, Krauss, 1964). In these families the parents themselves cannot serve as models for class-typed habits of speech, interests, and social skills that are required for successful upward mobility. Parents usually initiate development in prosocial directions by valuing and encouraging educational aspirations. By direct guidance and example, admired teachers and other prestigious adults further reinforce college ambitions in lower-class youths. Finally, selective association with college-oriented peers provides the role models and incentives for selectively acquiring the values and complex skills necessary to attain the desired status. When one's background is assigned an inferior status, the more successful the upward social transformation is, the greater the familial alienation will be. With increased legitimization of subcultural patterns and willingness of successful models to return to their own communities, members of minority groups may more easily attain educational aspirations without having to renounce their cultural heritage.

The preceding discussion was concerned with subcultural training in aggressive styles of conduct that are disavowed or condemned by the larger society. Most societies maintain elaborate social agencies to which they officially assign aggression-training functions. These include military enterprises with their many supporting subsystems. Military training practices, however, have received little psychological analysis. This is all the more remarkable considering that military establishments can, within a relatively short period, transform people who have been taught to deplore killing as morally reprehensible into skilled combatants who feel little compunction or even a sense of pride in taking human life. Such radical changes have more profound implications for accounts of aggression than the actions of assaultive individuals or youthful groups residing in dismal neighborhoods.

The task of converting socialized men into proficient combatants is achieved not by altering personality structures, aggressive drives, or traits. Rather, willingness and ability to kill in combat are attained by direct training combining several important features. In the first place, the moral value of killing is changed so that people can do it free from the restraints of self-condemning consequences. This is accomplished through indoctrination that assigns a high moral purpose to warfare. One must fight for his country to defend its survival, to preserve world peace, to save humanity from enslavement by cruel oppressors, and for national honor. The force of the moral appeals is strengthened by portraying the enemy as servile fanatics or subhumans driven by ruthless leaders. The moral redefinition of killing is nowhere more dramatically illustrated than in the case of Sergeant York, one of the most phenomenal fighters in the history of modern warfare (Skeyhill, 1928). Because of his deep religious convictions he registered as a conscientious objector, but his numerous appeals were rejected. At camp his battalion commander quoted chapter and verse from the Bible to persuade him that under certain conditions it was Christian to fight and kill. A marathon mountainside prayer finally convinced him that he could serve both God and country by becoming a dedicated fighter.

Self-censuring reactions to brutal acts are repeatedly neutralized by a variety of self-absolving devices that will be examined later, as well as by ideological justifications. Powerful social sanctions are also effectively used to promote acceptance of warfare. Combat heroism is glorified, while opposition to military mission is treated as an unpatriotic social disgrace. A nation that fails to convince its members of the justice of its cause encounters considerable difficulty in mobilizing them to fight.

The social influence process is greatly facilitated by immersing recruits in a totally new reality. Arrivals are promptly dispossessed of most civilian accouterments and outfitted with military gear. During the period of intensive training, rookies are isolated from family, friends, and normal community life, thus removing the customary social supports for their behavior and beliefs. Instead, almost every aspect of their daily life is closely regulated in accordance with the new reinforcement structure. Throughout this process they are subjected to obedience tests and firmly disciplined for noncompliance.

In addition to legitimization of military killing, recruits receive intensive training in the intricate techniques of warfare. A host of coordinated skills must be mastered, such as hand-to-hand fighting, tactical maneuvers, reconnaissance patrols, field fortifications, and artillery and aerial bombardment. Training proceeds by demonstrating how combat activities are executed and by having recruits practice attacks against simulated targets until proficiency is attained.

The third feature of military training is concerned with reducing fear of battle. Various methods are used for this purpose. Action extinguishes fear. Inductees are therefore drilled repeatedly in combat performances until they reach the level of automatic action. In some training programs (Rees, 1945) combat desensitization was aided by exposure to recorded sounds of actual warfare during mock battles. Frightening aspects of heavy bombardment were similarly neutralized by beginning with small fire and then gradually increasing its intensity until terrifying explosives could be discharged with equanimity.

The anxiety-neutralizing power of desensitization procedures is further revealed in successful extinction of anxiety disorders arising from terrifying battle experiences (Saul, Rome, and Leuser, 1946). In a secure setting, soldiers were shown a graded series of movies of battle scenes beginning with exposures they could tolerate. At first the films depicted preparatory combat activities, followed by scenes of surface and aerial bombardment from which displays of injuries and destruction were deleted. In later sessions the soldiers were gradually presented with more frightening combat scenes. Reexposure to the sounds of battle was regulated in a similar manner. At first the warfare was shown silently, and only gradually was sound introduced. Day by day the noise of gunfire and aerial bombardment was increased until full intensity was reached. As a further safeguard against excessive emotional arousal, each soldier was provided his own volume control with which he could regulate the amount of aversive stimulation. After about a dozen showings the soldiers, who earlier exhibited acute anxiety, hypersensitivity, and recurrent nightmares, were unperturbed by battle scenes that had previously terrified them. Moreover, the emotional extinction effect generalized to everyday situations. The soldiers were able to attend commercial movies, which most of them had avoided because of newsreels, and they no longer responded agitatedly to loud sounds or music. Schwartz (1945) also extinguished battle anxieties by repeated exposure to combat films graded in intensity as part of a larger treatment program.

Soldiers are returned to civilian life without putting them through a resocialization process designed to reinstate aggression restraints or to restore commitment to the dignity of human life. Nevertheless, the vast majority promptly revert to their civilian self-reinforcement systems so that they are deterred from behaving cruelly by self-condemning consequences. Achievement of such marked shifts in destructive behavior through moral sanctions without greatly changing the person provides striking testimony for the social control of aggression.

Symbolic Transmission of Aggression

The field studies cited earlier identified some of the familial conditions that breed antisocial aggression when the prevailing subculture is not conducive to such behavior. People can learn varied forms of aggression even when examples and direct tuition of assaultive actions are lacking in both the home and the immediate subculture. The advent of television has greatly expanded the range of models available to the growing child. Whereas his predecessors, especially those in middle-class homes, had limited opportunity to observe brutal aggression, the modern child has witnessed innumerable stabbings, shootings, stompings, stranglings, muggings, and less blatant but equally destructive forms of cruelty before he has reached kindergarten age. If parents could select from diverse alternatives the kinds of symbolic models they would wish to influence the development of their children, it is exceedingly improbable that they would choose Western gunslingers, remorseless psychopaths, deranged sadists, and unprincipled racketeers, unless they harbored odd ambitions for their growing progeny. The types of symbolic models regularly furnished to households are evidently determined more by economic than by moral values. Therefore, both children and adults, regardless of their social backgrounds, have unlimited opportunities to learn from televised modeling aggressive coping styles and the whole gamut of felonious behavior within the comfort of their homes.

Evidence that people can learn as much from symbolic as from actual models indicates that television is an important source of social behavior. Indeed, underdeveloped countries, in which educational resources are limited, rely heavily upon televised tutors for expanding children's cognitive functioning. Consistent with findings of studies on aggression, television-mediated learning is usually as effective as that achieved by actual tutors (Chu and Schramm, 1967).

Several field studies (Stein, Friedrich and Vondracek, 1972; Steuer, Applefield, and Smith, 1971) have shown that exposure to televised violence increases interpersonal aggressiveness, but the authors do not report the extent to which the aggressive acts are explicitly imitative. From time to time, however, numerous incidents in which people have patterned their aggressive behavior directly on that of televised models are reported. Children have been apprehended for writing bad checks to obtain money for candy, for sniping at strangers with BB guns, for sending threatening letters to teachers, and for injurious switchblade fights after witnessing similar performances on television (*San Francisco Chronicle,* 1961; Schramm, Lyle, and Parker, 1961). Cousins (1949) cites examples in which children were prepared to carry out televised homicidal solutions to their own problems. After receiving an uncomplimentary report card, a youngster suggested to his father that they send the teacher a box of poisoned chocolates for Christmas as he had recently seen on television a man successfully kill his wife with poisoned candy, and "she didn't know who did it."

That repeated portrayal of slayings may devalue human life is suggested in the case of a policeman's son who asked his father for actual bullets because his sister "doesn't die for real when I shoot her like they do when Hopalong Cassidy kills 'em." In still another case, "a housemaid caught a seven-year-old boy in the act of sprinkling ground glass into the family's lamb stew" to determine whether it would work as effectively as it did on television. Children have been maimed and sometimes killed while attempting to reenact the heroics of televised superstars, and many pets owe their shortened lives to the influence of televised Western hangings.

The modeling effects of televised aggression apparently are not restricted to the games of youngsters. It is not uncommon for criminal activities to be patterned after ingenious styles portrayed on television. Members of an assaultive gang styled themselves after the gangsters on the television series, "The Untouchables," under the same name (*Cleveland Press,* 1961). Another ring of youths successfully employed burglary tactics learned from the program "It Takes a Thief" (*Washington Post,* 1971). The specific entry procedure, adopted from a televised model, involved taping a window to avoid the noise of shattering glass and then breaking it with a blowtorch. Susan Atkins, a member of the infamous Manson family, later confessed that the Sharon Tate killings were committed partly out of love, in the belief that new murders might cause police to free another member of their family who had been jailed for an earlier slaying. She reported that the idea for the "copycat" murders was suggested to them by a television movie in which police concluded they were holding the wrong suspect after additional murders were committed in the same manner (*San Francisco Chronicle,* 1971a).

Television often introduces highly novel forms of aggression, the effects of which could be easily measured given advance knowledge of the content and time of showing. When the depicted activities pose serious social dangers, the occurrence of analogous actions must be recorded by requirement of law. One such experiment was inadvertently conducted with the showing of the program "Doomsday Flight," over vigorous protests by the airline pilots' association. The televised drama depicted an extortionist threatening airline officials that a pressure-sensitive bomb would explode on a transcontinental airliner as the plane descended to a certain altitude while landing. In the end the pilot outwits the bomber by selecting an airport located at an elevation above the critical altitude setting. A substantial increase in telephoned bomb threats occurred in the week following nationwide presentation of the program (*The New York Times,* 1966e). Shortly after reruns of "Doomsday Flight" were shown in Anchorage and in Sydney, Australia, two airlines in these cities received extortion threats that a barometric bomb was concealed on planes in flight and set to explode at a certain altitude. The extortion bomb hoax cost Western Airlines $25,000 and Qantas $560,000 for information on where the bombs were planted in the aircraft and how they could be defused. In the Australian incident the anonymous caller added force to his demand by also placing a bomb with a barometrically controlled trigger system in an airport locker and directing aviation officials to it.

National Airlines also received telephoned threats in San Francisco and Miami patterned after the television plot when it was rerun in these cities (*San Francisco Chronicle,* 1971c). Following a showing of the "Doomsday Flight" on Montreal television, an extortionist used the bomb plot in an effort to extract a quarter of a million dollars from the British Overseas Airways by warning that a barometric bomb was set to explode on a jet bound from Montreal to London when it descended below 5,000 feet. The hoaxer was unsuccessful, however, because airline officials, having gained thorough familiarity with the oft-repeated scenario, diverted the plane to a high-altitude landing at the 5,339-foot elevation airport in Denver (*San Francisco Chronicle,* 1971d). A California extortionist came closer to succeeding by not disclosing the altitude at which the pressure-triggered bomb would detonate (*Palo Alto Times,* 1971). During this period there was a dramatic rise in airline extortion attempts from a normal baseline of approximately 2 per month to an average of 16 per month for the next two months (Murphy, 1971). Frequency data could similarly be collected for baseline and post-showing rates of other dramatic forms of violence, such as stabbings in subways and the like.

Instigation of felonious acts in foreign countries by exported American programs illustrates the potential influence of cross-cultural modeling through television. The medium of television enlarges the range of models available to members of other societies for better or for worse, depending upon the modes of behavior that are portrayed. The impact of foreign television on the habits of a society can be verified by measuring the appearance of styles of behavior alien to the native culture until the advent of transcultural televised models. As is true of intrasocietal modeling, one would expect the power of foreign televised models to vary with the international prestige of the exporting nation and the utilitarian value of the modeled practices in the new cultural setting. Susceptibility to foreign modeling is also likely to be increased when the indigenous culture is assigned an inferior status, thus prompting aspiring members to accept external media portrayals as exemplifications of modernity.

People who ordinarily dismiss the psychological impact of televised influences nevertheless protest vigorously when its contents pose personal threats. Airline pilots and travelers object to portrayals of bomb plantings on airplanes; subway riders denounce programs depicting subway stabbings; and members of different ethnic and occupational groups condemn televised characterizations that repeatedly portray representatives of their groups in an unfavorable light.

Modeling Effects in Collective Aggression

Social responsiveness is extensively guided by modeling influences, a process that is particularly noticeable in collective aggression. The present chapter is concerned only with the forms that collective aggression takes. Its various causes and instigators will be analyzed later. Social contagion of new styles of aggression conforms to a pattern that characterizes the transitory changes of most other types of activities: New behavior is initiated by a salient example; it spreads rapidly in a contagious fashion; and after it has been widely adopted it is promptly discarded, often to be replaced by a new form that follows a similar course.

Modeled solutions to problems that achieve some measure of success are not only widely adopted by people facing similar difficulties, but tend to spread as well to other troublesome areas. The civil rights movement, which itself was modeled after Gandhi's crusades of nonviolent resistance, in turn provided the example for other protest campaigns aimed at eliminating injustices and undesired social practices. Through collective protest, blacks eventually gained lawful rights they had been dispossessed of in voting, in the use of public facilities, and in education. In addition, opportunities were opened up for which they were qualified but from which they had been barred by discrimination. Admittedly, the changes were slow in coming and fewer than desired, but much greater than if no coercive action had been taken. The model of collective protest as a means of forcing social reforms spread to the antiwar movement and to disadvantaged groups including Chicanos, Indians, homosexuals, and women.

The turbulent sixties provide numerous additional illustrations of the contagion of collective aggression. The urban disorder in Watts, for instance, grew rapidly into a national phenomenon following a common pattern of property burning, looting, and scattered sniper fire. Urban rioting ceased rather abruptly even though the desired social and political reforms were not secured and societal counterresponses, if anything, provided greater instigation and justification for violence than had existed originally. The campus protest movement at Berkeley served as the model for the sit-in method of protest in universities throughout the country. The peaceful sit-in was supplanted by progressively more aggressive forms of protest, graduating to combative disruptions of university functions, and eventually to a rapidly spreading "trashing." In this form of aggression, which was equally transitory, buildings were bombarded with rocks and firebombed by protesters employing mobile guerrilla tactics. Following a New York rally in which construction workers beat up antiwar demonstrators, assaults on dissident students by hard-hatters spread nationwide.

Airline hijacking provides another striking example of the rapid rise and decline of collective modeling of aggression. Air piracy was unheard of in the United States until a commercial airliner was hijacked to Havana in 1961. Prior to this incident there had been a rash of hijackings of Cuban airliners to Miami. These incidents were followed by a wave of hijackings both in the United States and abroad, a wave that reached its height in 1969, when a total of 87 airplanes was pirated (Figure 2.5). Thereafter, hijackings declined in the United States but continued to spread to other countries, so that international air piracy became relatively common. Foreign skyjackings then dropped precipitously. News of an inventive hijacker who successfully parachuted from an airliner with a large bundle of extorted money temporarily revived a declining phenomenon in the United States, as others became inspired by his successful example (*San Francisco Chronicle,* 1971e).

In Brazil a new form of political bargaining tactic was devised when a United States ambassador was abducted and later freed in exchange for political prisoners. This practice quickly spread across Latin America as other consular and ambassadorial envoys were kidnapped in Argentina, Brazil, Guatemala, Uruguay, and the Dominican Republic, and held hostage for the release of political prisoners. Canada and Spain, both containing separatist political factions, soon joined the ranks of South American countries in consular abductions.

There are several alternative explanations for the occurrence of analogous forms of aggression in close temporal proximity but in widely dispersed places. It might be argued that the likeness in events is sheer coincidence and that, in fact, they are in no way causally connected. While this is not inconceivable, the high stylistic similarity in tactics

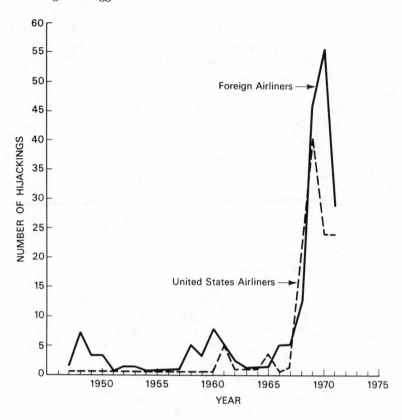

FIGURE 2.5   Incidence of hijacking over a span of 25 years. The rise in the foreign hijackings during the 1949–50 period occurred in Slavic countries at the time of the Hungarian uprising and the second flare-up between 1958–61 comprised almost entirely Cuban hijackings to Miami. A sudden widespread diffuson of hijackings occurred between 1969–71 eventually involving airliners from a total of 55 different countries. (Plotted from data furnished by the Federal Aviation Administration)

and simultaneity of episodes make the validity of such an interpretation highly improbable. A second explanation, most often advanced in political circles, is that the rash of aggressive incidents are related through a conspiratorial plan under the direction of revolutionary advocates. The spread of some types of collective aggression, as in campus protests and urban disorders, is sometimes aided by visits from militant spokesmen without any highly organized strategic collusion. Moreover, it is not uncommon for modeled violence to be adopted in settings where there has been no interchange of advocates. Although conclusive evidence for the determinants of mass social phenomena is difficult to obtain, congruence in the style of collective aggression can be best accounted for in terms of modeling influences.

New aggressive tactics are usually disseminated to members of a given community on the basis of direct contact with actual models. However, symbolic modeling serves to spread the modeled patterns to widely dispersed groups. Newspaper accounts, radio reports, and vivid televised portrayals furnish detailed examples of how the new modes of aggressive behavior are performed, as well as the consequences they are likely to produce. Hijackers, for instance, learn piracy behavior from the mass media rather than from direct observation of a hijacker in action on an airliner.

News of a sensational crime is often followed by a sharp rise in criminal violence that continues to grow at an accelerating rate for some time and then tapers off (Berkowitz and Macaulay, 1972). It is note-worthy, however, that the jump in violent offenses generally occurs a short time later rather than immediately after the horrifying incident. Assuming that the two sets of events are not coincidental, the delayed contagion may be interpreted in several ways. One possibility is that a heinous crime, by its shocking nature, temporarily increases restraints. A second interpretation is that it may require the cumulative impact of several modeling influences to initiate a significant rise in violent actions; thereafter, spreading violence breeds violence. Delayed effects may also occur because a variety of situational influences determines when violent acts will be performed. In the following example, a jealous husband lost his fear of killing by watching Oswald murdered on television, but he did not slay his wife's admirer until they met a short time later. The husband spontaneously commented on the disinhibitory effects of ob-serving an actual homicide: "I saw how easy it was to kill a man when Oswald was shot on TV" (Portland Press-Herald, 1963). Reports of a masterly extortion parachute skyjack did not send viewers running in-stantly to their local airports with demands for cash and parachutes. Within the next few months, however, a number of hijackers, embold-ened by the successful example, copied the specific tactics, including threats of bombing unless passengers were exchanged for ransom money and parachutes (Palo Alto Times, 1972). Any of the preceding explana-tions, either singly or in combination, may account for the temporal convariation between the inciting examples and subsequent imitations.

Cross-cultural Studies of Aggression

Variations in aggression training practices within a given society may cover a limited range of those found in different cultures. Causal rela-tionships can be further verified by comparing the incidence and form of aggression in cultures providing social learning conditions conducive to aggression with those in which they are much less prevalent.

The effects that aggressive modeling and reinforcement patterns have on cultural expressions of aggression are strikingly revealed in ethnographic reports of societies that pursue a warlike way of life and those that display a pacific style of behavior. The Dugum Dani, who live in the New Guinea highlands, exemplify a warrior society (Gardner and Heider, 1969). In the Dani culture men from villages separated by agricultural gardens regularly engage in intertribal warfare that is one of the most valued activities in Dani life. The Dani do not fight for land, food resources, or conquest of opponents; rather, fighting serves social and spiritual purposes.

Dani warfare, which is highly stylized, is performed in designated battlefields adjacent to the villages. Sentries maintain continuous surveillance from high watchtowers to safeguard against enemy ambushes. Men are armed wherever they go so they can be readily summoned to combat surprise raids. Indeed, much of Dani life is organized around warfare, including such activities as extended guard duty, fashioning weapons, cutting grass to prevent ambushes, and performing magical practices to secure defense systems. Formal battles are initiated by shouting a challenge across the no man's land. After ritualistic confrontations between advance bands of warriors, the combatants, armed with spears and bows and arrows, engage in repeated brief clashes of deadly fighting throughout the day.

Though the origin of the institutionalized warfare remains unknown, fighting is instigated and perpetuated largely by feared consequences of unavenged spirits. It is believed that when a dead warrior is cremated, a ghost is released that has the power to cause accidents, sickness, crop damage, and other misfortunes for living relatives until avenged by the taking of an enemy life. As a further method of placating malicious ghosts, a finger of a little girl is amputated and burned, so that females lose several fingers before they reach adulthood. In addition to threats of unavenged ghosts, fighting is prompted by the goading of women who seek retaliation for family deaths, and by the status rewards bestowed on able fighters.

Children of the Dani undergo a graduated training program in learning how to be warriors that bears on several issues discussed earlier. This step-wise training is illustrated photographically in Figure 2.6. Fighting skills are learned and perfected under simulated conditions long before the boys engage in actual combat. Young boys are initiated into fighting techniques by participating with older peers in a variety of war games that duplicate conditions of adult combat. In one of the battle games (spear the seed), berry seeds serve as opposing warriors who are "killed" by skewering them with sharpened sticks. The game even includes a miniature watchtower manned by a seed warrior. A second game (kill the hoop) is used to develop skill with spears. The object of this game is to impale with a lance a bounding vine hoop tossed by an opposing group. In another game that duplicates even more closely adult warfare patterns, groups of boys battle each other with grass-stem spears which are not firm enough to inflict injury. These simulated battles teach the boys, through example and practice, throwing and dodging skills, as well as defensive and raiding strategies of war. The final stage of aggression training involves observational learning on the battlefield itself. While warriors of a fighting unit are engaged in combat, young men watch the battle from a distance to learn tactics for later use when they join the ranks of professional warriors.

The Polynesians of the Society Islands present a marked contrast to the Dani in the socialization of aggression (Levy, 1969). In the Tahitian society, physical aggression is rarely modeled, aggressive behavior is devalued, and unlike the belief system of the Dani, ancestral spirits serve as punishers rather than inciters of aggression. Tahitians are characterized as affable people who are slow to anger, who quickly get over any ill feelings, and who lack vengefulness and hostile aggressiveness. They are disinclined to create anger-provoking situations, and when they show aggression, it is generally expressed in words rather than physical fights. On the infrequent occasions when they aggress physically, they do so in relatively harmless and designedly inept ways.

From an early age, Tahitians are made to fear the consequences of anger arousal and aggressive actions. Anger is presumed to have toxic effects on the body and is therefore best avoided. Moreover, if others are provoked, their spoken threats arouse ancestral spirits who can hurt the provocateur. Such anticipated consequences foster conciliatory behavior, even in highly irritating situations.

Although parents are initially permissive of mock aggressiveness in young children, they strongly discourage hurtful actions and prolonged anger. Control of aggression is largely achieved with threats of punishment, especially through the action of spirits who punish aggressors by causing illnesses and various injuries. Ordinarily, most verbal threats are ignored without any consequences, and hence they either lose their controlling power or retain their effectiveness only in the presence of the threatening agents. Tahitian parents, however, periodically reinforce their threats by capitalizing on false contingencies. When people get sick or suffer an accident, the misfortunes are depicted as caused by their earlier reprehensible behavior. Since the punishing spiritual agents are omnipresent, they serve as a more generalized source of control over aggression than parents or peers. Thus, by providing few opportunities for

A

B

C

FIGURE 2.6 A–E Graduated training program used by the Dani in teaching their children warrior fighting skills. The tutelage proceeds through war games with seed militia (A); practice of spear assaults on inanimate moving targets (B); simulated battles with actual combatants using grass-stem spears to safeguard against physical injury (C); and observational learning of fighting tactics by watching from a distance warriors fighting on the battlefield (D). The last photograph (E) illustrates a battle in progress. (Gardner and Heider, 1968)

D

E

learning aggressive behavior and by removing its functional value, aggression assumes a minor role in the Tahitian way of life.

Numerous other examples can be cited in which different societies foster different temperaments. In cultural settings where interpersonal aggression is discouraged and devalued, people live peaceably (Alland, 1972; Mead, 1935; Lantis, 1959; Turnbull, 1961). In other societies that provide extensive training in aggression and make it an index of manliness or personal worth, people spend a great deal of time threatening, fighting, maiming, and killing each other (Bateson, 1936; Chagnon, 1968; Whiting, 1941). That divergent cultural practices produce different human natures is even more convincingly demonstrated by the coexistence for generations of dissimilar aggressive patterns in people residing within the same segment or neighboring segments of a society. Contrasting socialization practices produced markedly different characteristics in the American Indian. The Comanche and Apache raised their children to be warriors (Goodwin, 1942; Linton, 1945), whereas the Hopi and Zuni, who embraced peaceful orientations, reared children with gentle dispositions (Goldfrank, 1945). To take a more contemporary example, among the American Hutterites, who stress pacifism as a style of life, aggressive conduct goes consistently unrewarded (Eaton and Weil, 1955). Even though children in this subculture are subjected to severe and presumably frustrating socialization pressures, they show virtually no interpersonal aggression. On the other hand, within the larger American society, where aggressive masculinity is widely promoted as a valued quality, combativeness is not uncommon. Social class differences in aggressiveness similarly reflect variations in the extent to which such conduct is modeled and reinforced.

One can only speculate on the origins of diverse cultural practices. Various explanations have been advanced in terms of geographic, biological, technological, and social determinism. To the extent that geographic conditions impose different survival demands, they may favor certain social and economic systems over others. Proponents of biological determinism ascribe cultural variations in behavior to inherent racial qualities of constituent members. As previously shown, man's biological endowment creates response potentialities, not preformed patterns of social behavior. Technological innovations can have profound consequences that extinguish old ways of life and force new social arrangements and practices. Finally, social events and the efforts of influential men can set in motion influences that alter the aims, the social organization, and the reinforcement practices of a society.

Whatever their origins, once social practices become institutionalized with authorized sanctions, they tend to be self-perpetuating long after the historical determinants cease to exist. The power of social determinism is clearly demonstrated by groups migrating to new societies where they transplant their traditional ways of life and, given sufficient collective isolation, preserve the patterns over generations. Thus, the Hutterites adhere to nonaggressive codes of conduct within a larger society in which rivalrous and aggressive behaviors have relatively high functional value. When a subgroup is unable to maintain its social isolation, as is commonly the case, the impact of powerful foreign influences produces fundamental changes in what is valued and in prevailing modes of behavior. Warlike tribes eventually adopted peaceful ways of life under government edict that removed all social supports for violent activities (Goldfrank, 1943). Cultures in which aggression is less firmly entrenched in prestige systems discard fighting even more rapidly under outside influence. The Fore, an equalitarian society in the New Guinea highlands, is a perfect case in point. They promptly gave up warfare on the arrival of Australian officials (Sorenson, 1971).

Individuals raised in aggressive societies are prone to attribute fighting to man's biological makeup and have difficulty conceiving of people living peaceably. Researchers coming from these settings who subscribe to the belief that man possesses an aggressive drive requiring periodic discharge selectively search for evidence of psychological disorders when they study the people of pacific societies. Considering the omnipresence of problems of living, the dubious validity of personality tests, and the elasticity of referents for psychiatric conditions, one who sets out to demonstrate that noncombativeness is hazardous to mental health should have no difficulty in finding confirmatory evidence, regardless of the merits of the belief. The reinforcement customs and habits of aggressive societies are rarely, if ever, studied by observers from gentle cultures. Were they to conduct anthropological field research revealing that in societies in which aggressiveness is idealized and cultivated people recurrently humiliate, injure, and kill each other, they would undoubtedly be struck with how aggression is generated by man's social customs. From the social learning perspective, human nature is characterized as a vast potentiality that can be fashioned by social influences into a variety of forms.

chapter three

INSTIGATORS OF AGGRESSION

People rarely aggress in blind, indiscriminate ways. Rather, aggressive actions tend to occur at certain times, in certain settings, toward certain objects or individuals, and in response to certain forms of provocation. As Toch (1969) has noted, if one wished to observe a stabbing, he could best do so by visiting a bar or a street corner frequented by a teenage gang in a slum neighborhood on a weekend night. Contrary to popular accounts of aggression as explosive emotional reactions, like other forms of social conduct, performance of injurious actions is extensively regulated by environmental cues (Bandura and Walters, 1959). A theory of aggression must therefore explain not only how aggressive patterns are developed, but also how it is that some stimuli become elicitors of aggression while others do not. This chapter examines the processes whereby originally neutral events acquire aggression-evoking potential. In addition, it reviews in some detail research on the types of incidents that function as predictable elicitors of aggressive actions as well as on the predisposing conditions.

ESTABLISHMENT OF STIMULUS CONTROL
OF AGGRESSION

Most of the events that evoke aggressive behavior in humans gain this capacity through learning experiences rather than from genetic endowment. Potent aggression elicitors, such as personal insults, verbal challenges, status threats, unjust treatment, and provocative aggressive displays, obviously do not instigate two-year-olds to fight. As development progresses, however, people no longer remain indifferent to either direct or symbolic assaults. A wealth of research findings shows how aggression can be provoked in others, but relatively few studies have been addressed to the issue of how elicitors that are not innately valenced acquire aggression-arousing properties in the first place. As is true of other types of behavior, aggression can be brought under stimulus control through either paired experiences or response consequences.

Stimulus-contingent Experiences

The discussion of learning principles in the introductory chapter explained how formerly ineffective stimuli acquire the capacity to control behavior through paired experiences. The operation of this learning process in aggression is illustrated by studies of conditioned fighting. Since researchers cannot record all the learning experiences of everyday life that serve to endow stimuli with controlling functions, the basic mechanism is best examined under laboratory conditions. In these experiments a previously ineffective stimulus, such as a tone, is repeatedly associated with pain-elicited aggression in pairs of animals (Creer, Hitzing, and Schaeffer, 1966; Farris, Gideon, and Ulrich, 1970; Lyon and Ozolins, 1970; Vernon and Ulrich, 1966). After a number of such paired experiences, in which the tone foreshadows provoked assault, the appearance of the tone alone tends to produce fighting. Delgado (1963) similarly found that aggressiveness in monkeys could be classically conditioned to a formerly neutral stimulus by associating it with aggressive behavior originally elicited by brain stimulation.

In natural situations physical assaults are ordinarily preceded by a sequence of provocative threats. Studies reported by Thompson (1969) show how anticipatory aggressive displays can be brought under discriminative stimulus control. Animals learned to exhibit aggressive threats in the presence of a red light that previously signaled aggressive activities, but they rarely behaved in a provocative manner to a green light that had never been associated with aggression-provoking experiences. The same learning mechanism is involved in neutralizing conditioned signals. Aggression elicitors lose their provocative value as a result of new experiences in which they are no longer associated with aggression (Farris, Fullmer, and Ulrich, 1970).

The learning histories of different individuals often vary substantially, and hence the incidents that set off aggressive actions in one person may have relatively little effect on another. Toch's (1969) studies of chronic assaulters give some indication of how aggression elicitors are conditioned in the course of natural social interactions. One of the cases reported suffered a humiliating beating as a youngster at the hands of an imposing opponent, a painful incident that determined his selection of future victims. Thereafter, he would become violent at any slight provocation by a large-sized person. These characteristics acquired such powerful control over his aggressive behavior that they often overrode the hazardous consequences of attacking powerfully built opponents.

Although people learn to dislike and to attack certain types of individuals on the basis of direct aggressive encounters with them, aggression instigators are perhaps more often established through symbolic and vicarious experiences. In the former case, the names and attributes of given individuals are paired with words or pictures likely to evoke in observers strong negative reactions on the basis of prior learning. Thus, for example, formerly neutral events take on negative valence through repetitive pairings with adjectives having repugnant connotations (for example, *ugly, dirty*), whereas the same things are evaluated favorably after they have been associated with words that conjure up pleasant reactions (Insko and Oakes, 1966; Staats and Staats, 1957). Likes and dislikes toward familiar names of persons and nations have also been created using emotionally charged words (Berkowitz and Knurek, 1969; Staats and Staats, 1958).

A study by Das and Nanda (1963) further reveals that evaluative responses established through symbolic means tend to generalize along previously established associative networks, thus producing effects that extend beyond the specific experience. After associating neutral syllables with the names of two aboriginal tribes, positive and negative reactions were developed toward the syllables by pairing them with affective words. The tribes took on positive or negative values in accordance with the evaluative responses attached to the syllables with which they had been associated. Similarly, by observing the hatreds expressed by others, people acquire strong emotional reactions toward certain things or classes of people on the basis of little or no personal contact with them.

Response-contingent Experiences

A second way in which aggressive actions are brought under the control of environmental cues is through association with differential response consequences. When the same behavior is treated differently depending on the times, places, or persons toward whom it is directed, these informative cues come to signify the probable consequences accompanying certain actions, and people regulate their behavior accordingly. They tend to aggress toward persons and in contexts where it is relatively safe and rewarding to do so, but they are disinclined to display such behavior when it carries high risk of punishing consequences.

The precision of stimulus control of fighting is again most clearly revealed in animal experimentation, where the requisite learning conditions can easily be created. Reynolds, Catania, and Skinner (1963) reinforced hungry animals with food whenever they attacked another animal in blue light, whereas fighting in green light was never rewarded. Under these conditions of selective reinforcement, animals fought predominantly in blue illumination, but rarely did so in green light. Later, opponents learned to fight in the presence of the green light as well when it signified that attack would bring rewarding results. Thereafter, the animals' aggressive behavior could be effectively regulated simply by changing color cues that signaled probable outcomes—one group attacked in blue light, the other attacked in green light. Dominance hierarchies created by the reinforcement contingencies could be repeatedly reversed simply by altering the discriminative fighting cues. In blue situations the blue-rewarded animals behaved in an aggressively domineering fashion, while the green-rewarded animals were submissive; under green circumstances, the social ranking was reversed. The latter findings would suggest that the relative stability of dominance relations noted among animals in their natural habitat partly results because the social circumstances under which domineering behavior is originally established do not change much over time. In a further extension of the aforementioned experiment, paired animals were reinforced for retiring to opposite corners of their cage when white light was present. By alternating the color fighting cues and white illumination, the animals could be induced to fight and then return to their corners during white light periods between rounds.

It has been shown that animals will aggress toward a companion when they must work hard in order to secure food reinforcement. After a time, stimuli that have been correlated with aversive work demands for meager rewards provoke attack reactions, whereas stimuli that signal a more beneficent rate of reinforcement virtually never produce combative behavior (Cole and Litchfield, 1969; Flory, 1969a).

The discussion thus far has focused on the development of aggression elicitors. Stimulus control also serves to regulate and reduce aggression. In social systems based on force, aggression largely determines social organization. This relationship is most strikingly illustrated in field studies of primate behavior. Past successes and defeats in combat establish a well-defined dominance hierarchy that inhibits intragroup fighting. As long as the social order is maintained, ranking members effectively control aggression of those subordinate to them by threat displays alone. Any overt aggression, when it does occur, is directed downward, usually to the immediately lower member who represents the most serious status threat. If the social order is disrupted by introducing strangers, intragroup fighting erupts and persists until a new dominance hierarchy is established (Southwick, 1967). Interestingly, status threats produced by social changes in membership have a much greater impact on levels of intragroup fighting than do environmental changes such as food deprivation and crowding.

It is easy to find parallels between aggression in the primate social order and in human functioning. Like primates, man often fights competitively for leadership when dominant figures depart or are overthrown; coercive threats are used extensively to constrain aggressive encounters between contending factions; and forceful challenges of those in positions of authority bring prompt counterattacks. It would be a mistake, however, to conclude that aggression is an inevitable determinant of social organization. Societies do exist in which the prevailing reinforcement systems actively promote nonaggressive qualities as the basis for social status (Alland, 1972). Perhaps even fighting among animals could be drastically reduced, if not eliminated, by removing the rewarding payoffs for aggression. If aggression is not inevitable, then social ranking by threat is adaptive for superiors in maintaining a privilege system to their liking, but detrimental to the hapless subordinates who must content themselves with meager offerings. Writers who extol the adaptive benefits of ranking created and perpetuated by force are interpreting the situation from the perspective of victors rather than victims. Evidence for reinforcement control of animal aggression suggests that by making access to food, mates, and the like contingent upon sharing behavior, a primate society could conceivably be organized as well around cooperative as around fighting skills. Kuo's (1960) reported success in establishing stable equalitarian relationships among animals merits further investigation. Research on aggression must not only record what exists, but determine what is possible under different social conditions.

In everyday life the potential consequences of aggressive actions are most often conveyed by distinctive features of potential targets—the positions they occupy in dominance hierarchies, their social roles, their sex status, their familiarity, their combative reputation, their size, and so on. Aggressive behavior is therefore extensively regulated by anticipated consequences derived from informative social cues. Without this type of stimulus control, people would repeatedly aggress foolhardily without concern for the probable effects of their actions.

MODELING INFLUENCES

The preceding chapter contained an analysis of how new patterns of aggression are learned through the examples provided by aggressive models. The expression of preexisting aggressive responses, however learned, is also extensively regulated by the actions of others. Numerous experiments have investigated the effects of exposure to live and symbolic models on subsequent interpersonal aggressiveness.

A major difficulty in studying the conditions that lead people to behave punitively arises because, for obvious humane reasons, one cannot incite individuals to inflict injury on each other. Buss (1961) has devised a procedure that provides individuals with opportunities to engage in physically injurious behavior without the victim experiencing any pain. The aggression apparatus used for this purpose consists of a panel containing ten shock buttons arranged in increasing intensity, together with lights that signal right and wrong responses ostensibly made by the victim in an adjacent room. The task is typically presented as a study of the effects of punishment on learning, in which participants shock the "learner" every time the apparatus signals that he has made a mistake. They are free to vary the length and the intensity of the shocks administered. In some studies, participants simply judge the quality of another person's performance by administering more shocks of their own choosing the more they devalue his work. Aggressors usually sample a few shocks at the outset to familiarize themselves with the severity of pain corresponding to the different shock buttons. Unknown to the aggressor, however, there either is no target person in the adjacent room or the shock electrodes are inoperative and the intended victim suffers no pain.

During the task a given number of wrong responses is signaled on the aggressor's panel, and the duration and intensity of the shocks he inflicts on the victim are recorded. Since aggressors are clearly aware of what shock intensities they are administering, whereas they may be relatively inaccurate in judging the duration of each shock, the intensity measure generally yields stronger relationships to variables that are known to determine aggressive responsiveness. Participants who do not wish to behave cruelly can easily meet the task requirements by choosing low-intensity buttons that would cause no discomfort and by curtailing their duration. On the other hand, those who select painful shocks and keep their thumbs on the shock button for relatively long periods are acting in an unnecessarily punitive manner.

In a somewhat different procedure (Taylor, 1967; Shuntich and Taylor, 1972), participants compete in a task ostensibly with another person in an adjoining room, though in fact there is no opponent. Participants select at the beginning of each trial any of five intensities of shock they wish their opponent to receive when he is defeated. On trials in which the opponent presumably wins, the participants receive the shock their opponent set for them. With this type of procedure one can study initiation and retaliation of aggression in sequential interchanges under varying degrees of opponent provocation.

A number of studies using some of these approaches have been conducted to elucidate how modeling influences, either singly or in conjunction with other determinants, affect people's interpersonal aggressiveness. Epstein (1966) investigated the interaction effects of observers' authoritarian attitudes and the models' ethnic and socioeconomic characteristics on aggression directed toward a black victim. White college students varying in authoritarianism observed either a white or a black model aggressing toward a black person. For half the students the models represented, in dress and interview replies, a lower-class rank; for the remaining students the models conveyed a middle-class status. On the assumption that high authoritarians tend to be conforming and sensitive to power relations, they were expected to be more imitative of punitive models, especially middle-class ones, than low authoritarians. It was further reasoned that seeing a minority model attack a member of his own group would legitimize such behavior; a black aggressor would elicit from white observers more punitive treatment of a black victim than would a white aggressor.

Compared to students who had no exposure to aggressive modeling, those who observed punitive models subsequently administered two to three times as many shocks that were labeled "very strong" and that evoked vocal expressions of pain from the victim. Although the models' social status did not exert a differential effect, the observers' authoritarianism and the models' ethnic characteristics were important determinants of imitative aggression. High authoritarians were more imitatively aggressive than lows, and the black model evoked greater punitive behavior than the white aggressor. Some data also suggested evidence that the imitative aggression of people who have strong authoritarian attitudes is relatively indiscriminative. Whereas low authoritarians refrained from imitating the white model but were responsive to the influence of the black one, high authoritarians readily adopted the punitive actions of the models regardless of their ethnic characteristics.

The present study cannot establish whether the black model induced more imitative aggression because the victim of his attack was ethnically similar, was of minority status, or because of other factors. To clarify this relationship would require an experimental design in which the ethnic characteristics of observers are varied and the target persons include whites as well as members of minority groups that differ from the model's ethnic affiliation.

Modeled punitiveness can disinhibit aggression in children as well as in adults. Hoelle (1969) measured the willingness of young boys to shock a peer for incorrect answers after they observed a model using either high or low shock intensities exclusively, or when no model was observed. Punitive modeling produced more intense aggressive responsiveness than displays of subdued aggressiveness or no modeling, which did not differ from each other.

Most studies of the behavioral effects of modeling present the aggressive models on film either to ensure standard portrayal of the action or because of intrinsic interest in the influence potential of symbolic modeling. In an early experiment of this type, Walters and Llewellyn-Thomas (1963) found that both adults and adolescents who watched the knife-fight scene from the motion picture *Rebel Without a Cause* behaved more punitively toward another person, whereas a control film on art work had no influence on their aggressiveness. The aggression-enhancing effects of both real-life and symbolic aggressive modeling have since been abundantly documented by other investigators studying diverse populations.

It has been assumed by advocates of the catharsis hypothesis (Buss, 1961; Feshbach, 1964, 1970) that the cathartic or drive-reducing effects of aggressive modeling occur only under certain specified conditions. Observation of aggression supposedly reduces subsequent injurious behavior only if observers are angered at the time of exposure. If, on the other hand, the aggressive drive has not been aroused, vicarious participation in aggressive activities will heighten ensuing aggressiveness. The catharsis theory thus presupposes that the functional properties of aggressive modeling can be radically altered by transitory emotional states of the observer.

An aggressive response sequence generally contains two important elements—the aggressive actions of the attacker, and the pain expressions of the victim. Although a number of researchers have reported changes in punitiveness following exposure to fight sequences, no attempt had been made to determine whether the pain expressions or the instrumental aggression depicted were primarily responsible for the obtained effects. It is apparent from results of experiments employing inanimate targets that observation of aggressive acts in the absence of pain cues can produce substantial increases in aggressive behavior. There are conflicting views, however, on whether expressive pain reactions augment or counteract the effects of aggressive displays. According to the theory of aggression proposed by Sears, Maccoby, and Levin (1957), signs of pain and injury resulting from a child's aggressive behavior occur sufficiently often in conjunction with the removal of his frustrations that seeing others in pain can acquire rewarding value and thus enhance aggressiveness. In contrast, it would be predicted from principles of generalization and vicarious arousal that expressions of pain would elicit empathetic and anxiety reactions that serve as aggression inhibitors. Functional relationships could be even more complicated if the rewarding and inhibiting properties of witnessed pain were significantly altered by the observers' level of anger arousal.

Hartmann (1969) examined the independent and interactive effects of anger instigation, aggressive actions, and pain expressions on subsequent interpersonal punitiveness. Adolescent delinquent boys who had or had not been angered were shown one of three films, each of which portrayed two adolescent boys tossing balls on a basketball court. In the control film the boys engage in active but noncompetitive play, whereas in the other two films the boys get into an argument that develops into a fist fight. The pain-cues film focuses almost exclusively on the victim's pain reactions as he is vigorously pummeled and kicked by his opponent. The instrumental-aggression film, on the other hand, centers on the assailant's actions, including angry facial expressions, foot thrusts, flying fists, and hostile remarks. After exposure to their respective films, the boys were provided with an opportunity to shock the peer who earlier had either angered them or treated them in a considerate manner.

Results of this experiment, based on several indexes of aggressiveness, are contrary to the catharsis hypothesis, but consistent with social learning theory. Boys who had observed either the aggressive acts or the pain expressions administered more severe shocks, both under aroused and nonaroused conditions, than boys who watched the nonaggressive film (Figure 3.1). Moreover, angered viewers behaved more aggressively than nonangered ones after observing aggressive activities, a result that is directly counter to the catharsis hypothesis. Prior anger arousal also heightened aggression in control subjects but not significantly. The find-

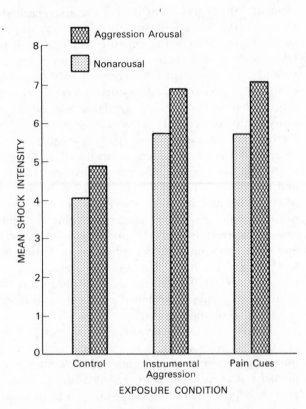

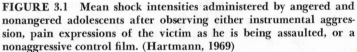

FIGURE 3.1 **Mean shock intensities administered by angered and nonangered adolescents after observing either instrumental aggression, pain expressions of the victim as he is being assaulted, or a nonaggressive control film. (Hartmann, 1969)**

ing that anger instigation combined with aggressive modeling increased punitiveness, but anger alone did not, provides additional evidence for the role of modeling influences in determining aggressive responsiveness to emotional arousal.

Although boys who watched either aggressive actions or their painful consequences showed similar increases in the intensity of shocks administered, these two groups differed when punitiveness was measured in terms of both intensity and duration of shock stimulation (Figure 3.2). Nonangered boys were more punitive when they had witnessed another person severely beaten. The relationship between punitiveness and suffering feedback will depend upon, among other factors, who the assailant is, the strength of his aggression restraints, and the severity of the injuries he causes. Evidence will be cited later indicating that a victim's

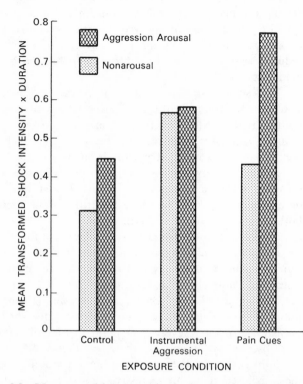

FIGURE 3.2 Mean punitiveness (shock level × duration) displayed by angered and nonangered adolescents after observing either instrumental aggression, pain expressions of the victim as he is being assaulted, or a nonaggressive control film. (Hartmann, 1969)

suffering is more likely to lessen attacks when the injurious consequences are produced by the aggressor's own actions than by observed assaults. Moreover, seeing horrid results of aggression by others may reduce punitiveness in observers by exposing the potential dangers of such conduct, whereas expressions of suffering alone may have few or no inhibitory effects (Goranson, 1970).

It will be recalled that in the motivational analysis of aggression from a social learning perspective, the expression of aggressive behavior is partly controlled by emotional arousal and by reinforcement influences. A number of modeling studies have been reported that are pertinent to these assumptions. One would expect people to aggress more freely toward victims who cannot retaliate than toward those who are apt to counteraggress. Baron (1971b) examined the extent to which responsiveness to modeling influences is affected by threat of retaliation. Seeing another person inflict punishment on a provocateur raised the level of punitiveness in angered observers when they were also given an opportunity to get back at him, but threat of retaliation significantly reduced aggression only in subjects who had no exposure to aggressive modeling.

It is surprising that the almost certain likelihood of reprisal did not significantly attenuate the instigative effects of modeling. Possibly this finding reflects the operation of arousal processes. Under high anger arousal, aggressive behavior may be under relatively poor outcome control. That is, an enraged person is likely to attack and then to worry about possible consequences of his actions if he sees others aggress unconcernedly toward a common antagonist. Under low instigation, however, observers are likely to be more heedful of how their actions may affect both themselves and their victims.

The research discussed thus far demonstrates that aggressive modeling raises the level of aggression shown by others. Conversely, aggression can be reduced in observers by exposure to models who behave in a restrained, nonaggressive fashion in the face of provocation. This is revealed in a study by Baron and Kepner (1970), who measured the punitiveness of angered college students after they had seen a model punish the insulter severely, respond to him in a nonaggressive way, or had observed no models. As shown in Figure 3.3, students who watched the punitive model exhibited the highest amount of aggression, whereas those exposed to a nonaggressive model performed relatively little aggression and were significantly lower in this respect than students who did not see the reactions of others. Whether observers liked or disliked the model had no appreciable effect on the degree to which they were affected by his behavior. The latter finding is consistent with previous results showing that aggression can be readily disinhibited by models regardless of their attractive qualities (Bandura and Huston, 1961; Madsen, 1968), and even by successful but disliked models (Bandura, Ross, and Ross, 1963b).

Baron (1971a) presents additional suggestive evidence that under multiple modeling influences, the presence of a restrained model can counteract the instigative effects of an aggressive one. Thus, angered students exposed successively to a model who aggressed against their annoyer and one who behaved temperately were not only less punitive than those observing only an aggressive example, but did not differ in this respect from subjects provided with no social guides for their actions. Although modeled restraint can often serve to avert violence, it is apt to be less effective when observers are highly angered (Waldman and Baron, 1971) or when aggression produces good results.

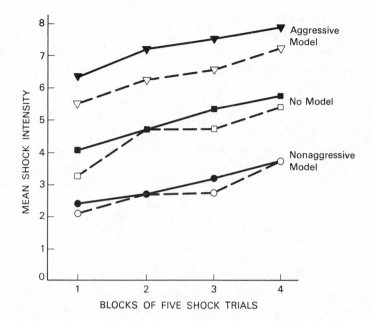

FIGURE 3.3 Mean intensity of shocks administered by adults depending on whether they had previously observed aggressive models, nonaggressive models, or no models, and whether they had high or low attraction toward the model. Within each of the three modeling conditions, the solid lines represent the high attraction subgroups and the dashed lines represent the low attraction subgroups. (Baron and Kepner, 1970)

Explanation of Modeling Effects

Social learning theory postulates several processes whereby modeling influences enhance expression of previously learned aggressive responses. As noted earlier, the actions of others function as social cues in facilitating similar behavior in observers. People often do what they see others doing. In this *response facilitation* process, a model's behavior simply provides an external inducement for similar actions that can be performed with ease.

Modeling influences acquire response-activating power through prior differential reinforcement. The behavior patterns widely adopted within a given culture are usually those of proven functional value, so that new members are spared the hazards and travail of unguided trial-and-error groping. In most instances, therefore, behaving like others is rewarding, whereas dissimilar actions are often less effective or may even bring disapproval. As a result of such differential consequences, modeled actions come to serve as informative cues that similar performances are likely to be positively reinforced. Conversely, when contingencies are reversed, so that analogous responses are never reinforced but dissimilar behavior is consistently rewarded, imitativeness is rarely exhibited (Miller and Dollard, 1941).

Observers obviously differ in the extent to which their behavior is guided by the actions of others, and not all models are equally influential in evoking the types of behavior that they themselves exemplify. Responsiveness to modeling influences is largely governed by three sets of variables. These include, in decreasing order of importance, the reinforcement contingencies associated with matching behavior, the attributes of models, and observer characteristics.

The principles that explain how modeling stimuli acquire the capacity to evoke similar responses account as well for the differential influence of various model and observer characteristics. Models differ in the extent to which their behavior is likely to be successful in producing valued outcomes. People are most frequently rewarded for following the behavior of models who are intelligent, who possess certain social and technical competencies, who command social power, and who, by virtue of their adroitness, occupy high positions in various status hierarchies. In contrast, the behaviors of models who are ineffectual, uninformed, and who have attained low vocational, intellectual, and social status are apt to have considerably less functional value. Identifying attributes and status-conferring symbols thus assume informative value in signifying the probable consequences resulting from behavior modeled by different people. Through a process of generalization, the effect of a model's prestige carries over from one area of behavior to another and to unfamiliar persons, to the extent that they share similar characteristics with models whose behavior has been effective in the past. Similarly, individuals who achieve better outcomes with minimal effort costs from following the examples of others than from their own independent endeavors are apt to be most responsive to modeling influences.

Aggressive behavior, especially when cruel, invidious, and lacking adequate justification, is often socially censured if not self-condemned. Consequently, anticipated punishment exerts a restraining influence on aggressive actions. A second major function of modeling influences is to *strengthen* or to *weaken inhibitions* of responses that already exist in observers' repertoires (Bandura, 1971c). The effects that modeling exerts on behavioral restraints are largely determined by observing the consequences engendered by the models' responses. Seeing the behavior of models punished generally suppresses similar responsiveness in observers. On the other hand, observing models engage in threatening or disapproved activities without experiencing any adverse consequences reduces observers' restraints toward behaving in a like manner. In social groups where aggressive conduct is regarded as emulative behavior, aggressive modeling influences are primarily instigational, whereas in those groups that censure such actions, modeling may also serve a disinhibitory function. Usually both instigational and disinhibitory processes are involved.

Modeling may produce disinhibitory effects in several different ways. When people respond approvingly or even indifferently to the actions of assailants, they convey the impression that aggression is not only acceptable but expected in similar situations. By thus legitimizing aggressive conduct, observers anticipate less risk of reprimand or loss of self-respect for such actions. In addition, observing models perform anxiety-provoking responses without experiencing any untoward consequences results in vicarious extinction of fears and behavioral inhibitions. These sorts of changes are most strikingly illustrated in the treatment of severe phobic conditions through modeling procedures (Bandura, 1971a). People who are terrified of snakes, for instance, and cannot approach them are generally able to handle them without experiencing fear arousal after seeing bold performers engage in threatening interactions with snakes. Cline, Croft, and Courrier (1972) report a similar extinction process in response to aggressive modeling. Children initially showed high emotional arousal to filmed aggression, but they exhibited progressively less emotional responsiveness during successive viewings of the same violence.

Reduction of inhibitions does not mean that observers will attack people indiscriminately, as some authors mistakenly contend (Berkowitz, 1965b; Berkowitz and Geen, 1966). Nor does the appearance of aggressive behavior as a result of restraint reduction imply that a formerly bridled urge to attack is set free or that individuals are internally impelled to aggress by liberated "habits" (Berkowitz, 1970). These misunderstandings can best be clarified by considering cases in which rigid restraints over other forms of behavior are eliminated. Obviously, snake phobics who have had their inhibitions removed do not go around randomly stroking reptiles, whether venomous or not. On the occasions when they do handle snakes, they are externally prompted to do so rather than internally propelled by aroused serpent-caressing habits seeking expression. Indeed, how can "habits," whatever they may be, activate themselves?

When inhibitions are reduced, behavior is more subject to cognitively mediated control. Actions are now self-regulated by anticipated social and other external consequences, by self-evaluative responses to one's own behavior, and by other considerations. Behavior is not only discriminatively performed in accordance with the effects it is likely to produce, but must still be activated and guided by various stimulus conditions. What a disinhibitory interpretation does imply is that, given appropriate instigation, responses will be performed more rapidly, more strongly, or more often when behavioral inhibitions are weak than when they are strong.

Aggressive modeling can have additional psychological effects, though these may be of lesser importance. The behavior of models directs observers' attention to the particular objects used by performers. As a result, observers may subsequently use the same objects to a greater extent, though not necessarily in an imitative way. In one experiment (Bandura, 1962), for example, children who had observed a model pummel a plastic figure with a mallet spent more time pounding other things with a mallet than those who did not see a person handle this particular weapon. *Stimulus enhancing effects* are distinguished from response facilitation in that the observers' behavior in the former case, although the same implements are used, may bear little or no resemblance to the modeled activities.

It has been further shown that observation of others fighting produces *emotional arousal*, as measured physiologically, in children (Cline, Croft, and Courrier, 1972; Osborn and Endsley, 1971), in adults (Zillmann, 1971), and in animals (Welch and Welch, 1968). The resultant emotional arousal may augment the strength of aggressive responding. Much of the effects of exposure to violent displays is, in fact, attributed by Tannenbaum (1972) to their arousal rather than their content properties. This interpretation, though partially valid, requires certain qualifications. Social conduct is learned from modeled contents, not from physiological activation per se. Combat strategies, for example, are better acquired by observing the actions of skillful fighters than from seeing equally arousing amorous behavior enacted in a boudoir. Differential sanctions for aggressive behavior, conveyed through content, can substantially affect the degree of punitiveness elicited by assaultive models under the same level of excitation. And finally, depicted catastrophic consequences tend to reduce aggressiveness even though they generate higher emotional arousal than less frightening outcomes resulting from the same assaultive actions. The empirical evidence, taken together, reveals that models can serve as teachers, as elicitors, as disinhibitors, as stimulus enhancers, and as emotion arousers. A complete account of how models affect observers must encompass the diverse functions of modeling influences.

Researchers who have advanced views on aggression differ in the relative emphasis they place on the eliciting and disinhibitory functions of modeling influences. In explaining contagion of aggression, Wheeler (1966), for example, assigns a prominent role to the reduction of internal restraints against aggressive actions. People who have been provoked presumably experience a conflict between an urge to aggress and their fear of displaying such behavior. Observation of others responding aggressively reduces observers' fears, thereby enabling them to perform similar actions.

Wheeler and his associates have explored several implications of an explanation of aggressive modeling in terms of disinhibitory processes. In the procedure employed, which is concerned solely with modeling of verbal aggression, adults (typically naval recruits) express opinions on a number of topics via an intercom system and then supposedly evaluate each other's judgments. Unknown to the listener, however, the verbal interchanges he hears are prerecorded to create different social influences. One of the recorded participants, who assumes the instigator role, arrogantly voices offensive views, while the second recorded participant, the aggressive model, derides him with varying outcomes. Following exposure to aggressive modeling, listeners' verbal aggression toward the obnoxious annoyer is measured.

As previously noted, behavioral restraints are largely determined by the effects that modeled aggression produces. Results of these studies provide only partial support for a restraint reduction process. Listeners were equally verbally abusive toward the obnoxious character regardless of whether they heard him counterattack, temper his original remarks, or show no response after the aggressive model berated him (Wheeler and Caggiula, 1966). Although listeners were more restrained after hearing an authority figure reprimand the model for attacking the provocateur, neither model self-censure nor peer disapproval of the model affected hostile responsiveness in the listener (Wheeler and Smith, 1967). Wheeler and Levine (1967) hypothesized that in circumstances where restraints arise from fear of punishment by an external agent, similar and dissimilar models will disinhibit aggression with equal ease. As it turned out, subjects who observed a dissimilar aggressor later expressed more hostility than those who heard an aggressor resembling them in many characteristics. The authors reasoned that seeing a person who is quite different get angry at an irritator provides greater justification for one's own annoyance than observing someone with a similar outlook.

Some of the discrepancies between Wheeler's findings and those of others regarding the inhibitory effects of model punishment are probably attributable to the nature of the treatment conditions. The annoyer behaved so obnoxiously that the modeled reprimands would appear justified regardless of the sentiments of others. Model punishment, of course, does not automatically produce response inhibition. The degree to which observed outcomes affect aggression restraints will be largely determined by the comparability, assumed or real, of response consequences customarily applied to models and observers. Social learning theory therefore assigns greater weight to similarity of probable consequences than to similarity of personal attributes in predicting modeling effects. Those who censured the model for his hostile attack differed in potential control over subjects' future well-being. The authority figure, presented as a commanding officer, could produce repercussions for naval enlistees beyond the experimental situation should they misbehave, whereas unfamiliar peers could in no way get back at them. It would be of interest to study the effects of observing response consequences to aggressors under different levels of provocation, and where the characteristics of censuring agents and their controlling power are varied. It might be noted parenthetically that aggression can be most effectively disinhibited by praising and otherwise rewarding the aggressor for his daring actions.

Berkowitz (1965a; 1970) conceives of modeling stimuli principally as activators of implicit aggressive responses, although sometimes he ascribes changes in aggression to disinhibitory processes as well. According to his motivational analysis, aggressive responsiveness requires both a state of anger arousal and the presence of environmental stimuli that possess aggression-activating properties. Anger arousal "primes" the organism for aggressive actions; the stimuli trigger them off. Under low anger arousal a powerful releaser is considered necessary to elicit aggressive responses, but a relatively weak external stimulus will suffice under high instigation. Berkowitz's formulation thus provides a revised frustration-aggression theory that differs from the traditional hypothesis mainly in the role assigned to external cues. Whereas the traditional version depicts aggression as largely impelled by internal excitation, Berkowitz views frustration produced arousal as merely a predisposing state requiring an appropriate external releaser for aggression to occur.

The assumptions of Berkowitz's formulation have been tested in a series of experiments in which punitiveness toward an antagonist is measured as a function of anger arousal and exposure to stimuli varying in aggressive cue value. In the standard design (Berkowitz, 1970), college students are treated insultingly or neutrally and then shown a prize fight scene from the movie *Champion* or a nonaggressive film. In addition, the provocateur's cue value for aggression is increased either by assigning him the same name as the victim of the filmed violence or an aggressive role such as a college boxer. The combined influence of anger arousal, aggressive modeling, and aggressive labeling of the antagonist generally produces the highest level of aggression. However, evidence that punitiveness can be enhanced by anger arousal and aggressive modeling in the absence of aggression-activating cues and by aggressive cues in the absence of anger arousal (Berkowitz, 1965b; Berkowitz and Geen, 1967) indicates that these factors should be regarded as facilitative rather than necessary conditions for the occurrence of aggression.

The justifiability of modeled aggression was varied in some of the above studies in order to determine whether modeling influences may produce their effects partly through reduction of inhibitions. For half the observers the victim in the filmed fight was portrayed as an unprincipled scoundrel who presumably deserved the thrashing; for others, the victim's behavior was depicted as an outgrowth of adverse circumstances that made the aggressor look somewhat malevolent. Observation of socially justified aggression evoked more punitive reactions in observers than unwarranted assaults.

In a related study, Hoyt (1970) found that exposure to filmed aggression in which the victorious aggressor was portrayed as avenging a past unfair beating generated more aggression in viewers than exposure to a film in which the aggressor was portrayed as defending himself against a dangerous attack, or to the same film shown without references to any justifying circumstances. Evaluation of these results with respect to the disinhibitory effects of justifiability must await independent evidence that aggression for vengeance is more excusable than for self-defense. The finding that self-defense justification did not produce more aggression than portrayal of brutal assault without extenuation presents difficulties for an interpretation of the data solely in terms of justification processes. A study by Geen and Stonner (1972) reveals further complexities of the problem. Modeled assaultiveness depicted as vengeful was more effective in disinhibiting retaliatory aggression in angered individuals than if it was presented as a professional activity devoid of animosity. Unangered people, on the other hand, rated themselves as less restrained and behaved more aggressively after seeing professional rather than vengeful violence. The direction of the causal relationship is uncertain, however, because self-reported restraints were measured after the people had aggressed, and it is conceivable that they judged their restraints from their punitive actions.

Taken as a whole, the data indicate that modeling of defensible violence adds legitimacy and thereby weakens restraints over the use of aggressive solutions for social problems. Findings of this line of research suggest that broadcasting codes requiring eventual punishment of criminal acts can inadvertently reduce aggression restraints in viewers when respected enforcement agents inflict violence on culprits with justified impunity. There is always the uncertainty as to whether righteous violence in the moral lesson will legitimize aggressive conduct or depicted punishment will inhibit transgressive behavior.

At this point, it might be instructive to compare the different views advanced on the conditions under which aggressive modeling will enhance punitive responsiveness. Both Wheeler and Berkowitz postulate anger provocation as necessary for aggressive modeling to have an effect. Social learning theory, on the other hand, regards anger provocation as one form of emotional arousal that serves as a facilitator rather than as a prerequisite for aggressive modeling. There is substantial empirical evidence that differs from the former line of theorizing, but lends validity to the social learning interpretation. Although both Wheeler and Berkowitz generally find that modeling without provocation is relatively ineffective, other investigators (Epstein, 1966; Hartmann, 1969; Hoelle, 1969; Walters and Llewellyn-Thomas, 1963) working with diverse populations have clearly demonstrated that unangered observers behave more aggressively after seeing aggressive models than those who have had no such exposure.

The divergent results may arise in part from different procedures in measuring aggressive responses. In Berkowitz's studies subjects are asked to evaluate the victim's solution of a problem by delivering shocks ranging from one shock for an excellent solution to ten for a poor solution. The task therefore requires subjects to administer multiple shocks when they judge the solutions insufficient regardless of whether or not they may want to hurt the target person. The measure thus incorporates both performance evaluations and punitiveness. Some people may administer many shocks because they judge the performer's solution in fact inadequate, while others may do so because they want to hurt him. This ambiguity about what the shock response represents does not exist in studies where subjects are free to respond to the victim's performances by administering very weak shocks that produce no discomfort or highly painful ones that clearly represent needlessly punitive treatment. The possible confounding effects of performance evaluation could be easily reduced in the Berkowitz procedure by allowing subjects free choice in the intensity of shocks they may deliver. Of subjects who considered a given solution sufficiently inadequate to warrant seven shocks, for example, those who selected the weakest intensities would be behaving nonaggressively, whereas those who inflicted painful shocks would be acting punitively. Studies employing unequivocal measures of aggression probably yield the more conclusive findings.

Interpretive problems also arise when anger arousal is induced in subjects by shocking them, because it introduces modeling influences. Receiving many or few shocks for one's own solutions in an ambiguous situation can significantly alter the standards for judging the work of others, independently of whether one is angered or not. Provocateurs administering many shocks are conveying a much higher achievement requirement than those delivering few shocks. Observers tend to match the shock intensities administered by others (Baron and Kepner, 1970; Epstein, 1966; Hoelle, 1969). There is every reason to expect that they would match the frequency of shocks as well. A person who receives many shocks may therefore deliver many because he has been angered, because the behavior of the other person sets a high standard for him, or because of both factors. Confounding of stringent modeling by the antagonist with the anger aroused by his treatment makes it difficult to evaluate findings of studies in which aggressors are presumably angered by differential shocks from the person who later serves as their target. Differences obtained in such experiments are attributed to anger arousal, whereas they may reflect, in varying degrees, the influence of differential aggressive modeling. This methodological problem does not exist when arousal is induced by insult, by arbitrary thwarting, or by other means that differ from the form in which aggression is later measured. When the provocateur angers verbally and the assailant attacks him physically, specific modeling is essentially precluded. In any event, substantial evidence exists that contagion of aggression does not require anger arousal.

Another issue that deserves comment concerns the conceptualization and functional role of external stimuli in the regulation of aggressive behavior, especially as they relate to symbolic modeling. Wheeler conceives of modeling influences principally as disinhibitors of aggression. Berkowitz considers aggressive modeling stimuli to be elicitors, but incapable of producing aggressive actions. In this approach, even the combined effect of anger arousal and aggressive modeling is considered insufficient to increase aggressive responding. As Berkowitz summarizes his own view: "Observed violence serves mainly to arouse the observer's previously acquired aggressive habits—to set them in operation, but only in 'low gear,' so to speak. Before these habits can erupt into a manifestly aggressive act, certain elicitory cues must also be present in the environment" (Geen and Berkowitz, 1966, p. 456). The implied mechanisms that limit the function of modeling stimuli are not explained, however. If aggressive habits are activated but not in action, where are they manifested and in what forms? In more recent elaborations of his position (Berkowitz, 1972), the implicitly evoked events include aggressive thoughts. The question remains, however, if aggressive modeling stimuli can activate implicit aggressive responses, why is it that they cannot evoke aggressive actions as well?

Unlike Berkowitz's theory, which assigns response-priming functions to anger provocation and modeling stimuli, and response-eliciting functions to other environmental stimuli, social learning theory regards all three sources of influence as having response-activating properties. Aversive stimulation, in the form of personal insult or physical assault, is in fact a much more potent elicitor of aggression than some environmental cue that has merely been previously associated with anger-arousing experiences. Thus, people often counteraggress when insulted or struck without requiring additional stimulus prompts; they aggress on slight provocation when they see that such actions are effective in gaining desired outcomes. And individuals who possess certain characteristics that are disliked by others as a result of past experiences are quick to elicit aggressive responses. In the social learning view, the more of these instigators that are present, and the greater their potency, the higher the likelihood that aggression will occur. The tendency to view anger provocation as a predisposing drive state rather than as a response activator probably stems from the fact that its effects on behavior may persist after the inciting incident has ceased. The point will be developed later that the effects of instigation endure not because of an undischarged drive, but because the provocation is re-created symbolically and, analogously to their environmental counterparts, infuriating thoughts also serve as symbolic stimuli for aggressive actions.

The equation of aggression with aggressive drives and injurious aims has restricted the range of determinants typically investigated in laboratory studies. Since, in social learning theory, aggression has multiple determinants and multiple functions, comparative tests of the predictive power of alternative theories require a greater array of experimental treatments than is ordinarily employed. Aggression ascribed specifically to anger may be more generally determined by emotional arousal. Data on this issue are sparse, but the evidence that does exist is consistent with the latter position. Aggression has been enhanced by sexual arousal (Zillmann, 1971), by nonirritating noise (Geen and O'Neal, 1969), by epinephrine (Schachter and Singer, 1962), and by success experiences (Christy, Gelfand, and Hartmann, 1971) in much the same way as by anger provocation. Empirical tests of catharsis and frustration-aggression hypotheses should therefore include conditions containing nonfrustrative sources of arousal as well.

In social learning theory, response consequences constitute a powerful determinant of aggressive responsiveness. It would be of theoretical interest to compare the relative power of anger arousal and positive reinforcement without anger provocation in producing aggressive behavior that is socially injurious. Considerable evidence showing that hurtful aggression can be enhanced, sustained, and eliminated simply by altering its consequences calls into question theories that postulate anger arousal as an essential and primary determinant of aggression.

In Berkowitz's formulation disliked persons serve as releasers of aggressive responses as a result of verbal and other associations with previous instigators. It will be recalled from an earlier section that there are two basic operations by which formerly neutral stimuli can acquire aggression-controlling functions. They can become *informative* or *discriminative* stimuli through association with differential response consequences. People experience different outcomes for aggressing toward

individuals who differ in status, power, age, sex, and many other attributes. A variety of personal characteristics come to signify probable
consequences for aggressive behavior. Through a similar process of
selective reinforcement, situational, temporal, and other cues acquire informative value that aid in regulating one's actions. People therefore
attack not only those whom they have learned to dislike, but also those
whom it is relatively safe to attack and those whom it is advantageous to
attack. The effects of anticipated consequences, depending on their
nature, may enhance, attenuate, or even override the eliciting power of
social characteristics. A less disliked person who cannot easily counteraggress is more likely to be selected as a target than a highly provoking
person who has the power to retaliate.

Cues can become *eliciting* stimuli for aggression through contiguous
association with aggression-provoking experiences. Classically conditioned
stimuli presumably elicit aggressive behavior regardless of its consequences. Berkowitz (1970, 1972) favors a classical conditioning explanation, though his speculations about how the control process works carry
additional implications. He advances the view that aggressive responses
are automatically and involuntarily elicited by aggressively valenced
stimuli. On the other hand, he notes further that such stimuli are not
in fact directly connected to overt behavior; rather, they evoke thoughts
and feelings according to the meaning attributed to them, and it is these
intervening events that serve as the prompts for aggressive responding.
In a two-stage causal process, external stimuli may very well function as
reliable elicitors of hostile thoughts, but there is abundant evidence that
thoughts do not automatically produce corresponding actions. A major
reason for the weak relationship is that irritating treatment arouses not
only retaliatory ideas, but also thoughts of likely response consequences
which, depending on their nature, can either facilitate or inhibit hurtful
actions. The two stimulus functions are not mutually exclusive. Indeed,
as the preceding analysis shows, both eliciting and response-regulating
influences usually operate jointly. Hence, a complete theory of aggression
must consider both stimulus functions in the activation of aggressive
responses.

In the social learning formulation, stimulus control is extensively
cognitively mediated by judgments of how particular behavior is likely
to be received under different circumstances. Therefore, aggressive actions are not automatically and rigidly controlled by external cues. This
view of the regulatory process has a bearing on the controversy of
whether the mere presence of aggressively valenced cues, such as a gun,
enhances expression of other forms of aggression (Berkowitz, 1971; Buss,
Booker, and Buss, 1972; Page and Scheidt, 1971). Stimulus prompts of
this sort will facilitate aggression if presented in ways that convey permis-

sive or expectant reactions toward such behavior, but not if they are introduced in a manner that makes the behavior either personally or socially unacceptable.

Before turning to other substantive issues, some of the reservations that have been raised concerning the generality of results from the shock paradigm deserve comment. Critics of this approach (Feshbach and Singer, 1971) question the import of injurious behavior when it is performed in a permissive setting as part of a sanctioned social task. What this argument overlooks is that these are precisely the conditions under which aggression is usually elicited and encouraged in everyday life. Aggressors are not recruited by being told to perform acts designated as ruthless, despicable, criminal, or bloodthirsty. Punitive treatment is typically carried out in the name of discipline rather than personal vengefulness; military slaughter is structured as a patriotic endeavor rather than as unconscionable murder; political activists win supporters by presenting their coercive tactics as principled protest against social injustice rather than as willful destructiveness; and people are prompted to assaultiveness by designating it as a sign of manliness rather than psychopathy. It therefore comes as no surprise that aggressive modeling increases aggressiveness in everyday situations in much the same way as it does in laboratory settings (Harris, 1972). While it is of interest to study aggression when such conduct is explicitly defined as human cruelty, it would be a mistake to regard dissuading conditions as prerequisites for identifying determinants of aggression as they operate in natural circumstances.

Another questionable practice is to invoke "demand characteristics" as a cause of behavior in experimental settings. This type of explanation recognizes that people infer from cues the kind of behavior that may be expected in particular situations and act compliantly or oppositionally to the perceived "demand." It is true that cues guide conduct in the laboratory as they do in everyday life. People often behave on conjectures of what others want them to do, but when this happens outside a laboratory it is rarely dismissed as a "demand effect."

The term "demand characteristics" has been used in two ways. Sometimes it is applied to possible *determinants* of behavior and other times to the *processes* by which designated determinants produce their effects. In poorly designed studies it is difficult to evaluate whether behavioral changes result from the conditions deliberately altered or from some other uncontrolled factors. It makes little difference whether unsuspected determinants are called demand characteristics or by some other name. Confusion arises when the effects of social influences that are explicitly varied are ascribed to demand characteristics. To designate changes as demand effects does not explain them. Moreover, all forms of social influence (for example, comments, instructions, persuasive appeals, conditioning, reinforcement, modeling) represent demands in the sense that they function as prompts for particular actions. Social influences might be better analyzed in terms of their explicitness and coerciveness and in terms of whether they change behavior directly or through cognitive processing.

The significance of controlled investigations of violence portrayed in symbolic form is more vigorously debated because of its social implications for television programming. Media spokesmen are especially quick to minimize such findings, on the grounds that the inputs do not involve standard television programs and injurious behavior is not assessed in spontaneous social interactions. It is doubtful that medical researchers, or those in other branches of science, would have made much headway in discovering general laws if their experiments adhered to the naturalness criteria. The determinants of a phenomenon isolated by controlled inquiry must, of course, also be examined under naturally occurring conditions. Unfortunately, much time is expended in unproductive controversies over the virtues of laboratory and field studies when, in fact, knowledge is best advanced by using both approaches in a complementary fashion.

Aggressive Modeling and
Vicarious Catharsis

Numerous field studies have been conducted to determine whether the causal relationships established under controlled conditions are replicated under more natural circumstances. According to Feshbach, a leading proponent of the catharsis hypothesis, televised violence operates through fantasy functions to decrease the likelihood of aggressive behavior (Feshbach and Singer, 1971). Fantasied injury, it is argued, partially substitutes for actual infliction of damage as a means of discharging the aggressive drive. The resultant drive reduction reinforces violent thoughts, which are considered to be incompatible with overt aggression. By delivering violent material, television thus furnishes rewarding substitutes for aggressive action. This service is presumably most beneficial to the less intelligent and unimaginative, who, lacking symbolic capacities, need external aids for generating violent fantasies.

In a large though loosely controlled field study, for six weeks Feshbach and Singer (1971) showed either aggressive or predominantly nonaggressive television programs to boys enrolled in residential private schools and in homes for the underprivileged. During this period supervisory personnel in these settings rated the boys' verbal and physical aggression; they were also administered a variety of personality tests.

The authors report that their findings provide evidence that exposure to televised violence reduces aggressive behavior. Actually, when boys in the two viewing conditions are statistically equated for initial differences in aggressiveness, those in the private schools did not differ on any of the measures of overt aggression. Institutionalized boys shown the violent offerings expressed less verbal aggression toward peers than those in the control condition, but they did not differ in physical aggression toward peers, nor did high aggressors, who should be experiencing the greatest cathartic discharge from violence viewing, express less physical or verbal aggression toward authorities. Even the few significant findings are difficult to interpret, however, because the boys assigned to the control condition were more aggressive toward each other to begin with. As Ball-Rokeach (1971) points out, a higher proportion of hyperaggressive boys in an ongoing group is likely to generate an elevated level of hostile interaction among the members that cannot be corrected statistically.

Relatively few differences were obtained on the personality variables and, in the instances in which some television effects are reported, the relationships vary depending upon subjects' age, institutional affiliation, and personality subgrouping. Given a diverse pattern of results in which many of the comparisons fail to support hypothesized relationships and the few obtained effects hold only for small subsamples, such data permit any variety of interpretations. However, the fact that the televised influence had a consistent impact on fantasy behavior deserves brief comment because of its direct relevance to the catharsis hypothesis. Feshbach, among other personality theorists, has generally regarded fantasy aggression as an index of aggressive drive that is presumably reduced by viewing televised violence. Contrary to expectation, Feshbach and Singer found that exposure to televised violence produced a higher level of fantasy aggression than the control offerings. They reconcile the contradictory evidence by reinterpreting fantasy activities as serving to delay and to control impulse expression. The absence of any television effects on overt aggression of boys in private schools is likewise attributed to their greater cognitive capacities that enable them to self-generate violent fantasies without the aid of television. Since the authors do not report any significant differences between the two samples of boys in their production of aggressive fantasies on thematic tests administered at the beginning of the study, the assumption that underprivileged boys are deficient in this cognitive capacity does not seem borne out by the data.

Research evidence indicates that fantasying goal responses serves neither drive-reduction nor cognitive-control functions. The notion that fantasy provides substitute gratifications that reduce corresponding behavior has been extensively tested and found wanting. Fantasying desired goal activities tends to increase rather than to reduce actions designed to produce them (Mischel and Baker, 1972; Mischel, Ebbesen, and Zeiss, 1972). For this reason, athletes in combative sports deliberately conjure up angry fantasies toward their opponents just prior to a contest in order to heighten aggressive responsiveness. Based on evidence that angry thoughts can instigate aggressive behavior, therapists have successfully reduced intractable violent actions by eliminating their fantasy determinants (Agras, 1967). Drive-reducing functions are further disconfirmed by evidence cited later that not only does fantasy fail to reduce anger arousal, but injurious actions, which presumably should be even more powerful drive reducers, rarely lower aggressiveness.

A number of methodological deficiencies, which are discussed in detail elsewhere (Ball-Rokeach, 1971; Liebert, Sobol, and Davidson, 1972) and will be only briefly noted here, most likely account for the variable results of this project. One of the more serious problems arises from the failure to control, or at least to measure, the aggressive contents the two groups of children were in fact viewing. Programs were classified as aggressive or nonaggressive on the basis of general format rather than in terms of their actual content. Thus, cartoons, which contain the highest violence rates, were assigned to the nonaggressive viewing condition. And in some of the serialized programs control boys were watching, the characters do resort from time to time to threats, verbal abuse, and aggressive actions (Gerbner, 1972a). Although the action-adventure type programs viewed by the aggressive group undoubtedly contain more expressions of lethal violence, they may present fewer examples of moderate aggression that would be immediately serviceable to boys in coping with their own interpersonal conflicts. Seeing people handle familiar problems through coercive means may have greater effects on aggressive behavior in institutional situations than viewing killers shoot victims in exotic settings.

Televised influences were additionally confounded by inadequate control of what shows were watched, with the result that control boys admitted viewing some of the aggressive programs. Without detailed recording of program selections, the amount of unacknowledged violence viewing by the controls cannot be determined. Results of an experiment are uninterpretable when the amount and type of aggressive portrayals remain unknown. This is analogous to studying the effects of protein intake on physical health by serving two sets of smorgasbord, both containing varying amounts of protein food, under loosely supervised conditions permitting some cross-over eating, without measuring how much protein the two groups actually consumed. To confuse further the televised input, in three of the institutions the experimenters yielded to demands from the controls to reinstate a then popular serial saturated with violent episodes. Not only was their so-called "nonaggressive diet" further enriched with violent offerings, but the rewarded protest demonstrated that aggression does pay. These factors, along with the initial higher aggressiveness of the controls, might partly account for some of the aggression they displayed.

This sudy is plagued by numerous other methodological problems, including nonrandom assignment of institutionalized boys to treatment conditions; many subjects withdrew from the experiment at different periods; aggressive behavior was recorded retrospectively by relatively untrained personnel whose ratings are of unknown reliability; there were inadequate controls for possible rating biases arising from knowledge of treatment conditions; and wide variations occurred in the number and types of measures administered to subjects both within and across institutions. Considering the deficiences in the regulation of the television input, in the implementation of procedures, and in the assessment of effects, it is hoped that the publisher's claim that the findings "will undoubtedly have a serious bearing on future programming" are not seriously accepted as guides either for therapeutic practice or for social policy. Indeed, the findings of Feshbach and Singer are disconfirmed by Wells (1971), who replicated their study with better controls for some of the major methodological defects. In two field studies conducted by Parke and his associates (Parke et al., 1972) delinquent adolescents who had been repeatedly exposed to filmed violence became more physically assaultive than those who received a nonviolent fare.

Feshbach (1972) reports a laboratory study designed to test the hypothesis that exposure to realistic violence facilitates aggression through modeling and disinhibition, but fictional violence reduces aggressiveness by delaying and substituting for action. Children watched a filmed sequence of a campus riot presented as either a fictional or a realistic event. Compared to a no-film control, the realistic set stimulated aggression while the fantasy set reduced aggressive behavior, as measured by children's administration of louder sounds to an adult for incorrect guesses on a game. If these differences are reproducible, further research would be needed to determine how unrecognized factors in what the children were told created the differences, because the view that fictional violence reduces aggression is disputed by a large body of evidence. In previously cited experiments innumerable college students have been stimulated to punitive action by viewing familiar actors behaving violently in presentations they know are fictional. None, for example would mistake Kirk Douglas for a real boxer fighting an actual championship bout in the often used segment from the movie *Champion*. Furthermore, children have been shown to become more interpersonally aggressive as a result of exposure to violent cartoons that bear little resemblance to reality. Although realistic violence may function as a more effective aggression activator, exposure to fictional violence does not reduce such conduct (Ellis and Sekyra, 1972; Hapkiewicz and Stone, 1972). Aggression is enhanced through observation of filmed violence mainly by its justification, not by whether it is real or fictional (Meyer, 1972).

There have been several well-designed experiments in which children are exposed daily over an extended time either to commercially televised aggression or to nonviolent offerings. The amount of aggression that children display in their everyday interactions during this period is systematically observed and recorded. Results of these field studies essentially corroborate those of laboratory investigations. Steuer, Applefield, and Smith (1971) found that repeated exposure to aggressive cartoons increased children's physical assaultiveness, whereas nonviolent contents produced no change in interpersonal aggression. In an experiment by Stein, Friedrich, and Vondracek (1972) employing a similar design, nonaggressive children showed no behavioral effects of viewing violent cartoons over a four-week period, but those above average in aggressiveness were more physically and verbally aggressive when exposed to televised violence than to neutral or socially positive programs. A follow-up assessment disclosed that television-heightened aggressiveness persisted after the violent programs were discontinued. The authors speculate that the passive children may have undergone severe inhibitory training which, if true, would require extended exposure to successful violent conduct to weaken restraints over behaving aggressively. Other studies (Ellis and Sekyra, 1972; Liebert and Baron, 1972) showing that even short exposure to violent scenes can increase children's interpersonal aggression lend further weight to the instigative potential of televised aggression.

Correlational studies relating television viewing to social behavior as it occurs under natural conditions provide supplementary evidence concerning television effects. Because of the gross indexes of violence viewing and aggressive behavior used in these studies, it is difficult to estimate how closely the obtained correlations approximate the true relationship. Their consistency, however, is noteworthy. Several projects based on large samples representing different communities, age levels, and sexes have found modest positive correlations between amount of violence viewing and interpersonal aggressiveness (Chaffee and McLeod, 1971; McIntyre and Teevan, 1972; Robinson and Bachman, 1972). The higher the exposure to televised violence, the more children are willing to use aggressive behavior, to suggest it as a solution to interpersonal conflict, and to view it as effective (Dominick and Greenberg, 1972).

Correlational data do not, of course, identify causal links between covarying events. Whether aggressive children are attracted to violent contents, whether repeated observation of people resorting to violence cultivates an aggressive disposition, or whether both activities are products of a common influence cannot be conclusively answered by a correlational study. Experimental evidence is sparse for the former relationship, though it is well founded experimentally that exposure to aggressive modeling increases aggressiveness. As part of a large field study exploring the social determinants of aggression, Eron (1963) correlated children's television viewing habits with their tendency to behave aggressively, as rated by their peers. Boys who preferred television programs containing a high level of violence displayed significantly more interpersonal aggression than those who regularly viewed programs low in violence. Not surprisingly, the overall findings reveal that the critical factor is the content of what children are observing, not the sheer amount of exposure to televised stimulation. No consistent relationships were noted between the viewing habits of girls and their aggressive conduct. Since aggressiveness in adolescent girls has been shown to correlate positively with amount of violence viewing but not with high preference for violent programs (Chaffee and McLeod, 1971), differential results may be partly attributable to the measure of violence viewing used as well as to other factors, such as more severe socialization of aggression in girls and preponderance of televised male aggressors.

In a follow-up study conducted ten years later, Eron and his associates (Eron, Huesmann, Lefkowitz, and Walder, 1972) report longitudinal correlations that help clarify the direction of causal relationships. High exposure to televised violence at age eight was positively related with interpersonal aggressiveness in boys at age nineteen (Figure 3.4). The positive correlation remains significant when level of childhood aggression is partialled out, thus removing the possibility that initial aggressiveness determines both child viewing preferences and adult conduct. Other partial correlations, controlling for a variety of familial causal contributors, further indicate that habitual exposure to televised violence promotes aggressive habits and eliminates alternative hypotheses that aggressiveness causes attraction to violent portrayals or that the obtained association is due to some other common determinant. Chaffee and McLeod (1971) arrive at a similar conclusion after demonstrating that significant correlations between amount of violence viewing and aggressiveness persist after ruling out the potential influence of socioeconomic variables, level of intellectual functioning, and a host of familial relationship factors. Model preferences and behavioral dispositions are more likely reciprocally interrelated for real life than for televised models. That is, aggressors may selectively gravitate toward aggressive models who, in turn, further shape and disinhibit aggressive modes of conduct.

In the controlled field studies interpersonal aggression is measured

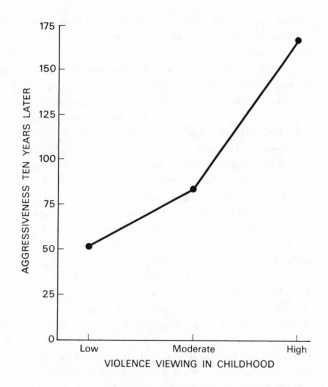

FIGURE 3.4   Relationship between boys' violence viewing at age eight and their interpersonal aggressiveness as measured ten years later. (Plotted from data by Eron, Huesmann, Lefkowitz, and Walder, 1972)

solely as a function of televised influences without regard to the social consequences that aggressive actions produce. The course that aggression takes over a period of time will be determined by the combined effects of televised inducements and the reinforcing consequences of a reactive environment. The same televised input can therefore result in different outcomes under diverse reinforcement conditions. Accurate prediction of television effects on either group or individual performance depends on how the concurrent influences interact. If television-prompted aggression proves effective for users in their daily interactions, aggressive modes of behavior are likely to increase and persist long after the televised influence has ceased. That television can give impetus to a long-term process is suggested by Eron's finding that exposure to televised violence in early formative years predicts aggressiveness in boys ten years later. These correlational data are corroborated by a short-term experimental demonstration by Stein, Friedrich, and Vondracek (1972) that televised influences can contribute to the formation of enduring aggressive styles of behavior.

Under conditions where television-stimulated aggression is firmly disapproved or creates new sanctions against injurious conduct, the instigative effects of television are counteracted by environmental punishment. The net effect of aggressive modeling in such circumstances may be little noticeable change or even a decline in the incidence of aggressive actions. Since reinforcement influences are mediated by stimulus control, prediction of outcomes must be situation specific. Televised aggression that is suppressed in prohibitive settings may be displayed when there is little risk of punishment (Hicks, 1968a).

Considering the multiple control of aggression, further progress in understanding television effects is unlikely to be achieved by additional studies in which media inputs are systematically varied but concurrent reinforcement determinants go unrecorded. Finer analysis of interacting influences is required to bring orderliness to variable results. For example, individual data reported by Steuer, Applefield, and Smith (1971) show that four of the five children exposed to televised violence became more assaultive toward peers than did their matched partners who watched nonviolent programs (Figure 3.5). However, they varied considerably in rate and level of aggression increments. Some showed immediate increases, whereas others required multiple exposures before the effects upon behavior were evident. It might be noted parenthetically that experiments in which observation of a single violent cartoon increased interpersonal aggression, but short of conventional significance levels (Siegel, 1956), would probably have produced stronger effects with longer exposure. The two weak responders in Steuer's study exhibited no aggression during baseline assessments, which suggests that limited impact of televised violence on their overt behavior may be attributable to low aggression proneness arising from deficient skills, strong aggression restraints, or both factors. Some displayed continuing marked increases in assaultive behavior with repeated exposure, and others manifested comparable heightening of aggressiveness, but eventually stabilized at an intermediate level.

When rate of aggression rises with longer exposure to violent conduct, the elevation may reflect the increasing cumulative impact of television, or viewers may be adopting aggressive solutions they saw modeled and using them more often because they produce good results. To elucidate the causal processes would require behavior observations of the frequency with which aggressive actions bring rewarding or punishing consequences. In sum, the impact of televised violence would be best predicted by taking into account viewers' preexisting aggression

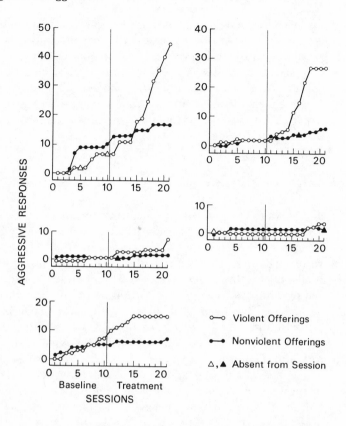

FIGURE 3.5 Cumulative frequency of physical interpersonal aggression by children who were exposed either to violent cartoons or to nonviolent offerings. (Steuer, Applefield, and Smith, 1971)

skills, their aggression restraints, and the proportion of positive and negative reinforcements provided for aggressive conduct in daily interactions. Multiple causation can be even better unraveled by experimentally varying exposure to televised violence in conjunction with environmental reward, extinction, or punishment of aggression for subjects differing in aggression skill and inhibition.

Exposure to modeled violence presented in ways that legitimize its use not only raises the probability of aggressive conduct, but also tends to increase preference for aggressive toys (Larder, 1962; Lovaas, 1961), stressful mood states (Tannenbaum and Gaer, 1965), and selection of aggressive solutions to depicted conflicts (Leifer and Roberts, 1972).

The combined findings of laboratory experiments, controlled field studies, and correlational investigations provide substantial testimony that violence viewing tends to foster aggressiveness. Research that clarifies causal relationships increases rather than reduces the level of controversy when profitable practices of a major industry are shown to have some adverse effects. Vested interest groups become understandably apprehensive about the implications of research findings for social policy. Although the issues continue to be vigorously debated in terms of empirical verification, at this stage the dispute is more a political matter than a scientific one.

Performance Catharsis

The catharsis hypothesis assumes that the drive to behave aggressively is reduced not only by vicarious experience, but also by direct expression of aggression. Although performance catharsis does not necessarily involve modeling processes, it is discussed in the present context because results of this line of research have an important bearing on the mechanism presumed to operate in vicarious catharsis through modeling.

The hydraulic model of personality and belief in the benefits of cathartic drainage of aggressive impulses were widely accepted in both professional and lay circles. Guided by this view, many parents, educators, and mental health workers urge hyperaggressive children to engage in aggressive activities and to aggress in psychotherapeutic playrooms, in the hope of reducing aggressive impulses that are presumably maintaining the troublesome behavior. Failure to release pent-up drives, it is contended, risks explosive aggressive discharges.

Evidence from research studies of children indicates that, far from producing a cathartic reduction of aggression, participation in aggressive activities within a permissive setting maintains the behavior at its original level or actually increases it (Feshbach, 1956; Freeman, 1962; Kenny, 1952, Mallick and McCandless, 1966; Nelsen, 1969). Early studies with adults in which evidence for cathartic processes was claimed relied on indirect indexes of aggression, such as replies to word association tests that are subject to response set biases (Feshbach, 1955; 1961) or quality of intellectual performance, on the assumption that anger arousal diminishes functioning (Worchel, 1957). Since emotional arousal can facilitate as well as disrupt performance, depending on its level, the complexity of the task, and the stress coping habits of subjects, the indirect indicators of aggression reduction have dubious value. In some studies presented as demonstrating a catharsis effect the data do not, in fact, support the conclusions. Angered subjects exhibit the same level of dislike of their tormentor after seeing him undergo either painful, neutral, or euphoric experiences (Bramel, Taub, and Blum, 1968). Reported substantiation of catharsis effects in other instances depends more on selective analysis of data than on what they actually show.

Results of experiments with adults using direct measures of aggression are essentially similar to those obtained with children. When adults are given repeated opportunities to shock a person under nonretaliative conditions, the more they aggress, the more punitive they become (Buss, 1966a). Angered aggressors, who should be achieving drive reduction if catharsis were operative, exhibit greater increases in punitiveness on successive attacks than nonangered subjects (Loew, 1967). Further evidence that encouraged or permissively viewed aggressive displays reduce restraints over such conduct is provided by Zimbardo (1969) in an experiment of a direct interpersonal nature. Intense verbal and physical assaults directed at passive resisters by disguised assailants tended to increase their subsequent hurtful actions.

Nor has the catharsis hypothesis fared well when the effects of aggressive displays are measured in terms of changes in hostile attitudes rather than injurious actions. De Charms and Wilkins (1963) report evidence that angered people who vent their hostility become increasingly hostile. The higher the volume of unpleasant remarks they direct at their tormentor, the more they dislike him. Hearing others berate the offender for his inconsiderate behavior increased hostility in maltreated observers even more powerfully. Kahn's (1966) results are especially relevant to the catharsis issue because subjects voiced their resentment to a sympathetic person, an interaction similar to those that occur in everyday experience. Those who expressed hostility with support and encouragement disliked their annoyer significantly more and were slower to calm down physiologically than equally angered subjects who were left to themselves for an equivalent period.

Under certain conditions expression of aggression can, of course, decrease its incidence, although the reductive effects do not occur through drainage of aggressive drive forces. Angry displays, especially if accompanied by threats, may intimidate antagonists so they cease behaving in provocative ways. Aggressive action may not only turn off abuse but promote beneficial improvements in social treatment, thereby removing chronic instigators of the behavior. Interpersonal interactions are somewhat ambiguous as to exactly who did what to whom and why, with the result that events can be easily misjudged or distorted. When malign intent is misattributed to the actions of others, anger arousal can be ruminatively generated to the point where the aggrieved person acts with inappropriate hostility—as if he had been deliberately maltreated. To the extent that verbalized resentment clarifies misconceptions or creates new understanding of why others behaved as they did, it can diminish autistically produced aggression. Moreover, behaving aggressively can arouse fear and self-censure over the injurious consequences of one's actions, and thus have reductive effects through inhibitory processes. After a provocateur has been duly punished for his insulting actions, a counteraggressor may temper further assaults on him without reducing his anger or dislike because the culprit has already paid sufficiently for his wrongdoings. Finally, repeated unrewarded expressions of a behavior produce a decrease in responsiveness due to aversive fatigue and declining attraction of the activity. Extinction is an operative factor in all nonreinforced performances.

The belief that human behavior is impelled by inner aggressive forces is nonetheless so strongly ingrained in psychological thinking that aggression decrements, when they do occur, are automatically attributed to cathartic discharges without measuring more plausible processes (Doob and Wood, 1972; Konecni and Doob, 1972). Progress in the understanding of how observed or performed aggression affects subsequent punitiveness would be better advanced if a moratorium were declared on catharsis explanations until proponents of the catharsis hypothesis devise a measure of aggressive drive independent of the behavior it supposedly causes. Attributing response decrements to drive reductions provides a ready explanation; one need therefore search no further for the determinants of aggressive behavior.

The discussion thus far has examined the behavioral and attitudinal effects of aggressive displays. Another aspect of the catharsis hypothesis is concerned with the physiological changes accompanying expressions of aggression. A series of experiments reported by Hokanson (1970) and others (Baker and Schaie, 1969; Gambaro and Rabin, 1969) demonstrate that angered adults often achieved faster decrease in blood pressure to baseline levels if they counteraggressed toward their antagonist than if they were given no opportunities to respond. However, venting aggression did not facilitate decline in vascular arousal if the aggression was expressed in fantasy, if the attack was displaced to substitute targets varying in similarity to the tormentor, if the aggressor was female, or if the attacked frustrator was a person of high status. The latter finding illustrates the difficulties of measuring aggressive drive strength in terms of physiological arousal because it does not distinguish between anger arousal and aggression-produced fear arousal—or other sources of activation, for that matter. Further studies, reported by Kahn (1966) and Holmes (1966), disclosed that direct aggression, even toward nonthreatening targets, does not always bring physiological relief. On the contrary, counteraggression sustained elevated arousal, whereas nonaggressive activities reduced it.

The catharsis hypothesis is more seriously challenged by the arousal reactions of angered nonaggressors than by the diverse physiological effects of counteraggression. After an aggressive drive is aroused, presumably it should remain at an elevated state until discharged through some form of aggressive activity. In reality, all angered subjects, regardless of whether or not they vent their hostility, display rapid decline in physiological arousal. Given that arousal reduction is the general rule, theories should perhaps be more concerned with explaining what prolongs arousal rather than what reduces it. Social learning theory explains both phenomena in terms of self-arousal mechanisms. It also specifies the additional experimental controls required to demonstrate a catharsis effect.

As previously noted, the anger arousal created by maltreatment dissipates, but it can be sustained and reactivated symbolically on later occasions by dwelling on past angering experiences. Persistence of elevated anger arousal, in the social learning view, arises from self-generated stimulation rather than from an undischarged reservoir of aggressive energy. If a person should become immersed in activities that take his mind off past provocations, the arousing ruminations are thereby eliminated and he experiences a noticeable reduction in tension. Similarly, on the assumption that diminution of emotional arousal accompanying observed performances results from changes in symbolic engagement, not vicarious energy releases, one would expect aroused individuals to experience equally salutary effects from getting involved in absorbing books, movies, or television programs lacking aggressive displays.

Subjects who have been treated insultingly and then left with nothing to occupy their attention are more likely to dwell on affronts they have just experienced than those assigned a task that provides opportunities to express aggression. To confirm that arousal decrements attributed to energy discharges are not due to differences in opportunities for resentful self-stimulation requires an experimental design in which changes in physiological arousal are compared in angered subjects who counteraggress and in those who engage in equally absorbing but nonaggressive activities. An idle group left either to foment their resentment or to distract themselves with irrelevant trains of thought does not furnish a neutral baseline against which to evaluate the effects of counteraggression.

Results of numerous experiments lend support to the self-arousal interpretation. When people are given an opportunity to respond to provocation they reduce their hostility, but the decrease cannot be attributed to catharsis because most voice little or no hostility (Rosenbaum and de Charms, 1960; Thibaut and Coules, 1952). Elevated blood pressure levels are maintained more effectively by exposure to an antagonist, whose presence is likely to reactivate anger-provoking thoughts, than by a lack of opportunity to express aggression in response to indignant treatment (Vantress and Williams, 1972). A study by Zillmann and Johnson (1973) explicitly designed to test the self-arousal hypothesis provides the most pertinent substantiating evidence. Aggressive portrayals sustained elevated physiological arousal and punitive behavior in angered adults, whereas exposure to nonaggressive contents resulted in substantial reduction in both arousal and retaliatory aggression.

In experiments permitting different counterresponses, angered males experience faster arousal reduction by aggressive than by friendly reactions to a punitive opponent, whereas females achieve greater tension relief by friendly reciprocal actions (Hokanson and Edelman, 1966). The differential physiological concomitants of defensive reactions most likely reflect the residual of past reinforcement experiences. Having developed stronger aggressive restraints, females might be expected to generate fear-arousing thoughts after behaving in a physically aggressive manner. Sosa's (1968) finding that passive male prisoners are more apt to experience tension reduction by friendly than by aggressive reactions to provocation confirms the impact of socialization experiences.

Thus, from a social learning perspective, physiological tension level is determined not only by what one does, but also by what one thinks. Diverting or tranquilizing thoughts will reduce arousal, whereas those that revivify past provocations or dwell on threatening future consequences of contemplated or accomplished actions will generate high states of arousal. The consequences people anticipate for their actions are derived largely from observed or directly experienced reinforcements. Studies in which the outcomes of reciprocal interchanges are systematically varied demonstrate that the same counterresponse, regardless of its content, can acquire either arousing or tranquilizing properties depending upon its consequences (Hokanson, Willers, and Koropsak, 1968). Both kindly and aggressive responses to provocation produce cathartic-like physiological relief after they have consistently elicited positive reactions in others; conversely, they both become physiologically arousing when they consistently draw punitive responses. By reversing reinforcing outcomes, the tension relief value of the same mode of response is radically altered.

Self-directed aggression can also acquire relief value through its functional utility. When adults could avoid painful shocks from others by administering to themselves shocks of lesser intensity, self-punitive responses not only increased but were physiologically relaxing (Stone and Hokanson, 1969). The way in which self-punishment can be maintained by averting anticipated threats is graphically demonstrated with subhuman subjects by Sandler and Quagliano (1964). After monkeys learned to press a lever to avoid being shocked, a second contingency involving self-administered punishment was introduced. A lever press prevented the occurrence of the original shock, but it also produced an electric shock of lesser magnitude. As the experiment progressed, the self-administered shock was gradually increased in intensity until it equaled the one being avoided. The animals, however, showed no reduction in self-punishment even though this behavior no longer served as a "lesser of two evils." Even more interesting, after the avoided shock was permanently discontinued but lever-pressing responses (which had now become objectively functionless) still produced painful consequences, the animals continued to punish themselves needlessly with shock intensities that they had previously worked hard to avoid. This experiment reveals how self-punishment can become divorced from actual conditions of reinforcement and be maintained through its capacity to forestall imagined threats that no longer exist. A puzzled observer, who had no knowledge of the prior learning conditions for this apparently senseless behavior, would be tempted to attribute it to a misdirected aggressive drive.

In psychotic disorders, self-punishment is often powerfully maintained by delusional contingencies that have little relationship to reality. The case cited earlier (Bateson, 1961) illustrated how a man who judged trivial acts as heinous sins could relieve his fright of hellish torment and feelings of self-contempt only by performing exceedingly self-punitive behaviors for long hours. Responses that are reinforced by reduction of thought-generated distress tend to be self-perpetuating.

These findings indicate that the physiological accompaniments of aggression are explainable in terms of the same principles governing aggressive actions. When aggression succeeds in curbing attack, it becomes a preferred tension-reducing style of behavior. On the other hand, when aggressive actions beget punitive treatment, they become physiologically perturbing and are generally not favored. The physiological correlates of counteraggression further illustrate the differences between drive and social learning theories. The former view assumes that affective discharges diminish aggressiveness. In the social learning analysis, tension reduction can serve as a reinforcer to increase the likelihood that aggression will be used on subsequent occasions. Relief of aversive arousal may thus supplement, or even override, the effects of other consequences in maintaining aggressive responsiveness. Discomforting arousal, however, would tend to exert inhibitory effects on hostile actions.

Controversies over modeling influences are not confined to aggressive behavior. Although experimental data are scarce, there is every reason to expect, for example, that sexual modeling, which has begun to be studied, would affect sexual behavior in similar ways. By observing the sexual activities and accompanying reactions of others, people can learn specific amorous techniques; their sexual anxieties can be diminished (Walters, Bowen, and Parke, 1964); and the portrayals can shape the types of sexual expression that will be practiced in a culture by teaching which forms are permissible and which exceed socially acceptable bounds. Viewing erotic films produces transitory increases in sexual arousal and sexual activities such as masturbation, petting, and marital intercourse (Mann, Sidman, and Starr, 1971; Schmidt and Sigusch, 1970), but habitual exposure can reduce the sex-arousing potential of nudity or erotic displays (Reifler, Howard, Lipton, Liptzin, and Widmann, 1971). In addition, sexual viewing fosters more permissive attitudes toward erotic depictions (Lockhart, 1970).

Although the processes and outcomes of sexual and aggressive modeling are undoubtedly similar, the social implications may differ markedly depending upon the moral codes applied to these two areas of functioning. Because of the hazardous consequences of physical aggression, a society must continuously control injurious actions in children and adults alike. Harmonious functioning therefore requires reduction of social influences that promote cruelty and destructiveness. By contrast, most cultures, including our own, present discontinuities in the socialization of sexual behavior. Overt sexual expressions are firmly prohibited during childhood and adolescence, but are not only expected but considered essential to a satisfying heterosexual relationship in adulthood. Therefore, the more successfully inhibitory training is achieved in early formative years, the more likely is heterosexual behavior to serve as a source of guilt and anxiety in adulthood. Given prolonged negative conditioning of sexual attitudes and behavior, many people feel that exposure to sexual material under proper conditions may help to counteract ignorance and dysfunctional inhibitions. On the other hand, proponents of stringent moral codes, fearing that erotic viewing will propagate premarital intercourse and antisocial sexual transgressions, vigorously oppose any lessening of prohibitions against sexual modeling.

Taken together, available research findings indicate that when erotic stimuli are effective, they tend to activate established modes of sexuality (Lockhart, 1970). Thus, exposure to erotic material temporarily increases masturbation principally in unmarried persons who habitually engage in such activities and in the sexually conversant lacking amorous mates. Among married couples and sexually experienced persons with available partners, viewing erotic displays produces transitory increases in sexual intercourse. There is no evidence, however, that erotic viewing stimulates deviant sexual practices or sex offenses.

AVERSIVE TREATMENT

The concept of frustration, which is frequently invoked as a principal cause of aggression, is so broad as to have little value. As previously noted, the diverse events subsumed under this all-inclusive term do have one feature in common—they are all aversive in varying degrees. Since, however, they differ in other important ways that can produce dissimilar behavioral effects, the determinants of injurious behavior can be better ascertained by relating aggression to specific aversive antecedents rather than to the omnibus term. This section examines the extent to which aggressive behavior is aversively controlled by unpleasant, thwarting, offensive, and physically painful treatment.

Physical Assaults

If one wished to provoke aggression, the most dependable way to do so would be simply to physically assault another person, who would then be likely to oblige with a vigorous counterattack. To the extent that counteraggression discourages further assaults, it is powerfully reinforced by pain reduction and thereby assumes high functional value in social interactions. Although the pain-aggression relationship is well established, there is some dispute over whether it is innate or acquired.

Azrin and Ulrich, exponents of the nativistic view, have extensively investigated the relationship between shock-produced pain and aggression (Azrin, 1967; Ulrich, 1966; Ulrich, Hutchinson, and Azrin, 1965). In studies employing a social paradigm, pairs of animals are placed in a chamber containing a grid floor through which foot shocks can be delivered. At periodic intervals brief shocks are presented and any fighting responses displayed by the animals are recorded and compared with their behavior at times when shocks are not administered. During the attacks, which are typically brief and cease shortly after shock termination, animals stand erect on their hind legs, lunge at each other with bared teeth, and strike with their forepaws.

Elicitors of aggression are often difficult to assess in social situations because target animals can influence the course of fighting in uncontrolled ways by their own actions, especially if they manifest threatening gestures or strike back, as they understandably are inclined to do. Social paradigms also cannot be used with highly destructive animals that can fatally injure their victims. In some studies, therefore, aggression is measured in terms of biting attacks directed against inanimate objects. Results based on the latter measure, however, may have limited generality because it appears to be relatively insensitive to known determinants of fighting behavior.

A considerable amount of information has been accumulated over the years on the nature and generality of the shock-attack relationship. The more intense the shocks and the longer their duration, the greater is the likelihood that they will provoke stereotyped fighting. Attack responses tend to be performed somewhat indiscriminately toward targets of varying physical characteristics. Animals will assault their own species, members of other species, and even inanimate objects. Additionally, shock-attack reactions have been found to be present in a variety of species. Other studies disclose that attack can be provoked by different types of aversive stimulation including, in addition to painful shock, intense heat and physical blows. Unlike fighting under natural conditions, which is partly determined by sex of combatants, their inbred aggressiveness, and previous familiarity wth each other, the incidence of shock-induced fighting is essentially unaffected by such factors. Azrin and Ulrich reasoned that since combative behavior is elicited by aversive stimuli with some regularity, emerges without any prior training, and persists without any evident reinforcement, pain-induced aggression must be an unlearned reflexive behavior.

Although the pain-aggression relationship appears to have some degree of generality, negative findings—often minimized or dismissed as unexplainable—are also very much in evidence. The latter data, which are reviewed next, dispute the view that animals are genetically programmed to respond aggressively to painful stimulation (Ulrich, 1967). Close examination of research findings reveals that aversive stimuli do not exert the "push-button" control over aggression sometimes claimed. In some species noted for their aggressiveness, such as fighting cocks and Siamese fighting fish, pain not only fails to provoke aggression, but suppresses such responses (Azrin, 1967). Shock also fails to produce fighting in certain docile species (Ulrich and Azrin, 1962).

Shock-attack reactions are much too variable to be attributable to genetic determination. In fact, numerous environmental influences determine whether or not aversive experiences will provoke combativeness. Young animals rarely, if ever, fight when shocked unless they have had some fighting experience (Hutchinson, Ulrich, and Azrin, 1965; Powell and Creer, 1969), and in some studies repeated shocks produced little or no fighting in 20 to 30 percent of mature animals (Azrin, Hutchinson, and Hake, 1963; Azrin, Hake, and Hutchinson, 1965). The likelihood that physically painful events will provoke attack, especially at lower intensities, is partly determined by a number of accidental factors, such as whether animals happen to be facing each other at the moment of shock delivery, whether they are moving, standing upright, or are close to each other. Thus, rats that are physically restrained and forced to face an inanimate target placed immediately in front of their mouths consistently bite it when shocked (Azrin, Rubin, and Hutchinson, 1968), whereas they never do so when repeatedly shocked in a confined but free-responding situation (Ulrich and Azrin, 1962). The former procedure, which is increasingly used for the convenience of automatic recording, apparently produces behaviors quite unrepresentative of those occurring under circumstances the experiments were originally designed to explain.

If aggression is an unlearned dominant response to painful stimulation, then shock would be expected to elicit attack during initial trials. Unfortunately, the numerous studies that have been published contain no information on how animals initially respond to painful treatment, despite the relevance of such data to instinctual interpretations of aggression. But some findings in addition to those cited above cast doubt on the view that aversive stimuli are innate elicitors of aggression. In one report in which responding during initial trials is briefly described (Azrin, Hutchinson, and Hake, 1963), one pair of monkeys jumped and squealed but did not fight when shock was first presented; another pair never fought during the first ten trials; a third pair never attacked each other even though they were repeatedly shocked. They displayed shock-attack reactions only later, after they had been paired with trained sparring partners.

The most decisive evidence that pain-aggression reactions may be more situationally determined than innately programmed is provided by investigations of shock-induced fighting as a function of size of the chamber (Ulrich and Azrin, 1962). In a small enclosure (6 in. × 6 in.) approximately 90 percent of the shocks provoked fighting, whereas in a larger chamber (24 in. × 24 in.) animals ignored each other and only 2 percent of the shocks elicited fighting. Powell and Creer (1969) likewise found pain-attack reactions to be a rarity in young animals shocked in large cages. If animals, in fact, possessed an unconditioned fighting reflex, they should be equally combative in varying, though still relatively small, enclosures when subjected to painful stimulation.

Premature attribution of pain-induced fighting to reflexive mechanisms has retarded investigation of other possible determinants and the functional utility of fighting in the experimental settings. Pain-elicited attack appears to differ qualitatively from naturally instigated fighting. In the former case, fighting episodes are usually very brief; fighting ceases almost immediately after the shock is stopped; and it is conspicuously absent during periods between shocks. If pain consistently provokes aggression, one would expect the biting and mauling initiated by shock to be sufficiently painful to perpetuate reciprocal fighting for some time after shock stimulation has ceased. Given evidence that animals can acquire aggression-eliciting properties through association with combat experiences (Ulrich, Hutchinson, and Azrin, 1965), it is also surprising that fighting does not come under social stimulus control so that animals eventually attack each other when shock is absent. In many respects, pain-induced postures appear to be more closely related to escape and defensive responses in which the combative features are secondary (Reynierse, 1971).

Ulrich and Azrin (1962) have considered—and discounted—possible undetected sources of reinforcement of pain-induced fighting. By assuming upright postures and jumping on each other, animals may periodically reduce contact with the electrified grid and thus have their sparring intermittently reinforced by partial escape from painful stimulation. As the authors point out, this explanation would not account for fighting induced by shock delivered through electrodes attached to the animals' bodies. Findings of the latter studies are less persuasive, however, because they are based on response-constraining procedures that force biting attacks on inanimate targets, attacks which are not often duplicated under unrestrained conditions.

A second interpretation is that fighting is partly maintained by accidental reinforcement through occasional coincidences of attack reactions with shock termination. Protective behavior is most readily perpetuated by supersitious contingencies when threats cannot be controlled by one's actions; coincidences between actions and outcomes tend to be interpreted as genuine contingencies that regulate behavior as though a given action will, in fact, forestall a feared outcome. The authors doubt whether such a process is operative on the grounds that the shocks are too brief to provide much superstitious reinforcement. Evidence of sequential changes in fighting responses as a function of shock duration suggests, however, that the temporal relation between attack behavior and shock termination may be a critical factor in sustaining pain-provoked fighting (Azrin, Ulrich, Hutchinson, and Norman, 1964). Initially, brief shocks rarely elicited fighting responses, but long shocks almost always provoked attack. As the experiment progressed, long-lasting shocks rapidly lost their effectiveness, whereas short ones increased and maintained their power to instigate fighting responses. On the occasions when shock elicits attacks, they tend to appear immediately and cease quickly. If the assumption is valid that fighting sometimes coincides with pain reduction given short shocks, but with continued painful stimulation when shocks last a long time, the obtained changes in the evocative power of shocks are consistent with an adventitious reinforcement interpretation. This speculation is tentatively supported by research showing that the contingency, not pain per se, is the critical determinant of aggression. Noncontingent painful stimulation provokes aggression, but—contrary to the reflexive elicitation hypothesis—shocks presented after each attack reduce and eliminate rather than increase aggressive responding (Azrin, 1970; Baenninger and Grossman, 1969; Ulrich, Wolfe, and Dulaney, 1969).

Aversive stimulation ordinarily activates behavior designed to eliminate or at least to reduce the source of discomfort. Thus, if a room is unbearably hot, people will typically turn on air conditioning devices in preference to assaulting someone nearby. The experiments reported thus far permitted attack but not escape. In order to determine whether aggression predominates in aversive situations, researchers examined the relationship between combative and flight reactions to painful treatment. The results show that, given a choice, animals would rather escape than fight. Under conditions in which the escape response requires social confrontations, shock can provoke some fighting, but successful escape quickly displaces attack reactions and fighting reappears only when escape is not possible (Azrin, Hutchinson, and Hake, 1967; Wolfe, Ulrich, and Dulaney, 1971). If paired animals can flee without the necessity of confrontation, they do so when shocked without ever aggressing toward each other (Logan and Boice, 1969). Knutson (1971) has further shown that, even under close social contact, when environmental inducements to fight are minimized, avoidance and escape responses to shock stimulation take priority over attack.

In everyday situations the target person is usually the source of the distress rather than simply an innocent bystander. Under these circumstances successful counterattacks provide escape from injurious assaults. As might be expected, aggressive responses that serve a protective function are highly resistant to change (Azrin, Hutchinson, and Hake, 1967).

There are some further indications that as the determinants of pain-attack reactions are more critically examined, they will most likely be dispossessed of their reflexive status. Developmental studies (Hutchinson, Ulrich, and Azrin, 1965) reveal that painful events rarely produce fighting in young animals, and they are relatively weak elicitors of aggression in animals of all ages if reared alone after weaning (Figure 3.6). The authors attribute the increasing capacity of shock to elicit fighting with advancing age to higher levels of testosterone, the male sexual hormone. Evidence bearing on this issue would seem to favor experiential rather than hormonal factors. Daily injections of testosterone create sexual precocity but do not enhance the attack-eliciting potential of shock in young animals (Powell and Creer, 1969).

The role of fighting experiences in determining whether pain will provoke attack or nonaggressive reactions was examined by Powell and Creer (1969), who assessed the interaction of developmental and environmental variables in shock-elicited aggression. As illustrated in Figure 3.7, young animals in standard enclosures almost never fought when shocked, but those in small cages, who also at first responded nonaggressively,

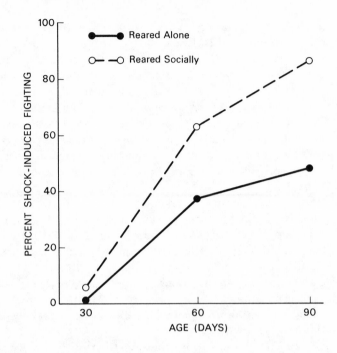

FIGURE 3.6 The percent of shocks that evoked fighting in groups of animals that were reared socially or isolated at 22 days of age and lived alone until tested for aggression to 100 shocks, presented at 30, 60, and 90 days of age, respectively. (Plotted from data of Hutchinson, Ulrich, and Azrin, 1965)

eventually became fighters as the sessions progressed. This differential combativeness indicates that young animals are physically capable of aggressing but that painful treatment alone is insufficient to elicit such behavior. Somewhat older animals yielded a similar pattern of results, whereas the oldest members, those most likely to have had previous fighting experience, increased their combativeness over the sessions regardless of enclosure size. A related experiment demonstrated that aversive stimuli essentially lose their capacity to arouse aggression if they have been previously experienced under social circumstances in which aggressive responses could not be performed. These findings are consistent with those of Maier, Seligman, and Solomon (1969); they show that after animals have been repeatedly shocked no matter what they do, they later respond passively to hurtful treatment even though successful coping responses are made available.

The overall results support the view that physically painful experiences are, at best, facilitative but not sufficient to provoke aggression

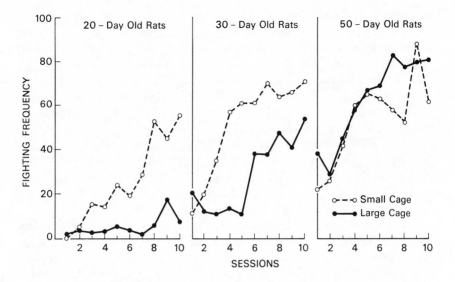

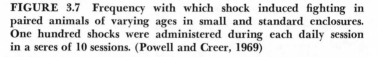

FIGURE 3.7 Frequency with which shock induced fighting in paired animals of varying ages in small and standard enclosures. One hundred shocks were administered during each daily session in a seres of 10 sessions. (Powell and Creer, 1969)

in animals. To produce regular fighting through painful treatment, animals must be directly confronted with the target in a constricted area, the aversive stimuli must be very brief and not follow attack reactions, the animals must have some fighting experience, and all flight reactions must be blocked. Fighting thus appears to be a forced rather than a primal unlearned response to pain. The restricted circumstances under which aversive stimuli apparently exercise control over aggressive responses cast some doubt on whether experimentation confined to such conditions will substantially advance understanding of what causes animals to aggress in their natural habitat, much less explain human aggressiveness. Under natural conditions aggression may be aversively controlled after animals have begun to attack each other and thus cause pain, but the factors that begin fights in the absence of any immediate aversive experiences still require explanation. Aggression is typically provoked by threats intruders pose to food supplies, to nesting sites, to offspring, to mates, and to dominance status, rather than by actual physical pain. In these instances, events that forebode painful consequences provoke combat. The latter phenomena can perhaps best be understood in terms of the response-controlling functions of informative stimuli and reinforcing consequences.

From field studies of social interactions resulting in violent conduct it is well documented that physical assault serves as a powerful instigator of aggression. For obvious humane reasons, virtually no experiments have investigated the conditions determining whether physical attack will elicit fight, flight, submission, or some other type of reaction in humans. The strength of anticipatory retaliative aggression is undoubtedly a critical controlling factor. The only studies that have included some physical provocation are ones in which adults could counteraggress toward either a punitive competitor or a person who had previously devalued their intellectual performance by administering painful shocks to them. People aggress more strongly toward their assailants when they are physically punished than when they are treated considerately (Berkowitz and Le Page, 1967; Pisano and Taylor, 1971). When escape from the situation is blocked, the more frequently they are attacked, the more physical aggression they inflict on their adversaries (Helm, Bonoma, and Tedeschi, 1972). It remains unclear, however, how much of the retaliation is provoked by the physical maltreatment, how much by the implied belittling of their intelligence, and how much by the aggressive modeling of the provocateur.

Verbal Threats and Insults

Social interchanges are typically escalated into physical aggression by verbal threats and insults. Toch (1969) retrospectively analyzed sequences of actions and reactions of chronic assaulters to determine what sets them off on a course productive of violence. Among those studied were assault-prone police officers, as well as parolees and prison inmates who recurrently get embroiled in acts of violence. Humiliating affronts and threats to reputation and manly status emerged as major precipitants of violence.

In the case of assaultive policemen, the interaction generally begins with the officer issuing orders coercively in some petty incident. Most people acquiesce to forceful show of authority, but individuals who are prone to violence respond to arbitrary commands as an unwarranted infringement of their rights. They regard their actions as perhaps mildly provocative but essentially within legal boundaries, and the policeman's coercive behavior as arbitrary and unjustified. Negative definition of police actions is especially prevalent among underprivileged youth who, due to experienced, observed, or affirmed harassment, are inclined to view police as guardians of an oppressive system. Consequently, they question the legitimacy of police authority. Policemen with a penchant for provoking fights also tend to assert their authority in inept ways that cause needless humiliation and defiance. As Toch puts it, assault-prone officers generally use last resorts as initial moves. Through his opening frontal approach the policeman thus places himself in a hazardous position where, given noncompliance, he has no alternative but to invoke additional force that eventually culminates in violence. Verbal orders are escalated to threats and physical struggles, in the course of which instigated antagonism is transformed into law violations. The policeman finally extricates himself from a dangerous situation largely of his own creation by overpowering his challenger and placing him under arrest.

Toch reports that in other types of social interactions people who are prone to act aggressively are similarly incited to violence when their reputation, status, and manliness are challenged or they are otherwise affronted and slighted. High sensitivity to embarrassing treatment is usually combined with deficient verbal and social skills for dealing with altercations that can easily erupt into violence. Where verbally skilled persons often resolve disputes and restore their self-esteem by verbal means without having to dispose of their antagonists physically, those who have impoverished coping techniques quickly resort to violent solutions.

Insult provokes counterattack as well in individuals who ordinarily eschew aggression (Berkowitz, 1965b; Geen, 1968). In the latter cases, however, insult alone is sometimes ineffective in increasing punitiveness, but it does heighten aggressive responding when supported by hostile modeling and other disinhibitory influences (Hartmann, 1969; Wheeler and Caggiula, 1966).

No one has traced, either developmentally or experimentally, the process whereby insults acquire aggression-provoking potential. The most plausible explanation is in terms of differential reinforcement. Affronts that are not successfully counteracted can have far-reaching consequences for victims. Among other things, ineffectual recipients become easy targets for further victimization; they are apt to forfeit their standing in social hierarchies along with the recognition and power to control resources that go with it; and they suffer a loss in self-respect because of their inability to curb humiliating treatment. To the extent that punishment of insults by counteraggression reduces the likelihood of further mistreatment, the insult-aggression reaction becomes well established. Conversely, when retaliative responses are consistently and severely punished, insult produces acquiescence with its attendant social and self-devaluative consequences.

*Unfavorable Changes in
Positive Reinforcement*

After individuals have come to expect their actions to be rewarded at a certain level, withdrawal or reduction of positive reinforcement serves as an aversive event. Like other types of unpleasant treatments, reinforcement withdrawal functions as both a punisher for responses and a conditioner of negative properties to formerly neutral events with which it is regularly associated (Azrin and Holz, 1966; Leitenberg, 1965).

Since aggression is to some extent aversively controlled, it is not surprising to find that unfavorable changes in reinforcement can provoke assaultive behavior. Hutchinson, Azrin, and Hunt (1968) report that hungry animals were disinclined to attack a member of their species located in the same chamber as long as their instrumental responses never produced food rewards. On the other hand, when food reinforcement was given and later withdrawn, they frequently attacked their companion upon transition to extinction. In successive phases of the experiment, attacks rapidly declined during times when food reinforcement was consistently withheld but quickly reappeared when food rewards were alternately given and revoked. The more prior reinforcement they received, the stronger was the assaultive behavior when rewards were terminated. Extinction-induced aggression was evident even in animals that were raised in social isolation and thus had no prior history of competitive battles over food. Close examination of temporal relations between different modes of response discloses that when customary rewards are first withdrawn, animals intensify instrumental responding that previously secured reinforcement; but as their energetic efforts fail, they resort to combative actions (Thompson and Bloom, 1966).

In the preceding studies attack reactions were precipitated by removing all positive reinforcement for performances that had been consistently rewarded. Less drastic reductions in conditions of reinforcement may likewise provoke aggression. Schedules of positive reinforcement requiring high expenditure of effort for minimal rewards are generally experienced as aversive. Hutchinson, Azrin, and Hunt (1968) found that, as work requirements for reinforcement were progressively increased, primates engaged in biting attacks even though their instrumental behavior was occasionally rewarded. Return to a more favorable payoff schedule reduced attack reactions. Other studies of schedule-induced aggression (Flory, 1969a; Gentry, 1968; Gentry and Schaeffer, 1969) verify that sparing reinforcements for effortful performances can act as elicitors of aggressive behavior. Physical attack is provoked by increasing the time between rewards as well as by raising work demands (Flory, 1969b). Although meager payoffs provoke aggression, terminating them altogether is also aggression arousing (Knutson, 1970). With continued nonreward, however, both work performances and assaultive behavior diminish and after a time virtually disappear. Thompson and Bloom (1966) have further shown that when efforts to secure reinforcement are repeatedly extinguished, behavioral responsiveness, instrumental as well as combative, is substantially depressed and not easily reinstated by occasional reward. These phenomena are not unlike naturalistic observations that people who are chronically subjected to adverse conditions of reinforcement develop a feeling of helplessness and become passively resigned to their dismal living conditions.

Extinction-induced aggression in humans has received little systematic study. A number of behavior therapists (Bucher and Lovaas, 1968; Williams, 1959; Wolf, Risley, and Mees, 1964) have noted that withdrawal of social reinforcement for deviant behavior sometimes produces a temporary intensification of aggressive reactions. An especially hazardous disorder, prevalent among autistic and grossly retarded children, involves self-injurious behavior. The conditions eliciting and maintaining self-mutilation are not fully understood, but case studies by Lovaas and his co-workers (Lovaas and Simmons, 1969) have established reinforcement withdrawal as one possible instigator of self-mutilation. Withholding positive attention for other behaviors was accompanied by substantial increases in self-hurtful actions. Lovaas speculates that through past experiences autistic children learned to behave self-destructively as a desperate way of reinstating attentiveness from unresponsive caretakers.

Overcrowding is an environmental condition often invoked as an aversive instigator of aggression. There are certain features of density groupings that could facilitate combativeness. At the familial level, children who live in cramped quarters are likely to spend more time on neighborhood streets than those residing in spacious households. To the extent that neighborhood influences foster antisocial styles of life, the probability of developing aggressive conduct is thereby increased. Moreover, parents who have to cope with many children in congested quarters are often forced to punitive measures to halt squabbles between family members who repeatedly get in one another's way. At the broader social level, the immense logistic problems of servicing hordes of people inevitably create annoyances. Crowding heightens competitiveness for services and desired resources, which can also be exasperating. Densely crowded conditions not only increase the likelihood of interpersonal friction, but pollute and otherwise intensify the aversive qualities of the physical environment. In addition to the irritants of crowded living, it fosters a sense of anonymity and impersonality conducive to inconsiderate behavior.

Despite widespread concern over the ecological dangers posed by overpopulation, the possible effects of population density on human aggressiveness have received little experimental attention. The psychological consequences of overcrowding are difficult to isolate because it is usually associated with, among other factors, poverty, ethnicity, unemployment, and inadequate law enforcement, which confound the causes.

The problem of untangling the multiple causation is further complicated by the fact that populousness may help to create some of the correlated conditions. Comparison of homicide rates for different nations and for different regions within the same country indicate that crowding in itself does not necessarily increase combativeness. Highly populated locales that traditionally eschew aggressive conduct have relatively low incidences of violence, whereas inhabitants of less crowded places who view aggressive conduct permissively and make lethal weapons easily available experience higher rates of interpersonal assaults. Such data indicate that the level of combativeness within a society can be better predicted from prevailing social sanctions than from population density. For reasons given earlier, crowding would be expected to enhance aggressiveness in conjunction with other aggression-promoting influences.

The problem is more complicated than it might at first appear, however. Crowded living is not invariably stressful. Man is immensely adaptable. People who become accustomed to a city life style may at first dislike isolated country living and vice versa. Those who discover sufficient rewarding features in the new environment eventually change their preferences. Interpersonal clashes are curtailed even under tremendous crowding through social organization and systems of control. Various segments of the population are spatially separated in different areas of a community on the basis of ethnic, religious, or socioeconomic characteristics, thus reducing the opportunity for conflict. The threat of personal retaliation and legal restraints additionally discourage people from taking what they want by forceful means. It is therefore not uncommon for extreme poverty to exist amid affluence without serious challenges to inequities. Similar patterns have been noted in the behavior of animals living in crowded colonies (Calhoun, 1950, 1962). Dominant animals gain control over resources, and after a few painful skirmishes, subordinate members resign themselves to a meager existence on the fringes of the colony. The probability of widespread aggression increases under conditions in which massive population growth overwhelms organizational constraints.

Thwarting of Goal-directed Behavior

Proponents of the frustration-aggression theory (Berkowitz, 1965a; Dollard et al., 1939; Feshbach, 1970) define frustration in terms of interference or blocking of goal-seeking activities. In this view, people are provoked to aggression when obstructed, delayed, or otherwise thwarted from getting what they want. Research bearing on this issue shows that thwarting can have a variety of behavioral effects, though under certain conditions it provokes forceful actions.

Frustrative conditions essentially prevent or delay desired reinforcement. The obstacles may take a variety of forms. Sometimes they are created by environmental barriers, physical or social, such as impoverished living conditions, obstructions and privations resulting from overcrowding, and restrictive laws and discriminatory social practices. Personal limitations, both physical and psychological, serve as other potential barriers. Positions in various status and power hierarchies are to a large extent determined by social and vocational competencies. The degree of control that a person can exercise over his own activities, the power to modify his environment, and the accessibility to, and control over, valued resources increases with higher status positions. People who lack sociovocational proficiencies are relegated to a subordinate status, in which not only is their welfare subject to arbitrary external controls, but they are irreversibly channeled into an economic and social mode of living that further restricts their opportunities to improve their lot in life. Self-restraints, arising from conditioned inhibitions and self-censuring reactions, may also curtail the types of gratifications that people can secure from among those that are socially permissible.

A number of experiments, conducted with both children and adults, in which blocking of goal-directed behavior and social learning factors are independently varied disclose that thwarting is a relatively weak and unpredictable determinant of aggression. Although it sometimes heightens aggression (Buss, 1963; Geen and Berkowitz, 1967; Mallick and McCandless, 1966; Ulrich and Flavell, 1970), thwarting often exerts no significant influence, whereas variables within the same studies such as modeling, prior aggressive training, and the functional value of aggressive actions emerge as major determinants of aggression (Buss, 1966a; Gentry, 1970; Jegard and Walters, 1960; Kuhn, Madsen, and Becker, 1967; Walters and Brown, 1963).

People are more easily provoked by insult than by blocking their goal-directed behavior. As was previously noted, they are also more inclined to respond aggressively to unwarranted than to justifiable hindrances, even though their goal-seeking behavior is equally thwarted. The latter findings suggest that in instances where thwarting arouses aggression, the implied insult rather than response interference is perhaps the more critical instigating factor.

The role of thwarting can be best understood by considering its effects on both aggressive and nonaggressive responses. A number of investigators have studied the intensity of responding after expected rewards have been withheld or delayed at different points from the goal.

Children blocked near to the goal respond more vigorously than if they are thwarted at some distance from it (Haner and Brown, 1955; Longstreth, 1966). In a related study, Penney (1960) showed that blocking may result in the intensification of a response which is not part of, but immediately succeeds, the thwarted instrumental activity, provided a strong expectation of reward was created. Holton (1961) similarly demonstrated that the more often children had been reinforced in the past, which presumably created reward expectation, the more forcefully they responded to nonreward, especially if blocked close to goal attainment.

The vigor of instrumental responses may be increased by delay as well as by omission of anticipated reward. The forcefulness with which children perform a behavior that brings them rewards is heightened with increasing delay of reward and reduced with decreasing delay. The effects of frustrative deprivation are not confined to performers. Observers also respond more intensely after seeing another person barred from achieving a goal that is within easy reach (Kobasigawa, 1965).

It is evident from these findings that thwarting can temporarily intensify performance. Since responses of high magnitude tend to be labeled as aggressive, when people react more vigorously after their efforts fail or are obstructed or their successful performances are simply nonrewarded, the strengthened responding is typically construed as aggression. The major questions of interest are twofold: Is intensified responsiveness, when it does occur, attributable to motivational or directive properties of frustrative events, and is the thwarting–vigorous-reaction relationship inherent or established through prior learning? There is some evidence (Amsel, 1958; Blixt and Ley, 1969) that thwarting can function as an aversive arouser that energizes behavior, but learning experiences appear to be the principal determinants of the kinds of responses that are activated (Bolles, 1967; Davitz, 1952). Forceful modes of behavior generally prove more successful in surmounting obstacles than dispirited efforts; consequently, people are differentially reinforced for responding vigorously to frustrative conditions. Various obstacles and thwarting agents may eventually become cues for forceful behavior independently of changes in motivational level. Natural contingencies ordinarily favor vigorous reactions to thwarting, and it is perhaps for this reason that the relationship is frequently observed. It can be reversed, however, by altering the contingencies so that weak rather than forceful responding to frustration pays off (Marx, 1956). Frustrative nonreward can thus come to elicit diverse reactions depending upon what has been found through repeated experience to work best.

In the preceding laboratory studies, thwarting failed to provoke forceful actions in people who had not experienced sufficient positive reinforcement to develop reward expectations and in those who were blocked far enough from the goal that it appeared unattainable. Indeed, prolonged thwarting and nonreward of efforts to secure valued outcomes eventually leads to apathy. These findings are in accord with field studies examining the influence of relative deprivation and behavioral efficacy on militant actions.

Explanations of civil disorders frequently invoke as principal causal factors the pervasive impoverishment, exploitation, and feelings of powerlessness to control conditions that affect one's life. Ransford (1968), for example, reports that, among black residents interviewed in Watts, those who felt most isolated, powerless, and dissatisfied were most willing to endorse violent methods. The view that discontent breeds disorder requires qualifications, however. It follows from this type of causal explanation that collective violence would be more likely to occur in cities where such conditions are prevalent than in those in which they are present to a lesser degree. Lieberson and Silverman (1965) provide some evidence, though admittedly based on gross measures, that adverse conditions of life are poor predictors of the location and timing of riots. Cities experiencing violent civil disturbances did not differ significantly in social and economic conditions commonly assumed to be sources of collective aggression from cities similar in size and region that had no riots. If anything, civil disruptions were more likely to occur where black-white differences in income and occupational pursuits were smaller, but discrimination practices remained in the system. Comparisons of rioters and nonrioters within the same communities yield essentially similar results. The groups did not differ on factors such as employment and income, but those who participated in urban violence were generally better educated, had greater racial pride, and favored coercive action to secure civil rights (Caplan, 1970). In considering why some strained situations erupt into riots and others do not, it should be noted that almost every urban disturbance was started by a police encounter with a ghetto resident that provoked onlookers to retaliatory violence. The fact that fortuitous events serve as precipitants of social disturbances makes prediction difficult from preconditions alone.

The major limitation of the privation theory of social unrest is clearly apparent when one considers that, despite condemnation of their degrading and exploited conditions of life, comparatively few of the sufferers take active measures to force warranted changes. A vast majority of the disadvantaged do not engage in disruptive public protest, and even in cities experiencing civil disturbances, only about 15 to 20 percent of ghetto residents actively participate in the aggressive activities (Bowen, Bowen, Gawser, and Masotti, 1968; Sears and McConahay, 1969; McCord and Howard, 1968). The critical question for social scientists to answer is not why some people who are subjected to gross maltreatment aggress, but rather why a sizable majority of them acquiesce to dismal living conditions in the midst of affluent styles of life. To facilely invoke the frustration-aggression hypothesis, as is commonly done, is to disregard the more striking evidence that severe frustration is generally accompanied by feelings of hopelessness and massive servility. Pervasive discontent may be a necessary but obviously not a sufficient cause of collective aggression.

Informal observation would indicate that discontent produces aggression not in those who have lost hope, but in those whose assertive efforts at social and economic betterment have been periodically reinforced; consequently, they have some reason to expect that coercive action will force additional social change. Psychological research on reinforcement processes has established that the value of given outcomes is determined relationally rather than by their absolute properties (Bandura, 1971b; Premack, 1965). The same level of compensation may thus be experienced as rewarding or punishing depending on the nature, frequency, and magnitude of past reinforcement. People not only compare their present gains with those they secured in the past, but also continually observe the rewards and punishments accruing to others. Unfavorable discrepancies between observed and experienced outcomes tend to create discontent, whereas individuals may be satisfied with limited rewards as long as they are equivalent to, or exceed, what others are receiving.

Selective processes operate in the standards used to evaluate one's outcomes. According to social comparison theory (Festinger, 1954; Pettigrew, 1967) people tend to select for comparison those who are somewhat similar to themselves. Disadvantaged people are therefore more likely to be dissatisfied with their life situations when members of their own group achieve differential advancements than when all remain subordinated. Upward mobility may also breed discontent, especially when self-betterment made possible by the development of requisite competencies raises aspirations, the attainment of which is then thwarted by prejudicial barriers. While the disadvantaged slowly improve their lot in life, the more affluent members of society usually make more rapid progress, so that the disparity between the groups widens. Hard-won gains become relative losses (Pettigrew, 1963). Betterment of social conditions can thus give rise to discontent. When coercive pressures are applied to secure further reforms, protesters are criticized as ungrateful for the benefits they have been granted, and warned that their militant actions will not only jeopardize additional advances but may even cost them what they have already gained.

Current explanations of violent protest emphasize relative deprivation rather than the actual level of aversive conditions as the instigator of collective aggression. In a survey study, Crawford and Naditch (1970) report that blacks who judged their present status as relatively close to their aspirations were inclined to disapprove of militant action and to believe that social changes could be better achieved through persuasion than through force. On the other hand, blacks who felt that their present life situation fell short of their aspirations displayed more militant attitudes. A majority of them regarded riotous actions as a legitimate and effective means of achieving reforms.

In an analysis of conditions preceding major revolutions, Davies (1962, 1969) shows that enduring severe privations is more likely to create resignation and despair than revolution. He attributes people's submissiveness to their preoccupation with physical survival. An alternative explanation is that their efforts to effect social change are extinguished to the point of apathy. Davies builds a convincing case that revolutions are most likely to occur when a period of social and economic improvement that instills rising expectations is followed by a sharp reversal. This pattern of changes would both create aversive social conditions that breed the widespread discontent required for collective action and reinforce a sense of behavioral efficacy that intensifies efforts to regain previously experienced benefits. Collective discontent, however, appears to play a more influential role in revolutionary violence than in protest activities, which are determined more by the coercive potential of challenging groups and the social sanction of forceful tactics (Gurr, 1970a, b).

Although aggression is more likely to be provoked by relative than by absolute deprivation, the predictive value of this determinant is limited by its conceptual and operational ambiguity. There is little consensus among theorists on the comparative standards used to measure level of dissatisfaction. Consequently, variable results may be obtained depending upon whether people evaluate their life circumstances in relation to their aspirations, to their past gratifications, or to the life situations of others whom they select for social comparison. Discontent created by raised aspirations, by reduction of rewards and privileges from accustomed levels, and by deceleration in the rate of anticipated improvement undoubtedly has variant effects. Moreover, different sources of inequity (for example, social, economic, political) may have differential aggression-activating power. A comprehensive theory would also have to specify the form of the relationship between size of negative disparity and likelihood of aggressive response. Informal evidence suggests a threshold rather than a linear function. That is, people lacking coercive power may acquiesce to considerable inequity only to respond violently when it exceeds a certain intolerable level.

The behavioral effects of aversive circumstances are determined not only relationally, but by their justifiability as well. Privations judged to be warranted are generally accepted without indignation, whereas less severe hardships regarded as unjustified are resented. It is inequitable deprivation of things people believe they rightfully deserve that is most conducive to aggressive action. Even unjustified inequities, however, may be accepted without undue protest given expectation either that the maltreatment will be corrected within the foreseeable future, or that opportunities will be created which promise eventual improvement in life circumstances. Hope thus reduces the aggression-arousing potential of aversive privation. To complicate matters further, response to inequitable deprivation is highly influenced by other controlling variables. A relatively low level of discontent combined with coercive power is more apt to produce vigorous protest than high, though powerless, dissatisfaction. Finally, variations in the scope and severity of aversive conditions partly determine whether people will attempt to force changes in specific practices within a system or more radical shifts in institutional principles.

Obviously, most people who feel relatively deprived do not resort to violent action. Unfortunately, researchers rarely examine the reinforcements that are provided for alternative means of securing desired goals. It would be predicted from social learning theory that people who are consistently nonrewarded or punished regardless of what they do would eventually lower their aspirations and acquiesce in their impoverished conditions of life; those who achieve some measure of success through the development of their potentialities would eschew violent tactics; and those who had found aggression to be the only effective means available for getting what they want or for expressing their grievances would favor violent actions.

Several lines of evidence indicate that some reinforcement of personal efficacy is an important factor in aggressive response to aversive social conditions. In many nations it is university students rather than the grossly underprivileged segments of the society who initiate protest movements that force social reforms and topple disliked governments (Lipset, 1966). Student activists in the United States came disproportionately from advantaged backgrounds and prestigious universities that attract the ablest students (Keniston, 1967). Admittedly, factors other than personal efficacy foster student activism. The lack of constraining responsibilities and availability of free time make it easier to act on idealistic convictions when risks are involved. By tradition, students are generally granted some degree of immunity from community control of their protest behavior. The broader awareness gained through critical study can create in highly principled students estrangement, if not outrage, over social inequities, even though they may occupy relatively privileged positions within the system. Since the vast majority of students, however, do not engage in protest activities, an adequate explanation of student activism must include personal as well as common organizational determinants. These issues are discussed at some length in the next chapter.

Studies of urban violence provide further evidence bearing on reinforced efficacy and aggressive responsiveness to maltreatment. Contrary to the popular belief that riotous behavior is performed by disreputable elements of ghetto society, those who participate in civil disturbances have achieved some economic and educational gains to reinforce a sense of racial pride, but they feel unjustly excluded from opportunities within their capabilities by a widespread system of discrimination (Caplan and Paige, 1968; Tomlinson, 1968). After collective aggression is begun, the disinhibiting effects of widespread modeling and the immediate rewards resulting from aggressive activities may instigate aggressive actions in ordinarily passive individuals. The personal determinants of social violence are therefore obscured when studies of the characteristics of participants in collective aggression fail to distinguish between initiators and followers.

People are usually discontented with many aspects of their life situation, but only a few of these, and not necessarily the most pressing ones, ever reach the level of public protest. Explanations of collective aggression must therefore address themselves to the timing and selection of specific problem areas for social action. Blumer (1971) distinguishes several stages in the selective process. The initial phase concerns problem recognition. A variety of factors may determine why a particular adversity attains visibility at a certain time, while other concerns receive little public attention. Adventitious events, coupled with the crusading efforts of reformers, often help to dramatize objectionable social conditions. Thus, prison revolts, mine disasters, shocking crimes, gross injustices, and incidents involving blatant misuse of power expose reprehensible practices. They gain further recognition through agitation of concerned groups. People generally learn about the plight of others through the press and television. Consequently, the mass media, with its immense dissemination capacity, serves as a powerful force in creating, mollifying, and reinforcing public concerns.

After a problem has gained public recognition, it must then survive the process of social validation. Unless the discontented can convince others of the justifiability of their cause, they will fail to gain the widespread sympathy and support needed to mobilize dissatisfaction into corrective action. Groups whose vested interests are threatened, of course, work actively to minimize the grievances and to discredit the protesters as self-serving agitators. Battles over the legitimation of social problems are fought in public assemblies, in the press, and on television by various advocates, including community organizers, students, lawyers, clergy, politicians, and other influential backers of contending factions. Since tactics that are good attention-getters tend to be self-discrediting by their immoderate nature, it is not uncommon for protesters to undermine the justification of their grievances in their effort to publicize them.

Problems can be well publicized and characterized in ways that win the support of socially concerned individuals as well as the aggrieved, but little is done about them. In fact, more often than not, drawing attention to warranted grievances generates a temporary outpouring of moral indignation but little social action. Discomfort over appalling disclosures is thereby relieved without incurring the costs of challenging individuals or institutions contributing to the problems. Personal influences must be brought to bear to get sympathizers to participate in forceful action. Since quick victories are difficult to achieve in confrontations with those who command authorized power, considerable positive reinforcement is also required to sustain reformative efforts in the face of repeated failure. When adequate supportive rewards are lacking, discouragement and weariness take a heavy toll of the ranks of activists.

Considering the complex interplay of opposing influences at each stage of the change process, it is hardly surprising that deprivation, whether defined in absolute or relative terms, is a weak predictor of collective aggression (McPhail, 1971). The substantial evidence reviewed in this section and elsewhere in this book supports the conclusion that aversive events commonly subsumed under the term frustration—be they physical assaults, insults, reinforcement withdrawal, or thwarting of goal-directed activities—are, at best, facilitative rather than necessary or sufficient conditions for aggression. "Frustration" is most likely to provoke aggression in individuals who have learned to behave aggressively and for whom aggression has functional value.

INSTRUCTIONAL CONTROL OF AGGRESSION

During the process of socialization people are extensively trained to obey orders. In the early formative years, when children cannot foresee the consequences of their actions, parents impose strict obedience demands, particularly in hazardous situations. Behavior is brought under verbal control through differential consequences for obedient and noncompliant reactions. By rewarding obedience to directives and punishing noncompliance, orders eventually acquire powerful response-controlling properties (Ayllon and Azrin, 1964). After this form of social influence is well established, people use it extensively to get others to do what they want them to do in a wide range of situations. Since verbal orders quickly lose their effectiveness if they go unheeded without penalty, defiance is seldom treated lightly. In order to preserve authoritative control, social agents are careful to avoid situations that risk open defiance, and they apply strong enforcement measures to ensure that the demands they do impose are obeyed. This is especially true in coercive societies where strict obedience is of considerable importance in maintaining the existing social system.

Given that people will obey orders, legitimate authorities can successfully command aggression from others, especially if the actions are presented as justified and necessary and the enforcing agents possess strong coercive power. Indeed, as Snow (1961) has perceptively observed, "When you think of the long and gloomy history of man, you will find more hideous crimes have been committed in the name of obedience than have been committed in the name of rebellion" (p. 24). He cites as an example the atrocities obediently perpetrated by agents of the Third Reich. The documentation of this thesis might also include the atomic holocausts at Hiroshima and Nagasaki, as well as the more recent wholesale slaughter at My Lai.

A series of controversial experiments conducted by Milgram provide graphic demonstrations of how demands of legitimate authorities can serve as powerful instigators of inhumane aggressive actions. In the obedience paradigm designed to study this phenomenon, well-meaning adults are told to administer increasingly severe shocks to a learner in an adjoining room, ostensibly to examine how memory is affected by punishment of mistakes. The apparatus contains thirty graded switches labeled with voltage ratings and verbal designations varying from slight shocks to dangerously severe ones. Each time the learner errs, the aggressor is ordered to increase the shock level one step. When the more painful levels are reached, the learner—actually a confederate of the experimenter, who never receives any shocks—vehemently protests the punitive treatment and emits increasingly agonized screams as the sessions progress. The experimenter, unperturbed by these reactions, instructs the aggressor to disregard the protestations and to step up the shock level after each error or refusal to respond. Whenever aggressors voice reluctance to continue the cruel actions, as they often do, they are simply told to go on, until they absolutely refuse to comply with the commands.

In the first experiment (Milgram, 1963), conducted with paid volunteers of different occupations, ages, and education, the experimenter provided the authoritative sanction. Much to everyone's surprise, 65 percent of the adults, though highly distressed over the suffering they caused by their brutal actions, nevertheless obeyed the orders to the end, and delivered shocks designated as extremely dangerous. Those who refused to go all the way did so only after the victim began pounding on the wall in desperation. Ordinarily sensible men will behave in a cruel and callous manner when told to do so by a seemingly legitimate authority in an organization of unknown character as well as in a university situation of high integrity (Milgram, 1965b). The following transcript from an obedient subject illustrates destructive compliance with verbal disclaimers for one's injurious actions:

> *150 volts delivered.* You want me to keep going?
> *165 volts delivered.* That guy is hollering in there. There's a lot of them here. He's liable to have a heart condition. You want me to go?
> *180 volts delivered.* He can't stand it: I'm not going to kill that man in there: You hear him hollering? He's hollering. He can't stand it. What if something happens to him? . . . I'm not going to get that man sick in there. He's hollering in there. You know what I mean? I mean I refuse to take responsibility. He's getting hurt in there. He's in there hollering. Too many left here. Geez, if he gets them wrong. There's too many of them left. I mean who is going to take responsibility if anything happens to that gentleman? (The experimenter accepts responsibility.) All right.
> *195 volts delivered.* You see he's hollering. Hear that. Gee, I don't know. (The experimenter says: "The experiment requires that you go on.") I know it does, sir, but I mean—uh—he don't know what he's in for. He's up to 195 volts.
> *210 volts delivered.*
> *225 volts delivered.*
> *240 volts delivered.* Aw, no. You mean I've got to keep going up with the scale? No sir. I'm not going to kill that man: I'm not going to give him 450 volts. (The experimenter says: "The experiment requires that you go on.") I know it does, but that man is hollering in there, sir . . . (p. 67)

This unusually high level of destructive obedience is especially astonishing considering that the experimenter had no coercive power to enforce his demands as is characteristic of authoritative control in everyday life. A number of factors undoubtedly contributed to the ruthless obedience. Included among them is anonymity, protection against retaliative aggression, the force of a contractual obligation, verbal dissociation of oneself from one's actions by assigning responsibility for them to the compelling authority, and the assurance that a qualified researcher would not demand perilous actions without necessary safeguards.

People are often induced to perform cruel acts by the collective pressures exerted by peers. A second experiment demonstrated that people find it difficult to behave counter to what the group wants just as they are averse to defying legitimitized authority (Milgram, 1964). In the absence of group influences, adults delivered only weak shocks; whereas under peer pressure calling for increasingly hurtful actions, men punished the victim with increasing severity despite his desperate cries. Seeing others carrying out punitive orders calmly likewise increases obedient aggression (Powers and Geen, 1972). Peer influences, depending on their nature, can also undermine authoritative control. Thus, under conditions in which others defy the experimenter's brutal demands, only 10 percent of the aggressors followed the issued commands unfailingly in the face of peer rebellion and victims' pleas (Milgram, 1965a). Modeled defiance, however, is less effective in reducing obedient aggression if resisters become emotionally upset than if they are unperturbed by their disobedience (Powers and Geen, 1972). Nervous defiance apparently conveys the impression that either opposition is risky or the challenger is faint-hearted and lacks conviction in the stand he has taken. The degree of compliance with demands for aggression shown by men under various social conditions is depicted graphically in Figure 3.8.

It is relatively easy to hurt a person when his suffering is not visible and when causal actions seem physically or temporally remote from their deleterious effects. Mechanized forms of warfare, in which masses of people can be put to death by destructive forces released remotely, illustrate such depersonalized aggression. When the injurious consequences of one's actions are fully evident, vicariously aroused distress and loss of self-respect serve as restraining influences over aggressive conduct that is otherwise authoritatively sanctioned. Milgram (1965b) obtained diminishing obedience as the harmful consequences of punitive actions became increasingly more salient and personalized. The percent of aggressors who eventually disobeyed brutal orders was 34 percent when the victim pounded the wall in an adjacent room; 38 percent when they heard agonized cries through a door left ajar; 60 percent when the victim expressed the same pleas and protests but in the aggressor's presence; and 70 percent when, in addition to seeing the victim's suffering, aggressors also had to place the victim's hand forcibly on the shock-plate in order to punish him as ordered. And when the commands to increase the severity of punishment were issued by telephone without social surveillance, subjects disregarded the authoritative orders by selecting the weakest shock levels.

When violence toward people designated as foes is not only legitimized but is a source of personal pride, as in warfare or sanctioned oppression of minorities, aggressors share the same values as their peers and superiors. Under such circumstances, there are no strong self-imposed restraints to counteract or circumvent cruel dictates. Malevolent authorities as well as those of good will who extenuate morally reprehensible practices, can, given proper conditions, get otherwise considerate people

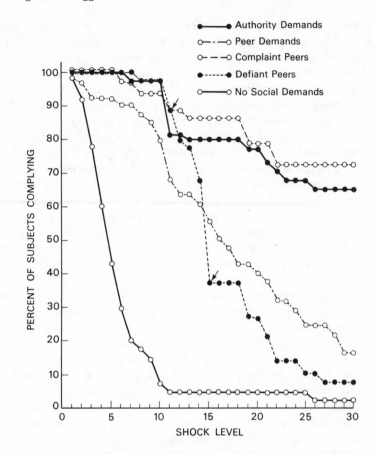

FIGURE 3.8 Percent of subjects who aggressed compliantly at different shock levels. The arrows on the graph for the defiant peers indicate the points at which each of the peers refused the authority's command to shock the victim more severely. (Plotted from data by Milgram, 1963, 1964, 1965a)

to behave inhumanely. In other words, it requires appropriate social influences rather than monstrous people to produce heinous deeds.

NONRECURRENT AGGRESSORS

Interpersonal violence is commonly viewed as an impulsive, irrational, and pathological type of behavior. Social learning theory, on the other hand, conceives of aggression as a learned conduct that, like other forms of social behavior, is under situational, reinforcement, and cognitive control. The view of aggression as a reckless explosive reaction is un-doubtedly reinforced by periodic dramatic episodes in which otherwise law-abiding persons perform heinous crimes. Bizarre mutilation of vic-tims, frenzied overkill of strangers, and sensational "crimes of passion" are striking examples that figure prominently in the mass media.

It has been repeatedly shown that, barring significant changes in social conditions, the best predictor of future behavior is past behavior (Mischel, 1968). This finding is consistent with the social learning view that a person's behavior is highly influential in creating social conditions that, in turn, tend to maintain the behavior. Previous performance has high predictive value for recurrent aggressors, but it is of no aid in identifying individuals who are likely to commit a monstrous act of violence without any prior history of assaultive behavior. Here the pre-dictive and analytic problems are complicated by the fact that unusual forms of violence generally have unusual idiosyncratic determinants.

An earlier analysis of grossly deviant behavior illustrated how behav-ior can come under bizarre symbolic control to the point where it re-mains refractory to external reality influences. Every so often tragic episodes occur in which individuals are led by delusional beliefs to commit acts of violence. Some follow divine inner voices commanding them to murder. Others are instigated to self-protective attacks by para-noid suspicions that the victim is conspiring to harm them. And still others are prompted by grandiose convictions that it is their heroic re-sponsibility to eliminate evil individuals in positions of power.

A study of Presidential assassins (Weisz and Taylor, 1970) shows that, with one exception, the murderous assaults were partly under de-lusional control. The assassins acted either under divine mandate, through alarm that the President was in a conspiracy with treacherous foreign agents to overthrow the government, or on the conviction that their own adversities resulted from Presidential persecution. Ordinarily, erroneous beliefs are modified through disconfirming evidence presented by others. The assassins, however, tend to be loners. Being unusually seclusive in their behavior, they effectively shielded their erroneous be-liefs from corrective influences. Serious personal failures, also a promi-nent feature of this group, further strengthened the tendency to assign their misfortune to pernicious external causes. In the case of autistically determined aggression, both the instigators of the violent acts and the dreaded consequences they are intended to forestall are to a large extent internally generated.

A number of studies have been conducted on whether chronic ag-gressors can be distinguished from occasional extreme assaulters by their personality characteristics (Blackburn, 1968; Fisher, 1970; Megargee, 1966; Megargee and Mendelsohn, 1962). The individuals included in the latter group tend to overinhibit aggressive responses, but when they are finally provoked by cumulative or extreme instigation to commit an aggressive act, they do so in a violent way. These two types of aggressors can be easily distinguished behaviorally, but they do not differ much in their responses to conventional psychological tests. The behavioral discontinuity of the obsequious murderer may be somewhat overemphasized because his past aggressive actions, unless they take blatant or antisocial forms, are seldom recorded. Incongruity is more characteristic of journalistic accounts than of the behavioral history of retiring assassins. It is not uncommon for mild-mannered assailants to be unusually well stocked with guns and to be highly proficient in their use. This requires some prior engrossment in activities productive of violence. Charles Whitman, the student sniper who went on a mass murder spree, is a good case in point.

Newspaper reports described Whitman as a former altar boy and Eagle Scout who exemplified the virtues of an All-American youth (*The New York Times,* 1966a). In fact, he was much less righteous than the summary characterization would imply (*The New York Times,* 1966b, 1966c). Whitman was raised in an atmosphere of familial violence. Like his father, who repeatedly beat his wife and displayed a "fanatic" interest in guns, Whitman was known to assault his wife and others with a minimum of provocation. From early childhood he also shared his father's fondness for firearms. As a marine recruit he was courtmartialed for insubordination and fighting. Upon discharge he had occasional brushes with the law in connection with aggressive activities. Whitman was once apprehended with two other students for poaching deer when they were caught dressing the carcass in a dormitory bathroom. On another occasion he threw an exchange student out of a classroom for sitting on his chair. At about the time of the murder spree, Whitman was drifting deeper into illegal activities, including, among other things, passing bad checks for heavy gambling debts and unsuccessful efforts to become a pornography supplier to local merchants. Contrary to journalistic accounts, Whitman's behavioral record was not that of a meek altar boy suddenly gone berserk.

Newsman similarly depicted Howard Unruh, who fatally shot thirteen people during a murderous rampage on a Camden street, as a "mild, soft-spoken veteran" with a reputation of being a "model boy" (*The New York Times,* 1949). Whatever other attributes he may have displayed, his intense engrossment with instruments of violence and neighborhood disputes belied the pacific journalistic characterization. He managed through various ruses to bring home from Europe an arsenal of weapons that he collected while in the Army. The walls of his room were adorned with crossed pistols and bayonets and pictures of armored artillery in action. Scattered about his room were pistols, machetes, and ash trays made of cartridges. In the months preceding the murderous episode, Unruh spent his time seclusively reading Scriptures, practicing pistol shooting in his back yard, and building up resentment against neighborhood shopkeepers who he believed were persecuting him by making derogatory remarks about his character. His persecutory beliefs were periodically reinforced by arguments with his neighbors over his disturbing behavior. After sitting through several showings of a double feature, *I Cheated the Law* and *The Lady Gambles,* into the small hours of the morning, Unruh returned home, whereupon he made up his mind to slay his tormentors. The next morning he walked down the street of the neighborhood shopping center methodically shooting merchants and their customers with the deadly accuracy that won him marksmanship medals in the Army.

Unruh displayed most of the distinguishing features of psychotic assassins. There is the deterioration in socioeconomic functioning; idleness and marked seclusiveness foster the development of persecutory and autistic resentments that become magnified in the absence of disconfirming judgments of trusted friends; eventually delusional constructions assume greater reality than the actual social events and, given appropriate instigating conditions, they take violent action. This conceptualization of homicidally extreme aggression by otherwise withdrawn individuals differs in many important respects from explanations in terms of undischarged aggressive drives exceeding rigid controls. Although they may have little prior history of criminally assaultive behavior, the allegedly quiet assassins such as Oswald, Whitman, and Unruh were all skilled riflemen who regularly engaged in far more aggressive activities that could "discharge pent-up aggression" than nonassaultive people who are also subjected to aggression instigation.

One can undoubtedly identify some distinguishing attributes among persons differing in aggressive patterns, but they may have limited value in predicting homicidal behavior in individual cases. For every psychotic or overinhibited person who behaves violently, there are countless others with similar characteristics who rarely display such conduct. People diagnosed as mentally ill, for example, are neither more nor less prone to acts of violence before, during, or after hospitalization than the general public (Gulevich and Bourne, 1970). Study of personality characteristics can yield valid predictors of homicidal behavior only if the causes reside primarily in the individual. If social conditions are major instigators of aggression, as is generally the case, then prediction of when, where, and by whom acts of violence will be committed cannot be achieved without assessment of instigating social influences. Bizarre homicides are usually produced by the coexistence of several unusual factors, such that if any one of them were absent the event would not have occurred. Unless there exist some common determinants of peculiar aggression across individual cases, the study of rare acts provoked by an idiosyncratic combination of influences will not yield much generalizable information.

chapter four

MAINTAINING CONDITIONS

The analysis of aggression has centered thus far on the development of injurious patterns of behavior and their various antecedent determinants. The third major feature of the social learning formulation is concerned with the conditions that sustain aggressive responding. Maintenance of behavior depends in large part on prevailing conditions of reinforcement. The principle that behavior is strongly controlled by its consequences applies equally to aggression. Aggressive actions that are rewarded tend to be repeated, whereas those that are unrewarded or punished are generally discarded. Thus, aggressive modes of response, like other forms of social behavior, can be produced, eliminated, and reinstated by altering the effects they produce.

This chapter discusses the wide range of rewards and punishments that determine whether or not people will behave aggressively under given circumstances. In traditional theories of learning, reinforcement influences are largely confined to the effects of external outcomes impinging directly upon the performer. Social learning theory distinguishes three forms of reinforcement control of aggression: the influence of direct external reinforcement, vicarious or observed reinforcement, and self-reinforcement.

EXTERNAL REINFORCEMENT

People aggress for a variety of reasons. Some resort to force to appropriate tangible resources they desire. Some behave aggressively because it wins them approval and status rewards. Still others may rely on aggressive conquests to bolster their self-esteem and sense of manliness. And some may derive satisfaction from seeing the expressions of suffering they inflict on their victims. Essentially the same aggressive actions thus may have markedly different functional value for different individuals and for the same individual on different occasions.

There are no conceptual or empirical grounds for regarding aggression maintained by certain reinforcers as more genuine or important than others. A complete theory must account for all aggressive actions whatever purposes they serve. The research findings reviewed in succeeding sections reveal that, like other forms of social behavior, aggression is maintained by diverse conditions of reinforcement. It appears, however, that aggressive actions are primarily reinforced by their functional value, whereas accompanying expressions of suffering by the victim tend, if anything, to have inhibiting effects. Extrinsic rewards assume special significance in interpersonal aggression because such behavior, by its very nature, generally creates a punishment contingency. A person who gets into fights will suffer some injury even though he eventually triumphs over his opponents. Under noncoercive conditions, positive incentives are therefore needed to overcome the inhibitions aroused by the inherent aversive effects of aggression. Rewards become increasingly important as the costs of aggression become greater.

Tangible Rewards for Aggression

Aggressive behaviors are often repeated because, if skillfully performed, they serve as effective means of securing desired tangible rewards. By threats of physical violence or aggressive actions children can forcibly appropriate possessions of vulnerable peers; delinquents and adult transgressors can support themselves or costly drug habits on income derived from aggressive pursuits; through forceful means protesters can secure social reforms that materially affect their lives; and nations are sometimes able to gain control over prized territories through warfare.

The degree to which individual or collective aggression is affected by its material consequences is difficult to evaluate under naturally occurring conditions. Unless one can observe the outcomes associated with all acts of aggression—an immense task—sample observations in a selected setting may provide an incomplete picture of the actual schedule on which aggression is reinforced. In the case of antisocial pursuits, delinquents are understandably averse to having the profits of their muggings recorded. Establishing reliable functional relationships is further complicated because aggressive actions ordinarily produce diverse effects that are not easily separable. Some of the concomitant consequences might augment the aggressive behavior, others might attenuate it, and still others might exert little influence on it. For these reasons, the reinforcement causes of aggression can be best understood by controlled experimental demonstrations.

Control of aggression by its material consequences has rarely been studied with humans, although several experiments with animals have been addressed to this issue. Ulrich, Johnston, Richardson, and Wolff (1963) report that initially docile rats who had been deprived of water attacked their partners with increased intensity when fighting responses won them drinks, but ceased aggressing when water rewards for such behavior were withdrawn.

The schedule and frequency of reinforcement apparently control aggressive behavior in essentially the same predictable way as they do nonaggressive responses (Azrin and Hutchinson, 1967). As shown in Figure 4.1, food-deprived pigeons displayed no aggression when food was made available on a noncontingent basis, whereas they readily fought when aggressive attacks produced food. The more often their fighting responses were rewarded, the more aggressive they became. When food was again given regardless of how they behaved, their attacks declined to a near zero level. Once fighting responses are established, they can be effectively maintained by occasional reinforcement (Stachnik, Ulrich, and Mabry, 1966). In the study cited earlier, Reynolds, Catania, and Skinner (1963) not only trained pigeons to fight for food rewards, but by reinforcing their aggressive responses only under designated circumstances, brought the fighting under precise situational control.

The power over fighting behavior wielded by positive reinforcement may be somewhat magnified in these studies because the opponents selected were either relatively docile or physically restrained. Pain resulting from more vigorous defensive combat by the victim would most likely attenuate the influence of rewards. However, repeated victories with progressively tougher opponents can produce vicious fighters not easily dissuaded by counterattacks.

In everyday life, people are rarely, if ever, rewarded every time

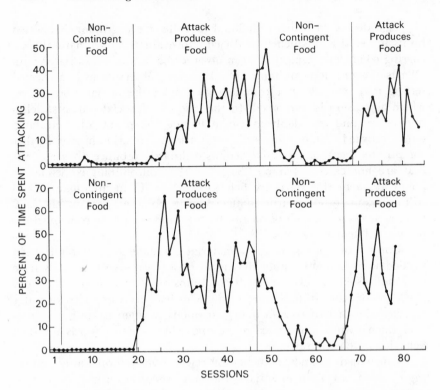

FIGURE 4.1   Percent of time spent by two hungry pigeons attacking a target pigeon during periods when attacks produced food and when food was given independently of how they behaved. (Azrin and Hutchinson, 1967)

they perform a given action. Forceful tactics do not always succeed. Aggressors, however skilled they may be, do not always emerge unscathed from their frays. Because of the variable nature of the social environment, behavior is characteristically reinforced on an intermittent basis. People respond quite differently depending on the pattern and frequency with which their actions are reinforced. Those who have been consistently rewarded become easily discouraged and give up quickly when their efforts fail. Individuals whose behavior has been reinforced only periodically tend to persist for a considerable time despite setbacks and only occasional success. In the absence of better alternatives, behavior that has been reinforced on a thin unpredictable schedule is exceedingly hard to extinguish because one's efforts are sustained by the belief that the actions will eventually prove successful.

The influential role of the reinforcement schedule in the maintenance of aggressive responses is revealed in laboratory studies with children. Cowan and Walters (1963) rewarded boys with marbles for punching an automated clown. They were reinforced after every punch, every third punch, or every sixth punch. Material rewards were then discontinued to see how long children would persist in their aggressive behavior. During this extinction phase, boys who were rewarded continuously were the least aggressive, whereas those who had to perform six aggressive responses to gain a reward displayed the highest number of punching attacks. Boys institutionalized for behavior disorders did not differ from noninstitutionalized youngsters in their initial aggressiveness; however, after rewards for aggression were withdrawn, institutionalized children continued to behave more aggressively and took longer to cease their punching assaults.

Intermittently reinforced aggressive responses not only are more persistent, but also tend to generalize to new situations. Walters and Brown (1963) reinforced boys with marbles for hitting the automated clown on a continuous schedule or after every sixth punching response, or they did not reward hitting behavior. Following aggression training, children in each condition underwent frustrating or enjoyable experiences and then their physical aggressiveness toward another child was measured in both competitive games and free responding situations. Boys who were only occasionally rewarded for aggression during training were about twice as interpersonally assaultive as boys who were continuously reinforced, never reinforced, or received no aggression training. Surprisingly, the latter three groups did not differ from each other. Nor did frustration, in which the experimenter interrupted an absorbing movie, confiscated the children's candy, and threw it away, influence the incidence of interpersonal aggression. Evidence that occasional reinforcement of physical aggression in nonfrustrating impersonal situations facilitates interpersonal aggression has important theoretical and social implications.

Social and Status Rewards

In every society some patterns of behavior are admired, others arouse no special interest, and still others are held up to ridicule. By behaving in ways that are highly valued, people can gain status in the circles in which they travel. There are certain advantages in holding a high position in a status hierarchy. Those who possess a superior rank enjoy greater power to control the activities of the group than do subordinate members; they are granted many privileges; they get better treatment; they have greater access to rewarding resources; and if their stature is secured through deserving accomplishments, they receive a great deal of rewarding attention and adoration. People therefore tend to aspire to higher standing by pursuing activities that are status conferring and by shunning those that lower their personal stature or bring disfavor. Once they gain advantageous positions, they will continue to do whatever is needed to maintain their status in the privilege system. For similar reasons, people will engage in costly retaliation to restore their social prestige following public humiliation.

Social rewards can be distinguished from status rewards, although they have some features in common. In the latter case, performance of valued behavior gains one a social rank that carries with it diverse benefits as long as that position is occupied. In the case of social reinforcement, a person wins approval for specific actions without necessarily changing his rank in a status hierarchy. In other words, one can be praised without being promoted in a status hierarchy.

Data are lacking on how strongly behavior is affected by these two types of reinforcement systems. Martin and her associates (1968), however, report a study that has some bearing on this issue. They compared the effectiveness of treatment programs for deliquents in which their academic and social performances were either rewarded individually or won them promotions to increasingly more privileged ranks. In the latter system, five levels that required progressively higher achievements were devised. As the adolescents advanced through these ranks by mastering the requisite patterns of behavior, they were granted greater freedom and more generous rewards. The rank-contingent reinforcement produced greater changes in behavior than previous practices in which specific responses were individually reinforced.

The relative superiority of status rewards may be attributed to several factors. If failure to perform a given action results in loss of a specific reward, the negative consequence is limited and of no great import. Maintenance of a status position typically depends on successful performance of a broad range of role behaviors. When a few foolhardy or faulty actions can produce a demotion in rank, thus creating pervasive negative consequences, the continuous threat of loss of status and its attendant rewards effectively maintains a wide repertoire of behaviors. Pressure for exemplary performance is especially great when status positions are limited and there are many eager competitors for them. Martin et al. (1968) ascribe some of the power of status reward systems to their inherent modeling influences. By designating the hierarchical role behaviors required for different status positions, members who aspire to higher status are provided with explicit symbolic and actual models of what they must do to gain more privileged ranks.

Some aggressive behaviors are controlled by the positive social reactions they elicit from others. Support for this interpretation comes from several sources. Children who are praised for hitting increase their assaultive attacks more than those who receive no approval for such behavior (Patterson, Ludwig, and Sonoda, 1961). The effects of social reinforcement on aggression are by no means confined to children. Adult males praised for administering high-intensity shocks to another person became progressively more punitive, whereas nonreinforced subjects displayed a relatively low level of aggression (Geen and Stonner, 1971). These differences are depicted graphically in Figure 4.2. Individuals rewarded for aggressive behavior continued to respond more punitively and generated more hostile thoughts to verbal aggressive cues after praise for injurious conduct was discontinued (Geen and Pigg, 1970).

Social reinforcement not only makes further aggression more likely, but can enhance other forms of aggression that were not explicitly rewarded. Both children (Lovaas, 1961) and adults (Loew, 1967; Parke, Ewall, and Slaby, 1972) who are socially rewarded for hostile remarks later exhibit more physical aggression than those reinforced for positive

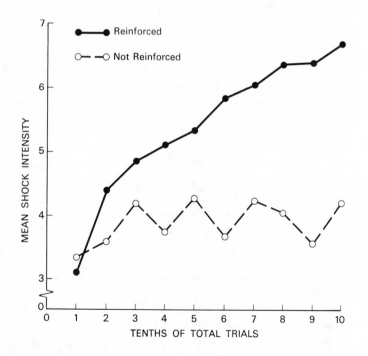

FIGURE 4.2 Mean intensities of shocks administered by adults when they were praised for behaving punitively or were never reinforced for escalating punitive responses. (Geen and Stonner, 1971)

or neutral verbalizations. Even seeing the aggressive remarks of others reinforced can increase physical aggression in observers (Parke, Wiederholt, and Slaby, 1972).

The generalization effects of reinforcement may be interpreted in several ways. It may be that different types of aggression represent a general response class so that rewarding any one form automatically strengthens other forms as well. An alternative, and more tenable, explanation can be cast in terms of the informative and incentive functions of reinforcement. Praising hostile expressions conveys permissiveness or even invitation to aggressive modes of response. The likelihood of aggression is increased on future occasions by expectations that such behavior, though ordinarily discouraged, is not only acceptable but brings commendation from others.

Geen and his associates advance the view that approval of reinforcement automatically strengthens aggressive habits rather than reducing inhibitions, on the assumption that disinhibition should increase aggressiveness to hostile and neutral situations alike. In point of fact, responses to markedly different stimuli are never uniformly rewarded in everyday life; disinhibition therefore tends to be selective rather than indiscriminate. Thus, rewarding attacks on peers will weaken aggression inhibitions toward them, but will not necessarily eliminate restraints against assaulting policemen. Since responding aggressively to hostile cues would be considered more appropriate and approvable than the same response to neutral or positive stimuli, the findings of Geen and Stonner (1971) are explainable in terms of differential restraint reduction. Staples and Walters (1964), indeed, demonstrated that inhibitory processes partly determine the effects of social reinforcement. Although females intensified shocks administered to a victim for praise, those exhibiting strong aggression inhibition were less responsive to the social reinforcement. Modeling studies cited earlier (Bandura, 1965b; Madsen, 1968) furthermore show that variations in aggression under different reinforcement conditions primarily reflect the effect of restraints and anticipated consequences rather than response availability. Whether generalization of aggression accompanying social reinforcement is attributable to its sanctioning or its habit-strengthening function can easily be tested by structuring aggression as commendable behavior without praising specific actions. The disinhibition hypothesis would predict comparable initial increase in aggressive responding under praise and sanctioning conditions. Since praise is not only a form of sanction but also conveys a sense of personal worth, it serves as a source of self-esteem rewards that can promote aggression over time more effectively than can a condoning attitude alone.

It has been amply documented in studies of verbal conditioning that the frequency with which adults engage in verbal hostility is partly determined by the positive interest shown in it (Binder, McConnell, and Sjoholm, 1957; Buss and Durkee, 1958; Simkins, 1961). Moreover, sequential analysis of interactions in psychotherapeutic interviews reveals that hostile remarks increase when they are positively received by therapists, and are either discarded or directed toward different targets when aggressive displays evoke disinterest or disapproval (Bandura, Lipsher, and Miller, 1960; Goldman, 1961). It is interesting to speculate whether, in interview treatments based on the catharsis model, clients are venting anger arousal or trying to please their therapists by telling them what they want to hear. Given evidence that positive reinforcement of verbal aggression increases the likelihood of aggressive action, ventilative therapies aimed at draining aggressive drives may inadvertently reinforce aggressive tendencies.

Analyses of social reinforcement of aggressive behavior in natural settings are in general agreement with results of laboratory studies. Bandura and Walters (1959) compared the reinforcement practices of parents of violence-prone adolescents and of nonaggressive boys. Parents of nonaggressive adolescents rarely reinforced their sons for resorting to physical aggression in response to provocation. Parents of assaultive delinquents, on the other hand, tolerated no aggressive displays whatsoever in the home, but condoned, actively encouraged, and reinforced provocative and aggressive actions toward others in the community. Similar findings emerged from a study of the reinforcement conditions prevailing in the families of young aggressive and inhibited boys (Bandura, 1960). Parents of inhibited boys consistently disapproved any type of aggressiveness, thus affording little opportunity for the development of such forms of conduct. By contrast, parents of the aggressive boys, while nonpermissive and punitive for aggression toward themselves, condoned a great deal of sibling aggression and encouraged and rewarded their sons' aggressive behavior when this was directed toward other children.

The effects of differential parental reinforcement were reflected in the boys' aggressive behavior. They expressed considerably more physical and verbal aggression toward their peers, displayed more oppositional behavior toward their teachers, and showed weaker restraints over aggression in the face of provocation than inhibited boys. However, they displayed no more aggression toward their parents, which is understandable, in view of the parents' punitiveness for aggression toward themselves.

Ordinarily, activities such as scholastic, artistic, and athletic accomplishments are highly valued, and it is noteworthy performances in such enterprises that win praise. For reasons given earlier, people willingly forego many personal gratifications in order to excel in status-conferring tasks. The countless hours of practice by aspiring musicians and stage performers, for example, are partly sustained by visions of future applause. Football players who have no professional aspirations nevertheless risk crippling injuries and endure grimy, arduous drills for social recognition and some brief moments of glory on the gridiron.

Cultures differ to some degree in what they value. Even the same society may, under unusual circumstances, radically alter its system of social rewards. During wartime, otherwise compassionate societies offer medals, promotions, laudatory press reports, and other social commendations for skill in killing. Those who refuse to participate in the sanctioned manslaughter, whether through fear or because they value the dignity of human life, are subjected to humiliating societal punishments. In the Nazi structure of reinforcement, where enslavement and execution of designated racial groups were viewed as meritorious acts of patriotism, promotions in concentration camps were made partly on skill in performing mass murders. Camp commandants proudly compared execution rates like industrial production figures (Andrus, 1969).

Most societies contain subgroups in which the members achieve status and recognition through their skill in fighting. That interpersonal aggression is often an approved form of conduct, rather than an impulsive frustration reaction, is nowhere better illustrated than in observational studies of delinquent subcultures (Miller, 1958; Short, 1968; Wolfgang and Ferracuti, 1967; Yablonsky, 1962). Among the personal qualities most highly prized in such groups are fighting prowess, toughness, ability to outsmart others, and a quest for excitement. Members are rewarded for fighting exploits and lose stature for faint-heartedness in the face of insults and combat challenges. Because aggression assumes such a central place in the system of values, active participants show continued concern about their fighting reputations. Status threats, from either challengers within the group itself or rival gangs, are quick to provoke aggressive actions. One need not be a member of a fighting gang to derive satisfaction from assaultive conquests. In circles in which physical prowess commands respect, beating up a person who has behaved irritatingly reinforces a sense of manliness and personal worth (Toch, 1969). Assaultiveness is most often equated with manhood among males in lower socioeconomic classes.

Many people have come to believe, on the basis of popular accounts of sensational episodes, that gang delinquents spend much of their time in perilous battles defending their "turf" against rival territorial intruders. Researchers who have observed daily gang activities over an extended period paint quite a different picture. Like the aggressive responsiveness of most other people, the aggression displayed by gang boys tends to be highly discriminative, is restricted to a narrow range of targets, and is largely limited to attenuated forms. Miller, Geertz, and Cutter (1961), who studied a representative example of a juvenile gang, found that most of the gang's aggressive actions (70 percent) are directed at one another, and only a small percentage of their attacks are aimed at either adults (16 percent) or other adolescents (12 percent). Not only does most of the aggression occur within the gang, but it is predominantly verbal. Of the total aggressive episodes recorded, 93 percent involved verbal attacks; physical assaults against persons or property were relatively rare (7 percent).

Intragang aggression is primarily used to maintain effective group functioning. Active members are typically chastised for such things as deviating from the group's standards of conduct, for unruly behavior that disrupts group activities, for ineptitude, for shirking obligations, for boastful self-aggrandizement, and for dealing dishonestly with compatriots. Miller notes parenthetically that these performance codes are not unlike the Boy Scout guide, though the types of behavior by which delinquents gain status and recognition obviously differ. Based on his painstaking observations, Miller concludes that aggressive gang behavior is inadequately explained in terms of either venting aggressive impulses or a lack of norms and identity. Rather, it serves a positive function to enforce adherence to the group's behavioral standards.

Any generalizations about gang aggression must, of course, be accepted with reservation, because gangs vary in a number of ways. Some of the more important distinguishing features include the size and stability of membership, the degree of consensus on standards of conduct, and the types of behaviors rewarded. Delinquent gangs that glory in fighting exploits will bear little resemblance to those valuing drug experiences. Nevertheless, the findings of Miller and others (Short, 1968) show the popular portrayal of members of fighting gangs as combative predators to be grossly exaggerated.

Getting smashed in the face or stabbed is doubtless as frightening and painful to delinquent boys as to persons leading more pacific styles of life. Therefore, to induce others to perform actions that can have self-injurious consequences requires some coercive or rewarding power over them. In the absence of strong reinforcement control, individuals would be reluctant to affiliate closely with a gang that confers status on the basis of fighting prowess if they were, in fact, often required to embark on perilous violence toward rival groups. As might be expected, close examination of intergang encounters reveals much verbal bravado but little actual combat, even by gangs whose status is built mainly around skill in fighting (Miller, 1958; Short and Strodtbeck, 1964).

Core members have to engage in some fighting from time to time when their status is publicly challenged in order to preserve their fighting reputation. However, it is the functional leaders who do most of the fighting. The main reason for this is that, as a rule, gang affiliation is relatively weak and unstable (Klein and Crawford, 1967). Many of the boys remain fringe members who hang around more for protection from rival gangs than for the rewards provided within the group. With weak rewarding control, the leadership does not have a sufficient hold on marginal members to enlist them easily in battle. Nor are they willing, for one reason or another, to risk beatings to enhance their standing in the gang hierarchy.

On occasions when gangs are provoked into physical violence by status threats, the combatants are usually relieved when police interventions or brandishing of guns provide them with legitimate alibis for cutting short the fray. Both forces can thus gracefully retreat with claims of victory that uphold or even boost their respective reputations. If intergang conflicts are skillfully orchestrated, gang boys can maintain their prestige as warriors on the basis of minimum actual combat. When one plays the violence game, however, miscalculations and unexpected circumstances sometimes result in serious injury to the participants. On such occasions, gang loyalties and preservation of reputation as a group not to be trifled with demand retaliatory violence despite high risk of further injury.

Expressions of Injury

Aggressive behavior usually produces, among other effects, expressions of pain and injury in victims. Several views have been advanced on how seeing the suffering caused by one's aggressive actions affects subsequent aggressiveness. Drive theories (Feshbach, 1970) consider infliction of injury the goal response that reduces the aggressive drive. Just as eating relieves hunger, hurting others presumably discharges the aggressive impulse and hence becomes satisfying in its own right. Sears, Maccoby, and Levin (1957) suggest two ways in which signs of pain and injury acquire rewarding value. In the first place, aggressive actions can reduce uncomfortable tensions resulting from conflict over desire to strike out and fear of punishing consequences. Second, aggressive behavior that removes frustrations is often accompanied by signs of pain and discomfort in those toward whom the attack is directed. Pain cues thus become rewarding through their repeated association with tension relief and removal of frustrations. As a result, people often behave aggressively for no other apparent reason than to produce signs of pain and distress in others.

At this point, it is important to distinguish between acquired reinforcers and acquired drives. If an aggressor achieves positive effects whenever he hurts others, there is every reason to expect that signs of suffering will develop reinforcing properties. What remains unexplained in drive theories is how people acquire a drive to inflict injury. If drives are invoked for everything people find satisfying, the result is an immense proliferation of drives that have no greater explanatory value than the conditioned reinforcers from which they are inferred. Moreover, as was shown earlier, frustration (which is presumably the prime inducer of the aggressive drive) is, at best, only a weak determinant of aggression. Nor is there any convincing evidence that people who refrain from aggressive activities necessarily experience a mounting urge to hurt others, as would be expected from the characteristics usually assigned to drives.

Feshbach (1970) interprets the rewarding value of pain expressions in terms of self-esteem processes. Through example and precept children learn a retaliation norm: Infliction of injury requires that the initial aggressor must be hurt. It is further assumed that perception of pain in one's tormentors is experienced as satisfying because retaliation restores self-esteem. Humiliating defeat of a foe can, under certain conditions, bolster aggressors' self-evaluations. Undoubtedly, there are also many instances in which reprisal is designed more to reestablish one's public image than to enhance one's self-regard. It is an open question, however, whether assailants derive much pride specifically from the agonizing cries and gory wounds caused by their actions. Retaliatory aggression can gain considerable value from its success in reducing or, terminating further victimization. In clarifying the functional properties of retaliation it would be important to assess its reinforcing value depending upon its successfulness and its injuriousness. These separable effects should be distinguished because they do not always occur together. That is, vengeful injury can be administered in defeat, and conversely, retributive triumphs can be achieved with minimal infliction of injury. A comparative analysis would reveal which combination of outcomes makes further aggression more likely.

A contrasting view is that signs of suffering ordinarily function as inhibitors rather than as positive reinforcers of aggressive behavior. Because of the potential dangers of violent and destructive actions, most societies prohibit physical forms of aggression except under specified conditions. As the process of social training takes effect, people learn to substitute the more readily tolerated verbal means of aggression for physical ones (Bandura and Walters, 1959; Sears, Maccoby, and Levin, 1957). Even direct verbal assaults meet with disapproval, so that people eventually learn to express aggression in subtler ways. Although defensive fighting may be permissible under certain circumstances, cruel and destructive acts of aggression are likely to bring swift punishment. Most people also adopt for self-evaluation societal standards in which ruthless aggression is morally reprehensible. Consequently, aggression that produces suffering in others elicits fear of retaliation and self-condemnation, both of which tend to inhibit injurious attacks. Examples can be cited of societal practices in which cruel, monstrous acts are considered praiseworthy by those in positions of power. Such bizarre reinforcement contingencies can breed people who take pleasure in inflicting pain and humiliation. Some of the most horrid illustrations of this phenomenon are documented in the proceedings of the Nuremberg trials. Rudolph Hoess, a former commandant of Auschwitz, for example, had a window installed in a gas chamber so he could watch the gruesome massacres (Andrus, 1969).

Lest the Nazi atrocities be dismissed as an anomalous product of a deranged social system, it should be noted here that otherwise socialized people can be led to behave brutally and to take pride in such actions under circumstances where reinforcement practices are instituted that favor sadistic forms of behavior. A United States infantry battalion in South Viet Nam adopted its own reward system for eliminating Viet Cong (San Francisco Chronicle, 1970). Infantrymen who could prove they had killed an enemy were not only rewarded with rest and recreation, but were also decorated with specially designed "Kill Cong" emblems formally presented at company formations. The barbarity of the reinforcement system adopted by this particular battalion is revealed by what had to be submitted as evidence of a kill. To lay claim to a badge one had to bring back an enemy ear. A string of ears was proudly displayed at the headquarters like huntsmen's trophies. Within any society certain individuals, or even subgroups, may function in a social environment subscribing to pernicious contingencies of reinforcement that make infliction of suffering a source of satisfaction.

Some experimental attempts have been made to assess whether signs of suffering by victims function as reinforcers. Feshbach, Stiles, and Bitter (1967) tested the notion that painful expressions assume rewarding value under conditions of anger arousal. Female students participated in a verbal conditioning task after being treated in either a hostile or a friendly manner by a confederate of the experimenter. For half the subjects in each condition the correct verbal response was reinforced by showing the confederate being shocked, while for the remaining students the correct words merely produced a light flash. Angered subjects increased verbal responses that brought displays of the provocateur undergoing pain, but the noninsulted subjects did not.

The above findings would seem to indicate that pain cues serve as positive reinforcers for angered people, but additional information is needed before the conditioning differences can be unequivocally attributed to the influence of anger arousal. Seeing others suffer pain evokes emotional reactions in observers (Berger, 1962). Angered subjects in the light flash condition were subjected to only one source of arousal, whereas those who also observed the suffering provocateur experienced two sources of emotion arousal. It has been shown that people become conditioned more easily under moderately high, as compared to low, emotional arousal (Bandura and Rosenthal, 1966; Spence, 1964). The obtained differences in conditioning could conceivably reflect differences in arousal level. Experiments examining the influence of anger should include other forms of arousal (for example, fear-aroused or sex-aroused conditions) to establish whether the results are due specifically to anger or to the general effects of emotional arousal.

Researchers who have studied how signs of injury influence further attacks on suffering victims do not find much evidence that pain expressions reinforce aggressive actions. Buss (1966b) analyzed whether knowledge that one's actions were physically injurious to an initial victim affects aggressors' tendency to behave punitively toward another victim. Aggressors were equally punitive toward both victims when they had no feedback on the results of their hurtful behavior. Neither male nor female aggressors reduced their punitiveness toward a male knowing that their aggressiveness had previously harmed a person. However, they behaved less aggressively toward a female after learning about the injurious consequences of their actions. Apparently, the cultural stereotype that men should be able to withstand painful treatment mitigates compassion toward them.

In the preceding study aggression was performed mainly in the service of social request. Pain feedback may have different effects on persons who are prompted to retaliatory aggression by insults or physical attacks. As previously noted, drive theories assume that expressions of suffering are likely to function as inhibitors of aggression in nonangered persons but to reinforce punitiveness in those harboring hostile feelings toward their adversaries. Several studies provide evidence on this point. Geen (1970) found that males who were treated considerately, as well as those who had been angered, behaved less aggressively toward their antagonist when he expressed anguished cries than when he suffered in silence. The aggression-inhibiting effects of hurtful reactions are shown even more convincingly by Baron (1971c), who varied anger arousal and the intensity of pain suffered by the victim. Both angered and nonangered adults lessened the strength of their attacks as the pain manifested by the victim increased.

In a closely related experiment, Baron (1971d) tested the notion that similarity between the aggressor and the victim would arouse empathy for the victim's suffering and thus reduce aggression directed toward him. Students were led to believe that the target person was either a fellow student with similar attitudes and opinions, or an apprentice electrician who advocated opposing views on such matters as environmental pollution and student power. The intensity of anger toward the victim and the intensity of his expression of pain were also varied. Signs of suffering on the part of the victim diminished interpersonal punitiveness regardless of whether the victim resembled or differed from the aggressor.

Although the scope of the experimental treatments and the populations studied are too limited to warrant sweeping generalizations, the evidence indicates that expressions of suffering serve as aggression inhibitors. These findings assume added significance considering that the pain reactions are conveyed only vocally or by readings on a pain meter without any visual contact with the victim. In actual life aggressors not only hear the tormented cries of their victims, but see the gruesome consequences of their actions. People are even less inclined to behave cruelly when they see their suffering victims than when they merely hear the distress they have caused them (Milgram, 1965b).

The conditions under which pain cues assume rewarding value still remain to be demonstrated. A gratuitous insult from a stranger in a laboratory may not create sufficient animosity for the victim to derive satisfaction from injurious retaliation. It is a quite different matter when an antagonist repeatedly tyrannizes others or wields his power in ways that make life miserable for them. In such instances, news of the misfortune, serious illness, or death of an oppressor is joyfully received by people who ordinarily respond more compassionately to the adversities befalling others.

Suffering of one's enemy is most apt to be rewarding when hurting him relieves discomfort or benefits aggressors in other ways. On the other hand, when aggressors suffer reprisals or self-contempt for harming others, signs of suffering function as negative reinforcers that deter injurious attacks. In other words, the alleviation of aversive treatment from an injured oppressor rather than his suffering may be the primary source of satisfaction. In studies showing that injury to the victim reduces aggression, pain expressions occur without the other extraneous rewards accompanying victory over antagonists.

The best evidence that pain cues themselves can become positively reinforcing comes from societies in which sexual partners bite, scratch, and lacerate each other during coital activities (Ford and Beach, 1951). Expressions of pain thus acquire rewarding value through repeated association with sexual gratification. As a result, erotic pleasure is derived from inflicting pain. Within our own society it is not unusual to find clinical cases who experience high sexual excitement from inflicting bodily pain on themselves or on others. From the standpoint of social learning theory, the victim's oppressiveness, the social sanctions for punitive behavior, and the consequences correlated with pain cues are more pertinent than transitory anger arousal in understanding the pleasurable value of injurious actions.

Experiments have been conducted with animals to determine whether opportunity to aggress can act as a reinforcer for instrumental behavior. Highly aggressive strains of animals will perform responses that produce an attackable target without much extraneous provocation (Hogan, 1967; Myer and White, 1965). In less aggressive species, however, opportunity to attack does not serve as a reinforcing event unless animals are subjected to aversive stimulation and have been trained for aggressive behavior (Azrin, Hutchinson, and McLaughlin, 1965; Cole and Parker, 1971; Dreyer and Church, 1970). It is under the combined influence of aversive arousal and high aggressiveness that fighting is most apt to be reinforcing (Legrand, 1970).

Although the preceding studies suggest that under certain circumstances fighting can be rewarding, this conclusion must be accepted with reservation for several reasons. Some of the experiments do not control for whether it is the escape provided by the activity in general or combat per se that serves as the reinforcer for disconcerted animals. Cole and Parker (1971) found that animals on whom unfavorable schedules of reward were imposed pecked a key to gain access to an attackable target but they also did so to get to an empty goalbox. If it were shown that aversively aroused animals do in fact work harder to secure an attackable target, it would be essential to include a condition in which they can see but not assault the target to assess whether combat or social contact is the source of reward.

Should the phenomenon survive the necessary experimental controls, its significance can be best assessed with paradigms that not only remove marked situational constraints, but allow alternative goal activities. Under natural conditions animals rarely go out of their way to secure victims; on the occasions when they do encounter opponents, they generally try to avoid fighting by resort to threat gestures. Given freedom of movement and a choice of flight, drinking, eating, courting, or fighting in response to aversive stimulation, fighting may very well turn out to be a weak reinforcer. When animals are treated aversively in a confined enclosure allowing only access to a restrained target, some blows will likely be exchanged. Aggression exhibited under these circumscribed conditions may, however, lack generalizability. Moreover, there are fundamental differences in the complexity of reinforcement control of human and animal behavior that make cross-species generalizations hazardous. Animal aggression is almost exclusively governed by direct physical consequences. If a human inflicts suffering on others, his actions not only produce immediate physical effects, but can arouse self-devaluative consequences and social reprobation, which serve as formidable negative reinforcers. Animals are not known to worry about what their cagemates might think of them, or to berate themselves for their cruelty. To the extent that inflicting suffering boosts self-pride and public acclaim, the self-rewarding effects of aggression will not be revealed by animal experimentation.

Alleviation of Aversive Treatment

People are frequently subjected to distressing treatment from which they seek relief. Forceful action that is not unduly hazardous is the most direct and quickest means of alleviating adverse conditions, if only temporarily. Pain reduction has been shown to be a powerful reinforcer of behavior. Indeed, many of the activities in which people engage are sustained by their functional value in eliminating various irritants and discomforts. Some aggressive behavior is undoubtedly reinforced by its effectiveness in removing the source of painful experiences.

Because of its aversive properties, aggression, if skillfully executed, can both secure rewards and remove painful stimuli. Evidence for this dual reinforcement process is provided by Patterson and his associates (Patterson, Cobb, and Ray, 1972; Patterson, Littman, and Bricker, 1967). In these field studies children's interactions are observed for extended periods in natural settings. The incidence of aggressive acts is recorded and their immediate consequences are classified as punishing, rewarding, or having no appreciable effect.

Patterson reports that aggressors are most likely to assault compliant peers. When attacked, these children cry, give up desired objects, or withdraw. If the victim does not immediately acquiesce, the aggressor intensifies his attack until the victim submits. Approximately 80 percent of the aggressors' assaultive actions produce rewarding consequences for them. The victims' submissiveness thus both invites and reinforces the aggressors' actions. This surprisingly high level of positive reinforcement of physical aggression by nursery school children remained stable over the nine-month period sampled by the observations.

Older children and adults are not always accommodating to the desires of aggressors. Assaults often elicit counterattacks. Observational studies of parent-child relationships (Patterson, Cobb, and Ray, 1972; Patterson and Reid, 1970), in fact, disclose a pattern of mutual coercion rather than quick acquiescence. These findings have led Patterson to conceptualize aggression as a form of coercive behavior that is primarily reinforced by reduction of aversive stimulation. In reciprocal fighting, for example, the victim attempts to terminate painful blows by defensive attacks of his own; the recipient, in turn, strikes back even more forcefully to escape the pain caused by his opponent's blows. Efforts at coercive control escalate in intensity until one of the combatants yields or is injured.

After people have begun to exchange blows, aggressive actions may be reinforced to some extent by their capacity to cushion or to reduce attacks. Immediate pain reduction, however, does not explain what initiates an aggressive course of behavior, or why combatants continue to suffer increasingly more painful beatings when any number of non-aggressive responses provide more effective means of escape. Explanation of aggression in terms of instant pain reduction is somewhat reminiscent of the view that people inflict injury on themselves because it feels so good when they stop.

In their reinforcement analysis of aggression Patterson, Cobb, and Ray (1972) discount the value of laboratory studies demonstrating that aggressive responses are increased by social and material rewards on the grounds that, in their field studies, aggression was seldom socially reinforced by peers or by adults. If this is the case, then the generality of the observational studies rather than the value of controlled experiments should be questioned. It is probably true that three- and four-year-olds rarely confer status rewards or commend their playmates for grabbing a prized toy and shoving other youngsters. Nor are onlooking wives likely to shower their husbands with praise for beating their children into submission. Other field studies, sampling a broader range of situations, show that parents often do praise their children for aggressing toward others outside the home; adolescents and adults win admiration and respect by demonstrated toughness; and in certain subcultures members achieve status through aggressive exploits.

In the social learning analysis, defensive aggression is sustained to a greater extent by anticipated consequences than by its instantaneous effects. People will endure painful treatment on expectation that their aggressive efforts will eventually succeed. In many instances, of course, performances are based on faulty assessment of probable consequences. Aggressive actions may also be partly sustained in the face of hurtful counterattack by anticipated costs of timidity. In aggression-oriented circles, failure to fight back can arouse fear of future victimization and humiliation. Moreover, cowardice, unless convincingly self-justified, can arouse anticipatory loss of self-esteem, especially when attacks are unjust and degrading. A physical pummeling may therefore be far less distressing than social derision or self-contempt. In other words, humans do not behave like unthinking servomechanisms directed solely by immediate response feedback. Rather, their cognitive capacity to represent future consequences enables them to regulate their actions by outcomes extended forward in time. Under aversive conditions of life, people will persist, at least for a time, in aggressive behavior that produces immediate pain but prospective relief from misery.

The manner in which aggressive behavior is reinforced by its success in terminating aversive treatment from aggressors is shown by Patterson, Littman, and Bricker (1967). Passive children who were repeatedly victimized and whose counteraggression often proved effective in halting attacks not only increased defensive fighting, but eventually began to initiate attacks of their own. On the other hand, passive children who were seldom maltreated because they avoided others and those whose counteraggressive responses to victimization were unsuccessful remained submissive in their behavior.

VICARIOUS REINFORCEMENT

People repeatedly observe the actions of others and the occasions on which they are rewarded, ignored, or punished. Observed outcomes influence behavior in much the same way as directly experienced consequences (Bandura, 1971b; Kanfer, 1965). In general, observed rewards increase, and observed punishment decreases, the tendency to behave in similar or related ways. Vicarious reinforcement not only influences similar performances in observers, but can markedly alter how they respond to the actual consequences accompanying their actions. Seeing other people's outcomes determines the nature and effectiveness of direct reinforcement by providing a standard for judging whether the treatment one customarily receives is equitable, beneficent, or unfair. The same consequence may therefore be experienced as a reward or as a punishment depending upon whether comparable actions by others are treated more or less favorably.

In experiments studying the influence of vicarious reinforcement on aggression, individuals observe aggressive models whose actions are rewarded, punished, or unaccompanied by any evident consequences (Bandura, 1965a; Bandura, Ross, and Ross, 1963c). The amount of imitative and nonimitative aggression that observers later spontaneously perform in a test situation is recorded. Witnessing aggression punished usually produces less imitative aggression than seeing it obtain social and material success or go unnoticed. However, performance of aggressive responses that differ from those displayed by the model is not greatly affected by observed negative consequences. Like the effect of directly experienced punishment, the inhibitory impact of vicarious punishment is thus largely confined to the modeled activities prompting negative sanctions. As we shall see later, the legal system of deterrence rests heavily on the restraining function of exemplary punishment (Packer, 1968).

Observed rewards generally produce a greater increase in similar responding than if the exemplified actions have no evident effects. It is noteworthy that in the case of reprehensible behavior—such as unprovoked physical assaults or violation of prohibitions—seeing transgressions go without consequences heightens analogous actions in observers to the same degree as witnessing the modeled behavior rewarded (Bandura, 1965a; Thelen and Soltz, 1969; Walters, Parke, and Cane, 1965). To the extent that absence of anticipated punishment conveys permissiveness and allays fears, behavioral restraints are thereby reduced and aggressive actions are performed more readily.

Because of the variety and complexity of social influences, people are not always consistent in how they respond to aggressive behavior. Rosekrans and Hartup (1967) examined the effects of discrepant observed consequences on imitative aggression. Children who saw assaultive behavior consistently rewarded were most aggressive; those who saw it consistently punished displayed virtually no imitative behavior; while those who saw aggression sometimes rewarded and sometimes punished exhibited a moderate level of aggressiveness. It is the latter mixed pattern of reinforcement that predominates in everyday life.

In the preceding studies the aggressive model was punished either verbally or physically by someone else. There are times when people respond with self-approving or self-devaluative reactions to their own behavior. Numerous experiments, discussed at length elsewhere (Bandura, 1971b), demonstrate that witnessing punishment self-administered by models has inhibitory effects on observers, whereas seeing others respond self-approvingly to their unmerited achievements and transgressions facilitates similar behavior in observers. Porro (1968), for example, reports that, of children who saw a model respond with self-praise to her transgressions, 80 percent subsequently violated a similar prohibition. By contrast, only 20 percent of the children deviated when they had observed the same model react self-critically to her transgressive behavior. Although relevant data are lacking, there is every reason to expect that aggressors' self-evaluative reactions toward their own conduct may have similar effects on aggressive dispositions of observers, especially if they hold the models in high esteem.

Most people, especially those residing in middle-class neighborhoods, rarely observe physical violence in their daily experiences. The vast majority have never directly witnessed any murders or muggings, and few encounter physical fights or violent confrontations between antagonistic groups. Rather, they learn about violence principally from televised portrayals and, to a lesser extent, from newspaper accounts. These symbolic sources provide abundant opportunities to observe aggressive conduct and its likely consequences.

A number of content analyses have been conducted to determine how fictional violence is portrayed on television. Larsen, Gray, and Fortis (1968) found that socially approved goals were achieved by illegal or violent methods 47 percent of the time in programs designed for adult audiences and 56 percent of the time in children's programs. Halloran and Croll (1972) similarly report that violent means are presented as both acceptable and successful in the short term, though villainous instigators fare less well in final outcomes. Witnesses to violence are more likely to approve of such behavior or to join in the fray rather than to seek alternative solutions. Violence is not only shown to pay off, but is repeatedly used by good characters who often dispose of adversaries in a quick perfunctory way, as though killing a human being were a routine act devoid of any moral implications or tragic consequences. Aggression is most readily legitimized as acceptable conduct by having good triumph over evil through aggressive means. When violent virtue kills, which is often, the killers seldom suffer negative consequences for their acts. On the contrary, good aggressors emerge victorious 66 percent of the time when they initiate assaults and 84 percent of the time when they reciprocate them. The physical effects of beating others are underplayed as less bloody or messy than in real life. Aggressive life styles are thus portrayed as exceedingly prevalent, highly functional, and relatively clean.

There has been surprisingly little analysis of how the functions and consequences of actual aggression are reported in news and documentary programs. The handling of criminal violence poses few dilemmas because it rarely arouses conflicts in how such behavior should be judged. On the other hand, it is difficult to remain impartial in the coverage of social disturbances arising from power conflicts within the community or society at large. Depending on what is selected for presentation and the manner in which the chosen events are evaluated, the media can convey support for coercive force either in the service of social control or social change. These issues, and other aspects of the legitimation of forcible means, are discussed at length in the concluding chapter of this book.

Explanation of Vicarious Reinforcement

Social learning theory posits several different mechanisms by which witnessed rewards and punishments alter the actions, feelings, and thoughts of others (Bandura, 1971c). A vicarious reinforcement event may vary in a number of aspects, including the characteristics of the aggressors and those who respond to them, the type and intensity of consequences, their justification, the situations in which the outcomes occur, and the counteractions of aggressors. The mechanisms that are operative in any given instance will therefore depend upon the nature and combination of these various factors.

One explanation of vicarious reinforcement is in terms of the *informative function* of observed outcomes. Response consequences accruing to others convey information to observers about the types of actions that are likely to be approved or disapproved. Given knowledge about probable response consequences, people will generally do the things they have seen well received and avoid those that they have seen punished.

Assessment of probable consequences from observed experiences is affected by comparability of sanctions customarily applied to models and to observers. In any social group aggressive behavior may be permitted for some members but prohibited for others depending upon, among other things, the status and legitimized roles they occupy. When models and observers differ in characteristics that foster different reactions to their behavior, observed reinforcement may not produce the usual effects. Knowledge gained from witnessing the outcomes experienced by models would be particularly influential in instances where the observer believes that the model's contingencies apply to himself as well. It is highly unlikely, for example, that seeing physical aggression approved in a person occupying a socially sanctioned role, such as a policeman, would prompt much imitative aggressiveness in citizens, because actions that are commended in law enforcers may be prohibited for others. For similar reasons, people are reluctant to adopt the behavior of models who occupy divergent occupational or social positions.

The same behavior can produce markedly different consequences depending on where, when, and toward whom it is performed. What is permissible on a street corner may be censurable in a church. Hence, adaptive functioning requires not only response information, but also knowledge about what actions are appropriate in what setting. When individuals are rewarded for aggressing in a given situation but ignored or punished for exhibiting the same behavior in a different setting, observers learn to *differentiate environments* in which it is relatively safe to behave aggressively from those in which such actions are hazardous. In this way, seeing the outcomes experienced by others facilitates aggression in settings correlated with observed rewards, and decreases aggression in situations in which the likelihood of punishment is high. Aggressive actions are accordingly regulated and modified on the basis of the successes and mistakes of others in designated settings.

Observed reinforcement is not only informative, but can also have *incentive motivational effects.* Seeing others positively reinforced can serve as a motivator by arousing in observers expectations that they will be similarly rewarded for analogous performances. Given appropriate reinforcement systems, people can be as much inspired by observed social acclaim and tangible benefits to aggress as to excel in athletic, artistic, or academic pursuits. The more highly observers value the rewards accruing to successful aggressors, the more likely they are to be prompted to aggressive actions when opportunities arise. The frequency with which others achieve desired outcomes can affect how long observers will persist in the face of discouraging results. Observational incentives play an especially important role in social activism, for here the chances of quick success are poor, but protest behavior is partly sustained by the long-range attainments of groups that have persevered in their efforts. Historical as well as contemporary successes in social change can provide motivational support for reform activities.

Models generally exhibit emotional reactions while undergoing rewarding or punishing experiences. Observers are easily aroused by the emotional expressions of others. Vicariously elicited emotions can eventually become conditioned either to the modeled behavior itself or to situations that are regularly associated with the performers' distress. As a result of vicarious emotional learning, situations in which aggressors were punished, or similar aggressive performances, are likely to frighten and to inhibit observers. Fears and inhibitions can also be extinguished by having fearful observers watch others engaging in threatening activities without experiencing any adverse consequences (Bandura, 1971a). *Vicarious conditioning and extinction of fear* may therefore partially account for increases and decreases in aggressiveness that result from observing affective consequences accruing to aggressive models.

People see not only the consequences of another's behavior, but also how he responds to his treatment. There is some evidence, presented by Ditrichs, Simon, and Greene (1967), that modeled responsiveness to social influence affects how observers later react when they themselves are rewarded for displaying similar behavior. Children who observed models express progressively more hostility for social approval later increased their own output of hostile responses under positive reinforcement. However, when models appeared oppositional by reducing hostile responses that brought them praise, or reacted in random fashion as though they were uninfluenced, observers did not increase their expression of hostility even though they were praised whenever they did so. Thus, *susceptibility to direct reinforcement influences* can be increased by observed responsiveness and reduced by observed resistance.

In addition to the foregoing effects of vicarious reinforcement, social status can be conferred on aggressors by the manner in which their behavior is reinforced. Punishment tends to devalue the model and his behavior, whereas the same model assumes emulative qualities when his actions are praised and otherwise rewarded (Bandura, Ross, and Ross, 1963c; Hastorf, 1965). *Modification of model status,* in turn, influences the degree to which observers pattern their own actions after behavior exemplified by different models. There are conditions, of course, in which observed punitive treatment enhances rather than lowers the recipient's social status. Members of protest groups who risk punishment for upholding their basic rights and beliefs gain the admiration not only of their peers but of others as well, especially when attacks are directed at social practices that violate the professed values of the society. It is for this reason that authoritative agencies are usually careful not to discipline challengers in ways that might martyr them.

Observed reinforcements can alter the *valuation of reinforcing agents* as well as recipients. When societal agents misuse their power to reward and punish, they undermine the legitimacy of their authority and generate strong resentment. Under these conditions, seeing inequitable punishment, rather than prompting compliance, may free incensed observers from self-censure of their own actions and thus increase aggressive behavior. This is most likely to occur when retaliative aggression is self-justified as rectifying past grievances or preventing further maltreatment. Otherwise considerate people can thus be readily provoked by observed injustice to behave cruelly without remorse.

SELF-REINFORCEMENT

The discussion thus far has illustrated how people regulate their aggressive behavior on the basis of response consequences that they either observe or experience at first hand. A theory that attributed performance of aggression solely to the influence of external rewards and punishments would be incomplete because humans can, and do, regulate their own actions to some extent by self-produced consequences. People do things that give them self-satisfaction and a feeling of self-worth; conversely, they refrain from behaving in ways that result in self-criticism and other self-devaluative consequences.

Self-reinforcement functions are acquired in several different ways (Bandura, 1971c). People learn to respond evaluatively to their own behavior partly on the basis of how others have reacted to it. Parents and other socialization agents subscribe to certain norms of what constitute worthy or reprehensible performances. They are inclined to respond approvingly when a child meets moral standards, whereas they are quick to reprimand him whenever he deviates from the way he is expected to behave. As a result of such differential treatment, children eventually come to respond to their own actions with self-approval and self-criticism in accordance with the standards originally set by others.

Individuals not only prescribe self-evaluative standards for others, they also exemplify them in response to their own behavior. Modeling has been shown to be another influential means of transmitting systems of self-reinforcement (Bandura, 1971b). People tend to adopt standards of self-reinforcement displayed by exemplary models, they evaluate their behavior relative to those standards, and they serve as their own reinforcing agents. Because of self-reactive tendencies, aggressors must contend with themselves as well as with others when they behave in injurious ways.

Self-reward for Aggression

One can distinguish several ways in which self-imposed sanctions enter into the self-regulation of aggressive behavior. First, there are individuals who have adopted a self-reinforcement system in which aggressive actions are a source of personal pride. Such people readily engage in aggressive activities because they derive self-satisfaction from aggressing successfully. Lacking self-reprimands for hurtful conduct, they are deterred from cruel actions mainly by fear of counteraggression and its other punishing costs. In the comparative study discussed earlier (Bandura and Walters, 1959), assaultive delinquents often showed little or no self-censure for their injurious behavior, even when it took severe forms.

> I: Have there ever been times when you felt you've got to do something just for the hell of it?
> B: Yeah.
> I: What kind of things?
> B: Well, I feel like going out and getting drunk, and going and beating the shit out of some guy.
> I: How often have you done this?
> B: About five or six times.
> I: How do you feel about it afterwards?
> B: I feel good. I always pick a person bigger than me, so I can't think I was picking up some guy smaller. I don't care if he's that much bigger. He's always bigger than me. (Pp. 288–89)

In the above case, it is the size of the unwary victim, not the suffering inflicted on him, that serves as the major deterrent and determinant of self-respecting reactions to physical conquest. The absence of self-reproof for cruel treatment of others in these boys stemmed not so much from failure to internalize parental standards of conduct, but rather from the adoption of their parents' positive valuations of aggressiveness. The following interview excerpt illustrates this process.

> **I:** Are there things about yourself that you're proud of, and wouldn't want to change?
>
> **B:** Motorcycle riding.
>
> **I:** Is there anything else?
>
> **B:** Say, something like you're proud of? You probably won't understand, but stomping. I'm proud of it because, I don't know, all the guys I hang around with do that. Do you know what stomping is?
>
> **I:** No, I don't.
>
> **B:** Fighting with two feet without using your hands, see. I'm not trying to be conceited or anything, but I know I can use my feet better than all the guys I hang around with, so I wouldn't want to change that. Like my Dad, he said, "If you know how to fight with your feet, then it's in your hands, you've got it made," or something like that. "You never need be afraid of anybody." (Pp. 121–22)

Studies of subgroups in which aggression is regarded as emulative behavior similarly report a high incidence of self-reward for inhumane actions. In the Nazi regime, under which horrific massacres were politically sanctioned, commandants of extermination camps felt tremendous pride when they surpassed the kill rates of other crematoria (Andrus, 1969). Indeed, Eichmann confessed that death lists were his favorite reading before he went to sleep (Wechsberg, 1967). Gang delinquents have been known to compile scrapbooks of newspaper articles about their aggressive exploits, which they regard with pride (Short, 1968). Toch (1969) vividly documents how violent men often derive self-satisfaction and enhanced feelings of worth from physical conquest. The chronic assaulter, quoted below, describes the tremendous boost in self-esteem he experienced from administering a brutal beating to a fellow prisoner over a trivial incident during a card game.

> And he turned around again, and he said, you know, "I told you not to stand behind me." And he said, you know, "Fuck you man." And the dude got up and we were both on him, man. And we beat him to a pulp. Fixed him up bad, man. . . . So we just, once we got going we just wasted the dude. And that was that. Sent him down to the hospital. And after that I felt like a king, man. I felt like you know, "I'm the man. You're not going to mess with me." . . . I felt like everybody looking up to me. (Pp. 91–92)

The above illustrations depict idiosyncratic self-systems of morality in individuals and deviant subgroups. Inhumane self-reinforcement codes are sometimes fostered on a society-wide basis. In aggressive cultures where prestige is closely tied to fighting prowess, members take pride in cruel treatment of fellow human beings.

Self-punishment for Aggression

In the course of socialization most individuals adopt, through example and precept, negative sanctions against cruel actions. As a result, they are restrained from injurious aggression by anticipated self-criticism. There is no more devastating punishment than self-contempt.

Results of the study by Bandura and Walters (1959) reveal how anticipatory self-reproach for repudiated aggression serves as a motivating influence to keep behavior in line with adopted standards. Adolescents who were compassionate in their dealings with others responded with self-disapproval, remorse, and attempts at reparation even when their aggressive actions were minor in nature. Assaultive boys, on the other hand, experienced relatively few negative self-reactions over rather serious aggressive activities. Hicks (1971) provides a laboratory demonstration of a similar self-regulatory process in young children. The more reprehensible girls judged aggressive actions to be, the less likely they were to adopt them when they were later exemplified by a peer model.

Neutralization of Self-condemnation for Aggression

Rarely is aggression uniformly self-rewarded or self-punished without regard to the victim or the circumstances under which it is performed. Humane, moral people sometimes behave cruelly without undue upset; and callous, brutal assassins may experience guilt over hurting pets and persons of whom they are fond. Like other reactions, self-reinforcing responses come under discriminative control. This is especially evident when social pressures impel people to act counter to standards of conduct that would ordinarily make them feel ashamed and self-contemptuous. By engaging in self-deceptive machinations, they can behave inhumanely without self-condemnation. The different forms that self-absolving practices take are discussed in the sections that follow.

Slighting aggression by advantageous comparison. A practice that is widely employed is to slight one's aggressive actions by comparison with more hideous deeds. American executors of Asian warfare and their ardent supporters, for example, minimized the slaying of countless Indochinese as checking massive Communist enslavement. Given such a benevolent definition of destructive practices, aggressors remained unperturbed by the fact that the intended beneficiaries were exterminated at an alarming rate. Militant protesters, on the other hand, characterized their domestic violence as trifling, or even laudable by comparing it with the widespread carnage perpetrated by military forces in foreign lands. Justification of aggression by comparison to outrageous acts is one of the more effective methods for making violence acceptable because it redefines the behavior in positive terms rather than relying on disguises of purpose or personal responsibility.

Since warfare requires collective contribution, however remote it may appear from military operations, almost anyone can be singled out as a party to the national crime. Unfortunately, the targets, whether they be national, institutional, or individual, are often selected for attack more on the basis of vulnerability and minimum risk than on degree of culpability. In such conflicts, reciprocal aggression usually escalates, with each side lauding its own violence but condemning the violence performed by its adversaries.

Justification of aggression in terms of higher principles. A closely related form of self-vindication is to construe one's aggression in terms of higher values. Given sufficiently noble aims, almost any form of aggression can be justified as righteous. To take a historical example, many massacres were devotedly perpetrated by crusading Christians in the service of religious principles. Groups that resisted the control of the clergy and the ambitious nobles who surrounded them were stigmatized as witches and heretics by the Pope, who encouraged all true believers to assist in their extermination (Mackay, 1932). Similarly, in contemporary times violence is frequently espoused in the name of freedom, social justice, equality, and civil order.

That high moral principles do not alone curb injurious behavior is shown more specifically in studies relating level of moral reasoning to aggressive conduct. Individuals exhibiting the highest moral viewpoints are inclined to resist arbitrary demands to behave punitively, but they will aggress against people who violate their personal principles (Keniston, 1970). Throughout history many have suffered at the hands of self-righteous crusaders bent on stamping out what they considered evil. By the same token, social reformers are able to use coercive, and even violent, tactics to change inhumane practices by reducing self-deterrent reactions through moral conviction in their cause.

The self-devaluative consequences of cruel deeds are sometimes eased by posing social conflict as involving issues of property values against human values. Little self-appeasement is required to destroy property belonging to adversaries if the destructive actions are justified as aimed at stopping maltreatment of humans. If this form of redefinition is to remain effective, the aggressor must disregard the threat to human rights created by the destruction of a man's belongings.

Displacement of responsibility.   People can be led to behave in injurious ways provided that a legitimate authority is willing to assume responsibility for their actions. Participants in Milgram's (1963) experiments, who were deterred from punitive assaults by distress over the suffering they had inflicted, continued to escalate the shocks to hazardous levels despite their victims' agonizing cries after the experimenter had assured them he would be fully accountable for the consequences of their behavior. Responsibility for cruel deeds is not always assumed so explicitly because no one wants to be answerable for such acts. To minimize risks to themselves, superiors more often invite and condone reprehensible conduct by their subordinates in insidious ways that allow them to claim ignorance for what was happening in the event that disclosures arouse public condemnation. The intended purpose of sanctioned destructiveness is also disguised so that neither issuers nor perpetrators regard their actions as censurable. When outrageous practices are publicized, they are officially dismissed as only isolated events.

Exemption from self-devaluation for heinous deeds is most gruesomely revealed in socially sanctioned mass executions. Nazi prison commandants and their staffs felt little personal responsibility for their unprecedented inhumanities. They were only carrying out lawful orders. Guiltless obedience to horrific orders is most evident in military atrocities. When questioned about the massacre of the entire population of the South Vietnamese hamlet of My Lai, the American lieutenant in charge replied, without any remorse, "That was my order, sir—that was the order of the day, sir. They were all enemy, they were all to be destroyed" (*San Francisco Chronicle,* 1971b). In an effort to deter institutionally sanctioned atrocities, the Nuremberg Accords were established declaring that obedience to inhumane orders even from the highest authorities does not relieve subordinates of the responsibility for their actions. However, since victors are disinclined to try themselves as criminals, such decrees have limited deterrent value without an international judiciary system empowered to impose penalties on victors and losers alike.

Diffusion of responsibility.   Exemption from self-criticism can be achieved to some extent by obscuring and diffusing responsibility for aggressive practices. Collective aggression requires numerous task functions that must be supported by an organizational apparatus. Departmentalization of destructive activities works in several ways to reduce participants' sense of personal responsibility for their complicitous behavior. Development, production, and use of instruments of destruction require the services of a considerable number of people, each performing a fragmentary job that in itself may appear harmless. The fractional contribution can be easily isolated from the end product, especially when one exercises little personal judgment in carrying out a subfunction that is related to the terminal aggression through remote, complex links. When the violence inflicted on victims is horrifying, guiltless functionaries in the destructive enterprise are quick to condemn and to take vengeance on the individuals assigned the gruesome task of performing the aggressive actions.

Another bureaucratic practice for relieving self-condemnation for aggression is to rely on group decision-making, so that no single individual feels responsible for what is eventually done. Indeed, social organizations go to great lengths to devise sophisticated mechanisms for obscuring responsibility for decisions that affect others adversely. Nor are people likely to experience much self-punishment for injurious outcomes resulting from direct participation in collective violence. The destruction of life and property can always be attributed to the other members of the group. Through division of labor, division of decision-making, and collective action, people can be contributors to cruel practices and bloodshed without feeling personally responsible or self-contemptuous for their part in it.

Dehumanization of victims. A further means of protection against self-devaluation is to dehumanize the victim. People selected as targets are often divested of human qualities by being viewed not as individuals with sensitivities, feelings, and hopes, but as stereotyped objects bearing demeaning labels such as "gooks" or "niggers." If dispossessing victims of humanness does not fully eliminate self-reproof, it can be further reduced by attributing subhuman or degrading characteristics to them. Foes become "degenerates," "pigs," and other bestial creatures. After victims have been so devalued, they can be cruelly attacked without much risk of self-punishment.

Bernard, Ottenberg, and Redl (1965) enumerate many conditions of contemporary life that are conducive to dehumanizing behavior. Bureaucratization, technology, automation, urbanization, and high social mobility all lead people to relate to each other in anonymous, impersonal ways. Under conditions of overcrowding, people inevitably become aversive, obstructive objects. It is difficult to remain sensitive to human qualities in individuals who are shoving you, blocking your progress, grabbing things you want, and in other ways reducing your comfort and freedom of movement. In addition, social practices that divide people into in-group and out-group members produce human estrangement conducive to dehumanization. Strangers can be more easily cast as sub-human villains than can personal acquaintances.

Attribution of blame to victims. Attribution of blame to victims is still another expedient that can be used for self-assuaging purposes. In this process, aggressors see themselves as essentially persons of good-will who are forced into punitive actions by villainous opponents. Victims are condemned for bringing the suffering on themselves either by their character defects or by their witless and provocative behavior. Violent encounters involve a series of reciprocally escalative assaults in which victims are rarely faultless. Self-vindication can therefore be achieved by selecting from the chain of causes an instance of defensive aggression by opponents and interpreting it as the original incitement.

Observers of victimization can be affected in much the same way as the aggressors. Seeing victims suffer punitive treatment for which they are held partially responsible leads observers to devalue them (Lerner, 1971; Piliavin, Hardyck, and Vadum, 1967). The indignation aroused by ascribed culpability, in turn, provides moral support for even more brutal acts by aggressors. When bad practices are well entrenched, efforts on the part of concerned individuals to halt them by publicizing their destructive effects are more likely to arouse derogation than sympathy for the victims. To acknowledge the inhumanities arouses self-critical reactions if one does nothing about the situation. It is easier to reduce the discomfort by designating the victim as a bad person than to challenge bad practices that are an accepted part of the social order.

Justified maltreatment can have more devastating human consequences than acknowledged cruelty. When blame is convincingly ascribed, victims may eventually come to believe the degrading characterizations they hear about themselves (Hallie, 1971). Negative attribution by itself may not be too persuasive, but it is usually accompanied by maltreatment that produces self-confirming evidence of the victim's defects or badness. Vindicated inhumanity is thus more likely to instill self-contempt in victims than if it does not justify itself.

Graduated desensitization. The practices cited above will not instantaneously transform a compassionate individual into a brutal aggressor. Rather, the change is usually achieved through a gradual desensitization process in which the participants may not fully recognize the marked changes they have undergone. Initially, individuals are prompted to perform aggressive acts they can tolerate without excessive self-censure. After their discomfort and self-reproof are extinguished through repeated performance, the level of aggression is progressively increased until eventually gruesome deeds, originally regarded as abhorrent, can be performed without much distress. Andrus (1969) describes this extinction process succinctly in his study of mass executioners: "Tentatively at first, then callously, and finally quite easily, they performed these terrible massacres" (p. 204).

The repetitive drills of military training, as in bayonet practice and shooting simulated targets, are intended not only to routinize fighting skills, but to extinguish deterring self-reactions to such behavior. Previously reported studies showed how traumatized soldiers could be desensitized within a brief period by reexposing them to progressively more terrifying battle scenes. It is perhaps increasing desensitization to injury more than frustration that accounts for the rise over time in military atrocities and the growing public indifference to them.

There exist a number of factors—many of them social and symbolic—that serve as disinhibitory devices over and above those already cited. Targets are usually presented as distilled military abstractions. In the hygienic verbal labels used to describe military slaughter, people are "wasted" rather than put to death. The inhumanity of the enemy, which makes it easier to kill him, is bolstered by accounts of atrocities and orientation training on how to deal with torture techniques as a prisoner. Even considerate soldiers can eventually be driven to brutal acts to avenge the deaths of fighting companions. And the prayers of clergy convey the symbolic impression that the vested agents of institutional morality are backing the combat enterprise. Finally, medicolegal procedures are available for controlling information sources and removing "undesirables" who might act as contravening influences.

The research of Davitz (1952) and Wright (1942) has shown that the presence of cooperative and friendly bonds between people serves to inhibit aggression toward each other in the face of provocation from external sources. An individual cannot easily mistreat a friend without holding himself in low regard, given a sense of implicit trust and heightened awareness of the personal suffering caused by such actions. However, just as high moral principles can be used to support ruthless behavior, positive social bonds can heighten aggressiveness under certain conditions. Wright (1942) found that whereas thwarting increased cooperativeness and reduced discord in close friends, it had little effect on the social behavior of those with weaker bonds of friendship. But the mutual support of close fellowship also counteracted restraints against aggressing toward the person who thwarted them. Close friends were more abusive toward their antagonist than the less close friends, the difference being particularly marked in the expression of physical aggression. The latter group often resorted to physical assaults, whereas the aggression displayed by those with a weaker friendship never went beyond hostile remarks. Thus, while close acquaintance with potential targets may serve as an inhibitor of aggression, the mutual social reinforcement inherent in comradeship can be effectively used, as in times of national warfare or intergroup strife, to strengthen aggression against a common foe.

Minimization and selective forgetting of consequences. The foregoing discussion reviewed the various self-absolving devices that permit otherwise socialized people to behave violently toward others without suffering self-condemning consequences. Once they have aggressed, additional self-placating measures are available that operate principally through distortion of the effects produced by one's actions. When people are prompted to self-disapproved conduct under conditions in which they have some choice on whether or not to behave that way, they tend to minimize the painfulness of its consequences; on the other hand, when they are forced to act punitively contrary to their values, they magnify the severity of the effects (Brock and Buss, 1962). Moreover, after being compelled to perform aggression of which they disapprove, individuals recall prior information given them concerning potential benefits of the punishment, but they are less able to recall its harmful effects (Brock and Buss, 1964). Both minimization and selective forgetting of consequences would be expected to reduce distress over conduct that is incompatible with one's self-evaluative system.

Examples taken either from military atrocities or political violence convey the impression that sanctioning of human cruelty occurs only under extraordinary circumstances. Quite the contrary. It is a common practice supported by financial profit as well as by governmental coercion or political disaffection. Exploitation of human brutality by the television industry illustrates the authorization of aggression for commercial purposes. Testimony of media practitioners at congressional hearings and in private interviews document how familiar self-absolving devices are used in conjunction with organizational sanctions to produce a heavy volume of violent material.

In the earlier days of television, producers and writers were issued explicit instructions by network officials to inject violence into their programs in ways that contributed neither to characterization nor to plot. In one such exchange a producer with humanitarian concerns was reminded that his program was scheduled against "Wanted Dead or Alive," a series in which the "hotrod cowboy kills a man a minute" (U.S. Senate, 1963, p. 1964). Scenes of violence, he was told, were therefore required for competitive purposes. Scenes were rearranged to begin with violent teasers repeating the fatal actions contained in the body of the programs. Other producers reported how plot development is often sacrificed for redundant brutality. Concerned writers expressed their indignation at being instructed to devise more interesting ways to kill people and at finding violence added to their scripts without their knowledge.

Eventually the production of violence became an occupational norm that no longer required special orders. Like other salable commodities, its manufacture required efficient routinization. Writers and producers who find the artistic constraints and exploitation of violence objectionable are selectively eliminated; those who remain as regular contributors become socialized into the practices of the system to use violence in amounts and forms that will not provoke troublesome criticism.

When one must produce material containing dehumanizing ingredients for money, losses in self-respect are reduced in many ways, as revealed in the remarks of media practitioners (Baldwin and Lewis, 1972). Diffusion of the production process reduces a sense of personal responsibility for the final product. Rewrite men alter writers' scripts; directors fill in the details of the scenarios; and editors take a part in how filmed events are depicted by what they select from the lengthy footage. If the original writers are offended by alterations of their scripts, they can use their registered pseudonyms and thereby avoid any personal embarrassment.

Producers often excuse commercialization of violence by contrasting it with outrageous inhumanities, as though one form of human cruelty absolves another. Why pick on television, the scapegoat disclaimer goes, when the government is slaughtering foreigners and the tobacco industry is disabling the natives ("To examine violence where the end result is a dead body on television glosses over the point. This evades the culpability of a whole society which permits wars" p. 343). Another variant in the justification process is to sanctify brutalizing excesses on television by pointing to revered masterpieces containing some violent episodes. The fact that people occasionally aggress in folk tales and in the Bible presumably exonerates the saturated overkill delivered daily to every household in the country year after year. Sometimes a high moral purpose is assigned to the taking of human life in the likeness of a national character-building service: "The government wants kids to think that there are values worth fighting for, and that's basically what the leads on our show are doing. . . . If people who break the society's code resist the law, we have to use violence to suppress them. In doing so we are in the mainstream of American morality" (p. 300). Modeling violent solutions to problems not only builds character and establishes the measure of man; it is also purported to serve a public therapeutic function by draining accumulated aggressive drives in viewers.

The term *violence* rarely appears in the vocabularies of media personnel. Rather, sanitized labels such as "action" and "adventure" are used in its place. Virtually all producers disclaim using gratuitous violence by attributing evident excesses to the characters they create. Ruthless individuals or even peaceful folks confronted with mortal jeopardy demand acts of violence. One of the more candid scriptwriters discounted the asserted dramatic requirement for violence as analogous to saying, "I never put cotton in a wagon that's not prepared for cotton—but I never use anything but a cotton wagon" (p. 311). In addition to sanitizing the product, media personnel tend to divest viewers of human sensitivities or invest them with base qualities that justify serving them gory offerings: "Man's mind is connected to his stomach, his groin, and his fists. It doesn't float five feet above his body. Violence, therefore, cannot be eradicated" (p. 300). . . . "Not as much action as some, but sufficient to keep the average bloodthirsty viewer fairly happy" (U.S. Senate, 1963, p. 2329).

Producers of products that may have some adverse consequences can avoid discomforting self-reactions by ignoring evidence about effects. It is therefore not surprising that most are unaware of the results of existing research, that they do not seem especially eager to find them, and that they can think of many reasons why the social effects of television can never be clearly demonstrated. As is true of any profit-oriented enterprise, some of the program manufacturers are not exactly plagued by bothersome standards of social morality: "Filmmaking for television is a business of merchandising and profit making. We are manufacturing a product and we want to attract the largest possible audience, short of prostitution" (p. 313).

The distributors and financial patrons of televised violence attribute the prevalence of such contents to the aggressive nature of man. Television is simply responding to the desires of its viewers, according to network officials. The fact that action programs attract mass audiences proves that people find violence inherently rewarding. This questionable diagnosis is usually accompanied by the democracy argument. Since there is such a substantial consumer demand for violence, the television industry has almost a mandate to serve the public what it wants. Social critics, accepting this causal analysis as valid, nevertheless contend that a public resource should be used for human betterment, not to reinforce destructive tendencies in the pursuit of profit.

These debates overlook that fact that the prevalence of action formats demonstrates neither that violence is the source of fascination, nor that violent offerings are necessarily the most popular. Suspense, excitement, conflict, and fast pace of action, all prominent features of such programs, attract and hold attention. The success of Westerns and crime series that rarely show people assaulting each other suggest that the nonviolent components of the characterizations are the more important sources of attraction. For example, in the dramatization of Wyatt Earp, which attracted a mass audience, this agent of the law shot only one man during the entire six years the program was on the air, and this single episode represented an actual event from history (U.S. Senate, 1963).

It is probably more accurate to say that people are fascinated with conflict and suspense rather than with brutality per se. For this reason, detective stories would hold little interest for readers or viewers if the outcomes of the plots were revealed to them in advance, even though the violent episodes remained unchanged. Nor are many sport fans willing to sit through complete reruns of football games knowing the outcomes of the contests. For years professional football, which is claimed to attract spectators by appealing to their inherent aggressiveness, in fact aroused little public interest until it was commercially promoted. If artificial sources of excitement created by league rankings, national ratings, and intersectional bowl games were discontinued attendance would drop, however much contestants shove each other around. On the other hand, spectators frequent competitive games such as baseball that involve little physical injury but sufficient uncertainty of outcome to hold their interest. Whatever the athletic activities might be, teams that rank low in the publicized standings typically draw small crowds regardless of their level of aggressivity.

The myth that program content is determined by the preferences of the viewing majority is widely accepted. Television preferences reflect what viewers are given to choose from. The offerings that are broadcast are determined by commercial considerations as well as popularity ratings, which do not always match. Programs that capture large audiences are discontinued if the people they attract do not fit the age (18–49) or income categories that advertisers wish to influence. Thus, popular programs that deliver the wrong kinds of viewers from a commercial standpoint are retired for unfavorable "demographics" despite their wide acceptance because they fetch low advertising rates (Brown, 1971). Since people who lack purchasing power hold little interest for advertisers, disadvantaged minorities tend to be underrepresented in survey samples of television preferences.

Within each broadcast hour approximately ten minutes are sold for commercial breaks. Popular shows that are expensive to produce will not make much of a profit even at high advertising rates. Program production cost per thousand viewers therefore strongly influences what gets televised. Action formats are prevalent because they are relatively cheap to produce. With a couple of horses, a makeshift saloon, a superhero, a transient evil-doer, and the open range a producer can grind out endless episodes at a price that yields higher profits than more popular programs incurring greater production costs. Many shows high in violent content are retained because they are financially attractive to the industry even though they draw smaller audiences than programs that do not feature violent action. We might note here in passing that television offerings, though generally accepted, fail to evoke much involvement or enthusiasm (LoSciuto, 1972). A good predictor of what viewers will watch is whatever appears on the same channel next, hardly the picture of a motivated search for violence.

Those who create the programs acknowledge quite candidly that conflict is essential for engrossing drama and physical violence is the easiest and intellectually nondemanding way of depicting it. As one producer put it: In dramatizing conflict on television, man against nature is too expensive, man against God is too intellectual, man against himself is too psychological and leaves too little opportunity for action, so man against man is what one usually ends up with (Baldwin and Lewis, 1972). Given severe time constraints, physical violence is a handy device for creating a conflict and a quick and decisive way of resolving it. Gifted writers and producers who could portray conflict more imaginatively are understandably reluctant to devote their talents to grinding our formula shows at costs that will yield high financial returns to stockholders.

When violence is routinely used as a substitute for creative plot development, it tends to increase if left unchecked. Producers resort to incremental violence to capture the attention of viewers who have grown accustomed to deadly combat: "Last week you killed three men; what are you going to do this week? So producers began to lean more heavily on the violence" (Baldwin and Lewis, 1972, pp. 321–22). It also forces them to create new ways of killing people to inject variety into overused formulas: "I wish we could come up with a different device than running the man down with the car as we have done this now in three different shows. I like the idea of the sadism, but I hope we can come up with another approach for it" (U.S. Senate, 1963, pp. 2302–32).

The answer to the abundance of televised violence perhaps lies more in production costs and in constraints imposed by time schedules, voluminous output, and limited talent pool than in viewers' cravings. The justifications of media violence in terms of social demand also misrepresents a two-way influence process as a one-way cause and effect relationship. Television creates as well as caters to preferences. In a major program of research Zajonc (1968), among others, presents several lines of evidence that mere repeated exposure to material increases liking for it. The abundant evidence that familiarity produces liking is confirmed by Himmelweit, Oppenheim, and Vince (1958) with regard to television offerings. Programs that initially held little interest for children and that they would not choose to watch if an alternative were available became more attractive with repeated viewing.

There exist many societal practices that have widespread injurious consequences, but because they are financially profitable or politically expedient, are institutionally sanctioned and routinely performed by decent people under self-exonerating disguises. Institutionalized discrimination takes a heavy toll of victims. A variety of industries, each with its public-spirited justifications, contribute to environmental destruction that causes harmful effects on a large scale.

Given the existence of so many self-absolving devices, a society cannot rely entirely on individuals, however noble their convictions, to safeguard against destructiveness. Just as aggression is not rooted in the individual, neither does its control reside solely there. Humaneness requires, in addition to benevolent codes of self-reinforcement, social reinforcement systems that continuously uphold compassionate behavior and discourage cruelty. Societies must create more effective organizational safeguards that function as restraining influences in the use of institutional power for exploitive or destructive ends.

PUNISHMENT CONTROL OF AGGRESSION

The earlier discussion has shown that aggressive actions persist because they are functional in producing rewarding effects, however lean or peculiar these outcomes might be in any given instance. Injurious forms of aggression can therefore be most effectively eliminated by removing the social conditions that instigate them and the positive reinforcements that maintain them. Unfortunately, most of the people who suffer the results of violence rarely exercise much direct control over the circumstances that continue to generate it. Ghetto victims, for example, lack the means with which to remove influences that breed violence. Similarly, university faculty, even if they could achieve high consensus on foreign policy, cannot by themselves promptly turn off military activities that arouse violent protests on campuses. People most often resort to punishment solutions when aggressive behavior is disturbing to them and the conditions fostering it are beyond their power to modify.

When aggression is either highly functional or personally valued, threatened consequences serve as its main deterrents. Behavior that produces aversive effects is generally performed less frequently, if not discarded altogether. There are two principal ways in which negative sanctions inhibit forbidden actions. Repeated punishment for aggressing toward certain persons, places, or things endows them with fear-arousing value. As a result, inclinations to aggress toward these threats evokes fear, which motivates inhibitory controls.

Man's cognitive capacities enable him to regulate his behavior to some extent without requiring fear arousal. Punishments that are either observed or experienced directly convey information about when certain forms of aggression are safe and when they are hazardous. Aggressive actions are thus partly regulated on the basis of anticipated consequences. Being under cognitive and situational control, aggression inhibition arising from external threats varies in its durability and in how widely it generalizes beyond the prohibitive situation.

The effectiveness of punishment in controlling behavior is determined by a number of factors (Bandura, 1969a; Campbell and Church, 1969). Of special importance is the level of reward achieved through aggressive conduct and the availability of alternative means of securing desired goals. The likelihood that aggression will be punished, the nature, severity, and duration of the aversive consequences, and the time elapsing between aggressive actions and negative outcomes also determine the suppressive power of punishment. Additionally, the level of instigation to aggression and the characteristics of the prohibitive agents influence how aggressors will respond to being punished. By considering these different influences one can predict, with some accuracy, what the effects of punishing aggression are likely to be in given circumstances.

Elimination of Aggression
Through Punishment

Under conditions in which alternative means are made available for people to get what they want, aggressive modes of behavior that carry a high risk of punishment are rapidly discarded. Findings reviewed in the concluding chapter demonstrate that selective reward of prosocial solutions combined with penalties for aggressive activities achieves enduring reductions in aggression without any adverse effects.

Societies rely heavily upon deterrent threats in their efforts to curtail behavior designated as criminal. Punishments are widely administered by enforcement agencies on the grounds that they discourage transgressors from committing future crimes and deter others should they be tempted by the sway of circumstances to engage in criminal conduct. Obviously if punishments for transgressive behavior were severe and certain, they would have strong deterrent effects. In reality, only about half of the criminal offenses that have been committed are ever reported by the victims (Ennis, 1967), and the chance of apprehension may be relatively low for the crimes that come to the attention of police. The deterrent potential of legal sanctions will vary depending on the risk of the threatened consequences.

The restraining effects of legal sanctions are difficult to evaluate because fluctuations in baseline crime rates arising from many contributory factors obscure the influence of threatened penalties. When severe punishments are instituted during periods of widespread infractions, as is often the case, predictable declines in contagious transgressions may be erroneously credited to the stricter control measures. Sometimes drops in offenses following the institution of more severe penalties turn out to be no greater than past fluctuations when compared over an extended time series (Campbell, 1969). Nor do high crime and recidivism rates necessarily refute the deterrent value of punishment, because the forbidden behavior might be much higher without the legal prohibitions. In neither case does one know what the crime rates would be if the threatened consequences were absent. Only by instituting and removing the penalties several times, or by comparisons with nonregulated situations, can the effects of legal sanctions be estimated. Zimring (1971) argues convincingly that legal and enforcement agencies bear some responsibility for measuring what effects their punishment prescriptions are having on people. When officials are granted punishment powers without being required to evaluate the results of their practices, aversive measures are more likely to be used vindictively than in ways that contribute to rehabilitative or preventive purposes.

Legal threats probably have greatest deterrent force for the more advantaged segments of the population. Individuals who have developed legitimate options that are reasonably rewarding are less attracted to criminal alternatives. They not only face weaker inducement to illegal conduct, but the punishment costs are more severe for them. After people have achieved a financial and reputational stake in their community, they fear the ruinous consequences of stigmatization and loss of standing as well as the hardships of imprisonment. Members of delinquent subcultures, or those relegated to an impoverished existence, do not risk status losses for engaging in criminal activities. In addition, high-status law-abiders are more likely to have adopted the moral standards of the larger society so that they are deterred from criminal conduct by self-reprobation, quite apart from the fear of external punishment. Finally, the deterrent efficacy of legal threats is weakened in high delinquency areas where residents see offenses committed repeatedly without detection. The chances of escaping punishment look pretty good.

The fact that threatened penalties work best for those who least need them does not mean that they do not serve a restraining function. Unlawful behavior and breaches of social prohibitions do occur among supposedly law-abiding citizens. Transgression rates would undoubtedly rise if negative sanctions were not in effect. However, control measures that punish forbidden conduct but offer no positive alternatives have serious limitations.

Selective inhibition and refinement of aggression through punishment. Aggression control through punishment becomes more problematic when aggressive actions are socially or tangibly rewarded, while alternate means of securing desired outcomes are either unavailable, less effective in producing results, or not within the capabilities of the aggressor. Here punishment must be applied in considerable force to outweigh the benefits of aggression. But even then it achieves, at best, only temporary partial control, with the risk of aggravating the problem.

When aggressive behavior that brings some rewards is consistently and severely punished, it is inhibited in the threatening situation. Functional aggression, however, tends to reappear after the punishment has been discontinued, and is readily performed in settings in which the chance of punishment is low (Bandura, 1960; Bandura and Walters, 1959). The inhibitory power of punishment is affected not only by prevailing conditions of reinforcement but also by those associated with aggressive behavior in the past. Deur and Parke (1970) report that children who had been consistently rewarded for hitting responses later reduced such behavior more when it was either ignored or consistently punished than did children whose aggression had previously been treated inconsistently by being rewarded and punished or rewarded and ignored. Comparison of the long-term effects of the two mixed patterns of reinforcements revealed that persistence of aggressive responding under unfavorable conditions of reinforcement was due mainly to the prior history of reward. Children who had come to expect that their aggressive behavior would always be rewarded were quick to abandon such actions when they no longer paid off. By contrast, children who learned that the benefits of aggression are obtained at the risk of some negative outcomes were not easily discouraged by nonreward or censure.

Evidence that punishment does not always reduce aggressive behavior has led some writers to characterize repetitive offenders as "psychopaths" who lack the capacity to learn from experience. This apparent learning deficiency might be readily refuted if information were available concerning the outcomes experienced for every transgression. The occasions on which antisocial aggression is punished are well publicized, but its successes remain unknown. Antisocial aggression is most likely to persist when the rewards it produces outweigh the inhibitory effects of occasional punishment.

Given some level of reward for aggression, the behavior of a person who is primarily deterred by fear is largely governed by his estimation of the probability of being caught and of the severity of the punishment that may follow. Most repetitive delinquents therefore do not commit offenses that bring extreme penalties, nor do they ordinarily carry out their antisocial acts under circumstances in which the chance of being apprehended is high. The accuracy with which probable consequences are assessed depends to a large extent on the aggressor's ability to profit from experience and to evaluate the reality circumstances at any given moment. Habitual offenders may more readily perform hazardous actions because they have altered their techniques on the basis of prior failures, thus gaining new confidence that they can get what they want with reduced risk of punishment. They often err by overestimating their chances of success (Claster, 1967). Failures normally occur because of unforeseen events that the aggressor could not have easily predicted even after careful assessment of the situation. Given limited options, the human mind is sufficiently facile to benefit from the successful examples of history but to discount its negative lessons.

Persons who have few alternatives that bring some payoffs will be slow to abandon them even though the behavior results in occasional adverse consequences. Under these conditions, punishment is likely to lead offenders either to adopt safer forms of antisocial aggression or to change their methods to avoid punishment on future occasions. An excellent example of how punishment results in refining rather than eliminating antisocial behavior that has functional value is provided in the autobiography of a talented habitual offender.

> My prison surroundings have been completely a life apart, something so far away that at times it was my real circumstances that seemed so fantastic. In between I went over jobs which I had pulled off and mentally surveyed them to see how they could be improved upon. Then I went over my mistakes again, and learned how they had occurred and let me down. So you see there was always plenty for me to do when I lay on the board with no occupation but thinking. And plan future jobs. Oh yes, if a survey could be taken it would be proved that most of the big criminal jobs, and thousands of small ones, are planned in gaol. Planned to the last detail because there is not sufficient alternative interest to occupy prisoners' minds. (Hill, 1955, p. 39)

Had this individual as ingeniously pursued a more socially acceptable vocation, he would undoubtedly have been admired for his flexibility and his ability to profit from failure experiences.

Modeling of aggressive tactics through punishment. Punishment is not only precarious as an external inhibitor of intermittently rewarded aggression, but its frequent use can inadvertently promote aggressive modes of behavior. In exercising punitive control, prohibitive agents model aggressive styles of behavior not unlike those they wish to discourage in others. Recipients may, on later occasions, adopt similar aggressive solutions in coping with the problems confronting them. Consistent with modeling theory, Hoffman (1960) reports that mothers who forced compliance through coercive means had children who likewise resorted to aggressive tactics in controlling the behavior of their peers. Numerous field studies have shown that parents of aggressive boys rely heavily on punitive methods of control, whereas parents of nonaggressive children favor nonpunitive verbal forms of influence (Bandura, 1960; Bandura and Walters, 1959; Glueck and Glueck, 1950). Although the direction of causal relationships cannot be unequivocally established from correlational data, it is clear from controlled studies that aggressive modeling breeds aggression.

Punitive treatment, in addition to furnishing aggressive examples of behavior, may reduce restraints over aggression in observers. Disinhibitory effects are especially apt to occur when aggressors in positions of influence convincingly justify their punitive actions. If empowered authorities can get what they want by aggressive means, the reasoning goes, why should such behavior not be acceptable for others in the pursuit of their own goals. Through modeling influences, institutionally sanctioned aggression, when misused in the service of behavior control, can thus promote the learning and legitimation of aggressive tactics. Moreover, authorities who exploit their coercive power to suppress warranted grievances create, by their actions, a cynical contempt for official condemnations of violence.

Capital punishment represents societal modeling of violence in the most brutal form, ostensibly for the purpose of homicide control. The moral and legal justifications offered for putting to death a prisoner against whom society is already protected by his imprisonment are essentially disguises for vengeance. Studies comparing murder rates in different areas that vary in their use of capital punishment and in the same area before and after the death penalty was abolished provide no evidence that presence of the death penalty reduces homicide rates (Bedau, 1967). It would appear that legal executions achieve mainly a lessened regard for human life.

In States that impose the death penalty only a fraction of those who have committed capital crimes are in fact executed. Discretionary power is exercised throughout the criminal process by prosecutors, judges and juries. As a result, the poor and disfavored minorities are more likely to be sentenced to death than the more advantaged for similar crimes. Execution rates of those committed to death row show the operation of selective influences in the commutation of death sentences (Johnson,

1957; Wolfgang, Kelly and Nolde, 1962). Thus, legal executions not only indicate how society regards human life but exposes the inequities in the administration of its system of justice.

Escalation of aggression through punishment. There are certain conditions under which neither threatened nor actual punishment deters people from behaving aggressively, at least in the short run. As might be expected, low aggressors inhibit hurtful actions when recipients can retaliate. In contrast, high aggressors do not temper their punitiveness under threat of counterattack (Edwards, 1967). In fact, the more self-assertive the opponent, the more aggressively they are inclined to treat him (Peterson, 1971). The different consequences anticipated by high and low aggressors is most likely the operative factor producing the diverse effects of threatened reprisal. Individuals who recurrently engage in aggressive behavior have experienced some success in controlling people through force. Strong attacks are designed to show potential challengers that the aggressor is a formidable person whose wishes should be heeded. Counterattacks merely evoke more forceful demonstration of power to gain eventual acquiescence. Given other options, people who have had little success in wielding coercive power are easily dissuaded from escalating the aggressive interchange by expectations of defeat.

The use of punishment as a control technique carries greater risks when applied to group aggression. Seeing others engage in aggressive conduct weakens the inhibitory effects of threatened retaliation (Baron, 1971b). Protest tactics, furthermore, have some legitimacy as an instrument of social change. After nonviolent means have proved ineffective, severe punishment of militant actions used to achieve laudable goals is likely to escalate collective aggression. These particular conditions are especially salient in campus protests and violence. Searle (1968) and Spiegel (1970) describe a common sequence of reciprocal escalation of aggression that was repeated with notable regularity on many college campuses, both in the United States and abroad. In the initial stage, a small group of students whose grievances have been slighted confronts a university administration with a set of demands relating to a fundamental issue (for example, war, free speech, racism, institutional policies) with which most nonprotesters sympathize, even though they are not moved to action. The demands are presented in a coercive style, often accompanied by provocative actions or by violations of campus rules that invite punishment.

Authorities refuse to give in under such pressure for a variety of reasons. Acquiescence to blatant or unlawful force will lose them the respect and support of other factions without whose backing they can no longer function effectively. They also fear that, however laudable the goals, granting demands under duress rewards violent tactics so that physical force will become a favored strategy rather than a method of last resort. Some of the ultimatums cannot be met within the specified time limits because decision-making procedures are unwieldly and universities may lack either the resources or the power to modify the causes of certain grievances. Partial rejection rather than full compliance is the predictable outcome. Protesters, in turn, become more resistant to negotiation because not only issues but their reputations in the face of perfunctory or unyielding response are now at stake. The net result is that some of the protesters, usually the most vocal leaders, are suspended or otherwise disciplined for campus rule violations.

Punitive measures escalate the level of aggression to the second stage. The original issue is now transformed so that the malevolence of the institution itself becomes the primary issue. Punishing individuals for protesting against evil practices, regardless of whether the protest is in good faith or to generate student revolt, mobilizes sympathizers to massive action against the university. The confrontation creates a strong sense of community in which provocative rhetoric is selectively rewarded, while concerns voiced over the morality of violence are silenced through justification or disregard. Restraints over aggressive actions are weakened by indicting the university for, among other things, scientific corruption, contributing knowledge and technology to pernicious societal practices, and self-serving ethical bias that favors existing systems causing social ills. Faculty members with similar sentiments give ideological and social sanction to forceful action. Additional directives are issued to the university to restructure its activities and decision-making; amnesty is demanded for individuals charged with disruptive actions. When these nonnegotiable demands are refused, as is invariably the case, protesters seize buildings, destroy facilities, or embark on other large-scale disruptions of university functions. Strong political and public pressure is then brought to bear on beleaguered administrators to put a halt to the unlawful behavior.

Lacking adequate internal mechanisms for dealing with major confrontations, university authorities call police onto campus, which elevates the conflict to the third, and final, stage. The sight of mass arrests, often carried out in a brutal manner, "radicalizes" many of those who had not publicly committed themselves one way or another, whereupon they too join the fray. The university is essentially shut down amid open hostilities between opposing factions, vigorous petitioning, emergency faculty meetings, and outpouring of grievances against the university. Few college presidents survive a major campus uprising without being seriously discredited.

After the predictable pattern became apparent, activists began to select tactics calculated to provoke authorities to punitive actions. Universities, in turn, adopted new countermeasures, principally in the form of quasi-judicial procedures and court injunctions. Administrators controlled disruptive activities without provoking more serious forms of aggression by reliance on legal deterrents rather than on personally administered punishments.

Aggression directed at social injustices in the society at large is frequently escalated and spread by the punitive actions of those in positions of authority. Violent response to extralegal protest provides manifest demonstrations of how coercive power can be misused by the social system itself. Protection of dissenters from encroachment of their civil rights by agents of control and the integrity of authoritative agencies become matters of concern in such struggles.

Disinhibition of Aggression by
Reducing the Risk of Punishment

When individuals are deterred from behaving aggressively mainly by fear of negative consequences, conditions that reduce anticipated risk of punishment weaken restraints over aggressive responding. This process, designated as disinhibition in social learning theory, has also been studied to some extent by social psychologists as "deindividuation" (Festinger, Pepitone, and Newcomb, 1952; Zimbardo, 1969). Although both concepts refer to a similar process, they differ in that disinhibition encompasses a wide range of determinants, whereas deindividuation is largely confined to restraint reduction arising from loss of individuality by immersion in a group.

Disinhibitory conditions may take many forms, some of which are graphically described by Zimbardo (1969). By decreasing fear of detection and punishment, anonymity is highly conducive to transgressive behavior. It is not uncommon for otherwise law-abiding people to perform socially prohibited activities without too much resistance when there is little chance they can be identified. Restraints over aggression are further weakened by the actions of a group. Some of the contagious effects are doubtless attributable to the modeling influence of seeing others engage in antisocial behavior without experiencing any adverse consequences. Moreover, in a joint performance no one feels personally responsible for the effects of the collective action. There is an additional safety in numbers. Since huge crowds cannot be easily punished, even a feeling of shared responsibility for cruel deeds does not have much inhibitory power. This is especially evident in censurable societal practices, when individuals facilely admit guilt for their contributions by their support or inaction, knowing full well that such confessions serve mainly to placate critics. Confessions of collective guilt would decrease markedly if there were any chance of being punished for acknowledged complicity. Indeed, structuring the problem as a societal act implicating everyone safeguards against accepting personal responsibility for one's own conduct.

Zimbardo (1969) examined the combined effects of anonymity and distributed responsibility on aggressive behavior. Female college students administered painful shocks to a victim in groups of four, in situations in which all members need not have acted punitively to fulfill the demands of the experiment. Participants who were never recognized by name and wore hoods over their heads shocked other girls much longer than those who were clearly identified by name tags and had no disguises. Anonymity heightened punitiveness toward charitable and obnoxious victims alike.

Results of subsequent experiments suggest that probable consequences rather than concealment per se is the critical disinhibitory factor. Belgian soldiers aggressing in groups and female students performing alone were significantly *less* punitive when they wore hooded disguises than when they were publicly identified. The conflicting findings were explained by Zimbardo on the basis that concealment made aggressors feel conspicuous and self-conscious. An alternative, though not incompatible, interpretation is in terms of anticipated reprobation. Sly aggressors are usually judged more severely than those willing to accept the consequences of their actions without being secretive. A single aggressor can escape neither self-reproof nor social censure for underhanded cruel actions by concealing her face during the performance. Similarly, a group of soldiers behaving cruelly in disguise during an official assignment nevertheless remain known and subject to disciplinary measures. In their studies of interracial aggression, Donnerstein *et al.* (1972) further corroborate how anonymity and freedom from reprisal heighten interpersonal punitiveness.

Most of the conditions described earlier that obscure or redefine the relationship between one's actions and its effects to lessen self-condemnation reduce the chance of external punishment as well. People who are deterred by external threats can be persuaded to aggress when a recognized authority is willing to accept the consequences for their actions, when extenuating circumstances can be invented, or when reprehensible behavior is redefined in ways that make it appear socially acceptable. Dehumanization of potential victims likewise disinhibits externally restrained aggression, since punishment is not only less likely but is much weaker for aggressing toward devalued people than toward revered ones. In everyday situations, disinhibitory influences ordinarily increase aggressiveness by reducing both self-reprimands and external threats.

REINFORCEMENT INFLUENCES IN
COLLECTIVE AGGRESSION

Psychological explanations of collective aggression generally invoke historical causes or personality traits rooted in the individual. In contrast, specific instigational and reinforcement influences, which function as powerful contemporary determinants of behavior, are either assigned an incidental role or neglected altogether. Differences between theories in the relative emphasis they place on the conditions that produce protest or on the types of individuals who become protesters are reflected in studies of student activism. This phenomenon has special significance for theories of aggression because, unlike most mass movements, it represents revolt by advantaged rather than by underprivileged segments of society.

Individual Determinants of
Collective Action

Research in this area, guided by the characterological tradition, has been largely preoccupied with delineating the attributes and backgrounds of students who are disposed to protest activities. Given appropriate conditions, protest behavior can be elicited in almost anyone. However, as numerous survey studies have demonstrated, some students are provoked to forceful actions more easily than others (Astin and Bayer, 1971; Flacks, 1967; Keniston, 1968). For the most part, militant students come predominantly from upper-status professional homes. They are bright, and generally do well scholastically. However, they do not view the traditional options available as providing them the satisfactions in life they seek. Their interests are predominantly in the social sciences and humanities rather than in technically oriented pursuits. On the social side, they tend to be sensitive to arbitrary authority, to social injustice, and to hypocrisy.

Contrary to popular belief, student activists are largely modeling their behavior after parental values rather than rebelling against them (Flacks, 1967; Keniston, 1968). In comparative studies of political orientation, for example, nonactivists and their fathers typically endorse conservative political positions, whereas activists and their fathers tend to espouse liberal views. Attitudes of activists in other areas are likewise correlated with those of their parents. Flacks (1967) concisely summarizes the major differences in familial orientations as follows: "Whereas nonactivists and their parents tend to express conventional orientations toward achievement, material success, sexual morality, and religion, the activists and their parents tend to place greater stress on involvement in intellectual and esthetic pursuits, humanitarian concerns, opportunity for self expression, and tend to de-emphasize or positively disvalue personal achievement, conventional morality and conventional religiosity." (P. 68)

In other words, there exists about as wide a divergence in beliefs among parents as among their offspring, though the latter tend to assume somewhat stronger positions on issues. A similar diversity also exists in the ideologies of college faculty. Thus, the view that student activism represents intergenerational conflict is disputed by substantial evidence showing that, within a society, beliefs are not distributed like a layer cake in homogeneous layers; rather, each age layer contains analogous degrees of heterogeneity. For this reason, when youth eventually becomes the Establishment and must deal with the issues of their time, the customary factional conflicts are reproduced.

Generational similarities in value orientation tend to be obscured to some extent by behavioral disparities arising, paradoxically, from successful modeling. The behavior of parents who espouse "liberal" or "radical" views is not always congruent with their ideals. They adhere, though often grudgingly, to conventional authority. Most of them pursue traditional occupations in competitive ways that amass wealth. Though permissive toward self-expression, their own life style does not stray far from conventional social norms. In the face of conflicting influences arising from the multiple responsibilities of adulthood, they are often forced to compromise their values. And it is not uncommon for highly principled people to express verbal outrage but to take no action to rectify injustices. Students who have adopted magnanimous principles are easily disillusioned and angered when the social practices of elders fail to live up to their professed beliefs. Such discrepancies, which inevitably occur, typically elicit accusations of hypocrisy and of complicity with the established order for self-interest. Adults, of course, do not hold a monopoly on hypocrisy. Public critics of student activism are equally skilled in exposing self-righteous tyrants in student movements who often preach a different morality from what they practice.

Coupled with the liberalist origin, there is some evidence (Flacks, 1967) that students who are disposed to militant action have received greater parental reinforcement for self-expression conducive to the development of strong self-assertive behavior. As a rule, those who come from advantaged backgrounds are more likely to experience early success in realizing their wishes than the less privileged who lack the resources for controlling their environment. People with a strong sense of personal efficacy are especially prone to take action against conditions they do not like. There is another aspect of privilege that encourages oppositional response. To the extent that high status affords some protection against the negative consequences of one's behavior, students of elite backgrounds will more readily risk hazardous action (Powers, 1971).

Obviously not all students who participate in forceful protest necessarily fit the pattern described above. Nor do most students sharing the same general background and ideological perspective become militants. In point of fact, proportionately few students actively participate in demonstrations. The vast majority, between 90 and 95 percent, either remain uncommitted onlookers or oppose the protesters (Keniston, 1967; Peterson, 1966). Campus confrontations, depending on the issues in dispute and the manner in which grievances are handled, can recruit new supporters of diverse social learning backgrounds and attributes. Some of the attitudes and behavior of activists are shaped by repeated exposure to militant leaders or through direct participation in demonstrations. In his intensive study of student activists, Keniston (1968) documents the role of modeling in the process of radicalization. Novices drawn into the movement learn the specific tactics, rhetoric, and ideology to a large extent by emulating more experienced and committed figures.

The time, the place, and the form of collective aggression can be best understood by considering both the characteristics of potential protesters and the presence of aggression-promoting influences. The latter conditions are especially important because, if sufficiently strong, they can override the residual effects of prior learning in determining how one behaves.

The immediate instigators of protest behavior were specific events of a provocative nature related either to military activities or to discriminatory racial practices. Although campus demonstrations were initiated by such factors, inept or precipitous counterresponses by university authorities often generated a sequence of events culminating in violent confrontations. The poor quality and impersonality of higher education were widely cited as principal causes of student unrest. However, evidence from comparative studies did not lend much support for this popular interpretation. Student protesters were no more dissatisfied with their educational experiences than nonactivists (Somers, 1965). Moreover, student activism was more prevalent in universities noted for their academic excellence and progressiveness than in those of lesser caliber (Kahn and Bowers, 1970; Foster and Long, 1970).

Public critics were quick to attribute oppositional activities on such campuses to greater leniency toward student protest. Traditional disciplinary procedures were adequate for adjudicating petty infractions, but ill-equipped for handling large-scale disruptions, especially when strengthened by nonstudent recruits. Countermeasures were rapidly devised and students were in fact penalized for prohibited activities (Keniston and Lerner, 1971). In addition to initial indecisiveness, exercise of restraint in disciplinary actions so as not to escalate peaceful dissent to violent confrontation was viewed by some as laxness. It should also be recognized that universities of high academic stature selectively recruit large numbers of talented students who have low thresholds for inequities and moral compromise in others, if not always in themselves. Kahn and Bowers (1970) provide some evidence, however, that high rates of activism in prestigious institutions are not due simply to the kinds of students they attract. High-quality universities tend to foster social and political protest in students of varied backgrounds. Kahn and Bowers identify several conditions that may be conducive to developing activist subcultures. Leading universities, charged with educating gifted students, many of whom will become the decision-makers and social reformers of the future, are more inclined to encourage critical scrutiny of traditional systems than to defend them. Principled protest is therefore not only accepted, but supported in varying degrees by questioning faculty members. Through scientific discoveries and consultation, the faculty of prestigious universities contribute to the course of social life and national policies. When this knowledge is put to bad use, influential universities are more vulnerable to student attack than those having few ties with industrial and governmental agencies. After a visible activist subculture has evolved, new students sharing similar orientations are drawn to the university, thus perpetuating the subculture.

Modeling influences, another contemporary determinant, not only define the critical instigators at any given time, but shape the specific style and tactics of collective aggression. Demonstrations at a few salient universities established whether military and industrial recruiting, classified research, campus officer training, ethnic studies, or some other issue became the principal object of protest on other campuses throughout the country. Equally striking was the rapid contagion of the style of aggression. The forms became progressively more violent over time, beginning with peaceful sit-ins, and graduating to combative disruptions of university functions, to mobile trashing of buildings, and eventually to firebombing. There is another aspect of modeling influences that has received little notice, though it may constitute a strong motivating force. Reformers have a militant reputation to uphold. Failure to take forceful actions when others in similar settings are protesting threatens loss of status. Widespread modeling may thus compel activists to espouse aggressive measures as a means of retaining their integrity and stature in the eyes of their supporters.

Modeling influences can substantially alter the personality correlates of activism over time. Those who set a style of behavior usually differ in characteristics from later adopters. Initially, certain types of students in prominent schools may establish the mode of protest. Like most forms of prestigious modeling, the pattern is eventually adopted by all kinds of students in diverse institutions, especially if the actions produce some benefits. When modeling influences override the effects of personal and immediate situational determinants, different correlates will emerge for participants in early and late stages in the diffusion of aggression (Kahn and Bowers, 1970; Mankoff and Flacks, 1971).

Analysis of reinforcement supports for collective aggression requires separate consideration of the consequences of individual and of collective response. At the individual level, the reinforcements for participating in aggressive activities are varied and complex, and they can change even for the same person in the course of continuing activism. Some of the protesters, who adhere to high social and ethical principles, become distressed by institutional practices that exploit and oppress disadvantaged people. In such cases, coercive actions are sustained, even in the face of punishing consequences, by self-approval for upholding one's convictions and by expectations that continued pressure may eventually produce humane social reforms.

It would be naive to assume that all militant actions, even by idealists, are in the service of altruistic goals. Public-spirited reformers are often changed by the social recognition and power their activities bring them. Discontent is easily exploited for self-serving interests without genuine concern for the plight of others. Moreover, after a protest movement has been launched, it creates a powerful subculture that supplies a new source of reinforcement supports for aggressive actions. Participants are united into a cohesive community that impinges on every aspect of their lives. Here they experience close personal relationships that are rarely matched in the usual course of events. They share their money and resources in the best equalitarian tradition; they educate and entertain themselves; and they develop a strong sense of camaraderie in battle through mutual protection and legal support should they get "busted" by the police.

Valor in mock combat or open fighting can bring group recognition and status rewards, as in other subcultures valuing aggressive accomplishments. Faithful participants therefore strive, in word and deed, to display the qualities prized by the group. On the occasions when victors forcibly discomfit their adversaries, they are strongly reinforced by a feeling of potency, particularly if their past efforts were slighted or brought them a sense of helplessness (Powers, 1971). Although of much less import, it should nevertheless be recognized that campus protest activities bring welcome relief from the boredom of academic routines. Hence, springtime, when outdoor attractions hold greater interest than textbooks, is an especially opportune time for mobilizing collective action. In sum, militant protest may be instigated by adverse social conditions, but it is sustained from day to day largely by the interpersonal reinforcements derived from the activist subculture. Indeed, for some of the participants, the broader social issues in dispute are poorly understood or, at best, of secondary concern. Even for those more ideologically inclined, the political determinants usually fade into the background as the subcultural influences assume major reinforcing functions. Groups seeking vast revolutionary changes in an affluent society are unlikely to achieve any quick successes for their efforts, nor are the prospects of long-range benefits particularly encouraging. Nevertheless, violent actions can be maintained after hope of tangible results is abandoned by social rewards from an estranged cohesive group, especially if the acts are carried out in ways that minimize risk of detection.

The diverse personal influences that may lead one to adopt violent courses of action are vividly documented in the tragic case of Diana Oughton (Powers, 1971). This sensitive girl, who came from a privileged conservative background, was progressively shaped, by events and by selective association with militant peers, from dedicated social service to revolutionary violence. Her disillusionment with existing social systems began in Philadelphia ghettos and intensified among the destitute Indians of Guatemala, where she served as a volunteer in a Quaker service program. Seeing at first hand the devastating human costs of severe privation, Diana—who as a child was repeatedly taunted for her family's affluence—developed a growing dislike for American extravagance and foreign influence. Her tireless efforts to improve living conditions in the remote village were negated by friends grown cynical about the prospects for peaceful social change. They argued that the magnitude of the problems and the indifference of self-seeking politicians demanded revolutionary measures to achieve sweeping reforms. These experiences provided the ideological justification for militant action.

Upon her return to the United States, Diana became deeply involved in the Students for a Democratic Society, which at the time was splintering into opposing ideological camps. She was readily drawn into the militant Weatherman faction through attachment to her boyfriend, who served as one of the national officers of the organization. His open admiration of Bernadine Dohrn's toughness presented additional requirements for callousness. After issuing their manifesto, the Weathermen set out to precipitate the revolution by terrorism in the streets. Analysis of the antecedent influences illustrates how development into radicalism, like most other life styles, is determined by a series of fortuitous events, not by studied design. Long-term prediction of social functioning is difficult because adventitious branching influences are often more decisive than personal attributes in shaping the course of life.

Transformation of a normally compassionate girl into a tough street fighter was not achieved through humanitarian concerns and revolutionary rhetoric alone. To extinguish any residual self-censure and revulsion over ruthless behavior, the Weathermen created small collectives where they eradicated their "bourgeois morality" with a vengeance. The brutalizing process, carried out in barricaded houses, is described in gruesome detail by Franks and Powers (1970).

> Inside they lived a 24-hour existence of intense political discussion, marked by a complete abandonment of all the bourgeois amenities of their largely middle class childhoods. Clothes were strewn everywhere, food rotted on unwashed plates, milk turned sour in half-empty containers, toilets jammed, flies and cockroaches swarmed in kitchens filled with encrusted spoons and spilled food. . . . When the collectives needed money for bail or for buying guns and, later, explosives, and sometimes simply as a matter of discipline, the members would go without food for days. On other occasions they would stay awake for two days or even longer to harden themselves for life in the "Red Army." . . . On at least one occasion, partly from genuine hunger and partly to instill in themselves a kind of savagery, a collective killed, skinned, and ate a tomcat. . . . The military aspects of the training—karate, target shooting, practice in street fighting and, later, the making of bombs —suffered in the chaotic atmosphere of the collectives where everyone was always overtired and underfed. (P. 27)

Though estranged from her parents, Diana could rely on them to protect her against the legal consequences of her violent actions. They were always quick to bail her out of legal and financial difficulties and, as the activities grew more violent, she sought assurance that they would come to her aid should she be apprehended for serious offenses. When destructive rampages and street battles with police failed to produce the heralded revolution, the Weathermen resorted to underground bombing attacks. Diana's brief career as a revolutionary ended with tragic suddenness in a townhouse bomb factory, where an antipersonnel explosive intended to help destroy the society she had come to hate took her life instead.

Consequences of Collective Action

The actions of individuals, however varied their reinforcement determinants, produce a collective response that creates another set of consequences which can have widespread and enduring effects for protesters and nonparticipants alike. Changes in social practices that resist individual effort are attainable through the force of numbers. One can distinguish circumstances in which group action is likely to gain tangible results from those in which it not only proves ineffective, but may even retard beneficial reforms.

When legitimate demands and constructive efforts to produce needed changes are repeatedly thwarted by persons who benefit from the prevailing system, this usually evokes more intense disruptive actions that cannot be ignored. Conditions favorable to change occur when forceful action is taken against social practices that lack sufficient justification to withstand concerted protest. Once they are revealed, their defenders receive little public support for continuing them. Warranted changes may be temporarily blocked by suppressive countermeasures, at high costs to the society and at the risk of enlarging the oppositional activities. However, given high justification for protest and the strong coercive power of mass supporters, continued aggressive behavior eventually succeeds in securing desired goals.

Coercive group behavior can be powerfully reinforced by the enduring changes it produces in institutional contingencies that affect the lives of many people. Collective aggression can, for example, remove disliked aversive controls. It can restore lawful rights and privileges. It can force authorities to relinquish some of their power and to introduce organizational changes that make life more rewarding for those in less advantaged positions. The more compliant members, who tend to look with disfavor upon militant tactics, eventually profit from the noncomformists' protests.

Because the consequences of collective actions are varied and removed in time, their effectiveness is difficult to verify. It is not uncommon to find advocates of conflicting tactics defining the same incidents as successes and as failures. In situations where protest activities partly serve to boost personal stature and self-esteem, demands are often issued in a form that assures apparent success even though the victors may gain little in the way of tangible results for their efforts. Usually some of the conditions demanded already exist as part of the informal practices of the system, while others would be granted upon firm challenge without requiring incensed confrontation. But authorities do not ordinarily give in to major demands that appear unreasonable at the time, and they can therefore rally support to their side. Protesters can nonetheless claim victory by pointing to concessions on issues that could probably have been obtained without massive expenditure of time and resources in combative clashes.

Fundamental changes that are resisted by the established leadership are attainable by coercive measures when applied concertedly, unremittingly, and in less violent forms that enlist rather than alienate supporters. Unfortunately, far-reaching consequences are invariably delayed.

It takes time to institute organizational changes embodying the desired reforms. Their implementation may be further postponed by defeated factions through appeals to higher agencies in an effort to restore some of the power and privileges they have lost. After appeal processes have been exhausted, new practices are still forestalled while effective mechanisms are devised for their enforcement. The long delay between action and noticeable results can give rise to disillusionment and a sense of failure, even though changes of long-term significance are eventually achieved. The power gained through these initial reforms increases the success of more forceful tactics that gain little unless backed up with coercive potential. To complicate assessment of effects, protesters may clearly lose critical battles and yet, through their actions, create a repercussion of influences that change the system in the desired directions long after their coercive pressures have ceased. Moreover, authorities in comparable siutations, fearing similar confrontation, may initiate self-protective reforms on the basis of observed costly battles in which no clear victors emerged.

Forceful aggression, being more aversive, tends to produce faster, though often more superficial, victories. Since behavior is more powerfully controlled by its immediate than by its delayed consequences, prevailing conditions of reinforcement generally favor militant action over restrained forceful tactics. It is therefore easier to get people to aggress than to adhere stoically to nonviolent resistance when their efforts are slighted or derided without any foreseeable changes. Under conditions in which immediate effects of group action are distressing but benefits are considerably delayed, powerful intragroup reinforcement and self-reward are required to sustain members until sufficient changes accrue to assume the reinforcing function. Reliance on collective aggression as a preferred method of achieving social change will decrease not by decrying violence, but by ensuring that nonviolent methods produce faster results. Though most people condemn coercive means, they are not averse to using them when their own interests are threatened.

Group force is less successful when social practices violate the professed values of the society but secure popular support because they are sufficiently beneficial to a majority of its members. Many enterprises that create jobs, profits, or privileges for a sizable segment of the population flourish under majority preferences at the expense of minorities and even long-term costs to all. Given sizable public support for inequitable practices, repressive measures succeed in curbing challenges to the existing order. Such systems are usually resistant to coercive influences for change from within unless augmented by pressures from without. It is doubtful, for example, that the civil rights movement in the South would have achieved the results it did without the influx of large numbers of protesters from the North who, being outsiders possessing some power, were not as vulnerable to punitive countercontrol.

Collective aggression is least effective when existing practices are not entirely satisfactory but have sufficient justification to gain the backing of different interest groups. Lacking both coercive power and adequate grounds for disruptive protest, forcible actions tend to discredit the protesters rather than enlist supporters for their cause in the numbers required to challenge the system. Such miscalculation of probable consequences sometimes arises through indiscriminate modeling. Seeing people get what they want through forceful action prompts others to adopt similar tactics without realizing that conditions favorable for change may be lacking in their case.

The conditions identified as conducive to social change through coercive action have been shown by Gurr (1970b) to be significant predictors of the magnitude of civil disorder in Western nations. Gurr examined three sets of determinants. The first factor is the level of social discontent, defined in terms of economic declines, new oppressive restrictions, and persisting discriminatory practices that prevent people from improving their life circumstances. Not all discontented people aggress. Modeling and reinforcement conditions largely determine whether the discontent will take aggressive or some other behavioral expression.

The second factor—reflecting the combined influence of historical example and sanctions—is the degree of social justification for using force tactically to achieve desired reforms. In some political systems mass protests and coups are regarded as an acceptable modus operandi of change, whereas in other nations such tactics lack functional value because they are widely condemned. Acceptability of forcible means was coded by Gurr in terms of legitimacy of the political system and the frequency with which previous civil disorder produced favorable changes in policies or in regimes. The assumption here is that the past successes of aggressive tactics legitimate their use.

The third, and final, determinant is the balance of coercive power between the regime and the dissident groups. Coercive capacity was assessed by the ability of contenders to enlist and to organize support on their side. Loyalty of the military and police forces, economic influence, and political and labor support defined the regime's coercive power. The size and organization of dissenting groups, as well as their military, labor, and foreign support, served as the criteria of dissident coercive power.

In the correlational analysis, social discontent was found to be unrelated to disruptive protest, but positively associated with more violent forms of civil disorders, such as organized rebellion. Justification of forcible tactics correlated highly ($r = .71$) with civil disorder. Countries that have unpopular governments and traditionally embrace militant counterresponses experience frequent public protest, even under low levels of dissatisfaction. In other words, when aggression is a common style of life, people are quick to engage in disruptive actions though not burdened with hardships. The data further disclose that widespread violent strife, involving terrorism and rebellion, can be provoked by intense grievances regardless of the activist traditions of the country. The balance of coercive power favorable to dissenters also appeared as an important correlate ($r = .74$) of all forms of protest. Dissident power, which increases the likelihood of success, enhances the prospects for aggressive challenges of the established system. Although regime support from political and labor sources mitigates against all forms of violence, military coercive force is more effective in suppressing rebellion than in reducing lesser protest activities.

Taken together, the three sets of determinants account for approximately 70 percent of the variation in civil disorders. However, the relative contribution of the component influences differs depending on the severity of the protest activity. Widespread marked discontent and dissident coercive power emerged as the important determinants of revolutionary violence. In less extreme forms of collective aggression, endorsement of forcible tactics and coercive power are equally strong determinants, whereas variations in discontent have less effect.

Decline of Contagious Aggression

Earlier it was shown that new modes of aggression spread in a contagious fashion but, after being widely adopted, tend to be discarded. A number of reinforcement influences can contribute to abrupt decline of contagious aggression. Foremost among these factors is the development of effective countermeasures. For example, as hijacking escalated, airlines instituted behavioral screening procedures along with magnetometric devices for detecting ferrous metal. As additional deterrents to air piracy, it was widely publicized that concealed armed guards rode unspecified flights. News of hijackers killed aloft by security guards and the growing reluctance of nations to grant asylum further reinforced restraints against contemplated hijacking. The incidence of both domestic and international air piracy dropped markedly.

College administrators similarly improved their methods of countercontrol through repeated experience in dealing with provocative actions. Eventually they adopted the position that disruptive tactics were no longer an acceptable means of settling disputes. Unlawful actions were

promptly curtailed by invoking legal restraining orders that barred protesters from the campus or from participating in activities forbidden by
court injuctions. Violation of institutional rules by students and faculty
were also firmly discouraged by college judicial bodies empowered to
impose severe penalties, if necessary. Disruptive behavior now carried a
high risk of punishment. Just as coercive tactics were widely modeled,
so were the methods of countercontrol. It is difficult to estimate how
much of the decrement in contagious aggression is attributable to disciplinary countermeasures and how much to reduction in aggression-
promoting conditions. Deescalation of the war, reduction of student
grievances by institutional reforms, and increasing weariness over peren-
nial confrontations were undoubtedly contributing factors.

The discrepancy between anticipated and experienced consequences
plays an important role in determining the future course of aggression.
Direct observation and media portrayals of mass aggression are largely
confined to dramatic confrontation episodes, not to the long intervening
hours of boredom and fatigue. What is seen of the group's functioning
generally conveys the sense of solidarity and principled dedication rather
than the stress of pressures for conformity, the feeling of isolation that
accompanies estrangement from the larger community, and the discouragement arising from failure to achieve fundamental changes. Participants who are drawn into protest activities mainly by their apparent
excitement may drop out after experiencing at first hand the full consequences of the endeavor. Functional leaders, who share a sense of
purpose and camaraderie, derive adequate reinforcement supports to
sustain their behavior; the lower ranks, however, experience high turn-
over, making it difficult to sustain the same group action with constantly
changing recruits, some of whom vie for leadership of a different style.
Certain forms of collective violence produce consequences in such devastating proportions that they prevent repetition of similar actions. Burning a ghetto area to the ground precludes a repeat performance.

Group aggression, like other collective phenomena shaped by modeling influences, often follows the transitory cyclic pattern of fads. When
a new style of behavior first appears, it wins social recognition and thus
becomes the "in" thing to do. As its popularity spreads, however, it
rapidly loses its positive value. What was once highly fashionable becomes trite. After a practice grows stale through overuse, it is discarded
in favor of another pattern that undergoes a similar rise and decline in
popularity. There are additional effects of stereotyped imitation that
shorten the life span of a particular mode of aggression. When the same
rhetoric and tactics are used repeatedly, protest activities take on the
quality of staged productions rather than genuine expressions of principle. As leaders reduce their credibility by stereotyped appeals, their

exhortations tend to be viewed as manipulative and increasingly resisted. Unresponsiveness to trite rhetoric is often misread as indifference to the issues. Even among members of activist groups, some of the more idealistically inclined may eventually become disillusioned by the contriving of power plays that appear to be based more on strategic than on moral considerations.

The course of collective aggression is often misjudged on the basis of the linear projection error. Expecting a continuous heightening of aggression, control agencies resort to needlessly extreme counterattacks at the point at which the activities may begin to decline, thus prolonging the strife for a time. The eventual cessation of aggressive activities may be erroneously credited to the punitive countermeasures when, in fact, they temporarily bolstered a waning phenomenon.

chapter five

MODIFICATION AND CONTROL OF AGGRESSION

The social learning principles that account for the development of aggressive behavior apply equally to its modification. In recent years learning principles have been used widely to promote diverse changes in psychological functioning, including aggression (Bandura, 1969a; Kanfer and Phillips, 1970). Social learning approaches differ from traditional intrapsychically oriented techniques in several important ways. Since aggression is largely under situational, cognitive, and reinforcement control, these are the events to which treatment addresses itself, rather than to traits, to presumptive drive forces, or to historical causes.

Discourses on treatment of aggressive disorders often fail to distinguish between historical and contemporary determinants of behavior. As a consequence, potentially powerful influences are often misapplied with disappointing results. This issue is well illustrated in views regarding the essential conditions for modifying delinquent patterns. It is commonly assumed that because delinquents come predominantly from rejecting familial backgrounds, they require a great deal of unconditional love to remedy their problems. As Ackerman (1944) astutely observed years ago, delinquents repeatedly experience interpersonal difficulties not because they were unloved as children, but because these adverse conditions created hostile, distrustful conduct that currently prevents them from achieving rewarding relationships, even though there are plenty of friendly people in their immediate environment. To take but one example, a person who has learned to expect rejection is inclined to test expressions of friendliness and interest from others by making difficult demands and otherwise subjecting potential friends to provocative challenges. Alienating love tests eventually evoke rejection from most people, producing recurrent reinforcement for guardedness and hostility. Thus, antagonistic behavior, due to its negative character, creates the very conditions likely to perpetuate it long after the original determinants have disappeared. The causes of behavior, including aggression, reside in the here and now, not in the past. Favorable changes are therefore best achieved not by replenishing lost love, but by helping people develop new ways of relating that make them more lovable. Although interest and affection are important ingredients in fostering behaviors conducive to mutual friendship, it will be shown later that beneficial results are rarely achieved by indiscriminate and unguided interest, however well intentioned.

Change programs based upon social learning principles differ from those relying heavily on conversational methods in the *content,* the *locus,* and the *agents* of treatment. With regard to content, treatment procedures are mainly applied to the actual problem behaviors requiring modification, instead of to verbal reports of troubles. Change agents therefore devote their efforts to altering the social conditions producing aggressive behavior rather than conversing about them, as so often happens in approaches using the interview as the basic vehicle for modifying behavior.

To enhance successful results, treatment is typically carried out in the natural settings in which aggressive problems arise. It may be conducted in the home, in schools, in work situations, or in the larger community, depending on the source of the critical determinants. The same general principle applies even more importantly in modifying subcultural patterns of aggression. Group problems demand group solutions. The most fundamental and enduring changes in aggression are accomplished by altering the social instigators and reinforcement practices prevailing in the deviant subculture. However, owing to the individualistic bias of psychological treatments and to the difficulties in changing the contingency structure of groups, the common practice is to remove individual transgressors from their usual environment and subject them to competing social influences. Should the offenders adopt the institutional standards of conduct, they not only lose their original basis for self-evaluation but, since the new styles of behavior conflict with what is valued in their community, they also lose the means of gaining the approval and respect of their peers. For these reasons, delinquents ordinarily resist institutional influences and revert to their customary patterns of behavior upon their return to the community. From a social learning perspective, subcultural delinquents must develop, through provision of suitable role models and valued incentives, new modes of behavior that produce better payoffs than do delinquent pursuits if more constructive patterns are to be established and normatively sanctioned.

The third factor that partly determines the success of a change program is concerned with who implements the corrective practices. The most effective treatments are generally carried out under close professional supervision by persons who have intensive contact with the aggressor and can therefore serve as powerful change agents. Numerous applications will be cited later showing that, given adequate training, supervision, and reinforcing feedback, parents can effectively eliminate the injurious conduct of their children; teachers can change aggressively disruptive students into productive learners; nurses can help violently assaultive patients to gain control over dangerous behavior; and peers can regulate the level of aggressiveness in their social interactions. The potential influence of such persons derives from their close association with the aggressing individuals so that they can exercise substantial control over the very conditions that govern both aggressive and prosocial conduct. Unless influences promoting aggression are altered, changes produced by interventionists, whether professional or otherwise, may not endure for long.

By treating the actual problems in the contexts within which they arise with influential members in those settings, social learning procedures are ideally suited for achieving enduring changes in psychological functioning. The further one departs from these optimal conditions, the weaker the results are likely to be.

Another distinguishing feature of a social learning approach is the specification of explicit goals coupled with objective evaluation of the results remedial practices are producing. Perhaps because psychological interventions rarely have immediate spectacular consequences, a casual attitude toward subjecting people to untested programs has developed. New approaches are promoted enthusiastically, and it is not until the methods have been applied for some time by a coterie of advocates that objective tests of efficacy are conducted, if at all. By couching objectives in high-sounding terms and defining results as alterations in inner states, high success rates are claimed for methods that accomplish no demonstrable changes in interpersonal functioning (Bandura, 1969a). Now that the behavioral consequences of social practices are being measured systematically, some methods widely assumed to have beneficial value have been found to actually produce deleterious effects. As the system of accountability is extended to psychological services and financial support is made contingent upon tangible results, ineffectual methods and the weak theories from which they are derived should be retired more rapidly.

The initial task in a social learning program (Bandura, 1969a) is to delineate the desired changes in performance terms. Unless goals for action are clearly stated in demonstrable form, there is no adequate guide either for selecting optimal conditions or for determining whether the objectives have in fact been attained. Behavioral specification of objectives in no way restricts the range of goals. Change agents may legitimately pursue abstract objectives, provided they indicate how the effects their programs supposedly produce will be manifested. How will people behave when they are claimed to be self-actualized, internally integrated, self-accepted, personally reconstructed, homeostatically equilibrated, or emotionally matured? When goals are stated as abstract virtues devoid of recognizable manifestations, recipients have no basis for knowing how they will be changed or whether the agents have delivered what they promised.

The second step involves a causal analysis of the troublesome behavior to identify the antecedent conditions that produce it and the consequences that maintain it. After ascertaining the determinants, the changes required to achieve desired outcomes are instituted. Complex behavior is best modified by arranging the requisite learning experiences into a stepwise sequence that ensures continuous progress. Poorly organized change programs, as evidenced by haphazard and inadequate gradation of experiences, will produce discouraging results, however valid the principles guiding the social practices.

Objective assessment of results constitutes another important part of responsible interventions. By continually monitoring the effects produced by a given program, it becomes readily apparent when the methods are succeeding, when they are failing, and when they must be altered to increase their power. This self-corrective feature not only provides a safeguard against perpetuating ineffective procedures, but influences the rate of change itself. Behavior is generally modified in small incremental steps, so that individuals may not fully recognize the progress they are making. Objective feedback of progress reinforces participants' efforts and thereby accelerates successive improvement, whereas the same interventions prove weaker when their effects go unmeasured. As outcomes are monitored during the course of intervention, necessary adjustments can be made to optimize results.

Value Judgments in the Modification and Control of Aggression

In designing change programs it is important to distinguish between judgments in the empirical domain relating to strategies for altering aggressiveness and those in the value domain that are principally concerned with whether aggressive actions ought to be supported or eliminated in given situations. It is appropriate for change agents to select the means by which particular outcomes can be best achieved, but recipients of interventions should play a major role in determining the directions in which their behavior is to be modified (Bandura, 1969a). When beneficiaries select the goals they wish to achieve, ethical questions frequently raised about the manipulation and control of human behavior become pseudo issues.

The general principle stated above is readily applicable to instances of individual aggression in which people seek help with their social behavior. Some highly submissive individuals choose to increase their assertiveness and ability to cope with situations requiring force. Normally passive individuals may overinhibit warranted aggressive reactions to disparagement or exploitation only to respond violently under cumulative provocation. Learning to deal forcefully with lesser affronts reduces the likelihood of more explosive episodes. Still others aggress only too readily and seek ways of controlling their injurious behavior when it gets them into trouble.

Change agents are by no means value free. Occasionally individuals may select goals that change agents have no desire to promote because the intended outcomes conflict with their values. For this reason, they do not sell their services to felons who seek to improve their mugging skills, nor are they likely to desensitize assaulters to expressions of suffering to enable them to aggress without undue distress. On the other hand, counselors may serve those in power in devising better ways of aggressing against certain people when such practices are institutionally sanctioned.

Value conflicts arise when the rewards of aggression far exceed its costs for the user. Under these circumstances successful aggressors, or groups valuing aggressive accomplishment, resist pressures to modify their behavior from those who either suffer the negative consequences of their actions or object to them on moral grounds. A society has the right to protect itself from injurious transgressors by imposing legal sanctions, though it is not granted the psychological or legal power to compel prosocial behavior from them. By the same token, individuals are entitled to adequate protection against transgressions of coercive power by the social system. Agencies of social control generally try to discourage the use of aggression by increasing penalties and the surveillance of such conduct. Individuals thus have the choice of behaving aggressively and taking the consequences or adopting more socially acceptable means of getting what they want. From a social learning perspective, the most effective way of diminishing aggression without raising moral dilemmas is to increase the functional value of prosocial alternatives. By developing rewarding options, aggressiveness is reduced through enhancement of individuals' freedom of choice.

Disputes over the morality of aggression and its control arise most often in relation to collective action directed against established social systems. In such instances, not only is the legitimacy of the actions contested, but even the victims and aggressors are difficult to identify. Social institutions can, through use of coercive power, control the behavior of dissident members without having to resort to openly aggressive measures. Those in privileged positions are not easily persuaded to make needed social changes that conflict with their self-interest. As long as groups that believe the system is biased against them accept their subordinated position without unauthorized protest, peaceable order is maintained. However, when dissidents take oppositional collective action in extralegal ways against inadequate or harmful practices of the system, enforcement agencies respond with aggressive force likely to provoke physical violence. Indeed, the counterattacks of authorities who wield power are often more violent than the actions of the protesters (Grimshaw, 1969; Marx, 1970b).

Aggressors tend to extol their own violence as principled behavior but condemn that of their opponents as morally reprehensible. The moralizing rhetoric of protagonists usually goes as follows: Challengers define their coercive actions as justifiable forms of protest designed to bring about social change in a corrupt or oppressive system. Established authorities, in turn, condemn disruptive activism as impatient resort to aggressive solutions when alternative avenues of influence are open to rectify legitimate grievances. They argue further that many protesters use aggression for self-aggrandizement rather than as a selfless means to laudable goals.

Dissidents rebut the democracy argument with the countercharge that the institutionalized procedures of influence, while adequate in theory, do not work in practice because they are controlled by partisan functionaries of the inequitable system. Authorities, in turn, respond that if the enforcement system, or its laws, are indeed unjust and traditional means to modify them have failed, the moral solution is non-violent resistance including, if necessary, acts of civil disobedience designed to get the policies judicially rescinded. However, disobeying laws under these specified conditions can be justified only if transgressors do so publicly and willingly accept the consequences of their unlawful conduct. In this way specific unjust laws can be challenged while maintaining respect for the judicial process itself. It is presumably the suffering endured by aggrieved protesters that shakes the moral complacency of compassionate citizens, if not the oppressors themselves. In theory, this will mobilize the massive support required to force political agencies to institute warranted reforms. However, to demand amnesty for one's unlawful conduct not only defeats the purpose of civil disobedience, but is morally wrong. If individuals do not have to accept responsibility for their actions, violent tactics and threats of force will be readily used whenever a grievance arises. It is further argued that illegal defiance of the rules of a representative society fosters contempt for the principle of democratic authority. Anarchy would flourish in a climate in which individuals acted on the basis of private moral principles and considered coercive tactics acceptable when they disliked majority decisions. Almost any form of conduct can be justified in terms of private conscience. An additional moral objection levied against the use of force is that it corrupts the user and dehumanizes the victims.

Challengers refute such moral arguments by appeal to a higher level of morality derived from communal concerns that transcend the immediate political system. Their constituencies are expanded to include all people, both at home and aboard, victimized either directly or indirectly by injurious institutional practices. From the protesters' perspective they are acting under a moral imperative to stop inhumane treatment of victims who are outside the system and therefore have no way of modifying its destructive policies. Even the disadvantaged members within the system are powerless to influence it in any significant way. Some are disenfranchised, most have no voice in decision-making, and even the judicial procedures are partially administered so that efforts to remedy legitimate grievances are repeatedly thwarted. Not only is one not obliged to obey authorities lacking legitimacy and laws enacted either undemocratically or selfishly, so the reasoning goes, but one is morally right to disobey them. Although nonviolent resistance does not jeopardize democratic institutions, it is relatively ineffective when leaders who are not highly principled secure widespread support from a populace that benefits sufficiently from existing policies to remain morally unmoved by seeing a small faction acting in a civilly disobedient manner. When self-interest conflicts with common welfare, self-interest usually prevails. The majority principle, selfishly applied, thus is claimed to work against disadvantaged minorities. Submitting to the punitive consequences of disruptive protest, the challengers argue, places institutional procedures above the welfare of humans and simply allows the system to perpetuate its exploitation of the disadvantaged. They further contend that they cannot afford the protracted time and expenses required to exhaust legal remedies.

When moral and democratic arguments fail to dissuade people from using illegal tactics, force is questioned on practical grounds. People in privileged positions and those who consider aggression to be morally wrong, whatever its source, contend that aggression is tactically ineffective. Challenging groups, on the other hand, contest this empirical assertion by downgrading the value of nonaggressive solutions and pointing to instances in which others successfully obtain what they want through aggressive means.

As the preceding discussion shows, one can easily marshal moral reasons either for or against the use of collective aggression to force desired changes. When institutional authorities and dissidents alike act as aggressors, it is a debatable question which of the contenders must change its ways. In some instances, collective aggression can be effectively reduced only by correcting injustices in the social system and pressuring advantaged members to subordinate their interests to the common good. Other instances require discouraging dissidents from resorting to aggressive tactics before alternative means of influence have been adequately tested. When a malfunctioning authoritarian system collides with aggressive malcontents who ascribe moral superiority to their own personal principles, then both adversary groups are in need of change.

Traditional prescriptions for the modification of aggression are typically stated in broad general terms offering little guidance on the specific courses of action that ought to be taken. According to intrapsychically oriented practitioners, one must find the personal causes of aggression and interpret them to the client. Environmentalists, on the other hand, advise that the society must be changed. What is lacking is a detailed specification of the procedures best suited for altering aggression arising from different causes. The following sections of this chapter discuss how social learning principles can be used to alter conditions fostering injurious modes of behavior.

MODELING PRINCIPLES

The power of modeling influences can be utilized to modify, as well as to transmit, aggressive patterns of behavior. People will persist in ineffective conduct when they have not learned other ways of handling situational demands. Even partially successful behavior is often maintained and valued, not because it is highly preferred, but because better alternatives are lacking. Aggression can therefore be best reduced at the individual level by developing more effective means of coping with interpersonal problems. There are many different ways of implementing modeling principles, some of which are more effective than others.

The method that has yielded the most impressive results with diverse problems contains three major components (Bandura, 1972). First, alternative modes of response are repeatedly modeled, preferably by several people who demonstrate how the new style of behavior can be used in dealing with a variety of aggression-provoking situations. Second, learners are provided with necessary guidance and ample opportunities to practice the modeled behavior under favorable conditions until they perform it skillfully and spontaneously. The latter procedures are ideally suited for developing new social skills, but they are unlikely to be adopted unless they produce rewarding consequences. Arrangement of success experiences, particularly for initial efforts at behaving differently, constitutes the third component in this powerful composite method. After new skills have become functional through repeated reinforcement, they are habitually used even though they may not always succeed. Given adequate demonstration, guided practice, and success experiences, this method is almost certain to produce favorable results. The potency of reinforced modeling derives largely from the fact that individuals learn and practice effective modes of behavior under conditions similar to those they typically face in everyday interactions. An additional advantage of this form of treatment is that a broad range of nonprofessional resource people can be enlisted to serve as role models.

Modeling procedures are used in some traditional treatment approaches, but their potential value is negated by enactment of the wrong behaviors. In efforts to promote cathartic discharge and insight into neurotic patterns, clients are prompted to reenact their faulty patterns of behavior and to revivify the emotional reactions engendered by their inadequate functioning. Observing one's negative behavior and its likely consequences may temporarily reduce its use, but it is insufficient to produce constructive changes. What most people need is not the insight that they are behaving inadequately, but the means to learn more successful ways of behaving. It is understandable that many clients who find themselves in treatments oriented toward exposing deficiencies leave after a few sessions, and those who remain spend much of their time defending themselves against negative interpretations of their habitual conduct. The tendency to accentuate the negatives is even more prevalent in the modification of aggressive behavior disorders in young children. They are typically urged to perform in doll play and other expressive media negative assaultive reactions toward parents, teachers,

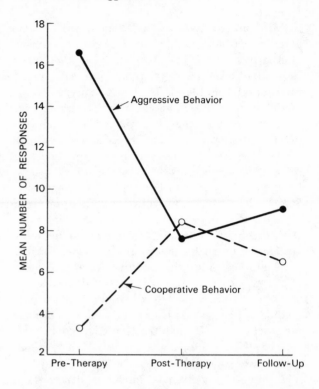

FIGURE 5.1 Amount of cooperative and aggressive domineering behavior displayed by hyperaggressive children before and after receiving a modeling treatment in which cooperative coping styles were favored over aggressive ones. (Plotted from data by Chittenden, 1942)

siblings, and peers that, if transferred to actual relationships, would further exacerbate their problems.

Chittenden (1942) shows how substantial benefits can be derived from modeling and practicing positive solutions to recurrent interpersonal conflicts. Children who were excessively domineering and hyperaggressive observed and discussed a series of portrayed interactions in each of which dolls, representing preschool children, exhibited alternately an aggressive and a cooperative solution to interpersonal conflicts that children frequently encounter. In addition to modeling these alternative modes of response, the consequences of aggression were depicted as unpleasant and those of cooperativeness as rewarding. In one of the modeled situations, for example, two boys engage in a fight over the possession of a wagon; during the struggle the wagon is broken, and both boys end up unhappy. By contrast, the cooperative alternative showed the boys enjoying themselves as they take turns playing with the wagon.

Children for whom the different reactions and consequences were modeled reduced their dominative aggressiveness in competitive situations, whereas similarly hyperaggressive children who received no treatment continued in their aggressive ways. The differential modeling of coping styles also decreased domination and increased cooperativeness as assessed from behavior observations in the nursery school made prior to treatment, immediately after treatment, and one month later (Figure 5.1).

This program relied primarily upon modeling influences. After desired patterns of behavior are transmitted through some form of modeling, whether they will be retained or discarded depends on the results they produce. Hence, it may be necessary to arrange favorable consequences to support newly acquired response patterns until they become well established. An approach combining modeling with reinforcement is well suited for achieving enduring changes in social behavior.

Reduction of Aggression Through Participant Modeling

Symbolic modeling, in which desired response patterns are demonstrated concretely through play activities, may be adequate for modifying the behavior of young children. In most cases, social skills are best acquired through repeated trials of behavioral demonstration, enactment, and performance feedback until a high level of proficiency is attained.

As Toch (1969) has shown, people who have a propensity for getting into fights are usually deficient in verbal and other social skills for coping with provocative situations. Socially adept individuals are able to defuse potentially explosive situations through pacifying moves, such as face-saving actions, friendly persuasion, and humor. Verbal skills not only reduce actions productive of violence, they can also help preserve one's integrity and self-esteem in embarrassing situations without having to dispose of antagonists physically. Social class differences in physical aggressiveness partly result because members of higher strata are taught to talk rather than to fight their way out of difficult situations.

Socially and verbally unskilled persons, having limited means for handling discord, are likely to become physically aggressive on slight provocation, especially in contexts where violent conduct is viewed favorably. Assaultive people can therefore profit greatly from a treatment program that teaches them nonviolent techniques for handling interpersonal conflicts. By enlarging their repertory of skills, aggressors achieve greater freedom in meeting present and future problems. The propensity to violence can be further reduced by changing the valuation of combativeness to make it signify ineptitude rather than manliness.

In the development of social skills, new modes of behavior are first modeled. Nonviolent ways of handling antagonists can be effectively demonstrated through role-playing simulating everyday experiences. Actual demonstrations may be supplemented with videotaped and filmed modeling of successful responses to common problems. To produce skills that can be applied to many situations, the treatment should emphasize general strategies rather than specific responses. Abstraction of a general style from individual examples is achieved by showing models handling diverse problems in similar ways.

After nonaggressive modes of response have been sufficiently portrayed, learners practice them while being variously insulted, goaded, thwarted, and threatened in role-playing exchanges. Social learning is retarded when performers fail to observe thoroughly the responses they are making, as is usually the case. Performance feedback, which provides information for corrective action, is thus required to realize the full benefits of behavior rehearsal. Reports of onlookers may be of some help, but the explicit feedback provided by audio and videotape recordings is ideally suited for this purpose. Through immediate videotape playback learners can observe their own performances, including their attitudes, tones of voice, and accompanying mannerisms. Successful accomplishments are noted, while aspects of their performance requiring further improvement are pointed out. Troublesome situations are then reenacted, with additional modeling if necessary, until they are handled satisfactorily. Through role reversal, participants can experience how their typical conduct affects others, and the greater understanding may perhaps reduce the aggression-arousing potential of antagonistic reactions in social interchanges.

Gittelman (1965) illustrates how modeling combined with behavioral enactment can be adopted for modifying aggressive behavior in older children. They first describe everyday situations that typically provoke them to aggression and belligerence. A hierarchy of irritating situations is then constructed, ranging from mild annoyances to enraging provocations. The participants enact these progressively aggravating situations and practice effective nonviolent means of coping with them. When certain events serve as unusually powerful elicitors of anger arousal, a stimulus neutralization procedure may also prove helpful. Herrell (1971) successfully treated a chronically assaultive adult who responded with uncontrollable anger to commands by pairing imagined scenes in which he was being told what to do with relaxation. Following the treatment the client, whose explosive reactions to directions from parents, teachers, police, and military personnel repeatedly got him into difficulty, was able to accept reasonable orders without becoming enraged or combative. Desensitization methods, which have proved effective in eliminating anxiety reactions, warrant further exploration as a means of neutralizing aggression elicitors.

Individuals may be reluctant to discard aggressive modes of response as long as such behavior remains personally valued. Cultivation of social competence may have to be accompanied by devaluation of assaultiveness. In altering a person's basis for self-evaluation one must, of course, consider the ethical issues involved. Anyone who sets out to modify standards of self-reinforcement should be prepared to teach new styles of behavior that serve as more self-satisfying alternatives. The self-evaluative consequences of aggressive behavior can be altered to some extent through the judgments expressed and modeled by change agents. It might be pointed out, for example, that the risk of permanent physical injury is an exorbitant price to pay for fleeting glory or a temporary boost in self-esteem; that it is much smarter to dispose of an antagonist by one's wits than by one's fists; and that hasty fighters become easily manipulable after others discover how to provoke them to foolhardy acts. An assaultive person is apt to exercise better control over his behavior if he also knows which things easily goad him into violent action. This knowledge is achieved through behavioral analyses of the social determinants of aggression in any given case.

Neither preaching nor example will be fully convincing unless backed up by corroborating rewarding experiences. Success endows activities with positive value (Breer and Locke, 1965). A number of methods can be used to make the control rather than the expression of aggression a source of self-pride. In one approach, described by Mahoney (1971), hyperaggressive boys each take turns being harassed and are rewarded in terms of how well they maintain their equanimity. One could similarly devise confrontation situations in which aggression-prone individuals are rewarded for tactful pacifying moves and adroitness of repartee.

When people are deliberately taught new ways of behaving, there may be a tendency to view the resultant changes as somehow artificial. Any new skill, regardless of how it was acquired, is initially performed awkwardly and self-consciously. With repeated use, however, the actions are executed spontaneously as part of one's natural style of behavior. But participant modeling does more than teach skills. If people behave in new ways, eventually their attitudes change in the direction of their actions. Indeed, numerous studies have shown that one of the most effective methods for altering attitudes and values is by producing a change in behavior (Bandura, 1969a; Elms, 1969).

Negative self-attitudes partly result from behavioral deficits and are repeatedly reinforced by failure experiences in handling common situations. No amount of self-exploration in therapeutic conversations will create esteem-producing vocational skills or social competencies required to support realistic positive self-evaluations. Here the primary concern must be with self-development rather than self-examination. With achievement of competencies that bring success, people revise their estimates of themselves in more favorable directions. Participant modeling, though primarily addressed to the acquisition of skills, improves self-evaluations as well. Without the requisite competencies people can be talked into thinking well of themselves, but positive self-evaluations are unlikely to survive for long in the face of disconfirming failure experiences.

Development of Assertiveness by Participant Modeling

Some forms of physical aggression result paradoxically from a lack of self-assertiveness. One can easily call to mind obsequious individuals who invite maltreatment through their passivity, only to respond explosively after being subjected to repeated humiliating affronts. These are the timid, indecisive people who cannot express their legitimate rights; who are disregarded, exploited, and victimized; and who harbor resentment rather than seek redress for justified grievances. People who are unable to behave assertively will suffer considerable aversive control by others, some of which may be of a sufficiently provocative character to force violent response. Under high states of emotional arousal, the risk of hazardous behavior is increased because anticipated response consequences, which ordinarily deter reckless actions, are given little consideration.

Venting anger and annoyance alone has little lasting benefit. Rather, a submissive person needs to develop assertive responses that enable him to control his social environment in ways that stop humiliating treatment. The modeling principles used to foster nonviolent responsiveness apply equally to teaching people how to behave assertively. Assertive modes of response must be modeled for the submissive. They must practice assertive styles with feedback that rewards their successes and corrects their errors. They must learn when and where assertiveness is appropriate. And they need positive reinforcement for asserting themselves in their daily interactions.

Some efforts have been made to assess the relative contributions to treatment outcomes of the various components in participant modeling.

Friedman (1972), for example, compared the effectiveness of different forms of modeling with and without guided practice for increasing assertive behavior in passive college students. Different groups had assertive response to provocation modeled in the form of either verbal descriptions or actual behavioral demonstrations, or they relied on reconstructed examples of assertiveness as guides for their behavior. Half the students in each of these treatments also received guided practice in behaving assertively toward an irritating associate. Untreated controls remained passive in the face of provocation. Behavioral modeling supplemented with guided practice proved to be the most powerful treatment; it produced approximately a triple increase in assertive behavior. The remaining procedures, which doubled the students' level of assertive responding, were found to be equally effective.

The above study set out to produce changes in a circumscribed range of assertive behavior. In formal treatment applications, of course, a number of assertive skills would be modeled and practiced. Depending on individual needs, these might include such things as complaining about inadequate service, returning purchases, refusing arbitrary or unreasonable demands, responding to unfair criticism, making rightful claims to goods and facilities, defending one's position in the face of opposition, and in other ways standing up for one's rights.

Fear of revealing one's inadequacies creates initial reluctance to engage in behavior rehearsals even under simulated conditions. There are several ways in which such resistances can be reduced. First, participant modeling is structured in a nonthreatening manner aimed at fostering new competencies and confidence rather than exposing weaknesses. Concern over poor performance is further decreased by noting that in all successful skill learning initial efforts are awkward; it is progressive improvement with practice rather than instant proficiency that is expected. In an optimistic, forward-looking program, people more readily accept and profit from their mistakes. Second, prior modeling provides a helpful guide for new styles of behavior. Needless failure is avoided because participants do not have to grope around for appropriate responses. Third, assertion tasks are graduated, beginning with relatively easy performances. As anxiety is extinguished through repeated practice, progressively more threatening encounters demanding more assertive actions are introduced.

Transfer of assertiveness from the training situation to the natural environment should be an integral part of the program rather than being left to fortuitous circumstances. A transfer program might proceed as follows: After the person has overcome his timidity, he accompanies the model on field excursions in which he witnesses further demonstrations of how to handle situations calling for assertive action. The change agent then reduces his level of participation to background support and guidance as the client tries his newly acquired skills under conditions likely to produce favorable results. By careful selection of encounters of increasing difficulty, the assertion requirements can be adjusted to the client's capabilities at any given time and so bolster his sense of confidence. As a final step, the client would be assigned a series of performance tasks requiring assertiveness to carry out on his own.

Reduction of Aggression by
Law Enforcement Agencies

Toch's (1969) studies of individual aggression provide ample evidence that violent incidents often are partly created by police through their inept handling of people who have brushes with the law. The contribution of police violence to collective aggression is equally well documented in analyses of past and more recent civil disturbances (Kerner *et al.*, 1968; Marx, 1970b). Urban riots are almost invariably set off by an incident involving harsh or humiliating police action against a ghetto resident. Spectators, sensitized to maltreatment by police harassment and unredressed grievances, retaliate against police and ghetto merchants singled out for their exploitive practices. Police forces under weak command control who are brought into a rampant situation are readily susceptible to aggression contagion. The anonymity afforded by concealed identity and the cover of darkness further reduces restraints against their behaving cruelly. When police violence gets out of hand, indiscriminate counterfire and brutal attacks on rioters and bystanders alike aggravate the riotous activities the police were sent in to quell.

Because police must deal with individuals prone to aggressive action and because misuse of coercive power can easily turn innocuous incidents into violent episodes, prescriptions for the curtailment of violence must address themselves as well to provocative aggression by law enforcement agencies. The most effective way of controlling unwarranted police aggression depends on whether it arises from individual ineptitude or social sanction.

At the individual level, police who recurrently provoke violent altercations respond to suspected transgressors with precipitous force that invites defiance from those who consider such blatant display of authority as humiliating and unjust harassment. The frontal approach eventually provokes fighting in belligerent transgressors (Toch, 1969). Policemen who are prone to provocative aggressive actions must be taught how to cope more constructively with potentially dangerous situations. This requires tactful routines for determining whether there is any cause for police action. Given that a transgression has occurred, the law can be better enforced, without risk of inciting assaultive reactions, by pacifying moves than by excessive application of force. Not only is the probability of police-generated violence reduced when aggressive measures are used as last resorts, but judicious police conduct reinforces responsiveness to their authority that generalizes beyond the immediate event.

The modeling procedures outlined earlier for training in nonviolence are equally well suited for police training. Skill in handling transgressors cannot be ensured by lectures and trial and error experiences on the street. Indeed, since most people acquiesce to police authority, forceful means are likely to be reinforced and selectively developed if police are left to their own devices.

Desired styles of conduct can be reliably established through demonstration and reinforced practice conducted initially under simulated conditions and later in field situations. After adept response patterns have been adequately modeled by exemplary police officers, recruits are given ample opportunity to perfect them through enactment of difficult situations they will encounter on duty. Videotape techniques provide a convenient means of both illustrating alternative courses of action and recording for analysis the conduct of trainees in simulated situations as they are called upon to secure identification and information from suspects, to mediate disputes, and to pacify, disarm, and arrest offenders. Since police are most prone to misuse force when their authority is challenged, special attention should be given to constructive ways of handling recalcitrant individuals to reduce the likelihood of escalating aggressive exchanges. During the performance analysis, adept responses are socially rewarded, while offensive and overaggressive ones are firmly discouraged. The process of demonstration, enactment, and corrective feedback is continued until the desired practices are performed skillfully and spontaneously. In order to add meaning to the formal instruction, recruits might accompany experienced officers into the field as observers during the period.

Police training must equip recruits with more than technical and interpersonal skills. They also require supervised practice in how to exercise discretionary power. A policeman on the beat must judge whether a given conduct performed under involved circumstances violates any one of many statutes. Judgmental errors are fraught with danger because it is disputable accusations that provoke the challenges to police authority most likely to end in violence. Police require detailed regulatory guidelines defining the types of behaviors that are forbidden by law. In training for judgmental accuracy, recruits might respond to descriptions of problematic situations and be informed, in each instance, whether they succeeded or erred in identifying transgressions. Offense recognition training should be continued until each recruit understands the range of conduct encompassed by the legal codes he is expected to enforce.

In addition to establishing social and judgmental skills, a police training program must instill sensitivity to the civil liberties of citizens. Judicial systems are designed to safeguard rights as well as to control crime. The balanced view of law enforcement is conveyed not by lofty rhetoric, but by the operating practices of the police department. Values of justice must be embodied in concrete guidelines for responsible conduct and procedural rules that make explicit what laws do not permit policeman to do. Unless behavioral guidelines are backed up by sanctions, they will have no lasting impact on police practices in the field. The behavioral enactments and judgmental tests used in training sessions should include incidents that raise constitutional issues. In this way, recruits can be sensitized to the conflicts they will repeatedly experience between the efficiency of disallowed methods and citizen rights.

The judicial aspect of training deserves serious consideration in view of evidence that policemen are disposed to make arrests partly on the basis of their own moral codes (Reiss, 1971). In effect, officers make a judgment of guilt influenced by such factors as mitigating circumstances, the public visibility of the offense, the officers' own personal standards of reprehensibility, and the attitudes of the offender. Many offenders are not arrested for unlawful conduct, whereas disrespectful individuals, or those whose transgressions violate the policeman's sense of justice, run a high risk of ending up in jail. Training and supervisory effort should be aimed at reducing the partiality of initial determinations of criminality.

After neophytes have demonstrated sufficient competence in the preparatory instruction, they need supervised field practice. Through modeling and differential reinforcement by supervisory officers, recruits are aided in handling actual incidents proficiently while performing their assigned duties. Since police quickly learn that they can extract obedience more easily through force than through tact, periodic monitoring of their performances is necessary to safeguard against abuse of their coercive power. Changes in laws and in societal standards of conduct may necessitate retraining from time to time. Considering the personal hazards and serious social consequences of police actions, it is remarkable that few police departments combine comprehensive recruit training with supervised field experience and periodic performance checks. A police agency that adequately trains and oversees its officers and that views harsh practices disapprovingly should not be plagued by provocative police practices.

Police aggression is much more difficult to control when such behavior is organizationally condoned. Because regional enforcement agencies are linked to local politics through appointment of the police chief, police forces tend to serve as partisan instruments of power interest groups. As Lohman succinctly puts it, "The police function to support and enforce the interests of the dominant political, social, and economic interests of the town" (Neiderhoffer, 1967). It is not uncommon for police to enforce the law differentially against rich and poor, against minorities and those in the majority, against superiors and subordinates, and against those who follow conventional and unorthodox life styles (Tieger, 1971). That police do not function impartially is most clearly revealed in their handling of collective protests against dominant interest groups. When dissidents challenge the traditional power system, as in the case of civil rights workers and antiwar demonstrators, police often become assaultive in the guise of curbing lawlessness (Marx, 1970b). Police attacks on unpopular targets may not only be viewed permissively within the police system, but may receive widespread public support (Blumenthal et al., 1972; Gamson and McEvoy, 1970). Societal antipathy toward dissenters obviously does not foster police restraint in the use of coercive power.

From time to time investigators report evidence of other forms of police misconduct which shows that enforcement agencies do not police themselves very well. Observers who have accompanied patrolmen on their daily rounds report that, although most perform their official duties properly, a substantial number engage in criminal conduct or behave abusively without provocation (Reiss, 1971). That some police transgress is hardly surprising considering they work under conditions that tax both restraint and virtue. Discretionary power is easily misused, especially when there are no witnesses to the social confrontations. Should the propriety of injurious actions be questioned in any given instance, it can always be justified as needed to apprehend defiant wrongdoers or to restore order. As an additional self-protection, the seriousness of arresting charges can be scaled to excuse unwarranted assaults. In situations of physical jeopardy, it is of course difficult to act with restraint. Apart from inducements to violence, there are many entrepreneurs of unlawful activities who are eager to provide policemen with attractive income supplements for protective services. Those who shun illegal subsidies have ready access to merchandise that can be pilfered with little chance of detection. It is to the credit of most policemen that they maintain their integrity under the circumstances. Nevertheless, transgression rates are sufficiently serious to require better regulatory mechanisms.

A citizen feedback system can function as a significant deterrent to police misconduct. Unless one knows how the clients on the street are being treated, corrective measures are unlikely to be instituted. Although to err is understandable, the lack of effective means by which citizens can control police misconduct is inexcusable in an open society. It is amply documented that police review procedures, where they do exist, serve more to discourage than to adjudicate grievances (Chevigny, 1969; Task Force Report, 1967). To begin with, people are dissuaded by fear of retaliation because they must lodge complaints through the offending agency. Should they choose to pursue the matter, the grievance procedures are inadequately publicized. Of the complainants who eventually find out where to go, many are discouraged, either by intimidation or bureaucratic harrassment, from filing their complaints. The record of adjudication of registered charges is perhaps the most serious indictment of the internal control system. Despite numerous charges and objective evidence that police infractions are common, in virtually all cases the policemen are exonerated of any misbehavior. Granted that many allegations are unwarranted and that corroborating evidence is sometimes difficult to obtain, nevertheless it strains credibility that patrolmen are that exemplary and complainants are that malicious.

It is not difficult to find reasons why policemen are averse to indicting themselves for delinquencies. Police transgressions are frequently witnessed by other patrolmen. Informal codes of the police subculture, however, prohibit informing on, or testifying against, fellow officers. The threat of peer sanctions is strengthened by promotion policies that tend to affect the quality of enforcement service as well. Advanced positions are filled by elevation within the ranks of the department, not by open competition for the best candidates. Barring lateral entry of personnel breeds conformity throughout the administrative hierarchy. Members of a closed system can ill afford to jeopardize their welfare by revealing infractions that many of their associates—and line officers, for that matter —may themselves have committed. Although police officials try to ferret out corruption in their ranks, few are apt to get exercised because of overzealous use of coercive force. On the contrary, policemen generally resent the legal restrictions imposed on the methods they can employ. In the private police ethic, the use of violent means to apprehend offenders is not viewed as a transgression. They are thus not about to indict fellow officers for roughing up argumentative suspects or infringing on the rights of dissidents. With law enforcement a major political issue, police administrators are quick to defend their officers in order to protect the public image of the department.

Overaggressive police behavior that is organizationally sanctioned is unlikely to be changed much by education, attractive salaries, or community relations programs. When police conduct is inadequately regulated from within, external influences are required to modify the policies of enforcement agencies. Responsible police conduct is best assured by holding patrolmen and their supervisory staff accountable for their actions, not only to vested interest groups, but to representatives of diverse segments of the community as well. However, insiders vigorously oppose having their actions reviewed by outsiders. And those most subject to police abuse unfortunately lack the political strength to institute monitoring procedures. Attempts to moderate police behavior therefore usually take the form of retaliatory threats and an occasional public exposé of police brutality that goes unpunished.

Efforts to improve police practices, like other endeavors at social reform, require a multifaceted approach. At the organizational level, changes in promotion policies allowing appointment of officials from the outside as well as from internal ranks can partially check perpetuation of police subcultures that subvert the purposes of the law. Corrective actions require an apparatus for assessing the performance of police departments by citizens outside the organization. If a monitoring system is to have much impact on police practices it must perform a broader function than merely processing complaints of police abuses. As Chevigny (1969) demonstrates convincingly, the individual case approach has limited value. Abusive police behavior is shielded by standard charges of disorderly conduct, resisting arrest, and felonious assault. Because allegations are difficult to prove, the unwieldy hearings rarely produce any disciplinary action. But although individual charges of misconduct can easily be dismissed, the accumulated complaints, if carefully evaluated, can reveal the types of transgressive behavior condoned by police mores and by the leading offenders in the system. Observers who have studied the problem in depth (Chevigny, 1969; Reiss, 1971) are of the opinion that complaint data should be used to change the regulations of police departments in ways that curtail future abuses. Since the credibility of complainants can always be challenged, such information might supplement broader periodic assessments that include interviews to secure citizens' reactions to the police services they are receiving. Community surveys should measure commendable performances as well as grievances arising from partiality or inaction in police work, from abuses of coercive power, and from controversial enforcement procedures. Public disclosure of current practices, along with annual trend data for different precincts, can exert pressure on police administrators to improve their field operations.

Judicial reviews provide an additional (though admittedly limited) measure of police performance that might be used in a formal way to correct unauthorized practices (Task Force Report, 1967). Courts can furnish a record of instances in which evidence was excluded because police behaved illegally. A high incidence of exclusionary rulings suggests that the departmental guidelines, the discipline, or both require administrative attention. Police, of course, exercise informal control over conduct that does not violate legal codes and is therefore not subject to judicial review. When the values shared by residents in a given neighborhood conflict with the standards of morality espoused by the policing agency, disputes over personally disliked behavior tend to get transformed into crimes against patrolmen. Some of the value clashes could be diminished by having community representatives participate in the formation of policies for police conduct toward the public they are serving.

It would be a mistake to assume that police abuses arise solely from malfunctions in enforcement agencies. A society gets the type of policing it wants. If a majority of citizens feel sufficiently threatened by social protest or deviant styles of behavior, they will condone unauthorized means of controlling the troublesome individuals. However, police can be less easily used as instruments of coercion if their performance is subject to public scrutiny than if it remains unexamined.

Contribution of the Mass Media

Various survey studies have shown American television to be a rich cultural source of violence. Gerbner (1972a, b), who has conducted the most sophisticated yearly analyses of televised violence, reports a stable violence rate of more than seven assaults per hour, with approximately 80 percent of dramatic programs containing some form of violent activity. Seasonal comparisons disclose some fluctuation in violence rates for the different networks and program categories, but no evidence of overall decline in this respect.

Evaluation of the impact of the mass media on individual and collective aggression has been impeded by fear that, should a relationship be demonstrated, such findings might prompt governmental regulation or even censorship of program content. As a result, many social scientists were quick to proclaim the innocuousness of televised influences long before there were any pertinent empirical data, and some continued to defend its impotence in the face of cumulative evidence to the contrary.

One prevalent disclaimer is couched in terms of multiple determination of behavior. Aggression, it is said, does not arise from any single source. To indict television as the cause of aggression is to find a convenient scapegoat for a complex problem. The force of this argument is usually bolstered by noting parenthetically that at one time some people (without supporting evidence, it should be added) imputed the roots of brutal aggressive acts to comic books. Since no behavior is ever completely controlled by a single psychological determinant, this type of argument applies equally to any other influence that might be invoked. It could be similarly contended, with justification, that broken homes, rejecting parents, impoverishment, oppression, and provocative police are not individually the sole and invariable causes of aggression. One does not advance understanding of media effects by posing nonsensical causal assertions that call for negative answers. Platitudes to the effect that televised influences operate through a variety of mediating factors are widely quoted in the literature in this field as incisive causal analysis. Obviously, portrayal of violent methods is neither a sufficient nor a necessary condition of aggression. The same can be said for every other determinant of aggression.

Closely related to the multiple cause disclaimer is the argument of secondary influence. Here, the possibility that modeled aggression might have some effect on viewers is acknowledged, but it is regarded as a relatively minor factor. The criteria by which such judgments are made unfortunately remain unstated. Subjective weightings of determinants actually have little meaning because the same stimulus can have weak or powerful effects for different individuals, and even for the same individual on different occasions, depending on the presence of other aggression inducements. The value of averaged influences calls to mind the apocryphal nonswimmer who drowned while crossing a river that averaged 4 feet in depth. To assign a general value to televised influences simply obscures their role in causal processes. A combination of influences is typically required to produce a violent act that otherwise would not have occurred if any of the contributing elements were missing. When behavior is evoked only by a particular set of coexisting conditions, determinants that prove ineffective alone or even in partial conjunction each play a decisive role in the multiform cause. As we have already observed, media influences have differential impact on different forms of individual and collective aggression.

Another common misconception is that aggressive modeling affects only disturbed people. This belief rests on the unsupported foundation that aggression is a manifestation of an emotional disorder. Since the presence of an "emotional disorder" is partly inferred from a person's violent actions, traditional explanations have a built-in circularity that reinforces such beliefs. Even a casual review of value judgments and social causes of aggression quickly dispels the notion that aggression is sick behavior generated by an internal pathology. A social system gets its members to aggress, whatever their personal makeup, by legitimizing, modeling, and sanctioning such behavior, not by inducing emotional disorders in them. For this reason, one would not contend that broadcasters make heavy use of violence because they are emotionally disturbed, have a weak sense of reality, or are homicidally predisposed.

Aggression is typically used because it is successful in getting people what they want. Although the industry is quick to attribute aggressive modeling to defects in children and parents, it doubtless ascribes increases in consumer behavior to the power of the medium rather than to pathologies in the viewers.

A popular variant on the dispositional theme is that only individuals already predisposed to aggression are susceptible to televised influences. In this view, predisposition is misconstrued as a property inherent in the individual when, in fact, it is a multifaceted determinant. First, dispositions take the form of response capabilities. People who have learned aggressive styles of conduct are more disposed to behave aggressively than those who lack such responses. Second, predisposition reflects self-control functions. Individuals who expect to derive rewards or self-satisfaction from combativeness are more inclined to aggress than those who anticipate punishing or self-condemning consequences. The third and most important feature of dispositions is concerned with how the behavior is socially sanctioned in the environment. People are more disposed to act aggressively in settings where such conduct is well received than in situations in which it is prohibited. Considering the fact that dispositional determinants operate through multiple interacting influences, it is misleading to depict aggression as primarily under internal dispositional control.

In evaluating the assumption of restrictive influence, one must distinguish learning from the performance effects of televised violence. Obviously, one does not have to be emotionally disturbed or hyperaggressive to learn aggressive tactics observationally. Mild-mannered children learn as much from aggressive example as do aggressive children. Girls, who ordinarily are less disposed to physical aggression than boys, nevertheless model patterns of aggression equally well, though they are less inclined to put them into practice unless given incentives to do so. To the extent that aggressive people spend more time watching televised violence, they have more opportunities to be affected by it. Under these circumstances, however, the effects of personal aggressiveness are mediated more through variations in self-exposure to violence than through differential susceptibility to such contents.

Aggression proneness is better reflected by spontaneous performance of modeled acts of aggression, but even here the differences are smaller than might be expected. Although modeled brutality more readily prompts authoritarians (Epstein, 1966) and those who have a history of assaultiveness or criminal offenses (Wolfe and Baron, 1971; Hartmann, 1969) to behave punitively, it can also increase cruelty in those who are less prone to harshness in their daily interactions. Contrary to what is frequently asserted, nondisturbed children are just as likely to imitate modeled forms of aggression as are emotionally disturbed children who have been hospitalized for severe "personality" disorders (Walters and Willows, 1968). Through the teaching and disinhibitory functions of symbolic modeling, television can create as well as activate "dispositions" to aggression.

It is often claimed that displays of violence may affect children because they are less able to foresee the full consequences of their actions, but that adults, who possess a greater reality sense, are relatively immune to such influences. This opinion is also refuted by numerous studies demonstrating that intelligent and otherwise considerate college students behave more punitively after seeing others act aggressively than if they have had no exposure to such modeling influences. Adult response to modeled violence is further shown in the rapid spread of new styles of collective aggression to people in widely dispersed areas who learn about them mainly through detailed media coverage. Nor are adults entirely unresponsive to fictional violence. It is adult rather than child extortionists who threaten to blow up airliners with altitude-triggered bombs in a manner copied from a televised plot. There is every indication that the actions of adults are shaped by example just as much as those of children. Fashion and taste industries flourish on the basis of adolescent and adult modeling.

Like many other issues in aggression, the impact of televised violence on viewers is better understood in terms of social influence than characterological factors. Although it is true that the psychological attributes of viewers can affect the likelihood that modeled aggression may be performed on future occasions, social conditions that increase the permissibility and functional value of aggression easily override the effects of personal dispositions. For this reason, it is primarily types of social inducements rather than types of people that should be examined in predicting who will put into practice what has been learned from television.

The familial antidote argument also appears with some regularity in commentaries on mass media effects. By providing a warm, secure home and wholesome peers, parents, it is claimed, can neutralize any potential negative impact of repeated exposure to human brutality. Fortunately, the medical profession never adopted an analogous stance in promoting the physical health of citizens. Had parents been told by specialists in preventive medicine that the best way to counteract any ill effects of contaminated water and milk supplies delivered to their households was to raise healthy children, the competence of such authorities would have been seriously questioned. If parents cannot create a counterenvironment, which is no easy task, they are told they should control what their children watch on television. To be most effective, parental monitoring requires advance information on the quantity of carnage contained in given programs. Parents would be greatly aided in this function if networks and TV guides reported the violence rates in the various offerings.

The antidote recommendations, even if they could be easily implemented, would not necessarily provide adequate safeguards against imitative assaultiveness. Aggressive acts, like other forms of behavior, are not exclusively under parental control. Children may refrain from imitative aggression in the presence of adults who disapprove of such actions, but perform them when the adults are no longer around (Hicks, 1968a). Interpersonal aggression is a social not a private matter. Nonviewers can be secondarily affected by television either by emulating the conduct of influenced viewers or as victims of their heightened aggression. In the controlled field studies, it is nonviewers who are physically assaulted by those exposed to aggressive models of behavior. In the case of adults, it would be far-fetched, for example, to claim that modeled extortion behavior toward airlines is mediated through maternal influences. Moreover, under certain conditions, parental warmth and compassion may facilitate rather than counteract aggressive modeling in their offspring. Students raised in principled, humanitarian homes were the most disposed to follow models of coercive action in attempts to rectify social injustices.

Disavowals of the aggression-promoting effects of televised modeling are usually accompanied by enumeration of the positive effects of displaying brutality. The cathartic function is listed as if this were a documented fact rather than a questionable belief. Even if there were evidence to show that a distinct aggressive drive existed and that watching someone commit physical violence upon others drained it, the wisdom of saturating the airwaves with displays of violence would still be questionable, if only because of their instructional function. Such sluicing operations would achieve, at most, temporary drainage at the price of teaching new techniques of cruelty, devaluing life by treating human beings like disposable commodities, and sanctioning violent solutions to interpersonal problems. A social influence must be judged on the basis of the multiple effects it can have on people. Concern with empirically demonstrable effects should not completely overshadow the morality of using cruelty to entertain people.

Material reviewed extensively in preceding chapters reveals that many vigorously debated issues are reasonably well clarified by controlled studies and corroborated by recurring modeling incidents in everyday life. The cumulative evidence provides answers to certain questions about the effects of television and increases the validity of probabilistic judgments of other effects. Given the abundant evidence for observational learning, there is no longer any justification for equivocating about whether children or adults learn techniques of aggression from televised models. People who watch commercial television for any period of time will learn a number of aggressive tactics and countless methods of murder. Television is a superb tutor. People do not, of course, perform everything they learn. Substantial progress has been made in identifying some of the factors that interact with modeling influences to foster or restrain aggressive actions. Individuals who have been exposed to displays of violence are more likely to act aggressively and with greater intensity than those who have not when they are subjected to provocation or emotional arousal; when they have received prior training in aggression; when adequate justification for aggressive conduct is provided; when threat of retaliation is reduced; when the injurious consequences of aggression are not fully evident; and when aggressive behavior has functional value in securing material rewards, social recognition, a boost in self-esteem, or successful retaliation against disliked antagonists.

Television does not control the aggression instigators experienced by its viewers or the reinforcement supports their environment provides for such conduct. Rather, it influences their aggressive tendencies primarily by teaching them how to aggress and by the way in which it portrays the functional value of coercive behavior. If violence were presented as a morally reprehensible and costly way of achieving desired goals, viewers might be discouraged from resorting to similar tactics should the temptation arise. Analyses of program contents show, however, that television is more inclined to condone than to devalue violent solutions.

Depicting punishing consequences for violence can reinforce aggression restraints in viewers, although it is an undependable inhibitor. Observed punishment may suppress, but does not erase, what viewers have learned. They may put this knowledge into practice on future occasions if sufficiently provoked or if the behavior is necessary to get what they want. Dramatic requirements further reduce the inhibitory potential of portrayed punishment. In the development of a plot villainous characters appropriate important resources and amass attractive rewards through variegated series of aggressive exploits. If they never succeeded, it would be difficult to sustain a plot. Thus, for example, through physical coercion protagonists gain control over grazing lands, gold mines, steers, nightclubs, attractive belles, the constabulary, corporations, and prominent figures. Aggressors are not usually punished—and then only once—until the end of the program, whereas their antisocial life styles prove highly profitable over an extended period. The message is not that "crime does not pay," but rather that the wages of violent sin are pretty good except for an occasional mishap.

It has been demonstrated that immediate rewards exert greater influence on behavior than delayed punishment. Moreover, observed successes weaken the inhibitory power of witnessed punishments wherever they may occur temporally (Rosekrans and Hartup, 1967). When commercials are inserted before the ethical ending, as is generally the case, young children fail to grasp the relationship between actions and outcomes and are therefore not dissuaded from adopting aggressive solutions (Collins, 1973). Finally, in some instances depicted punishment can sustain adherence to aggressive methods through its informative value. To the extent that observers profit from the mistakes of others, they may act on the belief that, with slight modification of tactics, they can gain the benefits of aggression without suffering the costs. For these various reasons, it is better not to teach violent methods than to teach them and try to inhibit their use. Affixing an ethical ending to a succession of aggressive triumphs in no way removes the enduring learning effects.

There has been much speculation but comparatively little research on the emotional and attitudinal effects of extended exposure to violence. Concerns have been voiced that viewing brutality day after day and week after week eventually produces callousness and insensitivity to cruelty. Repeated exposure to displays of violence can gradually extinguish emotional responsiveness. The power of filmed influences to diminish fears and behavioral inhibitions is most convincingly demonstrated in therapeutic applications of modeling. Phobic children lose some of their fears (Bandura and Menlove, 1968) and seclusive children overcome their social inhibitions by observing venturesome examples (O'Connor, 1969, 1972). As in other areas of functioning, adult inhibitions are susceptible to modification by modeling influences as are those of children. Adults who have suffered from severe phobias of long standing lose their fears and develop more favorable attitudes toward things they formerly abhorred after watching scenes of others interacting freely with threatening objects (Bandura, Blanchard, and Ritter, 1969). Results of these and other studies (Bandura, 1971a) attest to the positive potential of televised influences, were the medium to be used more constructively.

Of special interest are the behavioral effects of removing fears and aversions. Aggression anxiety inhibits a person from engaging in abhorrent activities. After aversions have been extinguished, he can more easily commit such acts, but whether or not he ever will do so depends on the social influences that impinge on him. This issue has some bearing on controversies over the cumulative effects of daily portrayals of combat activities in television news. Some people maintain that such scenes elicit shock reactions that condition aversion to war. Wertham (1966), a vigorous crusader against displays of violence in any form, contends that as a result of daily viewing of fragmented military scenes, people eventually become accustomed to warfare and indifferent to the suffering it causes. It therefore produces receptivity to war rather than revulsion against it. He argues further that most movie versions of warfare, with their glorification of patriotic violence, heroism, and adventure, are essentially war commercials. Through repeated exposure people can become emotionally habituated to depictions of horrific carnage (Hess, 1968). It remains to be demonstrated, however, whether the emotional desensitization leads them to accept or to abhor war. Emotional reactions and behavioral preferences are not perfectly correlated. That is, one can fear things he likes and deplore things he does not fear.

Ordinarily one might expect a widespread public outcry against corporations that provide continuous instruction in methods of murder for all ages and sanction aggression as a means of attaining goals or settling disputes. In reality, most of the viewing public have not only grown accustomed to a heavy dose of brutality on television, but having no comparative alternatives, accept what they are shown. Apart from its entertainment value, television serves as a most welcome baby sitter when parents want their children out of the way. If exposing children to human cruelty is the price for this function, then most preoccupied parents are willing to pay it, especially if they are reassured that it has no influence. Audience preferences partly shaped by television then serve as justification for similar offerings that produce further habituation to violence.

In contrast to the ready acceptance of televised violence by American viewers, representatives of other nations respond with incredulity to disclaimers that televised modeling has no influence and voice concern over the export of American violence abroad (Lejins, 1968). The amazement and uneasiness shown by other nations is well grounded, considering the massive evidence that the behavior of models can shape diverse classes of behavior including linguistic styles, moral judgments, self-gratification patterns, altruism, cognitive skills, inhibitions, emotional responsiveness, transgressive behavior, attitudes, tastes, and preferences, as well as aggressive modes of response (Bandura, 1969a, 1971d; Campbell, 1961; Flanders, 1968). The networks' unwavering uncertainty about the effects their programs have on people is captured in the story once told of a patient who consulted a psychiatrist concerning doubts over his wife's fidelity. During the next visit the patient reported seeing his wife accompany an amorous man into a hotel room, whereupon they promptly disrobed and jumped into bed. At that moment the lights were turned off, leaving the husband at the keyhole still feeling uncertain about his wife's fidelity.

In selling commercial time to sponsors television executives undoubtedly argue for the power of television to influence the behavior of viewers with the same strong conviction with which they disclaim its capability to affect aggressive responsiveness. Their public evaluations of research concerning social behavior often convey the impression that only demonstration of instant direct effects on viewers would constitute convincing proof that televised modeling can be a contributing influence to aggression. Evidence that exposure to aggressive models of behavior increases aggressive tendencies does not mean that after watching protagonists use aggressive methods, viewers leave the television set and assault the first person they meet, any more than smoking a package of cigarettes will produce instant cancer in everyone.

Since most behavior is under the multiple control of interacting influences, the coexistence of several factors is generally required to produce a given response. Multiple determination applies equally to television influence on consumer behavior. A well-endowed blonde entreats the viewing audience to "join the Dodge rebellion" while seductively enumerating the virtues of this brand of automobile. The commercial vendors obviously do not expect every viewer to dash off immediately to his nearest Dodge dealer. Most people will not instantly act on what they have learned because they do not need a car, are satisfied with the one they have, lack the money, or have other priorities at the moment. The idea has been planted, however, and given appropriate conditions some of the viewers will act in accordance with the televised directive on some future occasion. A rise in sales above a reliable baseline establishes television as a determinant, although the particular combinations of factors that prompt action in different individuals are not predictable in advance. The television industry justifiably sells commercial time even though it cannot specify beforehand exactly who will be influenced, at what time, and in what setting. Indeed, most policy decisions are made on the basis of group incidence rates rather than precise individual prediction.

The abundant evidence reviewed in this book and elsewhere (Goranson, 1970; Liebert, 1972; Maccoby, 1964; Siegel, 1970) supports the conclusion that televised aggressive modeling, through its instruction and sanction of aggressive methods, lowers the threshold of aggressive response and shapes its form. Exposure to televised violence increases the likelihood that some viewers will behave aggressively in the face of other inducements. As televised modeling is studied further in conjunction with other aggression-promoting conditions, greater accuracy will be achieved in predicting for which individuals and under what circumstances televised influences play a determining role in the occurrence of aggression.

Given the capability of television to influence behavior and the marketability of conflict, the use of brutal content is a proper matter of social concern. A sizable fraction of viewers from time to time register complaints against how the medium is used. Some of the criticisms represent moralizing and elitist preferences for what people should be taught to enjoy. Other critics are less concerned about negative effects than by the fact that pressures to maximize profits have deprived viewers of stimulating and creative experiences that develop the positive potentialities of man. In many instances the critical indictments reflect general concern over the commercial exploitation of violence. Members of minority groups, who find themselves victimized by being repeatedly portrayed in derogatory stereotypes, experience the effects of television more personally and pervasively. They have compelling reasons to seek change.

Television practices are under powerful advertiser control. As a commercial business, television networks must compete successfully to protect the financial interests of their stockholders. Most advertisers favor the competitor who can deliver the largest audiences at the cheapest rates. This in itself would not seriously prejudice programming against viewers' interests were it not for the contiguity problem. Advertisers are reluctant to purchase time adjacent to programs that attract small audiences because viewers tend to watch whatever comes on the channel next without much switching. Therefore sponsors willing to support quality programs that appeal to more limited audiences do not have equal access to prime viewing time even if they have the money to buy it.

When constitutional principles are used to defend television programming, the matter of restricted access to television is never raised. Freedom of expression combined with the right of public access to the medium would ensure a much broader expression of ideas on television than now exists. Exorbitant production costs further increase the force of economic control and curtail experimentation with varied dramatic contents. What catches on is widely copied, with the result that different networks counterprogram similar contents, leaving the viewer with few choices. Imitative proliferation of Westerns and crime series provide additional testimony to the influence of profitable aggressive modeling.

Without effective means of counterinfluence both the medium and the general public are subject to the abuses of excessive commercialization. There are four different ways in which the public can attempt to influence the operating practices of the television industry. The most popular—but minimally effective—method is to appeal to governmental agencies to control the commercial marketing of violence. Call for federal action produces few results for a variety of reasons. Constitutional guarantees of free communication restrict the government from regulating the content of television programming. Even if the government had such restrictive power, it would rarely be used because most people are, by tradition, opposed to having official agencies prescribing what they can watch. Although government cannot regulate program content, it can take action against grossly irresponsible performance through the licensing power of the Federal Communications Commission. There is little danger, however, that a television station would ever lose its license from commercial overuse of violence, whatever its effects. Not only would such rulings provoke endless semantic disputes over what is violence, but they would be challenged on constitutional grounds. Being subject to political pressures, regulatory agencies of government are usually heavily influenced by the very industries they are supposed to oversee. As militant consumer advocates have repeatedly shown, federal regulatory bodies are more likely to serve corporate than public interests.

In sum, broadcasting is a powerful industry subject to limited governmental checks in matters of program content. Official criticisms of the manner in which the medium is used elicit charges of impending governmental censorship in the image of notorious political dictatorships. Most countries have adopted some reasonable guidelines regarding the portrayal of brutality and some have set aside a portion of their broadcast time for different interest groups to present their views without producing any collapse of their democratic institutions. Indeed, increased public activism has raised the issue of corporate censorship. By restricting access to television time (Barron, 1967) and excluding things that conflict with sponsor interests, network officials exercise selective control over what people will be shown. Without some regulatory guidelines the commercial pressures for screening what will be telecast might well increase with conglomerate ownership of communications media by powerful interest groups. Johnson (1967), an outspoken FCC commissioner, was probably accurate in characterizing many of the disputes in this area as more concerned with profitable speech than with free speech. It is through concerted legal action that the public will probably eventually gain some control over access to television time.

Although the government has neither the sanction nor the desire to police television programming, it cannot ignore public protests. Governmental efforts to reduce the incidence of violence on commercial television usually take the form of congressional hearings. Like television reruns, at periodic intervals representatives of the broadcast industry are brought before a congressional committee, where they argue over various charges and documented evidence of exploitation of violence. Like standardized serials, congressional investigations have essentially the same protagonists, playing the same stylized roles, with the same outcomes.

After the networks are commended for serving the public well in many ways, their record of violence is presented along with testimony by researchers on the psychological effects of such influences. Broadcasters challenge the criteria for judging violence; industry researchers dispute the empirical evidence. The influence of the broadcast industry is brought to bear, if necessary, even on officially commissioned evaluations of research findings (Paisley, 1972). Some examples of television practices are usually presented at the hearings; this prompts network executives to register strong complaints against excerpting scenes for display on the grounds that the aggressive actions are distorted when shown out of context. At one of the hearings (U.S. Senate, 1963) this proved to be an impolitic complaint, because the industry itself makes heavy use of excerpts in the form of "teasers" (opening scenes of things to come in the program), "trailers" (previews of the action to be shown next week), and "promotionals" (clips shown throughout the broadcast day). The committee proceeded to show a collection of trailers that represented a gory catalog of human atrocities. People were bludgeoned to death, machine-gunned, attacked brutally with knives, meat cleavers, pitchforks, and stilettos, stomped, drowned, burned, whipped, beaten viciously, and ruthlessly tortured. When asked to comment on this carnage, the president of one of the networks staunchly maintained that the segments constituted scenes of "physical action," not violence, to the utter disbelief of his questioners. The hearing continued in this vein with much time spent quibbling about definitions of violence and categorization of programs. The testimony of producers, supplemented with industry memos documenting instances in which violence was callously exploited, could not be as easily dismissed semantically.

At the conclusion of such hearings, the presiding chairman predictably issues threats to the effect that if the industry fails to improve its procedures of self-regulation, federal controls will have to be imposed. Broadcasters, in turn, reaffirm that they have not been misbehaving; besides, the objectionable practices are a thing of the past, and they shall continue to abide by the industry code of good conduct. The reformed self-assessment is typically accompanied by righteous denunciations of the evils of governmental censorship, as though freedom carried no responsibility. In reality, the industry fears the adverse publicity more than the threat of censorship. Since no one bothers to maintain a check on violence rates in programs after hearings have concluded, there is little reason to discontinue the customary profitable practices. After a time public pressure on Congress again mounts, prompting another congressional rerun. The commotion generated by pseudo threats serves to evade a discussion of constructive changes that do not involve infringement of free expression. As a public service, some amount of broadcasting time could be set aside for children's programming without having advertisers using youngsters to pressure parents to buy products that they either don't want or don't need. Suitable funding arrangements would then be developed. Freed from the pressures of commercialism, producers could devote their talents to creating entertaining quality programs for children.

A second method for promoting social responsibility in television programming relies on the industry's system of self-regulation. In this approach discontented viewers are urged to write letters to networks and their sponsors threatening withdrawal of patronage if they continue to exploit themes of violence. A commercial business is highly responsive to economic threats, but the correspondence approach has little effect because the letters do not get written and the sponsors' products are rarely boycotted.

However well-intentioned media practitioners might be, when left to internal regulation, profits will dictate content. This is forcefully revealed in the operating principle stated by the president of a television network to the director of his news division: "They say to me [he meant the system, not any specific individual], 'Take your soiled little hands, get the ratings, and make as much money as you can'; they say to you, 'Take your lily white hands, do your best, go the high road and bring us prestige' " (Friendly, 1968, pp. xi–xii). Networks supervise the production process, but in the face of strong financial pressures and weak public sanctions, the operating guidelines are quite pliable. Monitors screen mainly the upper limits of violence, and even these are negotiable. Appeals to superiors in the system can overrule objections of the overseers. Some excesses in brutality get by because of the prohibitive costs of reshooting scenes. Righteous codes are fine for public relations, but neither the performance record nor frank statements by industry personnel (Baldwin and Lewis, 1972) inspire confidence that the broadcasters' self-regulatory practices are especially conducive to wholesome programming.

The third approach to corporate influence rests on the well-established principle that socially responsible behavior is produced through performance consequences. From time to time people knowledgeable in mass communications have proposed establishment of a private institute designed to report annually on the performance of the broadcasting industry and, whenever appropriate, to propose constructive reforms. A respected private body might gain some token concessions, but it is unrealistic to expect a global annual report to alter television practices in any significant way. The consequences, should any result, are too weak and remote.

Private individuals can promote socially responsible behavior in corporate enterprises through the power of publicity and constructive alternatives. If a change effort is to have much effect, it must combine continuing performance assessment with appropriate consequences. A company will behave differently when its performance is publicly evaluated than if no one examines what it is doing.

A public violence-monitoring service is the first step in fostering social responsibility in commercial television programming. A service of this type might be funded by foundation or private sources to preserve its independence from government and industry control. It would attempt to reduce some of the excesses of commercial control of program content by publicized assessments, since it would have no regulatory or enforcement power. Gerbner (1972a, b) has developed a sensitive method for measuring the amount of violence shown on television through content analysis of its output. The standard coding system records the number and kinds of violent actions, and provides an index of the rate of violent episodes per hour of broadcasting. The manner in which aggression is portrayed may be even more important than the amount presented. These qualitative features are measured in terms of the frequency with which righteous and villainous characters use violent tactics, and the percentage of leading characters involved in killing either as killers or as victims. Other ratable aspects of violence include its instigators, its rewarding and punishing consequences, and the types of people who are repeatedly victimized. The prevalence, rate, and role component scores are combined into an overall violence index. A multidimensional index, derived from depicted patterns of violent relationships, is much more difficult to circumvent than a simple prevalence or rate measure.

At periodic intervals a trained staff would conduct systematic analyses of the commercial fare. Otherwise responsible individuals feel less concerned over the production and marketing of violence for profit if their contribution to the total enterprise is not singled out. Analysis of media content should therefore restore accountability for violence wherever possible. This is achieved by computing separate violence rates for the different networks, sponsors, and programs.

The violence ratings, as well as seasonal trends, could be disseminated widely through TV guides, PTA publications, and—ideally—periodic televised reports to the public. Analyses of television practices should be concerned with more than just violence. The goal of improving the quality of television programming is better served by providing examples of creative uses of the medium that viewers find enjoyable.

It is through comparison with positive alternatives that the commercialization of violence is most forcefully revealed. Reports to the public also provide a suitable context in which to examine the broader issue of television as a cultural transmitter and innovator of attitudes and patterns of behavior.

Performance evaluation is a straightforward matter, but the promotion of consequences becomes a more sensitive issue. A violence rating service is likely to have greatest impact if conducted responsibly without assuming a strong advocacy position. The evidence of what viewers are being shown would be presented to them to use as they might wish without infringing on anybody's rights. As consumer advocates have demonstrated, disclosure of objectionable practices is, in itself, likely to mobilize some collective actions by citizen groups. Publicized violence ratings are most likely to achieve results through their effects on the principal force in the system, namely, the financial subsidizers. Since corporate sponsors are sensitive about their public image, publication of their violence ratings would prompt them to demand from producers engrossing drama without gratuitous use of violence. A business that employs violence to sell breakfast food to children, for example, could not afford to maintain that practice for long if it were widely and repeatedly publicized.

Any public efforts to diminish commercial control of television practices are easily discredited on misleading grounds. The most commonly used argument is that public influence will banish all violence from television, leaving a bland fare in its place. Fear-arousing appeals of this sort distort the nature of the public concern. It is not portrayal of conflict that people object to; rather, it is the unrelenting use of physical assaultiveness to convey human discord and fixation on violent solutions as the preferred remedies. Themes of conflict can, in fact, serve to counteract assaultive modes of conduct. Modeling prosocial solutions to conflict provides viewers with constructive options that tend to reduce their dependence on combative tactics (Chittenden, 1942).

The entertainment value of televised programs need in no way suffer by reducing violence as a salable commodity. Quite the contrary. Producers generally prefer creating nonviolent programs to those oriented around violent superheroes. Some acknowledge that limitations on routine use of violence are more likely to prod than to curtail creativity: "Sometimes these restrictions are challenging. How can I show tension in a fresh way without a punch in the gut?" (Baldwin and Lewis, 1972, p. 331). The more inventive producers, whose efforts deserve full support, welcome the creative challenge when network directives allow them to ease up on manufacturing violent contents: "You get sick doing that crap. We *had* to do it for two years because that is what the network wanted. . . . Now we are using our brains coming up with ways of doing things that do not rely on smashing, hitting, and banging. Now we are enjoying our work" (Cantor, 1972, p. 266). Analyzing bad programs is not necessarily going to produce good ones. A violence monitoring system may be required to create the opportunities for better offerings, but other vehicles are needed to bring this about.

Greater progress is achieved by rewarding desirable practices than by curtailing objectionable ones. Public efforts to improve the quality of television programming should not be limited to negative sanctions. The fourth, and most affirmative, approach relies on the power of positive example. Programs that use violence as the principal means for capturing audiences would be put out of business by providing people with more interesting alternatives. The influence of successful example is nowhere better illustrated than in children's programming, which has aroused the greatest public criticism. For years parents complained about the serial dramas and weekend commercial fare served their children, but did little to discourage them from watching it. The appearance of *Sesame Street* on noncommercial stations demonstrated that a program that is instructive as well as entertaining can attract large child audiences with parental endorsement.

A viable public broadcasting system, free of commercial pressures, is perhaps the best means of improving and diversifying television offerings. Within this context, a program development unit might be created for the purpose of testing new ideas as well as assessing the impact of programs, especially on young viewers. Close collaboration between producers and social scientists could serve the dual purpose of expanding the quality of television programming and advancing understanding of communication influences. The adoption of new formats by the commercial networks could be accelerated by displaying successful prototypes in the reports to the public mentioned earlier. Commercial networks can derive other benefits from a good public broadcasting service. It can function not only as a place for testing ideas, but for creating new interests which commercial television is understandably reluctant to undertake because of the initial financial losses. Under severe economic competition, programs are created for instant commercial success.

From time to time economic proposals have been offered on how to provide public broadcasting with adequate funding for facilities and professional talent. The most imaginative plan was developed by the Ford Foundation (Friendly, 1968). Satellites will replace land lines as the mode of transmission with considerable savings. Ford proposed that a nonprofit corporation operate the communications satellite service and reserve some of the revenues from commercial users to support public broadcasting. This plan was challenged by private carrier corporations that claim the right to operate a multipurpose satellite service. Whether any of the revenue from a communications satellite will be earmarked for noncommercial television remains to be seen.

There are other major developments in the offing that can alter the manner in which the medium is used. Technological innovations in the form of cable television and laser and satellite telecasting will permit simultaneous broadcasting of varied programs to audiences with diverse interests. The technical capacity for diversified programming can free viewers from the tyranny of the common denominator. Computer retrieval systems, wherein viewers can select programs from videotape libraries, will add another new dimension to broadcasting services. These systems, of course, will not be free of commercial pressures to maximize profits at the expense of public interests. If cost per thousand viewers continues to dictate program production, and there is every reason to believe it will, cable television is likely to duplicate the practices of the current system. The net result will be many channels ritualistically repeating similar formula shows, old movies, and reruns that, being cheaper, make more money than more entertaining programs requiring higher production expenditures. Whether the technical changes bring significant reforms in programming partly depends on whether the public is granted some right of access to the facilities and how actively it is exercised. A watchful public can increase the likelihood that new opportunities will change television from a mediocre entertainer and teacher of aggressive life styles to an instrument of human enlightenment.

Television Journalism

A high proportion of newscasting time is devoted to coverage of violent events in one form or another. Both local stations and national networks undoubtedly vary in the emphasis they give to violent incidents. Over an extended period Singer (1970) compared the proportion of news items of an aggressive nature reported by an American network and a Canadian network that has full access to the same content and frequently rebroadcasts a substantial amount of American material. American newscasts carried approximately twice as many aggressive items. Even when war reports were deleted from the data, American newscasts continued to offer substantially more aggressive items (36 percent) and devoted more time to them (40 percent) than its Canadian counterpart, for which the corresponding figures were 18 percent and 19 percent, respectively. Whether the heavy American emphasis on violence mirrors the cultural reality or the predilection of the medium itself cannot be determined from this study. A comparative analysis of the proportion of news items devoted to violence by the national networks and by local stations within the same city would provide some indication of broadcasting company preferences.

Heated debates have raged over the partiality of broadcast journalism and its social and political impact. Considering the central role played by television in public affairs, surprisingly little study has been made of these issues. Some researchers have analyzed the social influences operating within the media systems in determining the selection and presentation of news contents (Breed, 1955; Warner, 1971). The effects of the media output, however, remain largely unexamined. Reports of ordinary crimes rarely arouse controversy, except perhaps for their disproportionate emphasis as newsworthy items in the brief time allotted to television news. Rather, it is in conflicts for power between contending groups, where the medium can function as an instrument of influence, that charges of partisan treatment arise.

There are several ways in which accounts of violence might produce social effects. Detailed reports of activities have instructional potential. Previous analyses of aggression contagion, though complicated by many determinants, lend some substance to the view that mass media coverage of civil disturbances can shape the form of collective aggression and inadvertently contribute to its spread. Observers can learn from newscasts, among other things, how to firebomb with Molotov cocktails, how to conduct a sniper siege, and the steps required to hijack airliners successfully. Although the printed media disseminate information about acts of violence, television has the greater potential to influence behavior because it portrays events more vividly and concretely. Furthermore, most people learn about newsworthy incidents from watching television rather than from reading magazines or newspapers (Schramm, Lyle, and Parker, 1961). The power of pictures is confirmed by Barrow and Westley (1960), who found that young viewers learned more from television than from an equivalent radio version of the news events.

Media reports of violent episodes not only reveal the use of destructive weapons and aggressive tactics, but can also influence aggression restraints by their portrayal of the consequences of violence. In order to hold viewers' attention, the visual displays accompanying the news reports are selected to entertain as well as to inform. The outcomes of given courses of actions are easily misrepresented when graphic effects are favored over common, but less interesting, consequences. Thus, showing people running off with appliances and cases of liquor from looted stores in a jovial atmosphere is more likely to promote aggression in viewers living under similar circumstances than showing the terror and suffering caused by massive destruction of one's neighborhood.

Another way of affecting aggressive restraints in viewers is by the degree of justification given to violent activities in the narration of news stories. Meyer (1971) showed angered adults a filmed news item in which a wounded North Vietnamese prisoner was stabbed to death by a South Vietnamese soldier. Subjects who watched the newsfilm with a voiceover narration that justified the execution subsequently behaved more punitively than those who observed the same news event with either no commentary or verbal portrayal of the stabbing as unjustified. These results suggest that reporters' descriptions of newsworthy violence can influence viewers' readiness to behave aggressively.

Televised reports of violence, depending on what they accent, may in some instances affect the course of collective aggression for better or for worse through their sanctioning potential. Because of the scarcity of newscast time, only a few items from a vast array of events can be presented. Selective processes are similarly involved even in reporting the violent episodes chosen, since only a few aspects of the sequence of events can be introduced. One can highlight the social conditions provoking strife, the specific tactics of aggression used, the immediate or delayed consequences accruing to aggressors, the injurious effects to the victims, the pronouncements of leading protagonists, or the types of countermeasures employed by control agents. From knowledge of social influence processes one would expect the potential consequences of media presentations to vary depending on what aspects are selected for public display and how they are characterized in accompanying commentaries. Ball-Rokeach (1972) attaches special significance to media transmission of evaluative reactions concerning violent events. The reason for this is that relatively few viewers experience sufficient inducements to emulate portrayed violent conduct, but the modeled justifications and evaluative responses can help to mobilize public support for policy actions that have widespread social and political consequences.

If disruptive actions are depicted as lawlessness and the coverage selectively emphasizes the revolutionary rhetoric of extremists and the injuries suffered by the targets, most viewers will deplore the protest activities and demand punitive controls. In contrast, reports that attend to the causes of aggression and characterize the group action as a means of securing needed reforms will produce a more sympathetic response in viewers toward improving social conditions. Visual documentation of police practices can partly determine the sides viewers will take in a social conflict. Early in the civil rights movement, for example, the sight of policemen brutally attacking nonviolent protesters probably did more to arouse a hitherto complacent populace than all the moral appeals or democracy arguments combined.

The foregoing presumptions follow plausibly from existing knowledge, but they require experimental verification with studies offering differential reports of the same aggressive incidents. The behavioral and attitudinal consequences of media practices could be assessed by varying the amount of attention given to causes, tactics, consequences, and countercontrols in the coverage of newsworthy events. Should the predicted relationships be confirmed, such findings would sensitize television journalists to the specific effect that differential emphasis of news content is likely to have on the viewing public.

The discussion thus far has dealt with how the mass media may influence the course of aggression through selective or incomplete portrayal of newsworthy violence. Informal observations suggest that the presence of reporters and television cameras at the scene of aggressive altercations can exert some effect on the incidents themselves. Cameras tend to invite and to give greater attention to the provocative rhetoric of extremists than to less colorful moderates. It has been shown that selective attention to certain members of a group, who ordinarily received little recognition, confers leadership status on them (Hastorf, 1965). To the extent that such an influence process is operative in picking engrossing news shots, television may contribute to the emergence of a leader from among the various contenders. In a continuing conflict, selective editing of performances having dramatic appeal may distort the nature or purpose of the contending groups in ways that promote divisive stereotyping and angry polarization. Acrimonious retorts performed for television audiences would further prolong the aggressive struggle. Although claims of misrepresentation abound, no one has systematically compared the actual events and what is chosen for television news coverage.

With camera crews around, challengers are apt to become more exhibitionistic and police more restrained in their behavior. Indeed, the inhospitable reception that reporters typically receive from police at the scene of a conflict suggests that the presence of cameras reduces the incidence of unauthorized police aggression. It would be of considerable interest to measure changes in the behavior of contending groups when television camera crews are present and when they are absent.

The preceding discussion concentrated on how media output can affect public opinion and action. Because of its influence potential, the communication system itself is subject to constant pressure from various interest groups within the society. A complete analysis of communication processes must encompass the reciprocal influence between transmitters and recipients. Conflicts over coverage of newsworthy events inevitably arise from a multitude of sources. Since television is a competitive industry, concern over advertising revenue partly dictates how the medium will be used (Friendly, 1968). Political officials apply leverage in efforts to sway the reporting of domestic and foreign events in their favor. Additionally, there are the pressures from the viewing public that criticize the industry for slanted treatment of the news. Conservatives view newscasters as advocates of liberal causes, whereas dissidents contend that television, being controlled by privileged groups, avoids controversial issues that conflict with their corporate or political interests. Finally, the newsmen, who become the unenviable targets of the opposing pressures, have to contend with their own ideological commitments in choosing what to show the public.

Television journalism undoubtedly serves as an instrument in aiding social reforms or reinforcing prevailing customs by how it presents controversial issues. Few serious students of journalism espouse the illusion of neutrality. In commenting on the matter of balanced reporting, the distinguished broadcast journalist Edward R. Murrow, rightly pointed out that one cannot do equal justice to contending points of view because rarely are they equally justifiable. The different segments of society are better served by striving for communication pluralism rather than neutrality. As long as there are alternative channels of information to which the public has access, divergent views can be adequately aired.

A number of conditions, some organizational and others social, limit the pluralistic possibilities of television journalism. Media ownership is concentrated in the higher ranks of society. Although newsmen strive for fairness, diverse interests would obviously receive greater exposure if the media were under more varied proprietorship. Relatively little time is devoted to news coverage because it produces a low financial yield. Even with the best of intentions, time pressures preclude the type of analytic reporting required to explain the interplay of forces creating and maintaining violent conflicts. As a result, complex issues are essentially reduced to headlines with fragmented pictorial accompaniment interspersed with numerous commercials. Public affairs programs treat selected topics in greater depth, but this format is only sparingly used. Although television coverage is not intended to substitute for the depth and range of newspaper reports, most people do rely on television as their main source of information about matters that affect their lives.

In addition to organizational constraints, those who espouse unpopular views encounter social barriers to gaining a satisfactory hearing on television. This is because societal reinforcements are heavily weighted in favor of neglecting dissident groups. The television industry can enjoy public support by airing matters that fall within the bounds of popular sentiment, whereas providing a forum for dissenters brings condemnation and economic threats. Such differential reinforcements tend to shape broadcast policies in conservative directions. This is not to say that dissident factions are rarely heard. By resorting to coercive and outlandish behavior they command attention that they would not otherwise receive. Thwarted access to the media thus selectively reinforces disturbing forms of conduct that capture attention at the expense of a sympathetic hearing.

Changes in the communication industry should be directed at reducing inequities in access to the means by which the public can be informed and influenced. Diversified control of television facilities is one way of creating greater access opportunities for diverse aggregations in the society. This goal can also be served, though less completely, by officially designating a block of time on television as a forum for minority or controversial views. Here spokesmen for different interest groups could freely express the aspirations, the felt grievances, and the remedies sought by their constituencies. Since the public forum would be conducted by the participants themselves rather than by industry personnel, the networks are afforded protection against criticism for expression of dissenting views.

Good television journalism would require increasing the depth of news coverage and sacrificing some of the exciting features of violence. Knowing the causes of actions can reduce vindictiveness; seeing their long-term consequences can discourage ill-judged adoptions of the behavior. Unfortunately, such moderating influences are not only more difficult to portray, but have less audience appeal than the actions themselves. Brief newscasts do not provide time to dwell on causes, nor can the aftermath of violence, which remains in the distant future, be reported at the time when it would have the greatest impact on potential adopters and controllers alike. Given the demonstrated power of example, the news media must exercise caution in displaying detailed aggressive techniques and their immediate rewards if they are to safeguard against promoting the very things they are reporting.

DIFFERENTIAL REINFORCEMENT

Since aggression is partly under external reinforcement control, injurious behavior can be successfully modified by altering its customary consequences. The standard procedure begins with a baseline measurement of aggressive acts as they occur under the usual social practices. A change program is then instituted in which constructive behavior is positively reinforced while rewards for aggressive conduct are withheld or withdrawn. The findings generally show that aggressive behavior continues at a high rate during baseline conditions but declines when it is no longer positively reinforced. In order to confirm that the aggressive conduct is in fact supported by its consequences, the original reinforcement practices are reinstated, whereupon aggressive responding typically reappears. In the final phase of the program the beneficial contingencies are reintroduced so that aggression is again rendered ineffective through nonreward, whereas constructive modes of response are strengthened. Demonstration of replicative control by varying response consequences is essential in research for establishing the influence of outcomes, but in social applications it is unnecessary, if not unwise, to reinstate aggression temporarily after it has been reduced.

In implementing reinforcement practices one must select suitable reinforcers for alternative styles of behavior. The types of incentives likely to be most appropriate and effective are largely determined by the developmental level at which people are functioning. As people change, the type, amount, and source of reinforcement supporting their behavior are gradually modified. Hence, the incentives used initially in change programs may differ considerably from those that ultimately assume rewarding functions.

Some of the criticisms that have been levied against reinforcement practices fail to recognize the complexity and developmental changes in the consequences that influence human behavior. At the lowest developmental levels behavior is primarily responsive to tangible consequences. As physically rewarding experiences are repeatedly associated with expressions of interest and approval and punishments with disapproval, social reactions themselves acquire reinforcing properties.

A number of symbolic reinforcers other than social reactions take on reinforcing functions. Credits attainable through designated performances, which may be exchanged for countless things that people want, serve as dependable generalized rewards. This type of incentive system essentially involves negotiating a social contract with an individual to help him bring his aggressive behavior under control or to develop other skills that displace aggression because they are more functional (Cohen and Filipczak, 1971; Colman, 1971; Steffy et al., 1969).

Ordinarily, concrete rewards are employed in initial stages with individuals who are not reinforceable in other ways and would gain little from treatment efforts. Many of the contentious reactions of hyperaggressive individuals to task requirements, which are often attributed in clinical theory (Redl and Wineman, 1951) to high impulsivity, weak ego control, and low frustration tolerance, may in fact result from inadequate incentives. Aversive actions become an effective means of avoiding or turning off environmental demands that bring little or no reward. Thus, for example, belligerent boys who remained unmotivated by praise worked productively when their efforts were concretely rewarded and continued to do so even after the tangible reinforcers were progressively reduced and eventually discontinued altogether (Levin and Simmons, 1962). Another illustration of the change of reinforcement supports for behavior during the course of treatment is provided by Wahler (1968), who assisted parents in modifying extreme antagonism in their children. An initial program in which parents ignored defiance and commended cooperativeness proved ineffective. A subsequent reinforcement system combining parental approval with credits exchangeable for valued items produced dramatic and enduring increases in cooperativeness. Thereafter, the credits were gradually eliminated and cooperative behavior was maintained by expressions of appreciation alone.

At the highest level of functioning people regulate their own behavior by self-evaluative and other self-administered consequences. Several researchers (Goodlet and Goodlet, 1969; Bolstad and Johnson, 1972) have shown that aggressiveness can be eliminated by having boys reward themselves for reductions in aggressive conduct as well as or better than by having adults evaluate and reward their behavioral improvements. Tangible self-reinforcement and symbolic rewards can be used to maintain new patterns of behavior until they become a source of personal satisfaction.

Reinforcement influences have been extensively employed with notable success in modifying hyperaggressive behavior in children. The case reports involve physically assaultive children who repeatedly disrupt ongoing activities and, when others do not accede to their wishes, become abusive or display violent temper tantrums until they get what they want. When disciplined, they respond with aggressive defiance that discourages adults from attempting corrective action.

Treatment programs are generally implemented (under professional supervision) by those who regularly deal with the problem behavior, because it is their reactions that largely determine the direction and future course of change, however induced. In a well-designed program a behavioral analysis is first conducted to identify the social conditions that maintain aggressive conduct. Change agents are then given detailed instructions on how they must alter their characteristic ways of reacting to the child's behavior to achieve desired outcomes. This usually involves a reversal of reinforcement practices. Whereas previously coercive actions commanded attention and compliance and prosocial behavior received little notice, they are now advised to ignore or, if necessary, to disallow aggression and to reward constructive behavior.

Prescriptive instructions alone are likely to produce limited results unless combined with other aids that facilitate adoption of remedial measures. Change agents may come to understand principles for modifying behavior but remain at a loss as to how to implement what they have learned. What they need is guided practice with corrective feedback that rewards their successes and corrects their mistakes. Remedial measures must not only be sketched out in concrete actions, but preferably modeled through videotape, role playing, or, if feasible, in actual demonstrations of how to deal with problematic behaviors. After the procedures have been sufficiently demonstrated, change agents are supervised until they attain proficiency in handling problems without external directions (Johnson and Brown, 1969; Russo, 1964; Wolf, Risly, and Mees, 1964).

Detailed instruction combined with demonstration and guided practice are well suited for altering reinforcement practices, but unless adequately rewarded, the efforts of change agents are unlikely to endure very long. This problem is especially critical in initial stages of treatment when withdrawal of rewards for aggression may temporarily increase abusive responses in efforts to restore the former benefits of coercive behavior. During this period social support is required. Later, reductions in disturbing behavior begin to provide natural rewards for change agents, until eventually the interpersonal patterns become self-sustaining through reciprocal satisfactions.

Given adequate training along the lines discussed above, the behavior of parents, teachers, and other influential people is much more changeworthy than traditional theories would lead one to believe. Any remedial program, whether directed at change agents or at the clients themselves, will encounter problems from time to time. When disappointing results are obtained, there is a tendency to attribute difficulties to pathologies in the change agents and to lapse into protracted conversations concerning their dysfunctional behavior. The remedies usually lie elsewhere. Sometimes change agents do not consistently apply what they have learned because it is bothersome to do so. They adopt the remedial practices, however, when social or tangible rewards are made contingent upon improvements in their performance (Ayllon and Azrin, 1964; Bernal, Williams, Miller, and Reagor, 1972). At other times change agents cannot alter their behavior sufficiently because of disruptive influences impinging upon them. Here, successful results require an action program directed at the interfering conditions as well.

Hawkins, Peterson, Schweid, and Bijou (1966) provide one of many illustrations of home-based modifications of aggressive behavior. The case involved an assaultive, belligerent boy who, though young in years, effectively controlled the household by aversive means. After completing a baseline measurement of aggressive behavior, the mother was instructed to go about her household activities. Whenever her son acted reprehensibly, the observer signaled the mother either to tell him to stop or to place him in his room for a brief time. In contrast, when he behaved commendably the mother was encouraged to express her interest and approval. As summarized in Figure 5.2, the new reinforcement practices

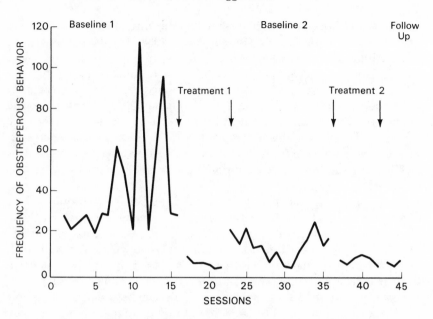

FIGURE 5.2 Number of 10-second periods in which the boy be-haved aggressively during each one-hour session. (Hawkins et al., 1966)

produced a marked decline in aggressiveness. In the next phase the mother was asked to resume her customary habit of chastising antag-onistic actions while ignoring desirable ones. Having experienced suc-cess, she found it difficult to revert to her former style. The mother not only maintained the favorable changes without any further guidance, but the boy became more considerate and affectionate, a marked contrast with his former domineering control. As Hawkins points out, a major benefit of enlisting parents as therapists for their own children is that the skills they acquire can serve them well in meeting future developmental problems.

There is ample evidence that selective reinforcement reduces aggres-siveness, but it remains unclear whether it is the consequences associated with aggression, with prosocial behavior, or both sources of influence that contribute to the effectiveness of this approach. In some studies re-porting high success aggressive behavior is consistently ignored while considerate conduct is rewarded with social approval and attention (Bernal *et al.*, 1972; Johnson and Brown, 1969; Russo, 1964; Scott, Burton, and Yarrow, 1967). In other cases prosocial behavior is positively reinforced, but aggression is punished by removing the child from the situation for short periods immediately following the act or by some other negative consequences (Bernal *et al.,* 1968; Hawkins *et al.,* 1966; Sloane, Johnston, and Bijou, 1967; Wolf, Risley, and Mees, 1964; Zeilberger, Sampen, and Sloane, 1968). Still others (Staats and Butterfield, 1965) report that assaultive delinquents ceased behaving destructively when they acquired new competencies, even though no effort was made to alter the consequences for aggressive acts. To isolate the therapeutic ingredients would require a comparative study in which aggressive responses are ignored, punished, or not singled out for special treatment and, within each of these conditions, prosocial alternatives are either fostered or not.

Approaches to the modification of child behavior disorders have undergone many changes over the years. Intrapsychically oriented therapists, who assumed that personality patterns are permanently established in the first few years of life, practiced an exclusively child-centered treatment. Therapists analyzed children's social behavior and play patterns in their offices while the parents assisted passively by not interfering in the endeavor. With mounting evidence that social behavior is changeable at all ages and that parents exert a continuing influence on their children, a collaborative form of treatment came into vogue. Growing out of the psychodynamic tradition, this approach regarded the child's troublesome behavior as a symptom of the parents' internal pathology. Family members were segregated in treatment, with the child's therapist serving essentially as a baby sitter who played with the detached symptom amid sand boxes, doll families, finger paints, and an arsenal of aggression-eliciting toys, while the adult's therapist delved into the mother's intrapsychic life. Parents' requests for advice on how to alter their children's problems were ignored, evaded, or disapproved as resistance to self-exploration. Remedial action was thus deferred for self-analysis of dubious value.

Disappointing results with these time-consuming endeavors eventually gave rise to family therapy in which all family members were seen together. The focus on family interrelationships was a move in the right direction, but a joint interview technique does not necessarily guarantee better outcomes. If the time is spent mainly in ventilating complaints, assigning blame, and analyzing how each member contributes to familial malfunctioning, there is little reason to expect that improvements will occur with any consistency. If, on the other hand, family members receive guidance in rewarding ways of relating to each other, the prospects of favorable outcomes are good.

A number of studies have already been cited in which parents were taught child management skills for specific aggressive problems. Patterson and his colleagues (Patterson and Cobb, 1971; Patterson and Reid,

1970) have been evolving procedures for teaching parents how to deal with a wide range of problems exhibited by different family members. Initially, parents familiarize themselves with principles of learning that help them understand how social behavior is established and modified. Following this brief didactic instruction, parents select problem behaviors they wish to modify. They are then assigned a special time during each day to record the incidence of these behaviors, the various effects they produce, and the family members who provide the consequences. This observational phase is designed both to sensitize parents to social influence processes and to reinforce the set that they will serve as active agents rather than as passive recipients of treatment. Once they have learned to observe interpersonal contingencies accurately, they are taught, by demonstration and guided practice, constructive ways of handling their children's behavior. Family problems are modified in this manner usually one at a time.

When necessary, new reinforcement practices are also introduced in classroom settings and peer groups. Influence over deviant behavior in extrafamilial situations is typically achieved by a peer contingency procedure in which the child and his peers initially earn valued rewards for positive conduct on his part. Concrete rewards are then gradually reduced until eventually the child's behavior is maintained by natural social reactions of teachers and peers.

In one project reported by Patterson, Ray, and Shaw (1968), parents reduced the frequency with which they rewarded coercive behavior from an average rate of 35 percent during the baseline period to 10 percent during the intervention program. Modification of familial reinforcement practices not only lowered the families' output of aggressive behavior, but increased the level and reciprocity of positive interactions within the family system. Results of additional studies with families presenting severe problems of social aggression reaffirm the efficacy of this type of approach (Patterson, Cobb, and Ray, 1972). Through a combination of instruction, demonstration, and guided practice parents can acquire proficient skills for changing problem behavior. Difficulties sometimes arise, however, in their implementation of requisite practices. Efforts to enhance the effectiveness of this method might do well to concentrate on the development of parental incentive systems to ensure that parents apply the methods they have learned more widely.

Teachers must often deal with children whose assaultive and disruptive behavior seriously intrudes on the activities of others. In some instances these are domineering children who have been repeatedly reinforced for controlling their social environment through coercive means. More often, however, the children resort to aggressive ways of securing attention when they lack alternative means of gaining acceptance. Negative attention-forcing behavior is highly resistant to change because, to a child of limited skills who desires the recognition of others, even reprimands serve as rewards. Moreover, in group situations aversive behaviors that alienate teachers are frequently reinforced by the amusement of peers from whom attention is sought. Once cast in the role of class buffoon, one loses opportunities to develop his potentialities unless the detrimental contingencies are reversed.

Madsen and his associates (1968) illustrate how reprimands may reinforce the very troublesome behaviors they are intended to diminish. When teachers admonished students for disruptive activities, the number of transgressors promptly increased. In subsequent phases of the study the number of disrupters declined when teachers reduced their reprimands and rose again when they resumed their admonishments. The chronic problem was solved by ignoring annoying actions and praising engrossment in learning activities.

Many interventions intended as punishments actually serve as positive reinforcers that maintain troublesome behavior. Self-defeating practices usually go unnoticed by those who use them since they see the immediate results but rarely assess the full or long-term effects their behavior may have on others. Detrimental social systems are unknowingly created and mutually sustained because aversive behavior is rewarded by the attention it commands, while the ineffective control techniques are reinforced by their success in temporarily checking disturbing performances. In the preceding example, the teachers inadvertently rewarded annoying conduct in students who, in turn, rewarded the teacher's shouting by their momentary compliance, with the net result that both sets of performances were mutually escalated.

In modifying disturbing aggression in school settings professional personnel serve as consultants to teachers who are given the knowledge and skills with which to solve the problems confronting them. School-based treatments generally achieve reductions in aggressive and defiant classroom behavior by having teachers ignore disruptive activities and attend positively to educational pursuits (Becker, Thomas, and Carnine, 1969; Goodlet, Goodlet, and Dredge, 1970).

Whenever one or more children are singled out for special treatment in a social context, one must be sensitive to how other members may be affected by seeing another's actions differentially reinforced. Some teachers fear that increased attention to the behavior of a problem child will prompt others to behave in a troublesome way to secure similar solicitous interest. Such adverse effects would occur if the increased attention were given noncontingently or if it were gained through abusive behavior. When annoying conduct is ignored and constructive actions are commended, the treatment, in fact, provides others with positive models for emulation. Nothing is gained by behaving aggressively. Consistent with these expectations, research has shown that differential reinforcement of one child either has no effect on others (Ward and Baker, 1968) or leads them to adopt productive activities that they see well received (Reppucci and Reiss, 1970).

Extinction of Aggression

When reinforcement for a learned response is withheld, the behavior continues to be performed for a time, sometimes even briefly increasing in rate, depending on its prior reinforcement history. Under consistent nonreward, however, the behavior declines and is eventually discarded. The use of extinction in multiple procedures has already been touched upon in the previous section. Ordinarily, a method combining nonreward of negative behavior with positive reinforcement of competing patterns is more effective than extinction alone. Some of the problems that may arise in the use of extinction procedures, either singly or in conjunction with rewarded alternatives, merit discussion.

When the rewards gained through coercive behavior are first withheld, it is often intensified in an effort to restore former benefits. If the more aversive tactics should force compliant reactions, the results are worse than if no intervention had been attempted. In the latter instance the aggressor is not only rewarded for using more extreme measures but learns that persistence eventually pays off, thus increasing the resistance of aggression to extinction. A psychological principle, no matter how powerful, will yield weak or variable results if it is not applied consistently.

The importance of uniform social practice in implementing a change program based on extinction is revealed in Williams' (1959) treatment of aggressively demanding behavior in a young boy. The child had required special care during a severe illness and, upon his recovery, continued to demand the parents' undivided attention with intense tantrums and crying spells, especially at bedtime. The parents were instructed to put their son to bed in a leisurely, amicable way, but after completing the bedtime routine, to ignore his screaming and raging. The duration of the unrewarded tantrum behavior dropped markedly and ceased altogether within a few days. The child no longer created a scene at bedtime, but instead played happily until he dropped off to sleep. A week later an aunt reinstated the tantrum behavior by complying with the child's demands to remain in the room after being put to bed. A second extinction series produced complete and enduring remission of the tantrums.

A child's aversive control of his parents, if intermittently reinforced, is likely to generalize to other areas of behavior and to other people. As the above study shows, after alienating coercive behaviors are removed, the familial atmosphere changes from one of recurrent drawn-out battles to reciprocally rewarding interactions. This case illustrates several other interesting issues. Psychotherapy cannot be separated from the experiences of everyday life. No amount of insightful conversation will have much effect unless the reinforcement practices of influential people in the social system change. There are no psychological methods that can render a person permanently insensitive to the consequences of his actions. Nor would such an outcome be desirable, even if it were possible, because behavior that remained immune to its effects would be grossly maladaptive. A remedial intervention can correct a reciprocally reinforcing system gone awry, but whether induced changes generalize and endure depends upon the prevailing reinforcement practices in different social contexts. To continue with the preceding example, if parents ignore tantrums but others reward them, tantrums will occur to some extent unless others also alter their way of reacting to them. If, for whatever reason, the behavior of certain members of the social environment cannot be changed, significant though less generalized reduction in aggression can still be achieved. Given conflicting contingencies, individuals eventually distinguish between situations in which their aggressive actions succeed or fail and behave accordingly.

Some forms of aggression are more amenable to extinction treatment than others. One can render verbal attacks, annoying actions, and oppositional response ineffective simply by choosing not to respond to them. But a tough aggressor can get what he wants by physical force regardless of the interest or cooperation shown by his victims. Brown and Elliott (1965) report findings that have a bearing on this issue. They instructed teachers to ignore aggression and to reward cooperative behavior in an effort to reduce the combativeness of 27 boys in a nursery school class. Under these reinforcement practices both physical and verbal aggression declined. After the program was discontinued, physical aggression showed some recovery during a follow-up period. The authors attributed the recurrence to teachers' difficulty in refraining from intervening and interacting with the boys when they assaulted others. Although these results are explainable in terms of differential reactions of teachers, it is also probably true that physical aggression was intermittently reinforced by its success in extracting compliance from peers, apart from the teachers' interest. A second application of the reinforcement program produced additional reductions in physical and verbal assaults.

In cases in which aggressive behavior is injurious or seriously infringes on the prerogatives of others, a simple extinction procedure may not be feasible. Pinkston, Reese, Le Blanc, and Baer (1972) tested an extinction treatment that protects the victim from harm. It consists essentially of ignoring the aggressor while attending to the victim by shielding him from further attack and arranging interesting activities for him. An explosively violent boy who proved unresponsive to reasoning, imposed limits, and reprimands promptly reduced his physical attacks when this type of treatment was instituted. Hurtful conduct generally alienates one from others. In keeping with expectation, elimination of injurious behavior alone enhanced the boy's positive relationship with his peers.

Protective extinction may be feasible with young children but it would be difficult to apply either to older aggressors or to problems in which an entire group is victimized. In such instances aggressive actions are typically controlled by negative sanctions while other coping styles are being developed.

The behavior exhibited during the course of extinction is primarily determined by the response options available to the individual. As dominant aggressive responses prove ineffective, a person will try alternative courses of action that have been successful in the past. No special problems are created by the use of extinction alone when the available alternatives are constructive. If, however, the responses in an individual's repertoire are largely negative, a change agent may be faced with the arduous task of eliminating a succession of detrimental tendencies. This problem can be avoided by combining extinction with modeling and reinforcement procedures that foster alternative means of securing desired outcomes. Individuals undergoing extinction alone learn what no longer works but remain uncertain about, or unskilled in, better options, whereas the combined use of extinction and reinforced modeling provides positive guidance. These considerations apply equally to punishment control of aggression, which is discussed next.

PUNISHMENT CONTROL OF AGGRESSION

Punishing consequences are widely applied to people in all walks of life in efforts to reduce or to eliminate troublesome behavior. In many instances aversive control is favored because it is reinforcing to the punisher rather than beneficial to the recipient. A method that is quick and effective in stopping disturbing behavior will be sufficiently rewarding to the user to be retained even though it may have minimal or adverse long-term effects for all concerned.

In professional circles two major criticisms were levied against the use of punishment to modify behavior. It was argued, more from belief than from fact, that negative sanctions are relatively ineffective and that furthermore, they produce undesirable side effects. However, as empirical evidence accumulated on how negative consequences influence behavior, blanket rejection gave way to qualified acceptance. Many of the unfavorable properties ascribed to punishment are not necessarily inherent in the methods themselves, but result from the faulty manner in which they are usually applied. In everyday use punishments are typically excessive, ill-timed, erratic, and administered vengefully without providing any positive direction. Results of numerous studies show that under certain conditions detrimental behavior can be effectively modified by negative consequences and that adverse side effects need not occur.

Negative consequences may involve either withdrawal of rewards or administration of aversive effects. Aversive control through physical punishment and other painful outcomes is seldom employed in judicious change programs and then only to control seriously injurious behavior requiring active interventions. Withdrawal of rewards is more commonly used on occasions when negative sanctions are needed. In the latter case, the response costs of aggression may take the form of monetary penalties, temporary forfeiture of privileges and possessions, or brief removal from rewarding situations for assaultive or destructive actions.

The adjunctive use of punishment by reward withdrawal has certain advantages over physical aversive procedures. As previously shown, painful treatment may arouse counteraggression or avoidance of the punishers, thus weakening their potential influence. In contrast, interventions that chiefly involve removal of valued things not only generate weaker emotional disturbances, but foster contact with the disciplinarian who can reinstate the forfeited rewards. If restoration of positive reinforcers is made contingent upon constructive actions, rapid behavioral changes may in fact result. In addition, reward withdrawal techniques provide more acceptable and feasible alternatives to physical punishment, which most change agents are understandably loath to use.

Punishment is rarely employed as a sole method of modifying aggressive behavior. Rather, it is applied in conjunction with positive influences conducive to the development of more rewarding styles of conduct. In other words, in effective intervention one does not punish without offering better alternatives. For aggressors who have already developed other social skills that are potentially reinforceable, negative consequences can produce rapid, lasting changes. As long as the aversive outcomes of aggression override its benefits, it will not be utilized. If more effective options are practiced during this period, the behavioral changes initiated by punishment are likely to endure after the negative sanctions have been discontinued. For persons who have perfected mainly aggressive ways of achieving desired results, punishment alone produces, at best, selective inhibition. Disapproved actions will be suppressed in the punisher's presence but readily performed toward others and at times and places where the probability of adverse consequences is low. In treating aggressors with skill deficiencies, punishment serves as a temporary inhibitor of injurious behavior while rewardable competencies are being established and strengthened.

Reduction of Aggression by Reward Withdrawal

Reinforcement withdrawal has proved to be an effective means of managing deleterious behavior that impedes the aggressor's own development or seriously infringes on the well-being of others. In work with children short periods of social exclusion are typically used as negative consequences for transgressive behavior. The child is told in advance that whenever he misbehaves he will be sent to another room for a specified time. This is done immediately, naturally, and in a firm but nonhostile manner. To avoid arousing needless anger, only brief exclusion periods of 10 to 15 minutes are employed, and the timeout room is designed as a neutral rather than an aversive place. The source of influence should be the temporary loss of rewards rather than devaluation or vindictiveness, which are likely to create more serious problems than those the intervention was intended to remedy. If, during the exclusion interval, the person continues to act aggressively, the separation period is extended until after the behavior subsides. Under this type of contingency self-control is readily established.

Social attention accompanying a disciplinary intervention may unintentionally reinforce the preceding transgressive actions. Change agents therefore minimize social and verbal interaction as much as possible while the negative sanction is applied. They do not argue, moralize, or offer apologetic explanations. When prearranged contingencies are applied in a consistent, nonpunitive fashion, a person is more likely to regard the interventions as natural consequences of his behavior than as arbitrary or malevolent treatment by others. The effectiveness of a timeout procedure is, of course, determined by the rewarding value of the situation from which one is withdrawn.

Judicious use of reinforcement withdrawal as part of a broad program is illustrated in the treatment of an autistic boy by Wolf, Risley, and Mees (1964). In addition to grossly retarded social and verbal development, the boy exhibited violent temper tantrums during which he would inflict serious injury on himself. After a tantrum he was badly bruised and bleeding, and refused to sleep at night, forcing one or both parents to remain by his bed. Sedatives, tranquilizers, and physical restraints were applied without success. When it became clear that refusal to wear eyeglasses (necessitated by removal of cataractal lenses) might result in ultimate blindness, behavior therapists were invited by the hospital staff to devise a treatment program for him. Ward attendants, and later the parents, carried out the prescribed procedures under the guidance of the consultants.

Most of the serious recurrent behaviors, which obstructed any remedial efforts, were eliminated by combined use of extinction and brief separation. In modifying the tantrum behavior, for example, whenever the boy slapped himself and whined, he was placed in his room for ten minutes or until the disturbing action ceased. Under this contingency tantrums gradually declined and eventually disappeared. Eating problems, in which the boy grabbed food from others, threw it about the room, or ate with his fingers, were rapidly eliminated in a similar manner. The attendants simply removed him from the dining room for the remainder of his meal for snatching or tossing food after a warning, and withdrew his plate for a few minutes whenever he ate with his fingers. Normal sleeping patterns were established within a week by not acceding to his demanding behavior. Finally, destructive discarding of glasses ceased within five days when the boy was placed briefly in his room for throwing his eyeglasses, or if tantrums developed, until they abated.

The foregoing account describes the punishing consequences for destructive actions. In the total program, positive incentives were also extensively used to get the boy to wear glasses, and he was assisted and rewarded for positive responsiveness. Prior to treatment, he lacked any communicative skills. These were gradually established by reinforced modeling. The development of rewarding competencies undoubtedly contributed to the effectiveness of mild punishment.

As the boy's social functioning improved, contacts with the family and home were progressively increased. At first the parents visited the hospital and observed how tantrums and bedtime struggles were handled by the attendants. Subsequently the parents made several weekly visits, during which an attendant observed and instructed them in their handling of their son. Then the boy began short home visits accompanied by an attendant, followed by progressively longer visits. Initially, the child almost succeeded in reinstating control over the parents by aversive tantrums, but with the attendant's corrective guidance coercion no longer worked. After discharge, his extreme behavior problems ceased, he had become increasingly verbal, and the family interactions were considerably more enjoyable. The reinforcement practices were applied for several years in a nursery school setting where the boy made sufficient progress to enroll in public school (Risley and Wolf, 1966; Wolf *et al.*, 1967). Social withdrawal procedures were used occasionally in early phases to eliminate tantrum behavior, exhibited when he was asked to perform instructional tasks, and to control hurtful acts toward other children.

Following the general rule that problems are best treated in the environment in which they occur, hyperaggressive behavior has been successively eliminated in children by their parents (Allison and Allison, 1971; Zeilberger, Sampen, and Sloane, 1968), nursery school teachers (Clark, Rowbury, Baer, and Baer, 1970; Sloane, Johnston, and Bijou, 1967), and hospital attendants (Bostow and Bailey, 1969), by rewarding friendliness and punishing harmful actions with brief social withdrawal. Figure 5.3 presents illustrative documentation of results from treatments employing contingency reversals. Similar interventions have yielded favorable outcomes with older children when ignoring troublesome behavior failed to produce results (Sibley, Abbott, and Cooper, 1969; Sulzer, Mayer, and Cody, 1968). As injurious behavior is eliminated, positive interactions with peers become reciprocally rewarding so that aggression is rarely resorted to even after the negative sanctions have been discontinued (LeBlanc, Busby, and Thomson, 1971).

A variant of reward withdrawal is reported by Keirsey (1969) for handling seriously disruptive or injurious behavior that has resisted concerted remedial efforts. The method essentially involves a behavior contract that specifies clearly the distressing actions requiring control, the responsibilities that each participant must assume, and the consequences that transgressions will produce. In a joint meeting including the child, his parents, his teacher, and the principal, the supervising counselor enlists the child's help to control, as best he can, behavior that disturbs all concerned. Whenever his aggressive actions exceed acceptable limits, the teacher must ask him to leave the school for the remainder of the day. She is further instructed not to threaten, coax, urge, or scold the child, nor to engage in persuasive attempts to alter his behavior, all of which could function as attentional rewards for transgressing. Rather, the prearranged sanctions are applied immediately and consistently so that the child looks upon them as natural, predictable consequences of his misdeeds. When the child arrives home, the parents are told to keep him at home until the time he normally returns from school, but otherwise to refrain from scolding or applying other disciplinary measures.

High rates of success are reported for this method in reducing chronically disruptive behavior (Blackham and Silberman, 1971; Keirsey, 1969). However, no quantitative results are presented, nor have the

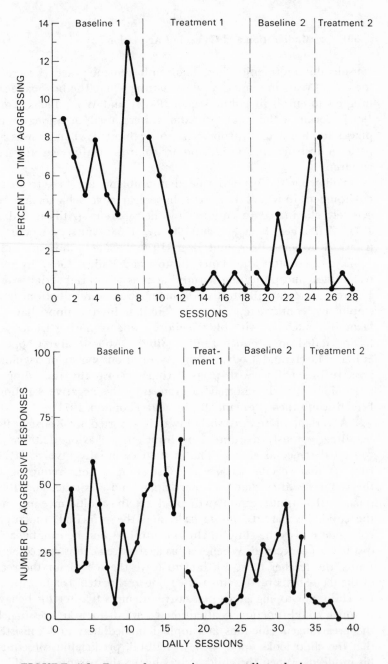

FIGURE 5.3 Rate of aggressive responding during treatment periods when positive responses were rewarded and injurious actions were punished by brief social exclusion. The upper figure shows the reductions in physical aggression achieved by a mother in her 5-year-old son (Zeilberger, Sampen, and Sloane, Jr., 1968); the lower figure presents the results for the treatment of an assaultive adult by hospital personnel (Bostow and Bailey, 1969).

conditions under which this method is most efficacious been systematically examined. An exclusion procedure will prove ineffective, or may
even augment deviant responsiveness, if the situation from which the
individual has been removed is unrewarding or unpleasant. Apparently
this problem has rarely arisen, which suggests that even children who
experience serious difficulties in the classroom find attendance at school
more attractive than sitting alone at home. Results of studies previously
cited suggest that short periods of exclusion might work as well as, or
even better than, prolonged suspension from classroom activities. When
misdeeds produce brief reward withdrawal, children have repeated opportunities to cope successfully with situational demands and thus to
improve their level of self-control. The corrective power of even the
extended exclusion method could probably be increased by rewarding
achievements as well as punishing transgressions.

In most of the cases discussed thus far the favorable changes induced
by parents or teachers are likely to be supported in peer relations. When
peer influences conflict with the behaviors promoted by the staff, as in
correctional institutions, negative sanctions achieve, at best, only temporary control over aggressive behavior. Tyler and his associates (Burchard
and Tyler, 1965; Tyler and Brown, 1967) greatly reduced aggressive
behavior in delinquent boys by means of brief social exclusion without
any threats, invectives, sermonizing or negotiations for a second chance.
However, when the negative sanctions were removed, the rate of offenses
increased rapidly. After the punishment contingency was again reinstated,
disruptive behavior subsided with equal rapidity and remained at a low
level. In a subsequent study, Brown and Tyler (1968) succeeded in dethroning a tough delinquent who exercised powerful intimidating control over his peers by excluding him whenever he or his cohorts forced
subservience from weaker members. The costs of autocratic delinquent
control proved too high to continue it. Since he was held accountable
for any trouble that might develop in the cottage, he not only ceased
promoting disruptive behavior but tried to dissuade others from it.
Given a powerful delinquent system, however, punishment may down-
grade one domineering leader only to elevate another one without restructuring the peer reinforcement system to any significant degree.

Aversive control can be an effective method for managing aggressive behavior in residential settings, but it is unlikely to have much
rehabilitative value in correctional institutions as they are constituted
at present. If negative sanctions applied by staff members are strong
enough to outweigh contravening peer influences, socially conforming
behavior may be achieved and sustained as long as the institutional
sanctions remain in effect. When aversive controls are removed, however,
peer reinforcement practices usually reinstate deviant patterns of be-

havior. It will be shown later that modification of antisocial aggression requires fundamental changes in the treatment systems themselves.

Reduction of Aggression by
Aversive Consequences

Physically painful consequences are sometimes applied to behavior so destructive to oneself or to others that it calls for drastic measures. Such behavior is most frequently found among institutionalized retardates and those suffering from gross behavior disorders. Ludwig, Marx, Hill, and Browning (1969), for example, curbed potentially homicidal behavior in a schizophrenic woman who terrorized fellow patients and staff alike by surprise vicious attacks upon them. After she had received every variety of psychiatric therapy to no avail, an effort was made to control her violent actions through aversive consequences. The aggressive episodes generally followed a common sequence: When asked to do something, the patient would become surly and resistive. If pressed further, she would successively cry, complain angrily that she was being persecuted and abused, and then threaten to harm or to kill the staff. After voicing threats she would calm down, causing the staff to lower their guard, whereupon she would strike out without warning. In the treatment program physical assaults, aggressive threats, and accusatory verbalizations were successively eliminated by administering a brief shock via a faradic stimulator upon their occurrence. As her violence was brought under control, the quality of her interactions changed from paranoid combativeness to a more warm and friendly responsiveness. Her general level of functioning also improved substantially. In many respects, the treatment achieved what the patient perceived its purpose to be: "You're trying to make a human being out of me." Unfortunately, sometimes this requires painful interventions.

Results of a study by Agras (1967) suggest that violent behavior may, in some instances, be controllable by eliminating its ideational precursors. A chronic schizophrenic had to be physically restrained because of uncontrollable tendencies to smash any glass in sight. He participated in a series of sessions during which he visualized himself breaking glass, whereupon he was administered a painful shock. As the treatment progressed, the latency of the destructive imagery increased and eventually he lost all urge to smash glass. A follow-up study revealed that, except for one minor incident, the destructive behavior never appeared again.

One of the most perplexing and dangerous disorders involves self-injurious behavior. In its more extreme forms, children pummel their faces repeatedly, bang their heads forcibly against hard or sharp objects, tear and bite off pieces of flesh from their bodies, or exhibit some other type of self-mutilating behavior. Because of the serious risk of permanent physical injury, such children are usually kept in continuous physical restraints.

The maintaining conditions of self-injurious behavior are not fully understood, but it is amenable to control through variation of reinforcing consequences. In a series of studies Lovaas and his colleagues (Bucher and Lovaas, 1968; Lovaas, Freitag, Gold, and Kassorla, 1965; Lovaas and Simmons, 1969) have shown that neither social deprivation nor social satiation have any appreciable effect upon self-mutilating responses. Contingent rewards, however, increased such actions, especially if given only periodically, as typically happens in understaffed institutions. Thus, self-injurious responses increase when they elicit solicitous attention and reassuring comments from adults, whereas such behavior is promptly reduced to its original baseline level after the positive reactions are discontinued. Self-injurious responses are also readily cued off by events signifying withdrawal of social reinforcement for other behaviors. Experiments with primates reported by Schaefer (1970) shed further light on reinforcement control of self-inflicted injuries. He was able to establish and to maintain a high rate of head-hitting by rewarding such performances with food initially for each self-hit and later for every fifth response. Moreover, by rewarding self-hits only when the experimenter emitted sympathetic remarks, but not in the absence of these words, self-hitting was brought under verbal stimulus control. Self-hitting could now be promptly evoked by the verbal cues alone.

Although self-injurious behavior may be partly maintained by its social consequences, the evidence is conflicting on this point. Subtle changes in social reinforcement, as when an adult remains with a child without attending to him when he hits himself, does not seem to affect the rate of self-injurious acts (Lovaas et al., 1965; Risley, 1968). Withdrawal of social contact for a brief period reduces self-injurious behavior, but occasionally children are unaffected even by these more powerful consequences (Risley, 1968). Whatever the controlling variables might be in any given case, preliminary findings indicate that chronic and intractable self-injurious behavior can be successfully eliminated with beneficial results by either ignoring or punishing it.

Lovaas and Simmons (1969) showed, with children who had been in continuous restraints, that if self-injurious behavior produces no social effects, it decreases gradually and eventually disappears. In some cases, however, when self-mutilating behavior is first placed on extinction it may temporarily increase in intensity, which could be potentially dangerous. Extinctions therefore cannot be safely employed unless adequate safeguards are available (Harmatz and Rasmussen, 1969). Self-destructive responses can be promptly and completely eliminated by contingent application of a few painful shocks. In one of several cases reported by Bucher and Lovaas (1968), a seven-year-old schizophrenic boy who had been self-injurious since the age of two performed approximately 3,000 self-pummeling responses during a period of 90 minutes when his physical restraints were removed. This behavior was almost totally eliminated in four sessions by the use of 12 contingent shocks. Self-destructive behavior that had persisted over a period of six years was also rapidly and durably removed in a schizophrenic after she received a total of 15 shocks for beating her head. In each case reported, contingent aversive consequences not only removed self-mutilating behavior, but the children decreased their whining and became more responsive to the therapists. Uniformly favorable results have been obtained with other retardates and autistic children who for years suffered severe self-inflicted injuries. Cessation of self-injurious behavior is often specific to the situation in which punishment is administered. Generalized reductions can be achieved, however, by a few punishments or verbal reprimands in other settings in which the responses occur.

Brief social withdrawal made contingent on self-destructive behavior is sometimes sufficient to remove it permanently. Hamilton, Stephens, and Allen (1967) were consistently successful in eliminating injurious aggressive and self-destructive behavior in severely retarded adolescents by social exclusion. In each instance, the individual was physically confined to a chair in a timeout area for a fixed period following an injurious act. In one case, a girl beat her head and back against the wall a total of 35,906 times during four 6-hour observations. While the timeout contingency was in effect, head-banging precipitously dropped to a negligible level of 7, 2, 0, 1, 0 for five successive weeks and never reappeared during nine months of follow-up study. Of considerable import, both from a clinical and an ethical standpoint, is that after the continual self-mutilating behavior was eliminated, the children participated with evident enjoyment in daily social and recreational activities.

It is noteworthy that brief programs of contingent punishment can remove self-destructive behavior of long standing and improve social functioning as well. After self-injurious behavior is eliminated, children generally become more socially responsive and display increased imitativeness, thus enabling them to acquire new patterns of behavior. If further studies support this conclusion, there will remain no justification for having children mutilating themselves or spending their early years uselessly in physical restraints.

Several factors may account for spontaneous improvements in social behavior following reduction of aggression. One explanation is in terms of the self-enhancing effects of increased freedom of action. When aggressors discard provocative activities that consume much time, they begin to make contact with potentially rewarding aspects of the environment that were always available and that automatically reinforce emergent patterns. A person's environment expands markedly after he has been freed from the restraints imposed by his aggressiveness toward himself or others. Not only is contact with positive features of the existing environment increased, but reduction in violent conduct changes the nature of the social environment. Others become more friendly when they are no longer being frightened or angered. Positive responsiveness, in turn, promotes cordial counterreactions. Once a reciprocally reinforcing interaction is initiated between nonviolent behavior and environmental rewards, widespread changes may result even though amicable conduct was never deliberately cultivated.

Another issue requiring comment is why relatively mild punishment used therapeutically can achieve lasting results, whereas even drastic punishment often fails to suppress aggressive conduct or even aggravates it. The discrepancy may be explained in several ways. In treatment, unpleasant consequences are used constructively to improve social functioning rather than vindictively or devaluatively. When aversive procedures are essential for alleviating detrimental conditions, they are generally viewed as an unpleasant though necessary part of treatment, comparable to the painful routines of physical medicine. If the therapeutic intent is clearly conveyed in the context of positive alternatives, negative sanctions will have fewer adverse side effects than when punishment is applied hostilely merely to suppress troublesome behavior with high functional value for the performer. The same punishing consequences may therefore be strongly resented or willingly accepted depending upon the perceived intent of the agent, and whether the sanctions are applied mainly for his own convenience or for the benefit of the recipient. If the initially painful ministrations of dentists and surgeons were seen as punishment for developing maladies, these practitioners would be feared and hated rather than sought out.

Undesirable emotional effects can be substantially reduced by arranging in advance explicit contractual contingencies that clearly define the broad limits of permissible and punishable behavior. Prearranged contingencies implemented in a responsible fashion will more likely be regarded as natural consequences of transgression than as arbitrary interpersonal assaults.

The power of punishment to create dysfunctional fears or defenses depends on the total context of experiences in which it appears. Occasional painful experiences occurring among many neutral or rewarding ones are generally ineffective in creating inappropriate fears (Rescorla,

1969). If change agents did little more than punish aggressive behavior, they would undoubtedly take on frightening or angering qualities. In well-designed treatment programs they, in fact, are highly supportive and rewarding so that a few circumscribed sanctions are unlikely to jeopardize the usually positive relationship. Punishment by an otherwise warm, rewarding person is more effective in reducing prohibited behavior than that by a nonnurturant one (Parke, 1969; Parke and Walters, 1967).

A third possible explanation concerns the manner in which negative consequences are applied. Ordinarily the contingency, certainty, and immediacy of punishment are more important than its severity. In therapeutic practice consequences are administered immediately and consistently for clearly designated transgressions. If generalized reduction in prohibited behavior is desired, the negative sanctions are applied in varied contexts by different individuals. In a comparison of certainty and severity of punishment, Pendergrass (1971) found that brief seclusion for each interpersonal attack was more effective in eliminating assaultive behavior than long seclusion applied periodically. Even weak punishment used in conjunction with rewarded alternatives can produce enduring positive changes where severe punishment alone fails. An additional factor contributing to the relative success of remedial sanctions is that rewards for aggressive behavior are removed as much as possible, whereas in usual efforts at social control punishment is simply superimposed upon rewards that remain operative. Any of these features may account for variations in the corrective power of punishing consequences.

MODIFICATION OF ANTISOCIAL AGGRESSION

Most youngsters who repeatedly engage in delinquent conduct eventually appear in correctional institutions. Such centers generally provide adequate custodial care, but they are severely limited by their structure and institutional practices in creating the kinds of experiences conducive to constructive personality change. Most are admittedly oriented toward custody and make no pretense at remediation. However, Polsky (1962) among others, documents how even well-intentioned treatment centers can become agencies for antisocial learning.

A sizable group of delinquents is typically assigned to a living unit with one or two adult supervisors. Within this social context a powerful peer subculture is formed containing status hierarchies based upon delinquent values and skills. Social ranking and control are achieved largely through intimidation and physical domination. Tough boys and their cohorts, having gained power through forceful means, bully and exploit weaker members who become subservient. Their victimization is usually facilitated by devaluing them as "queers" or subhumans. Newcomers are subjected to similar humiliating treatment from which they can escape by successful aggressive challenges of higher ranking members. Under a reign of force victors perfect aggressive styles of behavior, while the downgraded are demoralized.

The peer system receives support from various sources. The prevailing code of conduct effectively shapes and controls its members in directions that often subvert the treatment efforts of the staff. A contingency analysis by Buehler, Patterson, and Furniss (1966), for example, revealed that delinquents generously rewarded antisocial conduct but disapproved of actions that either deviated from their own norms or conformed to institutional standards. Nor does the residential staff escape the boys' coercive control. Being greatly outnumbered, supervisors need the cooperation of peer leaders to maintain order in residential units for which they bear responsibility. Supervisors are therefore inclined to patronize the delinquent leadership by accommodating to their reinforcement practices (Polsky, 1962). At periodic intervals the professional staff engage the boys in therapeutic conversations, while in their daily cottage life they are mutually reinforcing the very attitudes and behaviors that led to their incarceration.

Upon their return to society many continue a life of aggression that, sooner or later, sends them to more callous institutions in the correctional hierarchy. Eventually they end up serving long terms in walled prisons under subhuman living conditions. During this confinement prisoners are repeatedly subjected to degrading and brutal treatment at the hands of their keepers or fellow inmates.

Almost everyone acknowledges that the present correctional practices are antiquated. High recidivism rates attest to the fact that they do not accomplish the purposes by which they are justified. If anything, the dehumanizing prison experiences create obstacles to constructive change. It is incongruous that a society remains willing to underwrite, at enormous human and financial costs, penal systems that are admitted failures. Although the need for drastic reforms is repeatedly voiced by insiders and outsiders alike, the corrosive practices remain. Responsible indictments produce inaction perhaps because, despite the avowed aims, the public is more interested in punishing than in rehabilitating transgressors. One can point to evidence that public figures are applauded by large segments of the population more enthusiastically for advocating punitive controls than for humane remedial measures, which get criticized as "coddling." The public costs of punitiveness are too remote and obscure to be seen as doing more social harm than good.

Another explanation is that dysfunctional systems persist because they are not held accountable for the quality of their services. Agency practices tend to be adopted for the convenience of those who run the place at the expense of client benefits. As long as operating funds are not linked to accomplishments, there is little challenge for change. Popular sentiment regarding criminal offenders reinforces inaction even by dedicated personnel with the best of intentions. The remedial gains that accrue from lifting punitive restraints receive little notice, whereas occasional failures are widely publicized, often with political repercussions. This is hardly the climate conducive to innovative practice. Rather, it requires special effort to introduce reforms that carry some risk when efficient, though nonrehabilitative, custody suffices. Major accomplishments in the correctional field require a system of accountability that rewards program improvement. External audits of correctional practices and their degree of success would provide motivating incentives to devise more promising approaches.

It is difficult to alter huge malfunctioning agencies by internal modification alone because many of the functionaries in the system either have a vested interest in the existing procedures or are fearful of trying unproven alternatives. Agencies can be changed much faster by devising successful programs on a limited scale outside the system, and then using the power of superior alternatives as the instrument of influence. If officials are held answerable for the results of their treatments, ineffective practices cannot be long defended after new ones have been tried and proved superior.

Amelioration of antisocial aggression requires changing not only correctional systems, but also weak psychological theories that prescribe the remedial measures. Interventions must be reoriented from probing for internal malfunctioning to social treatment. By altering social practices in the family and school and changing community influences that foster aggressive behavior, the development of assaultive personalities can be largely prevented. Tharp and Wetzel (1969) provide many examples of the techniques of consultation and intervention in the natural environment. Serious forms of aggression that may initially require residential treatment will, of course, occasionally arise.

Home-style remedial programs based on learning principles are being developed as an alternative system to existing correctional facilities. Functioning units within the community contract with the court to treat juvenile offenders who would otherwise be sent to reformatories. In the prototype program (Phillips, 1968; Phillips, Wolf, and Fixsen, 1972), a pair of house parents, skilled in methods of behavior modification, resides with a small group of delinquent boys in a home located in the community. Beneficial changes are fostered initially through a system of immediate tangible rewards and later by more intrinsic and natural consequences. A positive learning environment is created in which boys earn points for designated social behavior, self-care, and academic activities that enhance their competencies, and lose points for transgressive actions. Various treats and privileges are secured with the points, first on a daily basis and later on a weekly arrangement.

Contingency reversals demonstrate the necessity of concrete rewards in early phases of the remedial program. Boys adopt and maintain constructive patterns of behavior when they result in point consequences linked to deferred rewards, whereas they quickly revert to their old patterns when all privileges are made available noncontingently (Phillips, 1968). Home-based reinforcement is likewise highly effective in improving class-room performance (Bailey, Wolf, and Phillips, 1970). In the absence of special incentives boys spent about 65 percent of their time disrupting classroom activities and only 35 percent of their time studying. In contrast, when they earned privileges in the home for working productively in school and lost privileges for disrupting the place, they studied better than 90 percent of the time, a notable achievement for students formerly regarded as unmotivated and uneducable.

Contingency systems can vary on several dimensions, depending on whether performance tasks are assigned to individuals or if the group decides on the distribution of labor; whether reinforcements are given for individual performance or for the group's combined achievements; whether rewards and privileges are tied to specific performances or to levels of functioning encompassing multiple competencies; whether the system rewards desired performances, punishes transgressions, or arranges both types of consequences; and whether the contingencies are implemented by the staff or by peer members themselves.

Researchers have begun to examine how different organizational practices affect group functioning and satisfaction. The merits of a given system are measured against four standards. It should be *effective* in achieving changes in psychological functioning. It should be *preferred* by the participants. It should be *practical* in that participants assume responsibility for regulating their activities with minimal adult supervision. And it should be *educational* by developing competencies that will be useful for the participants in the future. Phillips, Wolf, and Fixsen (1972) found that a system combining group assignment of tasks with group consequences was of limited effectiveness. When performance by any member benefits the entire group, individual members come to expect somebody else to do the work, with the result that both individual and group performances progressively deteriorate. Individual assignment with group consequences produced somewhat better results, as did completely individualized systems in which adults assigned tasks to each boy and rewarded his individual accomplishments.

One limitation of an exclusively adult-implemented program is that it places the burden for managing conduct on the staff, which tends to create antagonistic positions. Greater progress can be achieved if peers are enlisted to further the values and goals of the treatment program. In this regard, Phillips, Wolf, and Fixsen (1972) report that the contingency system which proved most effective and which was clearly preferred was one in which the boys periodically elected a peer leader who assigned required tasks to them individually and rewarded or penalized them according to their performance. To ensure that the leader used his delegated power constructively, he earned or lost points depending on how well those he supervised carried out their obligations. Apart from its favorable short-term results, a self-governing reinforcement system has greater educational potential because it provides experience in responsible and cooperative social living. As a general rule, contingency systems combining rewards and negative sanctions were not only more effective but, surprisingly, were liked better by the boys than ones relying solely on rewards. An environment in which individuals can engage in transgressive behavior with immunity apparently holds lesser satisfactions for its members.

There is no single optimal system because different goals and variations in the functioning levels of groups require different reinforcement practices. A completely individualized system is well suited for creating autonomous, self-determined people. If, on the other hand, one wishes to promote shared responsibility and contribution to common goals, then this objective can be best accomplished by instituting reinforcement contingencies on a group basis. Here, individual benefits depend upon the level of group performance; conversely, with shared accountability censurable conduct by any given member produces negative consequences for the entire group. By having people share in the consequences of their decisions and actions, their level of social responsibility and involvement is increased. The negative by-products of excessive individualism or collectiveness can be minimized by including both individual and group-oriented reinforcement. In a double contingency system, a given member's outcomes are determined by both the extent of his own contribution and the group's overall attainments.

At higher levels of functioning, rewards and privileges are usually tied to ranks rather than to individual performances. In areas requiring specialized skills social ranking is conducted formally, but in many situations members are differentiated in status informally. In applying hierarchical contingency systems, successive phases that require progressively higher levels of functioning in a variety of activities are devised. As individuals progress through these sequential steps by developing the requisite skills, they receive increased rewards and freedom of action. In the study cited earlier, Martin and her associates (1968) found that a hierarchical reward structure was superior to one in which specific performances were individually reinforced. Indeed, the latter arrangement produced much wrangling over unfairness because, in an effort to support progress by youngsters at different competence levels, they received comparable rewards for differing achievements.

Programs aimed at increasing social and intellectual competencies in persons lacking self-regulatory skills may initially require immediate reinforcement of specific performances. However, as progress is achieved, individuals are promoted to phase systems analogous to those existing in community life. In the treatment approach developed by Phillips, Wolf, and Fixsen (1972), after youngsters increase their competence sufficiently, they are advanced to a higher system in which all privileges are given free as long as they exhibit responsible behavior. Should they revert to reprehensible conduct, they are returned to the more concrete system until they are better able to manage increased independence. When members reach the stage at which they can maintain self-directive behavior under natural consequences, they return home or, if that possibility does not exist, are placed in a foster home. Parents receive some training in constructive ways of relating to their children before they are discharged.

If the promise of home-style treatment is confirmed by follow-up studies, it will gain acceptance as a more effective and humane alternative to incarceration. This approach holds additional advantages. In reorienting life styles one is dealing with morals and values. Although heterogeneous communities have many shared values, different segments of the population favor different conduct norms and ideals. Because of their small size and flexibility, home-style, community-based programs allow for the modification of antisocial aggression within multivalued frameworks.

Institutional Remedial Systems

Most correctional institutions are conducted on a contingent-punishment, noncontingent-reward basis. That is, the residents obtain whatever rewards and privileges the place has to offer as long as they comply with the house rules, but the privileges are promptly withdrawn for uncooperative or disruptive behavior. Thus, the threat of punishment is ever present, whereas the positive incentives for behavior change, though available, are poorly managed. Under such circumstances, most participants comply halfheartedly with the minimum demands of the institution in order to avoid penalties for any breach of the rules.

In an effective program of change, reinforcement contingencies should be arranged to create competencies for future use, rather than to extract minimal compliance with situational demands. All residents receive humane treatment on a noncontingent basis, but they can earn valued rewards and privileges for progress in acquiring educational, vocational, and social skills that create effective alternatives to antisocial conduct. A remedial program so structured can be managed without resort to those punitive measures that are commonly employed in penal institutions. By placing the residents' living conditions on a self-determining basis, the system not only provides positive incentives for constructive change but renders nonfunctional peer control practices that subvert remedial efforts. When contingencies are arranged so that constructive behavior secures good results and antisocial conduct has limited payoff, little is to be gained from outwitting staff members or provoking them by crisis-producing transgression.

Competence Training

People are unlikely to adopt or to adhere to socially acceptable life styles if they lack legitimate means of gaining the things that are highly valued by the culture. Because of adverse learning histories and wasted years of incarceration, most inmates in correctional institutions are handicapped by gross deficits in educational and vocational skills. As a consequence, those who lack the necessities of life or who value costly possessions and the benefits of high status are forced to resort to deviant means of getting them. Regardless of whether other objectives may be selected in rehabilitative programs, little progress can be made unless habitual offenders develop broadly useful skills that enable them to participate successfully in the larger society. The program devised by Cohen and Filipczak (1971) demonstrates how a custodial environment can be transformed into one that develops human potentialities by restructuring institutional reinforcement practices. This program focused primarily upon development of basic intellectual skills required for expanding one's capabilities. Although the learning environment was created within the context of a penal institution, the procedures developed have general applicability.

From the reformatory Cohen and Filipczak selected a group of delinquent boys who had few means for maintaining their subsistence other than through antisocial activities, and they failed even at these. A positive incentive system based on a point economy was employed to foster acquisition of language facility, reading, mathematics, and other functional skills. Money points earned for learning achievements in self-instructional courses could be used to purchase preferred accommodations and a wide range of services and commodities.

Most coercive sanctions imposed on inmates in prisons were eliminated. Rather, heavy reliance was placed on positive incentives, individual initiative, and self-determination. Consistent with contingency systems in daily life in the society, boys paid for their private rooms and selected meal plans that varied in choice of foods. They also used point currency to rent recreational items and private offices, and to purchase phone privileges, admission to entertainment activities, and merchandise available in either the project store or through mail order catalogs. To help the boys learn to manage their finances, a banking system was included so that they could establish savings accounts with interest rates and negotiate loans to tide them over critical periods. Those who presented an inadequate work record were told that they constituted poor loan risks and were not granted loans until they established a better credit rating. Within this environment the boys were provided with considerable freedom: They determined their own study and bedtime routines; they selected their own leisure-time activities and planned their outside programs; they aided in planning menus; and they had open mailing and visiting privileges.

A boy was free to choose not to pursue any of the self-instructional activities. If, however, his points fell below a minimum level, he lost his private room, was served the regular institutional food, and enjoyed none of the extra luxuries earned by his peers. This problem rarely arose. In an environment designed to reward learning, delinquent boys, who had received few prior accolades for scholarship worked productively at self-managed educational activities. They studied conscientiously in their spare time, gained more than two grade levels on standard achievement tests within an eight-month period, and substantially raised their intellectual level as measured by intelligence tests. By making benefits attainable through their own actions, rather than by management fiat, the boys had few reasons to create disciplinary problems. If they lacked things they wanted, they had mainly themselves to blame.

The foregoing contingency system fostered intellectual development and, although favorable changes in attitudes and social behavior were noted, no concerted effort was made to increase interpersonal competencies. Contingencies can, of course, be easily extended to include social skills and self-discipline which supplemented with proficiency in a selected occupation, would remove the major personal barriers to a prosocial mode of life. Sarason and Ganzer (1969) report preliminary studies that make use of modeling procedures with delinquents to develop social and other skills requisite for effective vocational and interpersonal functioning. Models demonstrate and then the boys practice proficient ways of handling common problem situations such as coping with authorities, negative peer influences, vocational demands, situations requiring self-control, and a variety of social predicaments. Delinquents who have the benefit of constructive modeling achieve greater changes in attitudes and behavior than boys who do not receive such training.

Deviant behavior can be modified in custodially oriented facilities through differential reinforcement. When good conduct is imposed from without, the resultant conforming behavior is likely to persist as long as the institutional sanctions remain in effect. The residents may, in fact, come to behave irreproachably or even to perform obligingly whatever behavior is expected of them in order to improve their institutional subsistence and to expedite their release. A beneficent incentive system may thus extract considerable prosocial behavior from delinquents, but they may revert to their usually antisocial conduct in situations in which it is permissively viewed. Therapeutically oriented facilities that arrange outcomes on a self-determining basis promote responsible rather than compliant behavior.

The competency training approach assumes that by increasing a person's options, a prosocial way of life will prove more functional and supplant antisocial styles of behavior. Certainly a person who has a number of effective alternatives will be less likely to revert to illegitimate activities than if he is unemployable except for menial jobs and is unskilled at handling interpersonal problems. Competency training, though essential, is generally insufficient of itself. In the demonstration project conducted by Cohen and Filipczak (1971), for example, delinquents who participated in the incentive program displayed substantially lower recidivist rates than boys who received the regular penal treatment in the same institution, but over a period of years, the differences between the groups decreased. A person who has pursued a delinquent career for many years will find it difficult to alter his social orientation, especially if he can gain recognition easily by antisocial conduct while alternative avenues entail unpleasant responsibilities with uncertain or deferred rewards. A treatment program is likely to achieve greater success if, in addition to cultivating competencies, it changes association preferences and reduces susceptibility to the influence of delinquent peers.

Development of Self-regulatory Functions

The sway of external reinforcement can be diminished by establishing countervailing self-reinforcement functions. When new standards for self-evaluation are adopted as self-regulative influences, people adhere to prosocial styles of behavior because they derive self-satisfaction from them; conversely, they refrain from antisocial conduct because it produces self-devaluative consequences.

Social learning theory suggests several procedures for developing self-regulatory functions. First, valued patterns of behavior and standards for self-evaluation should be exemplified by change agents. Second, an explicit set of conduct guides linked with a graded system of incentives should be instituted, such that progressive adoption of more advanced behavior brings increased freedom, privileges, and access to rewarding activities. Participants will adopt new forms of behavior on the basis of their utilitarian value. However, provision of exemplary models and positive inducements alone may not be sufficient to create new self-directing capabilities in persons whose behavior has been governed by dissocial standards.

Conditions that provide explicit training in self-reinforcement should be arranged. This is achieved by gradually transferring evaluative and reinforcing functions from change agents to the individual himself. At the first transition stage the person judges whether his behavior warrants reward, but others still serve as the reinforcing agents. After accurate self-evaluation is established, the reinforcing function is likewise transferred so that the individual both evaluates his own behavior and reinforces himself accordingly. Concrete rewards are gradually reduced as the person's behavior is increasingly regulated by social, self-evaluative, and symbolic consequences. The ultimate aim of training in self-determination is to produce a level of functioning at which participants regulate their own actions with minimum external constraints and artificial inducements.

Another means of instilling self-regulatory functions is to provide ample opportunities for participants to perform role behaviors with peers that are ordinarily carried out by the supervisory staff. Specifically, this entails delegating progressively more of the standard-setting, evaluative, and reinforcement functions to members of the group as they progress in the program. Thus, with staff guidance, peers play an active role in implementing the treatment goals. In a system containing shared responsibility, games designed to outwit the staff become pointless. In order to enhance participants' willingness to adopt role behaviors that carry bothersome responsibilities, increased benefits must be associated with these higher positions.

Values and preferences are changed more effectively when members participate actively in decision-making, reward their own accomplishments, and discipline their transgressions than when standards of conduct are imposed by administrative authority on covertly resistant individuals. Research evidence further suggests that a person who takes on the task of reinforcing the behavior of others is likely to alter his own standards of self-reinforcement in the practiced direction. When peers assume responsible roles in their subcommunity it not only fosters changes in themselves, but advances the development of newcomers and subordinates by providing success models for valued conduct. Since peers are closer socially and more available to serve as guides in daily life, they are likely to be emulated to a greater extent than staff members. Additionally, there is less risk of being ostracized for adopting behavioral standards that are modeled by peers and staff alike.

Change in Association Preferences

Just as self-regulatory functions are socially transferable through modeling and reinforcement, they are also extinguishable unless given sufficient social support. In any given community an assortment of subgroups, which differ widely in their standards of conduct, are potentially available to individuals. The groups with which one chooses to affiliate largely determine the role models and sanctions to which one will be exposed and, consequently, the direction in which one's behavior will be further modified. Several researchers have documented how selective association shapes the course of one's life (Bandura and Walters, 1959; Ellis and Lane, 1963, Krauss, 1964). Attention to factors governing the selection of reference groups is of critical importance, especially when newly adopted patterns conflict with the behavior reinforced by former associates.

New competencies and self-evaluative standards can exert decisive influence on whether participants gravitate toward groups that reinforce prosocial or antisocial pursuits. Moreover, given increased options, which reduce dependence on any single group, and incompatible self-evaluative reactions, a person is better able to resist pressures for conformity to antisocial values. When the advocated conduct violates self-prescribed codes, the individual may attempt to alter the value placed on the activities, may remain a marginal member, or, if the rewards for membership are insufficient, may discontinue his association with the group.

If delinquents are to affiliate with prosocial groups, they must possess the means for securing the acceptance and recognition necessary to sustain their active involvement. Otherwise, they will be unable to fulfill the new roles and will either eventually withdraw from or be rejected by their new associates. Many rehabilitative programs concentrate on changing offenders' behavior in ways that lose them the satisfactions associated with a deviant career without providing alternative means of obtaining gratifications. An effective remedial program should establish the entry skills and provide whatever initial support and guidance is needed to succeed in the new milieu. After the person has developed a rewarding stake in the system, he is unlikely to revert to antisocial behavior, especially if it carries punishment costs, as it does for those who do poorly at it.

CHANGES IN SOCIAL SYSTEMS

It would be short-sighted to concentrate solely on the casualties of detrimental social systems without changing the conditions that foster widespread aggression. In the preceding discussion guidelines were presented for changing the practices of subsystems that can affect the level of aggression within a society. The present section is mainly concerned with the use of collective action as an instrument of social change. Interventions at the social systems level require group action against the individuals and institutions contributing to social problems. Collective action usually fails, however, because it is poorly organized, because efforts are dissipated on too many different problems or on factional disputes over leadership, and the group pressure is not sustained. Consequently, the sufferers of malfunctioning systems come to display much discontent and cynicism but little social action.

Social change must be approached in a number of different ways. At the neighborhood level, residents can reduce the amount of destructive behavior that plagues their community from within by instituting sanctions against such conduct. As we have already seen, aggression stems from its functional value as well as from aversive instigating conditions. People who lack power cannot easily change adverse social conditions, but the reinforcements that their community provides for aggressive conduct lie within their sphere of influence. Accordant community functioning is something that is maintained to a large extent by the general expectations and reinforcing reactions of residents toward each other rather than imposed from without by enforcement agencies. Most aggressive offenses in fact lend themselves more to informal control than to legal sanctions, which are applied too infrequently to serve as reliable deterrents. Community control of aggression through shared enforcement of sanctions is illustrated by Christopherson and Risley (1972). They assisted residents of a low income housing project in curbing vandalism by having them articulate a set of conduct codes and impose consequences on destructive offenders. Other problems of common concern can be similarly alleviated by building into social relationships a sense of community through neighborhood reinforcement practices.

Institutions designed to serve the community must be held more accountable for their practices. Given our present knowledge, educational systems, for example, should not be turning out sizable numbers of students so lacking in basic skills that their choices of livelihood are essentially restricted to menial pursuits, some form of relief, or a life of crime. Results reported earlier and elsewhere (Bandura, 1969a) demonstrate that methods exist for creating learning environments that can transform academic failure into success. If students are to acquire requisite skills for participating successfully in the society, communities must institute a system of accountability in which financial support is tied to demonstrated educational effectiveness. When educational agencies are held answerable for their results, instructional systems rather than students are failed.

The system of accountability should be extended to other community services as well. In public agencies that enjoy monopolies over given functions, the practices that evolve are more likely to serve the interests and convenience of the staff than to maximize benefits for their clientele. Internal rewards for conformity to operating procedures mitigate against external efforts to produce change. Improvements in social services are achieved more rapidly by rewarding superior accomplishments of alternative systems than by imposing negative sanctions for poor performance by a single system. Many community services could be placed under a voucher system in which citizens are given certificates to purchase the service from any one of several authorized sources. Providing options creates strong incentives for organizations to increase the effectiveness of their operations, for otherwise they lose their patronage. When functions are best conducted through a single agency, bureaucratic barriers to change can be lessened by creating a semi-autonomous unit under public jurisdiction empowered to devise better ways of doing the job. Procedures for measuring how well an agency is meeting stipulated performance standards should be an integral part of the system. Performance assessments that have budgetary or staff consequences provide additional inducements to improve the quality of services.

Maltreatment is most prevalent where marked imbalances of power exist. In seeking improvements in their life situation, neglected and disadvantaged people are faced with the difficult task of altering the practices of those who wield power and do not wish to relinquish it. In such situations change can be pursued through the organized strength of numbers.

The first task in the agenda for social change is to gain broad participation of people in the collective endeavor. Organizational methods vary depending on whose support is sought and whether influence will be exerted indirectly through moral persuasion or by use of social power. Exponents of direct influence by power tactics depend mainly on the efforts of the aggrieved. The work of Saul Alinsky (1971), an astute community organizer, exemplifies successful mobilization of subordinated groups for action against inequitable treatment. The organizational efforts in this approach are aimed at building community self-determination. Organizers enter the situation as consultants by invitation only. The residents play a major role in selecting common goals for which broad support is enlisted by appeal to their self-interest. To ensure that local power bases survive over time, indigenous leadership is developed along with serviceable problem-solving mechanisms.

Reformers seeking basic changes in the society at large rely on the force of intermediary influences, which they attempt to mobilize largely through persuasive appeals (Zaltman, Kotler, and Kaufman, 1972). By arousing sympathetic reaction in people with greater power to create rewarding and punishing outcomes for officials, public pressure is brought to bear on offending institutions to change their policies. Whatever direct actions are taken are designed more to dramatize nationally the grievances and need for reform than to solve a local problem expeditiously. Tactical power is thus sacrificed for public credibility. In this process of mobilization communications media play a prominent role.

Over time the change efforts of subordinated people are extinguished, with the result that most become apathetic though discontented with their way of life. A change program must therefore help them learn how to exercise control over their social environment. They need to practice skills in decision-making, learn influence tactics and how to tailor them to changing circumstances, develop disciplined ways of reacting to counterpressure, and allay their fear of adversaries. Skill acquisition is best promoted through group role-playing in simulated conflicts with experienced leaders acting as models. Having established competencies, the next task is to build a sense of efficacy through success in alleviating everyday problems. By selecting goals that can be realized with concerted effort, participants gain confidence for tackling tougher issues.

If apathy reflected only past failures in effecting change, training for constructive action would pose no special difficulties. Subordinated groups, however, are deterred from challenging injustices by fear of punishment and economic reprisals. Why risk dangers for uncertain benefits? Inhibitions of this sort are overcome by the example of success. Seeing others like themselves improve their living conditions by organized effort provides compelling demonstrations that they too have something to gain from contesting unwarranted practices. After a group develops its capacity for social action, its bargaining efficacy is enhanced so that it has less need to carry out protest tactics. This is because group pressure, successfully applied, makes threats credible. Consequently, in future disputes threats of collective action alone are usually sufficient to produce accommodating changes.

The political system is a major agency of social change. People improve their society through reform legislation. They rely on the sanctions of judicial and administrative agencies to enforce laws that affect their everyday life. The governmental apparatus, however, is often subverted from its public function by the pressure of vested interests. Legislative procedures built into the system enable influential entrepreneurs to use the powers of government to resist social changes that conflict with their self-interests. Efforts to improve the functioning of society must also be directed at governmental practices to make them serve the public more equitably.

Gardner (1972) created Common Cause as a public mechanism for exerting pressure on Congress and state legislatures. A major thrust of this citizens' lobby is focused on congressional reforms. Numerous changes are sought in congressional committee operations that currently make it easy to slight the public interest. These include abolishing the seniority system, reducing excessive power of committee chairmen, and ending secrecy in the conduct of legislative business by making committee votes public. Common Cause worked successfully for a law requiring disclosure of political expenditures so that the public can be informed of the financial interests backing various candidates. As a further step in reducing congressional control by special moneyed interests, Common Cause is advocating lobbying laws to monitor who is spending how much for what purposes. In addition to curtailing entrenched private sources of congressional control, this citizens' organization exerts its influence on legislative actions in promoting new solutions to a broad range of social problems. In some of these areas inequitable or potentially detrimental practices are sufficiently beneficial to large segments of the population to gain popular support. Efforts to legislate social change are therefore subjected to conflicting sources of public and private control.

The law can be used to preserve existing practices or as an instrument of social change. Legal means are heavily relied upon by people to secure their rights and to advance their welfare. It is by converting social demands into formal codes backed by sanctions that enduring reforms, which reduce the likelihood of civil strife, are achieved. In some discriminatory practices, individuals may be willing to change if everyone else does so but not individually because they would be singled out for attack. Personal threats supporting adherence to customs that have adverse effects on others are greatly reduced when modifications in behavior can be attributed to legal mandates (Zimring and Hawkins, 1971). Under these conditions, laws serve to accelerate widespread social change.

Passing laws does not necessarily ensure adequate enforcement of them. Efforts to eliminate inequitable practices are resisted by entrenched interest groups and elements of the general public. When legal prohibitions are instituted against activities that have influential backing, it is not uncommon for the laws to be reinterpreted, circumvented, or poorly administered (Friedman, 1967). Further litigation is therefore required to refine statutes into effective operating rules and to guarantee their active enforcement. In addition to inducing and monitoring the process of change, legal mechanisms can uphold a society's capacity for constructive change by protecting dissenters from unauthorized coercion.

Like so many other problems confronting man, there is no single grand design for lowering the level of destructiveness within a society. It requires both individual corrective effort and group action aimed at changing the practices of social systems. Since aggression is not an inevitable or unchangeable aspect of man but a product of aggression promoting conditions operating within a society, man has the power to reduce his level of aggressiveness. Whether this capability is used wisely or destructively is another matter.

REFERENCES

ACKERMAN, N. W. Psychotherapy and "giving love." *Psychiatry*, 1944, **7**, 129–37.

ADLER, L. L., AND ADLER, H. E. Age as a factor in observational learning in puppies. *American Dachshund*, March 1968, 13–14.

AGRAS, W. S. Behavior therapy in the management of chronic schizophrenia. *American Journal of Psychiatry*, 1967, **124**, 240–43.

ALINSKY, S. D. *Rules for radicals.* New York: Random House, 1971.

ALLAND, A., Jr. *The human imperative.* New York: Columbia University Press, 1972.

ALLISON, T. S., AND ALLISON, S. L. Time-out from reinforcement: Effect on sibling aggression. *Psychological Record*, 1971, **21**, 81–86.

AMSEL, A. The role of frustrative nonreward in noncontinuous reward situations. *Psychological Bulletin*, 1958, **55**, 102–19.

ANDRUS, B. C. *The infamous of Nuremberg.* London: Fravin, 1969.

ARDREY, R. *The territorial imperative.* New York: Atheneum, 1966.

ARONFREED, J. The problem of imitation. In L. P. Lipsitt and H. W. Reese (Eds.), *Advances in child development and behavior*. Vol. IV. New York: Academic Press, 1969. Pp. 210–319.

ASTIN, A. W., AND BAYER, A. E. Antecedents and consequents of disruptive campus protests. *Measurement and Evaluation in Guidance*, 1971, **4**, 18–30.

AX, A. F. The physiological differentiation between fear and anger in humans. *Psychosomatic Medicine*, 1953, **15**, 433–42.

AYLLON, T., AND AZRIN, N. H. Reinforcement and instructions with mental patients. *Journal of the Experimental Analysis of Behavior*, 1964, **7**, 327–31.

AZRIN, N. H. Pain and aggression. *Psychology Today*, 1967, **1**, 27–33.

AZRIN, N. H. Punishment of elicited aggression. *Journal of the Experimental Analysis of Behavior*, 1970, **14**, 7–10.

AZRIN, N. H., HAKE, D. F., AND HUTCHINSON, R. R. Elicitation of aggression by a physical blow. *Journal of the Experimental Analysis of Behavior*, 1965, **8**, 55–57.

AZRIN, N. H. AND HOLZ, W. C. PUNISHMENT. In W. K. Honig (Ed.), *Operant behavior*. New York: Appleton-Century-Crofts, 1966. Pp. 380–447.

AZRIN, N. H., AND HUTCHINSON, R. R. Conditioning of the aggressive behavior of pigeons by a fixed-interval schedule of reinforcement. *Journal of the Experimental Analysis of Behavior*, 1967, **10**, 395–402.

AZRIN, N. H., HUTCHINSON, R. R., AND HAKE, D. F. Pain-induced fighting in the squirrel monkey. *Journal of the Experimental Analysis of Behavior*, 1963, **6**, 620.

AZRIN, N. H., HUTCHINSON, R. R., AND HAKE, D. F. Attack, avoidance, and escape reactions to aversive shock. *Journal of the Experimental Analysis of Behavior*, 1967, **10**, 131–48.

AZRIN, N. H., HUTCHINSON, R. R., AND McLAUGHLIN, R. The opportunity for aggression as an operant reinforcer during aversive stimulation. *Journal of the Experimental Analysis of Behavior*, 1965, **8**, 171–80.

AZRIN, N. H., RUBIN, H. B., AND HUTCHINSON, R. R. Biting attack by rats in response to aversive shock. *Journal of the Experimental Analysis of Behavior*, 1968, **11**, 633–39.

AZRIN, N. H., ULRICH, R. E., HUTCHINSON, R. R., AND NORMAN, D. G. Effect of shock duration on shock-induced fighting. *Journal of the Experimental Analysis of Behavior*, 1964, **7**, 9–11.

BACH-Y-RITA, G., LION, J. R., CLIMENT, C. E., AND ERVIN, F. R. Episodic dyscontrol: A study of 130 violent patients. *American Journal of Psychiatry*, 1971, **127**, 1473–78.

BAENNINGER, R., AND GROSSMAN, J. C. Some effects of punishment on pain-elicited aggression. *Journal of the Experimental Analysis of Behavior*, 1969, **12**, 1017–22.

BAILEY, J. S., WOLF, M. M., AND PHILLIPS, E. L. Home-based reinforcement and the modification of pre-delinquents' classroom behavior. *Journal of Applied Behavior Analysis*, 1970, **3**, 223–33.

BAKER, J. W., II, AND SCHAIE, K. W. Effects of aggressing "alone" or "with another" on physiological and psychological arousal. *Journal of Personality and Social Psychology*, 1969, **12**, 80–96.

BALDWIN, T. F., AND LEWIS, C. Violence in television: The industry looks at itself. In G. A. Comstock and E. A. Rubinstein (Eds.), *Television and social behavior*. Vol. 1. *Media content and control*. Washington, D.C.: Government Printing Office, 1972. Pp. 290–373.

BALL-ROKEACH, S. J. Review of *Television and Aggression,* by S. Feshbach and R. D. Singer. *Public Opinion Quarterly*, 1971, **35**, 501–4.

BALL-ROKEACH, S. J. The legitimation of violence. In J. F. Short, Jr., and M. E. Wolfgang (Eds.), *Collective violence*. Chicago: Aldine-Atherton, 1972.

BANDURA, A. Relationship of family patterns to child behavior disorders. Progress Report, 1960, Stanford University, Project No. M-1734, United States Public Health Service.

BANDURA, A. Social learning through imitation. In M. R. Jones (Ed.), *Nebraska symposium on motivation: 1962*. Lincoln: University of Nebraska Press, 1962. Pp. 211–69.

BANDURA, A. Influence of models' reinforcement contingencies on the acquisition of imitative responses. *Journal of Personality and Social Psychology*, 1965a, **1**, 589–95.

BANDURA, A. Vicarious processes: A case of no-trial learning. In L. Berkowitz (Ed.), *Advances in experimental social psychology*. Vol. II. New York: Academic Press, 1965b. Pp. 1–55.

BANDURA, A. *Principles of behavior modification*. New York: Holt, Rinehart and Winston, 1969a.

BANDURA, A. Social-learning theory of identificatory processes. In D. A. Goslin (Ed.), *Handbook of socialization theory and research*. Chicago: Rand McNally, 1969b. Pp. 213–62.

BANDURA, A. Psychotherapy based upon modeling principles. In A. E. Bergin and S. L. Garfield (Eds.), *Handbook of psychotherapy and behavior change*. New York: Wiley, 1971a. Pp. 653–708.

BANDURA, A. Vicarious and self-reinforcement processes. In R. Glaser (Ed.), *The nature of reinforcement.* New York: Academic Press, 1971b. Pp. 228–78.

BANDURA, A. *Social learning theory.* New York: General Learning Press, 1971c.

BANDURA, A. (Ed.), *Psychological modeling.* Chicago: Aldine-Atherton, 1971d.

BANDURA, A. The process and practice of participant modeling treatment. Unpublished manuscript. Stanford University, 1972.

BANDURA, A., BLANCHARD, E. B., AND RITTER, B. The relative efficacy of desensitization and modeling approaches for inducing behavioral, affective, and attitudinal changes. *Journal of Personality and Social Psychology,* 1969, **13,** 173–99.

BANDURA, A., GRUSEC, J. E., AND MENLOVE, F. L. Observational learning as a function of symbolization and incentive set. *Child Development,* 1966, **37,** 499–506.

BANDURA, A., AND HUSTON, A. C. Identification as a process of incidental learning. *Journal of Abnormal and Social Psychology,* 1961, **63,** 311–18.

BANDURA, A., AND JEFFERY, R. W. Role of symbolic coding and rehearsal processes in observational learning. *Journal of Personality and Social Psychology,* 1972, in press.

BANDURA, A., LIPSHER, D. H., AND MILLER, P. E. Psychotherapists' approach-avoidance reactions to patients' expressions of hostility. *Journal of Consulting Psychology,* 1960, **24,** 1–8.

BANDURA, A., AND MCDONALD, F. J. The influence of social reinforcement and the behavior of models in shaping children's moral judgments. *Journal of Abnormal and Social Psychology,* 1963, **67,** 274–81.

BANDURA, A., AND MENLOVE, F. L. Factors determining vicarious extinction of avoidance behavior through symbolic modeling. *Journal of Personality and Social Psychology,* 1968, **8,** 99–108.

BANDURA, A., AND MISCHEL, W. Modification of self-imposed delay of reward through exposure to live and symbolic models. *Journal of Personality and Social Psychology,* 1965, **2,** 698–705.

BANDURA, A., AND ROSENTHAL, T. L. Vicarious classical conditioning as a function of arousal level. *Journal of Personality and Social Psychology,* 1966, **3,** 54–62.

BANDURA, A., ROSS, D., AND ROSS, S. A. Transmission of aggression through imitation of aggressive models. *Journal of Abnormal and Social Psychology,* 1961, **63,** 575–82.

BANDURA, A., ROSS, D., AND ROSS, S. A. Imitation of film-mediated aggressive models. *Journal of Abnormal and Social Psychology*, 1963a, **66**, 3–11.

BANDURA, A., ROSS, D., AND ROSS, S. A. A comparative test of the status envy, social power, and secondary reinforcement theories of identificatory learning. *Journal of Abnormal and Social Psychology*, 1963b, **67**, 527–34.

BANDURA, A., ROSS, D., AND ROSS, S. A. Vicarious reinforcement and imitative learning. *Journal of Abnormal and Social Psychology*, 1963c, **67**, 601–7.

BANDURA, A., AND WALTERS, R. H. *Adolescent aggression*. New York: Ronald Press, 1959.

BANDURA, A., AND WALTERS, R. H. *Social learning and personality development*. New York: Holt, Rinehart and Winston, 1963.

BARKER, R., DEMBO, T., AND LEWIN, K. Frustration and regression: An experiment with young children. *University of Iowa Studies in Child Welfare*, 1941, **18** (Whole No. 386).

BARNETT, S. A. Attack and defense in animal societies. In C. D. Clemente and D. B. Lindsley (Eds.), *Aggression and defense*. Los Angeles: University of California Press, 1967. Pp. 35–56.

BARON, R. A. Reducing the influence of an aggressive model: The restraining effects of discrepant modeling cues. *Journal of Personality and Social Psychology*, 1971a, **20**, 240–45.

BARON, R. A. Exposure to an aggressive model and apparent probability of retaliation from the victim as determinants of adult aggressive behavior. *Journal of Experimental Social Psychology*, 1971b, **7**, 343–55.

BARON, R. A. Magnitude of victim's pain cues and level of prior anger arousal as determinants of adult aggressive behavior. *Journal of Personality and Social Psychology*, 1971c, **17**, 236–43.

BARON, R. A. Aggression as a function of magnitude of victim's pain cues, level of prior anger arousal, and aggressor-victim similarity. *Journal of Personality and Social Psychology*, 1971d, **18**, 48–54.

BARON, R. A., AND KEPNER, C. R. Model's behavior and attraction toward the model as determinants of adult aggressive behavior. *Journal of Personality and Social Psychology*, 1970, **14**, 335–44.

BARRON, J. Access to the press—a new first amendment right. *Harvard Law Review*, 1967, **80**, 1641–78.

BARROW, L. C., JR., AND WESTLEY, B. H. "Exploring the news": An experiment on the relative effectiveness of radio and TV versions of a children's news program. In W. Schramm (Ed.), *The impact of edu-*

cational television. Urbana: University of Illinois Press, 1960. Pp. 143–50.

BATESON, G. *The Naven.* Stanford, Calif.: Stanford University Press, 1936.

BATESON, G. The frustration-aggression hypothesis and culture. *Psychological Review,* 1941, **48**, 350–55.

BATESON, G. (Ed.). *Perceval's narrative: A patient's account of his psychosis, 1830–1832.* Stanford, Calif.: Stanford University Press, 1961.

BEACH, F. A. It's all in your mind. *Psychology Today,* 1969, **3**, 33–35.

BECKER, W. C., THOMAS, D. R., AND CARNINE, D. *Reducing behavior problems: An operant conditioning guide for teachers.* Urbana, Ill.: Educational Resources Information Center Clearinghouse on Early Childhood Education, 1969.

BEDAU, H. A. *The death penalty in America.* Garden City, N.Y.: Anchor Books, 1967.

BERGER, S. M. Conditioning through vicarious instigation. *Psychological Review,* 1962, **69,** 450–66.

BERKOWITZ, L. The expression and reduction of hostility. *Psychological Bulletin,* 1958, **55,** 257–83.

BERKOWITZ, L. *Aggression: A social psychological analysis.* New York: McGraw Hill, 1962.

BERKOWITZ, L. The concept of aggressive drive: Some additional considerations. In L. Berkowitz (Ed.), *Advances in experimental social psychology.* Vol. 2. New York: Academic Press, 1965a. Pp. 301–29.

BERKOWITZ, L. Some aspects of observed aggression. *Journal of Personality and Social Psychology,* 1965b, **2**, 359–69.

BERKOWITZ, L. The contagion of violence: An S-R mediational analysis of some effects of observed aggression. In W. J. Arnold and M. M. Page (Eds.), *Nebraska symposium on motivation, 1970.* Lincoln: University of Nebraska Press, 1970. Pp. 95–135.

BERKOWITZ, L. The "weapons effect," deviant characteristics, and the myth of the compliant subject. *Journal of Personality and Social Psychology,* 1971, **20,** 332–38.

BERKOWITZ, L. Words and symbols as stimuli to aggressive responses. In J. F. Knutson (Ed.), *Control of aggression: Implications from basic research.* Chicago: Aldine-Atherton, 1972 (in press).

BERKOWITZ, L., AND GEEN, R. G. Film violence and the cue properties of available targets. *Journal of Personality and Social Psychology,* 1966, **3,** 525–30.

BERKOWITZ, L., AND GEEN, R. G. Stimulus qualities of the target of aggression: A further study. *Journal of Personality and Social Psychology*, 1967, **5**, 364–68.

BERKOWITZ, L., AND KNUREK, D. A. Label-mediated hostility generalization. *Journal of Personality and Social Psychology*, 1969, **13**, 200–206.

BERKOWITZ, L., AND LE PAGE, A. Weapons as aggression-eliciting stimuli. *Journal of Personality and Social Psychology*, 1967, **7**, 202–7.

BERKOWITZ, L., AND MACAULAY, J. The contagion of violence. In H. Hirsch and C. Leiden (Eds.), *Political micro-violence*. New York: Harper & Row, 1972, in press.

BERNAL, M. E., DURYEE, J. S., PRUETT, H. L., AND BURNS, B. J. Behavior modification and the brat syndrome. *Journal of Consulting and Clinical Psychology*, 1968, **32**, 447–55.

BERNAL, M. E., WILLIAMS, D. E., MILLER, W. H., AND REAGOR, P. A. The use of videotape feedback and operant learning principles in training parents in management of deviant children. In R. D. Rubin (Ed.), *Advances in behavior therapy*. Vol. III. New York: Academic Press, 1972. Pp. 19–31.

BERNARD, V., OTTENBERG, P., AND REDL, F. Dehumanization: A composite psychological defense in relation to modern war. In M. Schwebel (Ed.), *Behavioral science and human survival*. Palo Alto, Calif.: Science and Behavior Books, 1965. Pp. 64–82.

BETTELHEIM, B. Individual and mass behavior in extreme situations. *Journal of Abnormal and Social Psychology*, 1943, **38**, 417–52.

BEVAN, W., DAVES, W. F., AND LEVY, G. W. The relation of castration, androgen therapy and pre-test experience to competitive aggression in male C57 BL/10 mice. *Animal Behaviour*, 1960, **8**, 6–12.

BINDER, A., MCCONNELL, D., AND SJOHOLM, N. A. Verbal conditioning as a function of experimenter characteristics. *Journal of Abnormal and Social Psychology*, 1957, **55**, 309–14.

BLACKBURN, R. Personality in relation to extreme aggression in psychiatric offenders. *British Journal of Psychiatry*, 1968, **114**, 821–28.

BLACKHAM, G. J., AND SILBERMAN, A. *Modification of child behavior.* Belmont, Calif.: Wadsworth, 1971.

BLIXT, S., AND LEY, R. Force-contingent reinforcement in instrumental conditioning and extinction in children: A test of the frustration-drive hypothesis. *Journal of Comparative and Physiological Psychology*, 1969, **69**, 267–72.

BLUMENTHAL, M., KAHN, R. L., ANDREWS, F. M., AND HEAD, K. B. *Justifying violence: Attitudes of American men.* Ann Arbor, Mich.: Institute for Social Research, 1972.

BLUMER, H. Social problems as collective behavior. *Social Problems,* 1971, **18,** 298–305.

BOLLES, R. C. *Theory of motivation.* New York: Harper & Row, 1967.

BOLSTAD, O. D., AND JOHNSON, S. M. Self-regulation in the modification of disruptive classroom behavior. *Journal of Applied Behavior Analysis,* 1972.

BOSTOW, D. E., AND BAILEY, J. S. Modification of severe disruptive and aggressive behavior using brief timeout and reinforcement procedures. *Journal of Applied Behavior Analysis,* 1969, **2,** 31–37.

BOWEN, D. R., BOWEN, E. R., GAWSER, S. R., AND MASOTTI, L. H. Deprivation, mobility, and orientation toward protest of the urban poor. *American Behavioral Scientist,* 1968, **11,** 20–24.

BRAMEL, D., TAUB, B., AND BLUM, B. An observer's reaction to the suffering of his enemy. *Journal of Personality and Social Psychology,* 1968, **8,** 384–92.

BREED, W. Social control in the newsroom: A functional analysis. *Social Forces,* 1955, **33,** 326–35.

BREER, P. E., AND LOCKE, E. A. *Task experience as a source of attitudes.* Homewood, Ill.: Dorsey, 1965.

BROCK, T. C., AND BUSS, A. H. Dissonance, aggression, and evaluation of pain. *Journal of Abnormal and Social Psychology,* 1962, **65,** 197–202.

BROCK, T. C., AND BUSS, A. H. Effects of justification for aggression and communication with the victim on postaggression dissonance. *Journal of Abnormal and Social Psychology,* 1964, **68,** 403–12.

BROWN, G. D., AND TYLER, V. O., Jr. Time out from reinforcement: A technique for dethroning the "duke" of an institutionalized delinquent group. *Journal of Child Psychology and Psychiatry and Allied Disciplines,* 1968, **9,** 203–11.

BROWN, L. *Television: The business behind the box.* New York: Harcourt Brace Jovanovich, 1971.

BROWN, P., AND ELLIOTT, R. Control of aggression in a nursery school class. *Journal of Experimental Child Psychology,* 1965, **2,** 103–7.

BUCHER, B., AND LOVAAS, O. I. Use of aversive stimulation in behavior modification. In M. R. Jones (Ed.), *Miami symposium on the prediction of behavior, 1967: Aversive stimulation.* Coral Gables, Fla.: University of Miami Press, 1968. Pp. 77–145.

BUEHLER, R. E., PATTERSON, G. R., AND FURNISS, J. M. The reinforcement of behavior in institutional settings. *Behaviour Research and Therapy,* 1966, **4,** 157–67.

BURCHARD, J., AND TYLER, V. O., Jr. The modification of delinquent behavior through operant conditioning. *Behaviour Research and Therapy*, 1965, **2**, 245–50.

Buss, A. H. *The psychology of aggression.* New York: Wiley, 1961.

Buss, A. H. Physical aggression in relation to different frustrations. *Journal of Abnormal and Social Psychology*, 1963, **67**, 1–7.

Buss, A. H. Instrumentality of aggression, feedback, and frustration as determinants of physical aggression. *Journal of Personality and Social Psychology*, 1966a, **3**, 153–62.

Buss, A. H. The effect of harm on subsequent aggression. *Journal of Experimental Research in Personality*, 1966b, **1**, 249–55.

Buss, A. H., Booker, A., and Buss, E. Firing a weapon and aggression. *Journal of Personality and Social Psychology*, 1972, **22**, 296–302.

Buss, A. H., and Durkee, A. Conditioning of hostile verbalizations in a situation resembling a clinical interview. *Journal of Consulting Psychology*, 1958, **22**, 415–18.

Calhoun, J. B. The study of wild animals under controlled conditions. *Annals of the New York Academy of Sciences*, 1950, **51**, 1113–22.

Calhoun, J. B. Population density and social pathology. *Scientific American*, 1962, **206**, 139–50.

Campbell, B. A., and Church, R. M. *Punishment and aversive behavior.* New York: Appleton-Century-Crofts, 1969.

Campbell, D. T. Conformity in psychology's theories of acquired behavioral dispositions. In I. A. Berg and B. M. Bass (Eds.), *Conformity and deviation.* New York: Harper, 1961. Pp. 101–42.

Campbell, D. T. Reforms as experiments. *American Psychologist*, 1969, **24**, 409–429.

Cantor, M. G. The role of the producer in choosing children's television content. In G. A. Comstock and E. A. Rubinstein (Eds.), *Television and social behavior.* Vol. 1. *Media content and control.* Washington, D.C.: Government Printing Office, 1972. Pp. 259–89.

Caplan, N. S. The new ghetto man: A review of recent empirical studies. *Journal of Social Issues*, 1970, **26**, 59–73.

Caplan, N. S., and Paige, J. M. A study of ghetto rioters. *Scientific American*, 1968, **219** (2), 15–21.

Carrighar, S. War is not in our genes. In M. F. A. Montagu (Ed.), *Man and aggression.* New York: Oxford University Press, 1968. Pp. 37–50.

Carthy, J. D., and Ebling, F. J. (Eds.). *The natural history of aggression.* New York: Academic Press, 1964.

Chaffee, S. H., and McLeod, J. M. Adolescents, parents, and television violence. Paper presented at the meeting of the American Psychological Association, Washington, D.C., September 1971.

CHAGNON, N. *Yanomamö: The fierce people*. New York: Holt, Rinehart and Winston, 1968.

CHEVIGNY, P. *Police power: Police abuses in New York City*. New York: Pantheon Books, 1969.

CHITTENDEN, G. E. An experimental study in measuring and modifying assertive behavior in young children. *Monographs of the Society for Research in Child Development*, 1942, VII, No. 1 (Serial No. 31).

CHRISTOPHERSEN, E. R., AND RISLEY, T. R. Community controlled sanctions in an urban poverty area. Unpublished manuscript, University of Kansas, 1972.

CHRISTY, P. R., GELFAND, D. M., AND HARTMANN, D. P. Effects of competition-induced frustration on two classes of modeled behavior. *Developmental Psychology*, 1971, 5, 104–11.

CHU, G. C., AND SCHRAMM, W. *Learning from television*. Stanford University: Institute for Communication Research, 1967.

CLARK, G. R., TELFER, M. A., BAKER, D., AND ROSEN, M. Sex chromosomes, crime, and psychosis. *American Journal of Psychiatry*, 1972, in press.

CLARK, H. B., ROWBURY, T., BAER, A. M., AND BAER, D. M. Control of a preschooler's disruptive behavior through the use of time-out. Paper presented at the meeting of the American Psychological Association, Miami, September 1970.

CLASTER, D. S. Comparison of risk perception between delinquents and nondelinquents. *Journal of Criminal Law, Criminology, & Police Science*, 1967, 58, 80–86.

CLEMENTE, C. D., AND LINDSLEY, D. B. (Eds.), *Aggression and defense: Neural mechanisms and social patterns*. Los Angeles: University of California Press, 1967.

Cleveland Press. Untouchable gang. May 19, 1961, p. 1.

CLINE, V. B., CROFT, R. G., AND COURRIER, S. The desensitization of children to television violence. Unpublished manuscript, University of Utah, 1972.

COHEN, A. R. Social norms, arbitrariness of frustration, and status of the agent of frustration in the frustration-aggression hypothesis. *Journal of Abnormal and Social Psychology*, 1955, 51, 222–26.

COHEN, H. L., AND FILIPCZAK, J. *A new learning environment*. San Francisco: Jossey-Bass, 1971.

COLE, J. M., AND LITCHFIELD, P. M. Stimulus control of schedule-induced aggression in the pigeon. *Psychonomic Science,* 1969, **17,** 152–53.

COLE, J. M., AND PARKER, B. K. Schedule-induced aggression: Access to an attackable target bird as a positive reinforcer. *Psychonomic Science,* 1971, **22,** 33–35.

COLLINS, W. A. The effect of temporal separation between motivation, aggression and consequences: A developmental study. *Developmental Psychology,* 1973, in press.

COLMAN, A. D. *Planned environment in psychiatric treatment: A manual for design.* Springfield, Ill.: Charles C Thomas, 1971.

CONNER, R. L., AND LEVINE, S. Hormonal influences on aggressive behaviour. In S. Garattini and E. B. Sigg (Eds.), *Aggressive behaviour.* New York: Wiley, 1969. Pp. 150–63.

CORNING, P. A., AND CORNING, C. H. Toward a general theory of violent aggression. *Social Science Information,* 1972, 11, 7–35.

COUSINS, N. The time-trap. *Saturday Review of Literature,* Dec. 24, 1949, 20.

COWAN, P. A., AND WALTERS, R. H. Studies of reinforcement of aggression: I. Effects of scheduling. *Child Development,* 1963, **34,** 543–51.

CRAWFORD, T., AND NADITCH, M. Relative deprivation, powerlessness, and militancy: The psychology of social protest. *Psychiatry,* 1970, **33,** 208–23.

CREER, T. L., HITZING, E. W., AND SCHAEFFER, R. W. Classical conditioning of reflexive fighting. *Psychonomic Science,* 1966, **4,** 89–90.

CROOK, J. H. The nature and function of territorial aggression. In M. F. A. Montagu (Ed.), *Man and aggression.* New York: Oxford University Press, 1968.. Pp. 141–78.

CURRIE, E., AND SKOLNICK, J. H. A critical note on conceptions of collective behavior. *Annals of the American Academy of Political and Social Science,* 1970, **391,** 34–45.

DAS, J. P., AND NANDA, P. C. Mediated transfer of attitudes. *Journal of Abnormal and Social Psychology,* 1963, **66,** 12–16.

DAVIES, J. C. Toward a theory of revolution. *American Sociological Review,* 1962, **27,** 5–19.

DAVIES, J. C. The J-curve of rising and declining satisfactions as a cause of some great revolutions and a contained rebellion. In H. D. Graham and T. R. Gurr (Eds.), *Violence in America: Historical and comparative perspectives.* Vol. II. Washington, D.C.: U.S. Government Printing Office, 1969. Pp. 547–76.

DAVITZ, J. R. The effects of previous training on postfrustration behavior. *Journal of Abnormal and Social Psychology,* 1952, **47,** 309–15.

DE CHARMS, R., AND WILKINS, E. J. Some effects of verbal expression of hostility. *Journal of Abnormal and Social Psychology,* 1963, **66,** 462–70.

DELGADO, J. M. R. Cerebral heterostimulation in a monkey colony. *Science,* 1963, **141,** 161–63.

DELGADO, J. M. R. Social rank and radio-stimulated aggressiveness in monkeys. *Journal of Nervous and Mental Disease,* 1967, **144,** 383–90.

DELGADO, J. M. R., VERNON, M., SWEET, W., ERVIN, F. R., WEISS, G., BACH-Y-RITA, G., AND HAGIWARA, R. Intracerebral radio stimulation and recording in completely free patients. *Journal of Nervous and Mental Disease,* 1968, **147,** 329–40.

DENENBERG, V. H. The mother as motivator. In W. J. Arnold and M. M. Page (Eds.), *Nebraska symposium on motivation: 1970.* Lincoln: University of Nebraska Press, 1970. Pp. 69–93.

DEUR, J. L., AND PARKE, R. D. Effects of inconsistent punishment on aggression in children. *Developmental Psychology,* 1970, **2,** 403–11.

DITRICHS, R., SIMON, S., AND GREENE, B. Effect of vicarious scheduling on the verbal conditioning of hostility in children. *Journal of Personality and Social Psychology,* 1967, **6,** 71–79.

DOLLARD, J., DOOB, L. W., MILLER, N. E., MOWRER, O. H., AND SEARS, R. R. *Frustration and aggression.* New Haven, Conn.: Yale University Press, 1939.

DOMINICK, J. R., AND GREENBERG, B. S. Attitudes toward violence: The interaction of TV exposure, family attitudes, and social class. In G. A. Comstock and E. A. Rubinstein (Eds.), *Television and social behavior.* Vol. 3. *Television and adolescent aggressiveness.* Washington, D.C.: Government Printing Office, 1972. Pp. 314–35.

DONNERSTEIN, E., DONNERSTEIN, M., SIMON, S., AND DITRICHS, R. Variables in interracial aggression: Anonymity, expected retaliation, and a riot. *Journal of Personality and Social Psychology,* 1972, **22,** 236–45.

DOOB, A. N., AND WOOD, L. Catharsis and aggression: Effects of annoyance and retaliation on aggressive behavior. *Journal of Personality and Social Psychology,* 1972, **22,** 156–62.

DREYER, P. I., AND CHURCH, R. M. Reinforcement of shock-induced fighting. *Psychonomic Science,* 1970, **25,** 147–48.

DUBANOSKI, R. A., AND PARTON, D. A. Imitative aggression in children as a function of observing a human model. *Developmental Psychology,* 1971, **4,** 489.

DUFFY, E. *Activation and behavior.* New York: Wiley, 1962.

EATON, J. W., AND WEIL, R. J. *Culture and mental disorders.* New York: Free Press, 1955.

EDWARDS, N. L. Aggressive expression under threat of retaliation. Unpublished doctoral dissertation, University of Iowa, 1967.

EHRHARDT, A. A., EPSTEIN, R., AND MONEY, J. Fetal androgens and female gender identity in the early-treated adrenogenital syndrome. *Johns Hopkins Medical Journal,* 1968, **122,** 160–67.

ELLIS, G. T., AND SEKYRA, F. The effect of aggressive cartoons on the behavior of first grade children. *Journal of Psychology,* 1972, **81,** 37–43.

ELLIS, R. A., AND LANE, W. C. Structural supports for upward mobility. *American Sociological Review,* 1963, **28,** 743–56.

ELLISON, C. D., AND FLYNN, J. P. Organized aggressive behavior in cats after surgical isolation of the hypothalamus. *Archives of Italian Biology,* 1968, **106,** 1–20.

ELMS, A. C. (Ed.). *Role playing, reward, and attitude change.* New York: Van Nostrand Reinhold, 1969.

ENNIS, P. H. Crime, victims, and the police. *Trans-action,* 1967, **4,** 36–44.

EPSTEIN, R. Aggression toward outgroups as a function of authoritarianism and imitation of aggressive models. *Journal of Personality and Social Psychology,* 1966, **3,** 574–79.

ERON, L. D. Relationship of TV viewing habits and aggressive behavior in children. *Journal of Abnormal and Social Psychology,* 1963, **67,** 193–96.

ERON, L. D., HUESMANN, L. R., LEFKOWITZ, M. M., AND WALDER, L. O. Does television violence cause aggression? *American Psychologist,* 1972, **27,** 253–63.

FARRIS, H. E., FULLMER, W. H., AND ULRICH, R. E. Extinction of classically conditioned aggression: Results from two procedures. *Proceedings of the 78th annual convention of the American Psychological Association.* Washington, D.C.: American Psychological Association, 1970. Pp. 775–76.

FARRIS, H. E., GIDEON, B. E., AND ULRICH, R. E. Classical conditioning of aggression: A developmental study. *Psychological Record,* 1970, **20,** 63–68.

FESHBACH, S. The drive-reducing function of fantasy behavior. *Journal of Abnormal and Social Psychology,* 1955, **50,** 3–11.

FESHBACH, S. The cartharsis hypothesis and some consequences of interaction with aggressive and neutral play objects. *Journal of Personality,* 1956, **24,** 449–62.

FESHBACH, S. The stimulating versus cathartic effects of a vicarious aggressive activity. *Journal of Abnormal and Social Psychology,* 1961, **63,** 381–85.

FESHBACH, S. The function of aggression and the regulation of aggressive drive. *Psychological Review,* 1964, **71,** 257–72.

FESHBACH, S. Aggression. In P. H. Mussen (Ed.), *Carmichael's manual of child psychology,* Vol. II. New York: Wiley, 1970. Pp. 159–259.

FESHBACH, S. Reality and fantasy in filmed violence. In J. P. Murray, E. A. Rubinstein, and G. A. Comstock (Eds.), *Television and social behavior.* Vol. 2. *Television and social learning.* Washington, D.C.: Government Printing Office, 1972. Pp. 318–45.

FESHBACH, S., AND SINGER, R. D. *Television and aggression: An experimental field study.* San Francisco: Jossey-Bass, 1971.

FESHBACH, S., STILES, W. B., AND BITTER, E. The reinforcing effect of witnessing aggression. *Journal of Experimental Research in Personality,* 1967, **2,** 133–39.

FESTINGER, L. A theory of social comparison processes. *Human Relations,* 1954, **7,** 117–40.

FESTINGER, L., PEPITONE, A., AND NEWCOMB, T. Some consequences of de-individuation in a group. *Journal of Abnormal and Social Psychology,* 1952, **47,** 382–89.

FISHER, G. Discriminating violence emanating from over-controlled versus under-controlled aggressivity. *British Journal of Clinical and Social Psychology,* 1970, **9,** 54–59.

FLACKS, R. The liberated generation: An exploration of the roots of student protest. *Journal of Social Issues,* 1967, **23,** 52–75.

FLANDERS, J. P. A review of research on imitative behavior. *Psychological Bulletin,* 1968, **69,** 316–37.

FLORY, R. K. Attack behavior in a multiple fixed-ratio schedule of reinforcement. *Psychonomic Science,* 1969a, **16,** 156–57.

FLORY, R. K. Attack behavior as a function of minimum inter-food interval. *Journal of the Experimental Analysis of Behavior,* 1969b, **12,** 825–28.

FORD, C. S., AND BEACH, F. A. *Patterns of sexual behavior.* New York: Harper & Row, 1951.

FOSTER, J., AND LONG, D. *Protest! Student activism in America.* New York: Morrow, 1970.

FRANKS, L., AND POWERS, T., of UPI. Profile of a terrorist. *Palo Alto Times,* Sept. 17, 1970, pp. 26–28.

FREDERICSON, E. Competition: The effects of infantile experience upon adult behavior. *Journal of Abnormal and Social Psychology,* 1951, **46,** 406–9.

FREDERICSON, E., AND BIRNBAUM, E. A. Competitive fighting between mice with different hereditary backgrounds. *Journal of Genetic Psychology,* 1954, **85,** 271–80.

FREEMAN, E. Effects of aggressive expression after frustration on performance: A test of the catharsis hypothesis. Unpublished doctoral dissertation, Stanford University, 1962.

FREUD, A. *The ego and the mechanisms of defence.* Tr. by Cecil Baines. New York: International Universities Press, 1946.

FREUD, S. *A general introduction to psycho-analysis.* New York: Boni & Liveright, 1920.

FREUD, S. *Beyond the pleasure principle.* London: International Psychoanalytic Press, 1922.

FREUD, S. *The ego and id.* London: Horgarth, 1923.

FREUD, S. *New introductory lectures on psycho-analysis.* New York: Morton, 1933.

FREUD, S. Why war? In J. Strachey (Ed.), *Collected papers.* Vol. V. London: Hogarth Press, 1950. Pp. 273–87.

FRIEDMAN, L. M. Legal rules and the process of social change. *Stanford Law Review,* 1967, **19,** 786–840.

FRIEDMAN, P. H. The effects of modeling, roleplaying and participation on behavior change. In B. A. Maher (Ed.), *Progress in experimental personality research.* Vol. VI. New York: Academic Press, 1972. Pp. 41–81.

FRIENDLY, F. W. *Due to circumstances beyond our control.* New York: Vintage Books, 1968.

GAMBARO, S., AND RABIN, A. I. Diastolic blood pressure responses following direct and displaced aggression after anger arousal in high- and low-guilt subjects. *Journal of Personality and Social Psychology,* 1969, **12,** 87–94.

GAMSON, W. A., AND McEVOY, J. Police violence and its public support. *Annals of the American Academy of Political and Social Science,* 1970, **391,** 97–110.

GARATTINI, S., AND SIGG, E. B. (Eds.), *Aggressive behaviour.* New York: Wiley, 1969.

GARDNER, J. W. *In common cause.* New York: Norton, 1972.

GARDNER, R., AND HEIDER, K. G. *Gardens of war: Life and death in the New Guinea stone age.* New York: Random House, 1969.

GEEN, R. G. Effects of frustration, attack, and prior training in aggressiveness upon aggressive behavior. *Journal of Personality and Social Psychology*, 1968, **9**, 316–21.

GEEN, R. G. Perceived suffering of the victim as an inhibitor of attack-induced aggression. *Journal of Social Psychology*, 1970, **81**, 209–16.

GEEN, R. G., AND BERKOWITZ, L. Name-mediated aggressive cue properties. *Journal of Personality*, 1966, **34**, 456–65.

GEEN, R. G., AND BERKOWITZ, L. Some conditions facilitating the occurrence of aggression after the observation of violence. *Journal of Personality*, 1967, **35**, 666–76.

GEEN, R. G., AND O'NEAL, E. C. Activation of cue-elicited aggression by general arousal. *Journal of Personality and Social Psychology*, 1969, **11**, 289–92.

GEEN, R. G., AND PIGG, R. Acquisition of an aggressive response and its generalization to verbal behavior. *Journal of Personality and Social Psychology*, 1970, **15**, 165–70.

GEEN, R. G., AND STONNER, D. Effects of aggressiveness habit strength on behavior in the presence of aggression-related stimuli. *Journal of Personality and Social Psychology*, 1971, **17**, 149–53.

GEEN, R. G., AND STONNER, D. Context effects in observed violence. *Journal of Personality and Social Psychology*, 1972, in press.

GENTRY, W. D. Fixed-ratio schedule-induced aggression. *Journal of the Experimental Analysis of Behavior*, 1968, **11**, 813–17.

GENTRY, W. D. Effects of frustration, attack, and prior aggressive training on overt aggression and vascular processes. *Journal of Personality and Social Psychology*, 1970, **16**, 718–25.

GENTRY, W. D., AND SCHAEFFER, R. W. The effect of FR response requirement on aggressive behavior in rats. *Psychonomic Science*, 1969, **14**, 236–38.

GERBNER, G. Violence in television drama: Trends and symbolic functions. In G. A. Comstock and E. A. Rubinstein (Eds.), *Television and social behavior*. Vol. 1. *Content and control*. Washington, D.C.: Government Printing Office, 1972a. Pp. 28–187.

GERBNER, G. The violence index: A rating of various aspects of dramatic violence on prime-time network television 1967 through 1970. Unpublished manuscript, University of Pennsylvania, 1972b.

GERST, M. S. Symbolic coding processes in observational learning. *Journal of Personality and Social Psychology*, 1971, **19**, 7–17.

GILLESPIE, W. H. Aggression and instinct theory. *International Journal of Psycho-analysis*, 1971, **52**, 155–160.

GINSBURG, B., AND ALLEE, W. C. Some effects of conditioning on social dominance and subordination in inbred strains of mice. *Physiological Zoology,* 1942, **15,** 485–506.

GITTLEMAN, M. Behavior rehearsal as a technique in child treatment. *Journal of Child Psychology and Psychiatry,* 1965, **6,** 251–55.

GLUECK, S., AND GLUECK, E. *Unraveling juvenile delinquency.* Cambridge, Mass.: Harvard University Press, 1950.

GOLDFRANK, E. S. Historic change and social character: A study of the Teton Dakota. *American Anthropologist,* 1943, **45,** 67–83.

GOLDFRANK, E. S. Socialization, personality, and the structure of Pueblo society (with particular reference to Hopi and Zuni). *American Anthropologist,* 1945, **47,** 516–39.

GOLDMAN, J. R. The relation of certain therapist variables to the handling of psychotherapeutic events. Unpublished doctoral dissertation, Stanford University, 1961.

GOODLET, G, R., AND GOODLET, M. M. Efficiency of self-monitored and externally imposed schedules of reinforcement in controlling disruptive behavior. Unpublished manuscript, University of Guelph, 1969.

GOODLET, G. R., GOODLET, M. M., AND DREDGE, K. Modification of disruptive behavior of two young children and follow-up one year later. *Journal of School Psychology,* 1970, **8,** 60–63.

GOODWIN, C. *The social organization of the Western Apache.* Chicago: University of Chicago Press, 1942.

GORANSON, R. E. Media violence and aggressive behavior: A review of experimental research. In L. Berkowitz (Ed.), *Advances in experimental social psychology.* Vol. 5. New York: Academic Press, 1970. Pp. 1–31.

GRIMSHAW, A. D. Violence: A sociological perspective. *George Washington Law Review,* 1969, **37,** 816–34.

GRIMSHAW, A. D. Three views of urban violence: Civil disturbance, racial revolt, class assault. *American Behavioral Scientist,* 1970, **11,** 2–7.

GRUSEC, J. E. Demand characteristics of the modeling experiment: Altruism as a function of age, and aggression. *Journal of Personality and Social Psychology,* 1972, **22,** 139–48.

GULEVICH, G. D., AND BOURNE, P. G. Mental illness and violence. In D. N. Daniels, M. F. Gilula, and F. Ochberg (Eds.), *Violence and the struggle for existence.* Boston: Little, Brown, 1970. Pp. 309–26.

GURR, R. T. *Why men rebel.* Princeton, N.J.: Princeton University Press, 1970a.

GURR, R. T. Sources of rebellion in Western societies: Some quantitative evidence. *Annals of the American Academy of Political and Social Science,* 1970b, **391,** 128–44.

HALLIE, P. O. Justification and rebellion. In N. Sanford and C. Comstock (Eds.), *Sanctions for evil.* San Francisco: Jossey-Bass, 1971. Pp. 247–63.

HALLORAN, J. D., AND CROLL, P. Television programs in Great Britain: Content and control. In G. A. Comstock and E. A. Rubinstein (Eds.), *Television and social behavior.* Vol. 1. *Media content and control.* Washington, D.C.: Government Printing Office, 1972. Pp. 415–92.

HAMBURG, D. A. A combined biological and psychosocial approach to the study of behavioural development. In A. Ambrose (Ed.), *Stimulation in early childhood.* New York: Academic Press, 1969. Pp. 269–77.

HAMBURG, D. A. Recent evidence on the evolution of aggressive behavior. *Engineering and Science,* 1970, **23,** 15–24.

HAMILTON, J., STEPHENS, L., AND ALLEN, P. Controlling aggressive and destructive behavior in severely retarded institutionalized residents. *American Journal of Mental Deficiency,* 1967, **71,** 852–56.

HANER, C. F., AND BROWN, P. A. Clarification of the instigation to action concept in the frustration-aggression hypothesis. *Journal of Abnormal and Social Psychology,* 1955, **51,** 204–6.

HANRATTY, M. A., LIEBERT, R. M., MORRIS, L. W., AND FERNANDEZ, L. E. Imitation of film-mediated aggression against live and inanimate victims. *Proceedings of the 77th Annual Convention of the American Psychological Association.* Washington, D.C.: American Psychological Association, 1969. Pp. 457–58.

HANRATTY, M. A., O'NEAL, E. C., AND SULZER, J. L. Effect of frustration upon imitation of aggression. *Journal of Personality and Social Psychology,* 1972, **21,** 30–34.

HAPKIEWICZ, W. G., AND STONE, R. D. The effect of age, sex, and model characteristics on children's aggressive and cooperative play. Unpublished manuscript, Michigan State University, 1972.

HARMATZ, M. G., AND RASMUSSEN, W. A. A behavior modification approach to head banging. *Mental Hygiene,* 1969, **53,** 590–93.

HARRIS, M. B. Field studies of modeled aggression. *Journal of Social Psychology,* 1972.

HARTLEY, R. E. *A review and evaluation of recent studies on the impact of violence.* New York: Office of Social Research, Columbia Broadcasting System, 1964.

HARTMANN, D. P. Influence of symbolically modeled instrumental aggression and pain cues on aggressive behavior. *Journal of Personality and Social Psychology,* 1969, 11, 280–88.

HASTORF, A. H. The "reinforcement" of individual actions in a group situation. In L. Krasner and L. P. Ullmann (Eds.), *Research in behavior modification.* New York: Holt, Rinehart & Winston, 1965. Pp. 268–84.

HAWKINS, R. P., PETERSON, R. F., SCHWEID, E., AND BIJOU, S. W. Behavior therapy in the home: Amelioration of problem parent-child relations with the parent in a therapeutic role. *Journal of Experimental Child Psychology,* 1966, 4, 99–107.

HELM, B., BONOMA, T. V., AND TEDESCHI, J. T. Reciprocity for harm done. *Journal of Social Psychology,* 1972, 87, 89–98.

HERRELL, J. M. Use of systematic desensitization to eliminate inappropriate anger. *Proceedings of the 79th Annual Convention of the American Psychological Association.* Washington, D.C.: American Psychological Association, 1971. Pp. 431–32.

HESS, E. H. The relationship between imprinting and motivation. In M. R. Jones (Ed.), *Nebraska symposium on motivation. 1959.* Lincoln: University of Nebraska Press, 1969. Pp. 44–77.

HESS, E. H. Pupillometric assessment. In J. M. Shlien (Ed.), *Research in psychotherapy.* Washington, D.C.: American Psychological Association, 1968. Pp. 573–83.

HICKS, D. J. Imitation and retention of film-mediated aggressive peer and adult models. *Journal of Personality and Social Psychology,* 1965, 2, 97–100.

HICKS, D. J. Effects of co-observer's sanctions and adult presence on imitative aggression. *Child Development,* 1968a, 39, 303–9.

HICKS, D. J. Short and long-term retention of affectively varied modeled behavior. *Psychonomic Science,* 1968b, 11, 369–70.

HICKS, D. J. Girls' attitudes toward modeled behaviors and the content of imitative private play. *Child Development,* 1971, 42, 139–47.

HILL, B. *Boss of Britain's underworld.* London: Naldreth Press, 1955.

HIMMELWEIT, H. T., OPPENHEIM, A. N., AND VINCE, P. *Television and the child.* London: Oxford University Press, 1958.

HINDE, R. A. Ethological models and the concept of "drive." *British Journal of Philosophical Science,* 1956, 6, 321–31.

HINDE, R. A. Energy models of motivation. *Symposium on social experimental biology,* 1960, 14, 199–213.

HOELLE, C. The effects of modeling and reinforcement on aggressive behavior in elementary school boys. *Dissertation Abstracts,* 1969, 29B, 3483–84.

HOFFMAN, M. L. Power assertion by the parent and its impact on the child. *Child Development,* 1960, **31,** 129–43.

HOGAN, J. A. Fighting and reinforcement in the Siamese fighting fish (Betta splendens). *Journal of Comparative and Physiological Psychology,* 1967, **64,** 356–59.

HOKANSON, J. E. Psychophysiological evaluation of the catharsis hypothesis. In E. I. Megargee and J. E. Hokanson (Eds.), *The dynamics of aggression.* New York: Harper & Row, 1970. Pp. 74–86.

HOKANSON, J. E., AND EDELMAN, R. Effects of three social responses on vascular processes. *Journal of Personality and Social Psychology,* 1966, **3,** 442–47.

HOKANSON, J. E., WILLERS, K. R., AND KOROPSAK, E. The modification of autonomic responses during aggressive interchange. *Journal of Personality,* 1968, **36,** 386–404.

HOLMES, D. S. Effects of overt aggression on level of physiological arousal. *Journal of Personality and Social Psychology,* 1966, **4,** 189–94.

HOLMES, D. S. Dimensions of projection. *Psychological Bulletin,* 1968, **69,** 248–68.

HOLTON, R. B. Amplitude of an instrumental response following the cessation of reward. *Child Development,* 1961, **32,** 107–16.

HOYT, J. L. Effect of media violence "justification" on aggression. *Journal of Broadcasting,* 1970, **14,** 455–64.

HUNT, J. McV., COLE, M. W., AND REIS, E. E. S. Situational cues distinguishing anger, fear, and sorrow. *American Journal of Psychology,* 1958, **71,** 136–51.

HUTCHINSON, R. R., AZRIN, N. H., AND HUNT, G. M. Attack produced by intermittent reinforcement of a concurrent operant response. *Journal of the Experimental Analysis of Behavior,* 1968, **11,** 489–95.

HUTCHINSON, R. R., ULRICH, R. E., AND AZRIN, N. H. Effects of age and related factors on the pain-aggression reaction. *Journal of Comparative and Physiological Psychology,* 1965, **59,** 365–69.

IGLITZIN, L. B. Violence and American democracy. *Journal of Social Issues,* 1970, **26,** 165–86.

INSKO, C. A., AND OAKES, W. F. Awareness and the "conditioning" of attitudes. *Journal of Personality and Social Psychology,* 1966, **4,** 487–96.

JACOBS, P. A., BRUNTON, M., AND MELVILLE, M. M. Aggressive behavior, mental sub-normality and the XYY male. *Nature,* 1965, **208,** 1351–52.

JEGARD, S., AND WALTERS, R. H. A study of some determinants of aggression in young children. *Child Development,* 1960, **31,** 739–47.

JOHNSON, A. M., AND SZUREK, S. A. The genesis of antisocial acting out in children and adults. *The Psychoanalytic Quarterly,* 1952, **21,** 323–43.

JOHNSON, E. H. Selective factors in capital punishment. *Social Forces,* 1957, **36,** 165–69.

JOHNSON, N. *How to talk back to your television set.* Boston: Little, Brown, 1967.

JOHNSON, S. M., AND BROWN, R. A. Producing behaviour change in parents of disturbed children. *Journal of Child Psychology and Psychiatry,* 1969, **10,** 107–21.

KAHN, M. The physiology of catharsis. *Journal of Personality and Social Psychology,* 1966, **3,** 278–86.

KAHN, M. W. The effect of severe defeat at various age levels on the aggressive behavior of mice. *Journal of Genetic Psychology,* 1951, **79,** 117–30.

KAHN, R. M., AND BOWERS, W. J. The social context of the rank-and-file student activist: A test of four hypotheses. *Sociology of Education,* 1970, **43,** 38–55.

KANFER, F. H. Vicarious human reinforcement: A glimpse into the black box. In L. Krasner and L. P. Ullmann (Eds.), *Research in behavior modification.* New York: Holt, Rinehart and Winston, 1965. Pp. 244–67.

KANFER, F. H., AND PHILLIPS, J. S. *Learning foundations of behavior therapy.* New York: Wiley, 1970.

KAUFMANN, H., AND FESHBACH, S. The influence of antiaggressive communications upon the response to provocation. *Journal of Personality,* 1963, **31,** 428–44.

KEIRSEY, D. W. Systematic exclusion: Eliminating chronic classroom disruptions. In J. D. Krumboltz and C. E. Thoresen (Eds.) *Behavioral counseling: Cases and Techniques.* New York: Holt, Rinehart & Winston, 1969. Pp. 89–113.

KENISTON, K. The sources of student dissent. *Journal of Social Issues,* 1967, **23,** 108–37.

KENISTON, K. *Young radicals.* New York: Harcourt Brace Jovanovich, 1968.

KENISTON, K. Student activism, moral development, and morality. *American Journal of Orthopsychiatry,* 1970, **40,** 577–92.

KENISTON, K., AND LERNER, M. Campus characteristics and campus unrest.

346   References

Annals of the American Academy of Political and Social Science,
1971, **395**, 39–53.

KENNY, D. T. An experimental test of the catharsis theory of aggression.
Unpublished doctoral dissertation, University of Washington, 1952.

KERNER, O., et al. *Report of the National Advisory Commission on Civil
Disorders.* New York: Bantam Books, 1968.

KESSLER, S., AND MOOS, R. H. The XYY karyotype and criminality: A
review. *Journal of Psychiatric Research,* 1970, **7**, 153–70.

KLEIN, M. W., AND CRAWFORD, L. Y. Groups, gangs and cohesiveness.
Journal of Research in Crime and Delinquency, 1967, **4**, 63–75.

KLOPFER, P. H. *Behavioral aspects of ecology.* Englewood Cliffs, N.J.:
Prentice-Hall, 1962.

KNIVETON, B. H., AND STEPHENSON, G. M. The effect of pre-experience on
imitation of an aggressive film model. *British Journal of Social and
Clinical Psychology,* 1970, **9**, 31–36.

KNUTSON, J. F. Aggression during the fixed-ratio and extinction components of a multiple schedule of reinforcement. *Journal of the Experimental Analysis of Behavior,* 1970, **13**, 221–31.

KNUTSON, J. F. The effects of shocking one member of a pair of rats.
Psychonomic Science, 1971, **22**, 265–66.

KOBASIGAWA, A. Observation of failure in another person as a determinant of amplitude and speed of a simple motor response. *Journal of
Personality and Social Psychology,* 1965, **1**, 626–30.

KONECNI, V. J., AND DOOB, A. N. Catharsis through displacement of
aggression. *Journal of Personality and Social Psychology,* 1972, **23**,
379–87.

KRAUSS, I. Sources of educational aspirations among working-class youth.
American Sociological Review, 1964, **29**, 867–79.

KUHN, D. Z., MADSEN, C. H., Jr., AND BECKER, W. C. Effects of exposure
to an aggressive model and "frustration" on children's aggressive
behavior. *Child Development,* 1967, **38**, 739–45.

KUO, Z. Y. The genesis of the cat's responses to the rat. *Journal of Comparative Psychology,* 1930, **11**, 1–35.

KUO, Z. Y. Further study on the behavior of cats toward rats. *Journal of
Comparative Psychology,* 1938, **25**, 1–8.

KUO, Z. Y. Studies on the basic factors in animal fighting: VII. Inter-
species coexistence in mammals. *Journal of Genetic Psychology,*
1960, **97**, 211–25.

LAGERSPETZ, K. M. J. *Studies on the aggressive behavior of mice.* Hel-
sinki: Suomalainen Tiedeakatemia, 1964.

LAGERSPETZ, K. M. J. Aggression and aggressiveness in laboratory mice. In S. Garattini and E. B. Sigg (Eds.), *Aggressive behaviour*. New York: Wiley, 1969. Pp. 77–85.

LANTIS, M. Alaskan Eskimo cultural values. *Polar Notes*, 1959, 1, 35–48.

LARDER, D. L. Effect of aggressive story content on nonverbal play behavior. *Psychological Reports*, 1962, 11, 14.

LARSEN, O. N., GRAY, L. N., AND FORTIS, J. G. Achieving goals through violence on television. In O. N. Larsen (Ed.), *Violence and the mass media*. New York: Harper & Row, 1968. Pp. 97–111.

LEBLANC, J. M., BUSBY, K., AND THOMSON, C. The functions of time-out for changing the aggressive behaviors of a preschool child: A multiple baseline analysis. Paper presented at the meeting of the American Psychological Association, Washington, D.C., September 1971.

LEGRAND, R. Successful aggression as the reinforcer for runway behavior of mice. *Psychonomic Science*, 1970, 20, 303–5.

LEHRMAN, D. S. A critique of Konrad Lorenz's theory of instinctive behavior. *Quarterly Review of Biology*, 1953, 28, 337–63.

LEIFER, A. D., AND ROBERTS, D. F. Children's responses to television violence. In J. P. Murray, E. A. Rubinstein, and G. A. Comstock (Eds.), *Television and social behavior*. Vol. 2. *Television and social learning*. Washington, D.C.: Government Printing Office, 1972. Pp. 43–180.

LEITENBERG, H. Is time-out from positive reinforcement an aversive event? A review of the experimental evidence. *Psychological Bulletin*, 1965, 64, 428–41.

LEJINS, P. J. International opinions on American media violence. In O. N. Larsen (Ed.), *Violence and the mass media*. New York: Harper & Row, 1968. Pp. 168–72.

LERNER, M. J. Observer's evaluation of a victim: Justice, guilt, and veridical perception. *Journal of Personality and Social Psychology*, 1971, 20, 127–35.

LEVIN, G. R., AND SIMMONS, J. J. Response to food and praise by emotionally disturbed boys. *Psychological Reports*, 1962, 11, 539–46.

LEVY, R. I. On getting angry in the Society Islands. In W. Caudill and T.-Y. Lin (Eds.), *Mental health research in Asia and the Pacific*. Honolulu: East-West Center Press, 1969. Pp. 358–80.

LIEBERSON, S., AND SILVERMAN, A. R. The precipitants and underlying conditions of race riots. *American Sociological Review*, 1965, 30, 887–98.

LIEBERT, R. M. Television and social learning: Some relationships between viewing violence and behaving aggressively. In J. P. Murray, E. A. Rubinstein, and G. A. Comstock (Eds.), *Television and social behavior*. Vol. 2. *Television and social learning*. Washington, D.C.: Government Printing Office, 1972. Pp. 1–42.

LIEBERT, R. M., AND BARON, R. A. Short-term effects of televised aggression on children's aggressive behavior. In J. P. Murray, E. A. Rubinstein, and G. A. Comstock (Eds.), *Television and social behavior*. Vol. 2. *Television and social learning*. Washington, D.C.: Government Printing Office, 1972. Pp. 181–201.

LIEBERT, R. M., SOBOL, M. D., AND DAVIDSON, E. S. Catharsis of aggression among institutionalized boys: Fact or artifact. In G. A. Comstock, E. A. Rubinstein, and J. P. Murray (Eds.), *Television and social behavior*. Vol. 5. *Television effects: Further explorations*. Washington, D.C.: Government Printing Office, 1972. Pp. 351–59.

LINTON, R. The Comanche. In A. Kardiner (Ed.), *The psychological frontiers of society*. New York: Columbia University Press, 1945. Pp. 47–80.

LIPSET, S. M. University students and politics in underdeveloped countries. *Comparative Education Review*, 1966, **10**, 132–62.

LOCKHART, W. B. *The report of the commission on obscenity and pornography*. New York: Bantam Books, 1970.

LOEW, C. A. Acquisition of a hostile attitude and its relationship to aggressive behavior. *Journal of Personality and Social Psychology*, 1967, **5**, 335–41.

LOGAN, F. A., AND BOICE, R. Aggressive behaviors of paired rodents in an avoidance context. *Behaviour*, 1969, **34**, 161–83.

LONGSTRETH, L. E. Distance to goal and reinforcement schedule as determinants of human instrumental behavior. *Proceedings of the 74th Annual Convention of the American Psychological Association*. Washington, D.C.: American Psychological Association, 1966. Pp. 39–40.

LORENZ, K. *On aggression*. New York: Harcourt Brace Jovanovich, 1966.

LoSCIUTO, L. A national inventory of television viewing behavior. In E. A. Rubinstein, G. A. Comstock, and J. P. Murray (Eds.), *Television and social behavior*. Vol. 4. *Television in day-to-day life: Patterns of use*. Washington, D.C.: Government Printing Office, 1972. Pp. 33–86.

LOVAAS, O. I. Effect of exposure to symbolic aggression on aggressive behavior. *Child Development*, 1961, **32**, 37–44.

LOVAAS, O. I., FREITAG, G., GOLD, V. J., AND KASSORLA, I. C. Experimental studies in childhood schizophrenia: Analysis of self-destructive behavior. *Journal of Experimental Child Psychology,* 1965, **2,** 67–84.

LOVAAS, O. I., AND SIMMONS, J. Q. Manipulation of self-destruction in three retarded children. *Journal of Applied Behavior Analysis,* 1969, **2,** 143–57.

LUCHINS, A. S., AND LUCHINS, E. H. Imitation by rote and by understanding. *Journal of Social Psychology,* 1961, **54,** 175–97.

LUDWIG, A. M., MARX, A. J., HILL, P. A., AND BROWNING, R. M. The control of violent behavior through faradic shock. *Journal of Nervous and Mental Disease,* 1969, **148,** 624–37.

LYON, D. O., AND OZOLINS, D. Pavlovian conditioning of shock-elicited aggression: A discrimination procedure. *Journal of Experimental Analysis of Behavior,* 1970, **13,** 325–31.

MACCOBY, E. E. The effects of mass media. In N. L. Hoffman and L. W. Hoffman (Eds.), *Review of child development research.* Vol. 1. New York: Russell Sage Foundation, 1964. Pp. 323–48.

MACCOBY, E. E., AND WILSON, W. C. Identification and observational learning from films. *Journal of Abnormal and Social Psychology,* 1957, **55,** 76–87.

MACKAY, C. *Extraordinary popular delusions and the madness of crowds.* Boston: Page, 1932.

MCCORD, W., AND HOWARD, J. Negro opinions in three riot cities. *American Behavioral Scientist,* 1968, **11,** 24–27.

MCCORD, W., MCCORD, J., AND ZOLA, I. K. *Origins of crime: A new evaluation of the Cambridge-Somerville Youth Study.* New York: Columbia University Press, 1959.

MCDOUGALL, W. *An introduction to social psychology.* London: Methuen, 1931.

MCINTYRE, J., AND TEEVAN, J. Television violence and deviant behavior. In G. A. Comstock and E. A. Rubinstein (Eds.), *Television and social behavior.* Vol. 3. *Television and adolescent aggressiveness.* Washington, D.C.: Government Printing Office, 1972. Pp. 383–435.

MCMAINS, M. J., AND LIEBERT, R. M. Influence of discrepancies between successively modeled self-reward criteria on the adoption of a self-imposed standard. *Journal of Personality and Social Psychology,* 1968, **8,** 166–71.

MCPHAIL, C. Civil disorder participation: A critical examination of recent research. *American Sociological Review,* 1971, **36,** 1058–72.

MADSEN, C. H., Jr. Nurturance and modeling in preschoolers. *Child Development,* 1968, **39,** 221–36.

MADSEN, C. H., Jr., BECKER, W. C., THOMAS, D. R., KOSER, L., AND PLAGER, E. An analysis of the reinforcing function of "sit-down" commands. In R. K. Parker (Ed.), *Readings in educational psychology*. New York: Allyn & Bacon, 1968. Pp. 265–78.

MAHONEY, M. J. A residential program in behavior modification. Paper presented at the Fifth Annual Meeting of the Association for the Advancement of Behavior Therapy, Washington, D.C., September 1971.

MAIER, S. F., SELIGMAN, M. E. P., AND SOLOMON, R. L. Pavlovian fear conditioning and learned helplessness: Effects on escape and avoidance behavior of (a) the CU-US contingency and (b) the independence of the US and voluntary responding. In B. A. Campbell and R. M. Church (Eds.), *Punishment and aversive behavior*. New York: Appleton-Century-Crofts, 1969. Pp. 299–342.

MALLICK, S. K., AND McCANDLESS, B. R. A study of catharsis of aggression. *Journal of Personality and Social Psychology,* 1966, **4,** 591–96.

MANKOFF, M., AND FLACKS, R. The changing social base of the American student movement. *Annals of the American Academy of Political and Social Science,* 1971, **395,** 54–67.

MANN, J., SIDMAN, J., AND STARR, S. Effects of erotic films on the sexual behavior of married couples. In *Technical report of the Commission on Obscenity and Pornography. Vol. 8. Erotica and social behavior.* Washington, D.C.: U.S. Government Priting Office, 1971. Pp. 170–254.

MARK, V. H., AND ERVIN, F. R. *Violence and the brain.* New York: Harper & Row, 1970.

MARMOR, J. Psychoanalytic therapy as an educational process: Common denominators in the therapeutic approaches of different psychoanalytic "schools." In J. H. Masserman (Ed.), *Science and psychoanalysis. Vol. 5. Psychoanalytic education.* New York: Grune & Stratton, 1962. Pp. 286–99.

MARTIN, M., BURKHOLDER, R., ROSENTHAL, T. L., THARP, R. G., AND THORNE, G. L. Programming behavior change and reintegration into school milieux of extreme adolescent deviates. *Behaviour Research and Therapy,* 1968, **6,** 371–83.

MARX, G. T. Issueless riots. *Annals of the American Academy of Political and Social Science,* 1970a, **391,** 21–33.

MARX, G. T. Civil disorders and the agents of social control. *Journal of Social Issues,* 1970b, **26,** 19–58.

MARX, M. H. Some relations between frustration and drive. In M. R.

Jones (Ed.), *Nebraska symposium on motivation: 1956.* Lincoln, Neb.: University of Nebraska Press, 1956. Pp. 92–130.

MASLOW, A. H. Deprivation, threat, and frustration. *Psychological Review,* 1941, **48,** 364–66.

MEAD, M. *Sex and temperament in three savage tribes.* New York: Morrow, 1935.

MEGARGEE, E. I. Undercontrolled and overcontrolled personality types in extreme antisocial aggression. *Psychological Monographs,* 1966, **80,** No. 3 (Whole No. 611).

MEGARGEE, E. I., AND MENDELSOHN, G. A. A cross-validation of twelve MMPI indices of hostility and control. *Journal of Abnormal and Social Psychology,* 1962, **65,** 431–38.

MEYER, T. P. Some effects of real newsfilm violence on the behavior of viewers. *Journal of Broadcasting,* 1971, **15,** 275–85.

MEYER, T. P. Effects of viewing justified and unjustified real film violence on aggressive behavior. *Journal of Personality and Social Psychology,* 1972, **23,** 21–29.

MILGRAM, S. Behavioral study of obedience. *Journal of Abnormal and Social Psychology,* 1963, **67,** 371–78.

MILGRAM, S. Group pressure and action against a person. *Journal of Abnormal and Social Psychology,* 1964, **69,** 137–43.

MILGRAM, S. Liberating effects of group pressure. *Journal of Personality and Social Psychology,* 1965a, **1,** 127–34.

MILGRAM, S. Some conditions of obedience and disobedience to authority. *Human Relations,* 1965b, **18,** 57–76.

MILLER, N. E. The frustration-aggression hypothesis. *Psychological Review,* 1941, **48,** 337–42.

MILLER, N. E. Liberalization of basic S-R concepts: Extensions to conflict behavior, motivation, and social learning. In S. Koch (Ed.), *Psychology: A study of a science.* New York: McGraw-Hill, 1959. Pp. 196–292.

MILLER, N. E. Learning of visceral and glandular responses. *Science,* 1969, **163,** 434–45.

MILLER, N. E., AND DOLLARD, J. *Social learning and imitation.* New Haven, Conn.: Yale University Press, 1941.

MILLER, W. B. Lower class culture as a generating milieu of gang delinquency. *Journal of Social Issues,* 1958, **14,** 5–19.

MILLER, W. B., GEERTZ, H., AND CUTTER, H. S. G. Aggression in a boys' streetcorner group. *Psychiatry,* 1961, **24,** 282–98.

MISCHEL, W. *Personality and assessment.* New York: Wiley, 1968.

MISCHEL, W., AND BAKER, N. Cognitive stimulus transformations in self-control. Unpublished manuscript, Stanford University, 1972.

MISCHEL, W., EBBESEN, E. B., AND ZEISS, A. R. Cognitive and attentional mechanisms in delay of gratification. *Journal of Personality and Social Psychology,* 1972, **21,** 204–18.

MISCHEL, W., AND LIEBERT, R. M. Effects of discrepancies between observed and imposed reward criteria on their acquisition and transmission. *Journal of Personality and Social Psychology,* 1966, **3,** 45–53.

MISCHEL, W., AND LIEBERT, R. M. The role of power in the adoption of self-reward patterns. *Child Development,* 1967, **38,** 673–83.

MONTAGU, M. F. A. (Ed.), *Man and aggression.* New York: Oxford University Press, 1968.

MOSER, D. Screams, slaps and love. *Life,* May 7, 1965, 90A–101.

MUNROE, R. L. *Schools of psychoanalytic thought.* New York: Dryden, 1955.

MURPHY, J. T. Federal Aviation Administration. Personal communication, 1971.

MYER, J. S., AND WHITE, R. T. Aggressive motivation in the rat. *Animal Behaviour,* 1965, **13,** 430–33.

NEIDERHOFFER, A. *Behind the shield.* New York: Doubleday, 1967.

NELSEN, E. A. Social reinforcement for expression vs. suppression of aggression. *Merill-Palmer Quarterly,* 1969, **15,** 259–78.

NELSON, J. D., GELFAND, D. M., AND HARTMANN, D. P. Children's aggression following competition and exposure to an aggressive model. *Child Development,* 1969, **40,** 1085–97.

The New York Times. Veteran kills 12 in mad rampage on Camden street. September 7, 1949, p. 1.

The New York Times. Sniper in Texas U. tower kills 12. August 2, 1966a, p. 1.

The New York Times. Sniper told psychiatrist he had thought of going to tower and "shooting people." August 3, 1966b, p. 20.

The New York Times. Friends of Whitman reveal he often broke law. August 8, 1966c, p. 19.

The New York Times. Youth, 18, slays 4 women and child in beauty school. November 13, 1966d, p. 1.

The New York Times. TV show blamed by F.A.A. for rise in bomb hoax calls. December 21, 1966e, p. 79.

NISBETT, R. E., AND SCHACHTER, S. Cognitive manipulation of pain. *Journal of Experimental Social Psychology,* 1966, **2,** 227–36.

O'Connor, R. D. Modification of social withdrawal through symbolic modeling. *Journal of Applied Behavior Analysis,* 1969, **2,** 15–22.

O'Connor, R. D. Relative efficacy of modeling, shaping, and the combined procedures for modification of social withdrawal. *Journal of Abnormal Psychology,* 1972, **79,** 327–34.

Osborn, D. K., and Endsley, R. C. Emotional reactions of young children to TV violence. *Child Development,* 1971, **42,** 321–31.

Ostrow, M., and Ostrow, M. Bilaterally synchronous paroxysmal slow activity in the electroencephalograms of non-epileptics. *Journal of Nervous and Mental Disease,* 1946, **103,** 346–58.

Owen, D. R. The 47, XYY male: A review. *Psychological Bulletin,* 1972, **77,** 209–33.

Packer, H. L. *The limits of the criminal sanction.* Stanford, Calif.: Stanford University Press, 1968.

Page, M. M., and Scheidt, R. J. The elusive weapons effect: Demand awareness, evaluation apprehension, and slightly sophisticated subjects. *Journal of Personality and Social Psychology,* 1971, **20,** 304–18.

Paisley, M. B. Social policy research and the realities of the system: Violence done to TV research. Unpublished manuscript, Stanford University, 1972.

Panksepp, J. Aggression elicited by electrical stimulation of the hypothalamus in albino rats. *Physiology and Behavior,* 1971, **6,** 321–30.

Panksepp, J., and Trowill, J. Electrically induced affective attack from the hypothalamus of the albino rat. *Psychonomic Science,* 1969, **16,** 118–19.

Palo Alto Times. Jetliner bomb hoax backfires. July 17, 1971, p. 1.

Palo Alto Times. Hijackers flee to jungle, Cuba. May 6, 1972, p. 1.

Parke, R. D. Effectiveness of punishment as an interaction of intensity, timing, agent nurturance, and cognitive structuring. *Child Development,* 1969, **40,** 213–35.

Parke, R. D., Berkowitz, L., Leyens, J., West, S., and Sebastian, R. The effects of repeated exposure to movie violence on aggressive behavior in juvenile delinquent boys: A field experimental approach. Unpublished manuscript, University of Wisconsin, 1972.

Parke, R. D., Ewall, W., and Slaby, R. G. Hostile and helpful verbalizations as regulators of nonverbal aggression. *Journal of Personality and Social Psychology,* 1972, **23,** 243–48.

Parke, R. D., and Walters, R. H. Some factors influencing the efficacy of punishment training for inducing response inhibition. *Mono-*

graphs of the Society for Research in Child Development, 1967, Vol. XXXII, No. 1 (Serial No. 109).

PARKE, R. D., WIEDERHOLT, C., AND SLABY, R. G. The effect of exposure to a model's aggressive verbalizations on the observer's motor aggression. Unpublished manuscript, University of Wisconsin, 1972.

PASTORE, N. The role of arbitrariness in the frustration-aggression hypothesis. *Journal of Abnormal and Social Psychology,* 1952, **47,** 728–31.

PATTERSON, G. R., AND COBB, J. A. A dyadic analysis of aggressive behaviors. In J. P. Hill (Ed.), *Minnesota symposia on child psychology,* Vol. 4. Minneapolis, Minn.: University of Minnesota Press, 1971.

PATTERSON, G. R., COBB, J. A., AND RAY, R. S. A social engineering technology for retraining the families of aggressive boys. In H. E. Adams and I. P. Unikel (Eds.), *Issues and trends in behavior therapy.* Springfield, Ill.: Charles C Thomas, 1972, in press.

PATTERSON, G. R., LITTMAN, R. A., AND BRICKER, W. Assertive behavior in children: A step toward a theory of aggression. *Monographs of the Society for Research in Child Development,* 1967, **32,** No. 5 (Serial No. 113).

PATTERSON, G. R., LUDWIG, M., AND SONODA, B. Reinforcement of aggression in children. Unpublished manuscript, University of Oregon, 1961.

PATTERSON, G. R., RAY, R. S., AND SHAW, D. Direct intervention in families of deviant children. Unpublished manuscript, University of Oregon, 1968.

PATTERSON, G. R., AND REID, J. B. Reciprocity and coercion: Two facets of social systems. In C. Neuringer and J. L. Michael (Eds.), *Behavior modification in clinical psychology.* New York: Appleton-Century-Crofts, 1970. Pp. 133–77.

PENDERGRASS, V. E. Effect of length of time-out from positive reinforcement and schedule of application in suppression of aggressive behavior. *Psychological Record,* 1971, **21,** 75–80.

PENNEY, R. K. The effects of non-reinforcement of response strength as a function of number of previous reinforcements. *Canadian Journal of Psychology,* 1960, **14,** 206–15.

PETERSON, R. A. Aggression level as a function of expected retaliation and aggression level of target and aggressor. *Developmental Psychology,* 1971, **5,** 161–66.

PETERSON, R. E. *The scope of organized student protest in 1964–65.* Princeton, N.J.: Educational Testing Service, 1966.

PETTIGREW, T. F. Actual gains and psychological losses: The Negro

American protest. *Journal of Negro Education,* 1963, **32,** 493–506.

PETTIGREW, T. F. Social evaluation theory: Convergences and applications. In D. Levine (Ed.), *Nebraska symposium on motivation: 1967.* Lincoln: University of Nebraska Press, 1967. Pp. 241–311.

PHILLIPS, E. L. Achievement place: Token reinforcement procedures in a home-style rehabilitation setting for "pre-delinquent" boys. *Journal of Applied Behavior Analysis,* 1968, **1,** 213–23.

PHILLIPS, E. L., WOLF, M. M., AND FIXSEN, D. L. An experimental analysis of governmental systems at achievement place, a group home for pre-delinquent boys. *Journal of Applied Behavior Analysis,* 1972.

PILIAVIN, I., HARDYCK, J., AND VADUM, A. Reactions to the victim in a just or non-just world. Paper presented at the meeting of the Society of Experimental Social Psychology, Bethesda, Maryland, August 1967.

PINKSTON, E. M., REESE, N. H., LeBLANC, J. M., AND BAER, D. M. Independent control of a preschool child's aggression and peer interaction by contingent teacher attention. *Journal of Applied Behavioral Analysis,* 1972, in press.

PISANO, R., AND TAYLOR, S. P. Reduction of physical aggression: The effects of four strategies. *Journal of Personality and Social Psychology,* 1971, **19,** 237–42.

POLSKY, H. W. *Cottage six: The social system of delinquent boys in residential treatment.* New York: Russell Sage Foundation, 1962.

PORRO, C. R. Effects of the observation of a model's affective responses to her own trangression on resistance to temptation in children. *Dissertation Abstracts,* 1968, **28,** 3064.

Portland (Me.) Press-Herald. It looked easy on TV, says the man held in killing here. November 28, 1963, p. 1.

POWELL, D. A., AND CREER, T. L. Interaction of developmental and environmental variables in shock-elicited aggression. *Journal of Comparative and Physiological Psychology,* 1969, **69,** 219–25.

POWERS, P. C., AND GEEN, R. G. Effects of the behavior and the perceived arousal of a model on instrumental aggression. *Journal of Personality and Social Psychology,* 1972, **23,** 175–83.

POWERS, T. *Diana: The making of a terrorist.* Boston: Houghton Mifflin, 1971.

PREMACK, D. Reinforcement theory. In D. Levine (Ed.), *Nebraska symposium on motivation: 1965.* Lincoln, Neb.: University of Nebraska Press, 1965. Pp. 123–80.

PRENTICE, N. M. The influence of live and symbolic modeling on promoting moral judgments of adolescent juvenile delinquents. *Journal of Abnormal Psychology,* 1972 (in press).

PRICE, W. H., AND WHATMORE, P. B. Behaviour disorders and pattern of crime among XYY males identified at a maximum security hospital. *British Medical Journal,* 1967, 1, 533–36.

RACHMAN, S. *The effects of psychotherapy.* Oxford, Eng.: Pergamon, 1971.

RADKE-YARROW, M., TRAGER, H., AND MILLER, J. The role of parents in the development of children's ethnic attitudes. *Child Development,* 1952, **23,** 13–53.

RANSFORD, H. E. Isolation, powerlessness, and violence: A study of attitudes and participation in the Watts riot. *American Journal of Sociology,* 1968, **73,** 581–91.

RAUSH, H. L. Interaction sequences. *Journal of Personality and Social Psychology,* 1965, **2,** 487–99.

REDL, F., AND WINEMAN, D. *Children who hate: The disorganization and breakdown of behavior controls.* Glencoe, Ill.: Free Press, 1951.

REES, J. R. *The shaping of psychiatry by war.* New York: Norton, 1945.

REICH, P., AND HEPPS, R. B. Homicide during a psychosis induced by LSD. *Journal of the American Medical Association,* 1972, **219,** 869–71.

REICHARD, G. A. Social life. In F. Boas (Ed.), *General anthropology.* Boston: Heath, 1938. Pp. 409–86.

REIFLER, C. B., HOWARD, J., LIPTON, M. A., LIPTZIN, M. B., AND WIDMANN, D. E. Pornography: An experimental study of effects. *American Journal of Psychiatry,* 1971, **128,** 575–82.

REISS, A. J., Jr. *The police and the public.* New Haven, Conn.: Yale University Press, 1971.

REPPUCCI, N. D., AND REISS, S. Effects of operant treatment with disruptive and normal elementary school children. Paper presented at the meeting of the American Psychological Association, Miami, September 1970.

RESCORLA, R. A. Pavlovian conditioned inhibition. *Psychological Bulletin,* 1969, **72,** 77–94.

REYNIERSE, J. H. Submissive postures during shock-elicited aggression. *Animal Behaviour,* 1971, **19,** 102–7.

REYNOLDS, G. S., CATANIA, A. C., AND SKINNER, B. F. Conditioned and unconditioned aggression in pigeons. *Journal of the Experimental Analysis of Behavior,* 1963, **6,** 73–74.

RISLEY, T. R. The effects and side effects of punishing the autistic behaviors of a deviant child. *Journal of Applied Behavior Analysis,* 1968, **1**, 21–34.

RISLEY, T. R., AND WOLF, M. M. Experimental manipulation of autistic behaviors and generalization into the home. In R. Ulrich, T. Stachnik, and J. Mabry (Eds.), *Control of human behavior.* Vol. 1. Glenview, Ill.: Scott, Foresman, 1966. Pp. 193–98.

ROBERTS, W. W., STEINBERG, M. L., AND MEANS, L. W. Hypothalamic mechanisms for sexual, aggressive, and other motivational behaviors in the opossum, *Didelphis virginiana. Journal of Comparative and Physiological Psychology,* 1967, **64**, 1–15.

ROBINSON, J. P., AND BACHMAN, J. G. Television viewing habits and aggression. In G. A. Comstock and E. A. Rubinstein (Eds.), *Television and social behavior.* Vol. 3. *Television and adolescent aggressiveness.* Washington, D.C.: Government Printing Office, 1972. Pp. 372–82.

ROSEKRANS, M. A., AND HARTUP, W. W. Imitative influences of consistent and inconsistent response consequences to a model on aggressive behavior in children. *Journal of Personality and Social Psychology,* 1967, **7**, 429–34.

ROSENBAUM, M. E., AND DE CHARMS, R. Direct and vicarious reduction of hostility. *Journal of Abnormal and Social Psychology,* 1960, **60**, 105–11.

ROSENHAN, D., FREDERICK, F., AND BURROWES, A. Preaching and practicing: Effects of channel discrepancy on norm internalization. *Child Development,* 1968, **39**, 291–301.

ROSENZWEIG, S. An outline of frustration theory. In J. McV. Hunt (Ed.), *Personality and the behavior disorders.* Vol. I. New York: Ronald Press, 1944. Pp. 379–88.

ROSS, L., RODIN, J., AND ZIMBARDO, P. G. Toward an attribution therapy: The reduction of fear through induced cognitive-emotional misattribution. *Journal of Personality and Social Psychology,* 1969, **12**, 279–88.

ROTHBALLER, A. B. Aggression, defense and neurohumors. In C. D. Clemente and D. B. Lindsley (Eds.), *Aggression and defense.* Berkeley, Calif.: University of California Press, 1967. Pp. 135–50.

RUSSO, S. Adaptations in behavioural therapy with children. *Behaviour Research and Therapy,* 1964, **2**, 43–47.

San Francisco Chronicle. "James Dean" knifing in South City. March 1, 1961, p. 6.

San Francisco Chronicle. Klan rally—hate and fears. May 13, 1963, p. 17.

San Francisco Chronicle. A "club" for teen sadists. November 26, 1964, p. 3.

San Francisco Chronicle. A badge for killing Reds. June 11, 1970, p. 23.

San Francisco Chronicle. Tate killings—"Right thing to do." February 11, 1971a, p. 21.

San Francisco Chronicle. Calley says killing was order of day. February 24, 1971b, p. 1.

San Francisco Chronicle. Bomb hoax costs airline $560,000. May 27, 1971c, p. 1.

San Francisco Chronicle. BOAC knew the plot—and foiled the plotter. August 4, 1971d, p. 1.

San Francisco Chronicle. Hijacker's slick parachute escape. November 26, 1971e, p. 1.

SANDLER, J., AND QUAGLIANO, J. Punishment in a signal avoidance situation. Paper presented at the meeting of the Southeastern Psychological Association, Gatlinburg, Tennessee, 1964.

SARASON, I. G. AND GANZER, V. J. Social influence techniques in clinical and community psychology. In C. D. Spielberger (Ed.), *Current topics in clinical and community psychology.* New York: Academic Press, 1969. Pp. 1–66.

SARNOFF, I. Identification with the aggressor: Some personality correlates of antisemitism among Jews. *Journal of Personality,* 1951, **20,** 199–218.

SAUL, L. J., ROME, H., AND LEUSER, E. Desensitization of combat fatigue patients. *American Journal of Psychiatry,* 1946, **102,** 476–78.

SAVITSKY, J. C., ROGERS, R. W., IZARD, C. E., AND LIEBERT, R. M. Role of frustration and anger in the imitation of filmed aggression against a human victim. *Psychological Reports,* 1972, **29,** 807–10.

SCHACHTER, J. Pain, fear, and anger in hypertensives and normotensives: A psychophysiological study. *Psychosomatic Medicine,* 1957, **19,** 17–29.

SCHACHTER, S., AND SINGER, J. E. Cognitive, social, and physiological determinants of emotional state. *Psychological Review,* 1962, **69,** 379–99.

SCHAEFER, H. H. Self-injurious behavior: Shaping "head-banging" in monkeys. *Journal of Applied Behavior Analysis,* 1970, **3,** 111–16.

SCHENKEL, R. Submission: Its features and functions in the wolf and dog. *American Zoologist,* 1967, **7,** 319–29.

SCHMIDT, G., AND SIGUSCH, V. Sex differences in responses to psychosexual stimulation by films and slides. *Journal of Sex Research,* 1970, **6,** 268–83.

SCHRAMM, W., LYLE, J., AND PARKER, E. B. *Television in the lives of our children.* Stanford, Calif.: Stanford University Press, 1961.

SCHWARTZ, G. E. Voluntary control of human cardiovascular integration and differentiation through feedback and reward. *Science,* 1972, **175,** 90–93.

SCHWARTZ, L. A. Group psychotherapy in the war neuroses. *American Journal of Psychiatry,* 1945, **101,** 498–500.

SCOTT, J. P. An experimental test of the theory that social behavior determines social organization. *Science,* 1944, **99,** 42–43.

SCOTT, J. P. Hostility and aggression. In B. Wolman (Ed.) *Handbook of genetic psychology.* Englewood Cliffs, N.J.: Prentice-Hall, 1972.

SCOTT, J. P., AND MARSTON, M. V. Nonadaptive behavior resulting from a series of defeats in fighting mice. *Journal of Abnormal and Social Psychology,* 1953, **48,** 417–28.

SCOTT, P. M., BURTON, R. V., AND YARROW, M. R. Social reinforcement under natural conditions. *Child Development,* 1967, **38,** 53–63.

SEARLE, J. R. A foolproof scenario for student revolts. *The New York Times Magazine,* December 29, 1968, p. 4.

SEARLE, L. V. The organization of hereditary maze-brightness and maze-dullness. *Genetic Psychology Monographs,* 1949, **39,** 279–325.

SEARS, D. O., AND MCCONAHAY, J. B. Participation in the Los Angeles riot. *Social Problems,* 1969, **17,** 3–20.

SEARS, R. R. Non-aggressive reactions to frustration. *Psychological Review,* 1941, **48,** 343–46.

SEARS, R. R., MACCOBY, E. E., AND LEVIN, H. *Patterns of child rearing.* Evanston, Ill.: Row, Peterson, 1957.

SEARS, R. R., WHITING, J. W. M., NOWLIS, V., AND SEARS, P. S. Some child-rearing antecedents of aggression and dependency in young children. *Genetic Psychology Monographs,* 1953, **47,** 135–234.

SHAH, S. A. *Report on the XYY chromosomal abnormality.* Washington, D.C.: Government Printing Office, 1970.

SHORT, J. F., Jr. (Ed.). *Gang delinquency and delinquent subcultures.* New York: Harper & Row, 1968.

SHORT, J. F., Jr., AND STRODTBECK, F. L. Why gangs fight. *Trans-action,* 1964, **1** (6), 25–29.

SHUNTICH, R. J. AND TAYLOR, S. P. The effects of alcohol on human physical aggression. *Journal of Experimental Research in Personality,* 1972, **6,** 34–38.

SHUPE, L. M. Alcohol and crime: A study of the urine alcohol concentration found in 882 persons arrested during or immediately after the commission of a felony. *Journal of Criminal Law, Criminology and Police Science,* 1954, **44,** 661–64.

SIBLEY, S. A., ABBOTT, M. S., AND COOPER, B. P. Modification of the classroom behavior of a disadvantaged kindergarten boy by social reinforcement and isolation. *Journal of Experimental Child Psychology,* 1969, **7,** 203–19.

SIEGEL, A. E. Film-mediated fantasy aggression and strength of aggressive drive. *Child Development,* 1956, **27,** 365–78.

SIEGEL, A. E. The influence of violence in the mass media upon children's role expectation. *Child Development,* 1958, **29,** 35–56.

SIEGEL, A. E. Violence in the mass media. In D. N. Daniels, M. F. Gilula, and F. M. Ochberg (Eds.), *Violence and the struggle for existence.* Boston: Little, Brown, 1970. Pp. 193–239.

SILVER, L. B., DUBLIN, C. C., AND LOURIE, R. S. Does violence breed violence? Contributions from a study of the child abuse syndrome. *American Journal of Psychiatry,* 1969, **126,** 404–7.

SIMKINS, L. Effects of examiner attitudes and type of reinforcement on the conditioning of hostile verbs. *Journal of Personality,* 1961, **29,** 380–95.

SINGER, B. D. Violence, protest and war in television news: The U.S. and Canada compared. *Public Opinion Quarterly,* 1970–71, **34,** 611–16.

SKEYHILL, T. (Ed.). *Sergeant York: His own life story and war diary.* Garden City, N.Y.: Doubleday, Doran, 1928.

SLOANE, H. N., JOHNSTON, M. K., AND BIJOU, S. W. Successive modification of aggressive behaviour and aggressive fantasy play by management of contingencies. *Journal of Child Psychology and Psychiatry and Allied Disciplines,* 1967, **8,** 217–26.

SNOW, C. P. Either-or. *Progressive,* 1961, **25** (2), 24–25.

SOMERS, R. H. The mainsprings of rebellion: A survey of Berkeley students in November, 1964. In S. M. Lipset and S. S. Wolin (Eds.), *The Berkeley student revolt: Facts and interpretations.* Garden City, N.Y.: Doubleday, 1965, Pp. 530–57.

SORENSON, E. R. The evolving Fore: A study of socialization and cultural change in the New Guinea highlands. Unpublished doctoral dissertation, Stanford University, 1971.

SOSA, J. N. Vascular effects of frustration on passive and aggressive members of a clinical population. Unpublished master's thesis, Florida State University, 1968.

SOUTHWICK, C. H. An experimental study of intragroup agnoistic behavior in rhesus monkeys (Macaca mulatta). *Behaviour,* 1967, **28,** 182–209.

SPELT, D. K. The conditioning of the human fetus in utero. *Journal of Experimental Psychology,* 1948, **38,** 375–76.

SPENCE, K. W. Anxiety (drive) level and performance in eyelid conditioning. *Psychological Bulletin,* 1964, **61,** 129–39.

SPIEGEL, J. P. Campus disorders: A transactional approach. *The Psychoanalytic Review,* 1970, **57,** 472–504.

STAATS, A. W., AND BUTTERFIELD, W. H. Treatment of nonreading in a culturally deprived juvenile delinquent: An application of reinforcement principles. *Child Development,* 1965, **36,** 925–42.

STAATS, A. W., AND STAATS, C. K. Attitudes established by classical conditioning. *Journal of Abnormal and Social Psychology,* 1958, **57,** 37–40.

STAATS, C. K., AND STAATS, A. W. Meaning established by classical conditioning. *Journal of Experimental Psychology,* 1957, **54,** 74–80.

STACHNIK, T. J., ULRICH, R., AND MABRY, J. H. Reinforcement of intra- and inter-species aggression with intracranial stimulation. *American Zoologist,* 1966, **6,** 663–68.

STAPLES, F. R., AND WALTERS, R. H. Influence of positive reinforcement of aggression on subjects differing in initial aggressive level. *Journal of Consulting Psychology,* 1964, **28,** 547–52.

STEFFY, R. A., HART, J., CROW, M., TORNEY, D., AND MARLETT, N. Operant behaviour modification techniques applied to a ward of severely regressed and aggressive patients. *Canadian Psychiatric Association Journal,* 1969, **14,** 59–67.

STEIN, A. H., FRIEDRICH, L. K., AND VONDRACEK, F. Television content and young children's behavior. In J. P. Murray, E. A. Rubinstein, and G. A. Comstock (Eds.), *Television and social behavior.* Vol. 2. *Television and social learning.* Washington, D.C.: Government Printing Office, 1972, Pp. 202–317.

STEUER, F. B., APPLEFIELD, J. M., AND SMITH, R. Televised aggression and the interpersonal aggression of preschool children. *Journal of Experimental Child Psychology,* 1971, **11,** 442–47.

STEVENSON, H. W. Studies of racial awareness in young children. In W. W. Hartup and N. L. Smothergill (Eds.), *The young child: Review of research.* Washington, D.C.: National Association for the Education of Young Children, 1967. Pp. 206–13.

STONE, L. J., AND HOKANSON, J. E. Arousal reduction via self-punitive behavior. *Journal of Personality and Social Psychology,* 1969, **12,** 72–79.

SULZER, B., MAYER, G. R., AND CODY, J. J. Assisting teachers with managing classroom behavioral problems. *Elementary School Guidance and Counseling*, 1968, 3, 40–48.

TANNENBAUM, P. H. Studies in film- and television-mediated arousal and aggression: A progress report. In G. A. Comstock, E. A. Rubinstein, and J. P. Murray (Eds.), *Television and social behavior*. Vol. 5. *Television effects: Further explorations*. Washington, D.C.: Government Printing Office, 1972. Pp. 309–50.

TANNENBAUM, P. H., AND GAER, E. P. Mood change as a function of stress of protagonist and degree of identification in a film-viewing situation. *Journal of Personality and Social Psychology*, 1965, 2, 612–16.

Task force report: The police. Washington, D.C.: U.S. Government Printing Office, 1967.

TAYLOR, S. P. Aggressive behavior and physiological arousal as a function of provocation and the tendency to inhibit aggression. *Journal of Personality*, 1967, 35, 297–310.

THARP, R. G., AND WETZEL, R. J. *Behavior modification in the natural environment*. New York: Academic Press, 1969.

THELEN, M. H., AND SOLTZ, W. The effect of vicarious reinforcement on imitation in two social racial groups. *Child Development*, 1969, 40, 879–87.

THIBAUT, J. W., AND COULES, J. The role of communication in the reduction of interpersonal hostility. *Journal of Abnormal and Social Psychology*, 1952, 47, 770–777.

THOMPSON, T. Aggressive behavior of Siamese fighting fish. In S. Garattini and E. B. Sigg (Eds.), *Aggressive behaviour*. New York: Wiley, 1969. Pp. 15–31.

THOMPSON, T., AND BLOOM, W. Aggressive behavior and extinction-induced response-rate increase. *Psychonomic Science*, 1966, 5, 335–36.

TIEGER, J. H. Police discretion and discriminatory enforcement. *Duke Law Journal*, 1971, 717–43.

TINBERGEN, N. *The study of instinct*. London: Oxford University Press, 1951.

TOCH, H. *Violent men*. Chicago: Aldine, 1969.

TOCH, H., AND SCHULTE, R. Readiness to perceive violence as a result of police training. *British Journal of Psychology*, 1961, 52, 389–93.

TOMLINSON, T. L. The development of a riot ideology among urban Negroes. *American Behavioral Scientist*, 1968, 11, 27–31.

TURNBULL, C. M. *The forest people.* New York: Simon and Schuster, 1961.

TURNER, R. H. The public perception of protest. *American Sociological Review,* 1969, **34,** 815–31.

TYLER, V. O., JR., AND BROWN, G. D. The use of swift, brief isolation as a group control device for institutionalized delinquents. *Behavior Research and Therapy,* 1967, **5,** 1–9.

ULRICH, R. E. Pain as a cause of aggression. *American Zoologist,* 1966, **6,** 643–62.

ULRICH, R. E. The experimental analysis of aggression. Unpublished manuscript, Western Michigan University, 1967.

ULRICH, R. E., AND AZRIN, N. H. Reflexive fighting in response to aversive stimulation. *Journal of the Experimental Analysis of Behavior,* 1962, **5,** 511–20.

ULRICH, R. E., AND FLAVELL, J. E. Human aggression. In C. Neuringer and J. L. Michael (Eds.), *Behavior modification in clinical psychology.* New York: Appleton-Century-Crofts, 1970. Pp. 105–32.

ULRICH, R. E., HUTCHINSON, R. R., AND AZRIN, N. H. Pain-elicited aggression, *Psychological Record,* 1965, **15,** 111–26.

ULRICH, R. E., JOHNSTON, M., RICHARDSON, J., AND WOLFF, P. The operant conditioning of fighting behavior in rats. *Psychological Record,* 1963, **13,** 465–70.

ULRICH, R. E., WOLFE, M., AND DULANEY, S. Punishment of shock-induced aggression. *Journal of the Experimental Analysis of Behavior,* 1969, **12,** 1009–15.

U.S. Senate Hearings, Subcommittee to Invesigate Juvenile Delinquency. *Effects on young people of violence and crime portrayed on television.* Washington, D.C.: U.S. Government Printing Office, 1963.

VAN LAWICK-GOODALL, J. Some aspects of aggressive behavior in a group of free-living chimpanzees. *International Social Science Journal,* 1971, **23,** 89–97.

VANTRESS, F. E., AND WILLIAMS, C. B. The effect of the presence of the provocator and the opportunity to counteraggress on systolic blood pressure. The *Journal of General Psychology,* 1972, **86,** 63–68.

VERNON, W., AND ULRICH, R. Classical conditioning of pain-elicited aggression. *Science,* 1966, **152,** 668–69.

WAHLER, R. G. Behavior therapy for oppositional children: Love is not enough. Paper read at Eastern Psychological Association meeting, Washington, D.C., April 1968.

WALDMAN, D. M., AND BARON, R. A. Aggression as a function of exposure and similarity to a nonaggressive model. *Psychonomic Science,* 1971, **23,** 381–83.

WALTERS, R. H., BOWEN, N. V., AND PARKE, R. D. Influence of looking behavior of a social model on subsequent looking behavior of observers of the model. *Perceptual & Motor Skills,* 1964, **18,** 469–83.

WALTERS, R. H., AND BROWN, M. Studies of reinforcement of aggression. III. Transfer of responses to an interpersonal situation. *Child Development,* 1963, **34,** 563–71.

WALTERS, R. H., AND LLEWELLYN-THOMAS, E. Enhancement of punitiveness by visual and audiovisual displays. *Canadian Journal of Psychology,* 1963, **17,** 244–55.

WALTERS, R. H., PARKE, R. D., AND CANE, V. A. Timing of punishment and the observation of consequences to others as determinants of response inhibition. *Journal of Experimental Child Psychology,* 1965, **2,** 10–30.

WALTERS, R. H., AND WILLOWS, D. C. Imitative behavior of disturbed and nondisturbed children following exposure to aggressive and nonaggressive models. *Child Development,* 1968, **39,** 79–89.

WARD, M. H., AND BAKER, B. L. Reinforcement therapy in the classroom. *Journal of Applied Behavior Analysis,* 1968, **1,** 323–28.

WARNER, M. Organizational content and control of policy in the television newsroom: A participant observation study. *British Journal of Sociology,* 1971, **22,** 283–94.

Washington Post. Youth theft ring cracked. January 30, 1971, p. Bl.

WECHSBERG, J. (Ed.). *The murderers among us.* New York: McGraw-Hill, 1967.

WEISZ, A. E., AND TAYLOR, R. L. American Presidential assassinations. In D. N. Daniels, M. F. Gilula, and F. Ochberg (Eds.), *Violence and the struggle for existence.* Boston: Little, Brown, 1970. Pp. 291–307.

WELCH, A. S., AND WELCH, B. L. Reduction of norepinephrine in the lower brainstem by psychological stimulus. *Proceedings of the National Academy of Sciences,* 1968, **60,** 478–81.

WELLS, W. D. Television and aggression: Replication of an experimental field study. Unpublished manuscript, University of Chicago, 1971.

WERTHAM, F. Is TV hardening us to the war in Vietnam? *The New York Times,* December 4, 1966, p. D23.

WHEELER, L. Toward a theory of behavioral contagion. *Psychological Review,* 1966, **73,** 179–92.

WHEELER, L., AND CAGGIULA, A. R. The contagion of aggression. *Journal of Experimental Social Psychology,* 1966, **2,** 1–10.

WHEELER, L., AND LEVINE, L. Observer-model similarity in the contagion of aggression. *Sociometry*, 1967, **30**, 41–49.

WHEELER, L., AND SMITH, S. Censure of the model in the contagion of aggression. *Journal of Personality and Social Psychology*, 1967, **6**, 93–98.

WHITING, J. W. M. *Becoming a Kwoma*. New Haven, Conn.: Yale University Press, 1941.

WHITING, J. W. M., AND CHILD, I. L. *Child training and personality*. New Haven, Conn.: Yale University Press, 1953.

WHYTE, W. F. *Street corner society*. 2nd ed. Chicago: University of Chicago Press, 1955.

WILLIAMS, C. D. The elimination of tantrum behavior by extinction procedures. *Journal of Abnormal and Social Psychology*, 1959, **59**, 269.

WOLF, M. M., RISLEY, T., JOHNSTON, M. K., HARRIS, F., AND ALLEN, E. Application of operant conditioning procedures to the behavior problems of an autistic child: A follow-up and extension. *Behaviour Research and Therapy*, 1967, **5**, 103–11.

WOLF, M. M., RISLEY, T. R., AND MEES, H. Application of operant conditioning procedures to the behaviour problems of an autistic child. *Behaviour Research and Therapy*, 1964, **1**, 305–12.

WOLFE, B. M., AND BARON, R. A. Laboratory aggression related to aggression in naturalistic social situations: Effects of an aggressive model on the behavior of college student and prisoner observers. *Psychonomic Science*, 1971, **24**, 193–94.

WOLFE, M., ULRICH, R., AND DULANEY, S. Fighting and escape reaction in paired rats. *Psychological Record*, 1971, **21**, 59–68.

WOLFGANG, M. E., AND FERRACUTI, F. *The subculture of violence*. London: Travistock, 1967.

WOLFGANG, M. E., KELLY, A. AND NOLDE, H. C. Comparison of the executed and the commuted among admissions to death row. *Journal of Criminal Law, Criminology, and Political Science*, 1962, **53**, 301–11.

WORCHEL, P. Catharsis and the relief of hostility. *Journal of Abnormal and Social Psychology*, 1957, **55**, 238–43.

Wright, G. O. Projection and displacement: A cross-cultural study of folk-tale aggression. *Journal of Abnormal and Social Psychology*, 1954, **49**, 523–28.

WRIGHT, M. E. Constructiveness of play as affected by group organization and frustration. *Character and Personality*, 1942, **11**, 40–49.

WRIGHT, M. E. The influence of frustration upon the social relations of young children. *Character and Personality*, 1943, **12**, 111–22.

YABLONSKY, L. *The violent gang*. New York: Macmillan, 1962.

ZAJONC, R. B. Attitudinal effects of mere exposure. *Journal of Personality and Social Psychology Monograph Supplement*, 1968, **9**, (2), Part 2. Pp. 1–27.

ZALTMAN, G., KOTLER, P., AND KAUFMAN, I. (Eds.), *Creating social change*. New York: Holt, Rinehart and Winston, 1972.

ZEILBERGER, J., SAMPEN, S. E., AND SLOANE, H. N., JR. Modification of a child's problem behaviors in the home with the mother as therapist. *Journal of Applied Behavior Analysis*, 1968, **1**, 47–53.

ZILLMANN, D. Excitation transfer in communication-mediated aggressive behavior. *Journal of Experimental Social Psychology*, 1971, **7**, 419–34.

ZILLMANN, D., AND JOHNSON, R. C. Motivated aggressiveness perpetuated by exposure to aggressive films and reduced by exposure to non-aggressive films. *Journal of Research in Personality*, 1973, **7**, 261–76.

ZIMBARDO, P. G. The human choice: Individuation, reason, and order versus deindividuation, impulse, and chaos. *Nebraska symposium on motivation, 1969*. Lincoln, Neb.: University of Nebraska, 1969. Pp. 237–309.

ZIMRING, F. E. *Perspectives on deterrence*. Washington, D.C.: Government Printing Office, 1971.

ZIMRING, F., AND HAWKINS, G. The legal threat as an instrument of social change. *Journal of Social Issues*, 1971, **27**, 33–48.

author index

subject index

375

Military atrocities (*Cont.*)
  under reinforcement control, 192, 196
  self-absolving devices in, 212
Military training:
  desensitization by, 100, 214–15
  and drastic behavior change, 98–99, 101
  implications for personality theory, 98–100
  methods of, 98–100
  and moral sanctions, 99, 210–11, 215
  obedience tests in, 99
  social isolation during, 99
Modeling of aggression:
  adult-peer model differences in, 77
  in aggressive subcultures, 3–4, 97–98, 334
  of aggressive tactics, 85, 101–9, 233–35, 283, 287
  in airline hijackings, 105
  in animals, 17–18, 23
  of attitudes and values, 85–86, 117
  attitudinal effects of, 85
  and authoritarianism, 89, 121–22
  in capital punishment, 226–27
  in collective action, 73, 173, 233–35
  in concentration camps, 86–89
  in correctional institutions, 315–16
  cross-cultural, 103–5, 107–13
  cross-sex, 77
  in developing assertiveness, 258–60, 321
  ethnic, 121
  explanation of, 69–72
  familial, 93–94, 96–97, 180
  and familiarity, 80–82
  and fantasy-reality distinction, 73–74, 142–43
  field studies of, 104
  and frustration reactions, 58, 78
  as a function of:
    emotional arousal, 54–57, 77–79, 123–25, 271
    frustration, 78
    memory aids, 71, 74–78
    model characteristics, 69–70, 121–22, 126
    observer characteristics, 70, 89, 121–22, 268–69
    reinforcement, 71–72, 127–28, 146
    response consequences to the model, 65–67, 79–80, 86, 89, 128, 131–32, 283, 287
    social sanctions, 71–72, 78–79, 146–47
  and identification, 67, 70, 86
  in mass homocide, 77
  in mass media, 73, 93, 101–4, 139–48, 266–75, 283
  in military training, 100

Modeling of aggression (*Cont.*)
  and model nurturance, 80
  and model similarity, 131
  and response availability, 71
  and retaliation threats, 125–26, 131
  and self-reinforcing responses, 210
  sex differences in, 65–67, 76, 78–80
  social implications of, 139, 147–48
  and social justification, 99, 131–33, 143, 271, 284, 286
  and social power, 70, 88–89, 128
  in student protest, 105, 233–35
  symbolic, 122–25, 132–33, 139–42
  in urban riots, 105
  See also Mass media, Models, Observational learning, Social facilitation, Symbolic modeling
Models:
  activist, 233–35
  cross-cultural, 103–5, 107–13
  effects of exposure to:
    inhibitory and disinhibitory, 74
    observational learning, 64–67, 72–75, 101–7
    response facilitation, 127–28
  ethnic, 121
  homocidal, 45, 77
  influence of characteristics of, 69–70, 88–89, 121–22, 126
  military, 98–100
  multiple, 67, 70, 92, 126–27
  nonaggressive, 83, 126–27
  pictorial and behavioral compared, 72–74
  prestigeful, 69–70, 98, 103–4, 128, 234–35
  symbolic, 64–67, 101–7, 122–25, 132–33, 139–48
Modification of aggression by:
  aversive consequences, 221–30, 307–8
  cognitive restructuring, 57
  desensitization of aggression activators, 256–57
  differential reinforcement, 18, 58, 287–97, 310–13
  extinction, 58, 289, 295–97
  modeling procedures, 17–18, 58, 83, 252–87, 315–16
  positive bonds, 215–16
  reducing aversive instigators, 58, 319–23
  reducing ideational precursors, 58, 141, 304
  reward withdrawal, 58, 119, 290–92, 299–304
  self-reinforcement, 289, 316–18
Motivation:
  drive theory of, 2–3, 31–39, 195
  drives and acquired reinforcers distinguished, 40, 195